THE SPOILAGE

JAPANESE AMERICAN EVACUATION
AND RESETTLEMENT

The Spoilage

By Dorothy Swaine Thomas
and Richard S. Nishimoto

WITH CONTRIBUTIONS BY

Rosalie A. Hankey, James M. Sakoda
Morton Grodzins, Frank Miyamoto

UNIVERSITY OF CALIFORNIA PRESS

Berkeley and Los Angeles · 1946

UNIVERSITY OF CALIFORNIA PRESS
BERKELEY AND LOS ANGELES
CALIFORNIA

◇

CAMBRIDGE UNIVERSITY PRESS
LONDON, ENGLAND

PRINTED IN THE UNITED STATES OF AMERICA
BY THE UNIVERSITY OF CALIFORNIA PRESS

PREFACE

Early in 1942, a group of social scientists in the University of California undertook a study of the evacuation, detention, and resettlement of the Japanese minority in the United States. The study was conceptualized on an interdisciplinary basis: (*a*) viewed as a sociological problem, it was to include analysis of the social demography of forced mass migration and voluntary resettlement, with special reference to the dislocation of habits and changes of attitudes produced by the experience; (*b*) viewed as a study in social anthropology, it would be oriented around the modifications and changes in the two cultures represented in the group, first under the impact of constant, enforced association, and later in the process of dispersal into the "outside world"; (*c*) viewed as a study in political science, it would emphasize policy formation and administrative procedures: the interaction of state and national political forces, the part played by local government units in determining both state and national policy, the development of organized pressures and their result; (*d*) viewed as a problem in social psychology, the primary focus would be on the nature of the collective adjustments made by this population group, following the crisis of evacuation, to the way of life imposed by the government during detention and on the extent and kind of institutional reorganization and individual readjustment following resettlement; (*e*) viewed as an economic problem, it would be concerned with the economic conditions predisposing the formulation of policies, the economic consequences of the program upon the areas of evacuation and upon the evacuees themselves, and the governmental efforts to protect the interests both of the areas and of the classes of population involved.

This ambitious conceptualization was never realized to the full, partly because data on certain aspects as outlined a priori (e.g., much of the economic segment) were unobtainable, partly be-

[v]

cause of diversion of university personnel into other wartime activities,[1] but mainly because the course of events which were to be investigated could not be anticipated. The staff of the Evacuation and Resettlement Study began their researches in February, 1942, when the program of evacuation and detention was initiated, and continued to make field observations through December, 1945, by which time the program of resettlement was about completed. Problems for research were defined and redefined during this period. Planning was on a point-by-point basis: old questions were discarded and new questions raised as the ramifications of a highly dynamic situation became apparent; ad hoc techniques had to be devised to meet the exigencies of data collection in an ever-changing, emotionally charged situation.

One problem was to obtain an accurate record of governmental regulations, of the development of policies underlying these regulations and of the interpretations of these policies at various points, both by the administration and by the evacuees. Because policies were formed and applied at several levels—in Washington, in regional offices, at relocation projects—frequent field trips to these various points were made by a political scientist on our staff. Because many governmental agencies participated in policy formation and policy direction, and because the policies so developed were often conflicting in purpose and application, multiple lines of contact had to be established and maintained.

The main problem of the study was to record and analyze the changes in behavior and attitudes and the patterns of social adjustment and interaction of the people to whom these policies and regulations were applied. Since most of the people concerned were detained and confined in government-operated camps for periods up to three and a half years, the camps became, for our purposes, social laboratories. Having prior knowledge of the stratification of the population groups we were studying (e.g., urban-rural, state-wise, occupational, and generational distributions), we had hoped

---

[1] In addition to the senior author of this volume, Professors Robert H. Lowie of Anthropology, Charles Aikin of Political Science, Milton Chernin of Social Welfare, and Frank L. Kidner of Economics participated in the early stages of planning. Professor Lowie was drawn out of the Study by activities connected with the Army Specialized Training Program; Professors Aikin and Kidner obtained leave of absence from the University to work for the Office of Price Administration; Professor Chernin was inducted into the Army.

to make a judicious selection of camps and, within camps, of classes of people as the subjects of our investigation. For various reasons we concentrated our main efforts on three camps and obtained spot observations in most of the other camps.

Our three major "laboratories" were at the Tule Lake project in northern California, the Poston project in Arizona, and the Minidoka project in Idaho. We were able, also, to make spot observations in five of the other seven War Relocation Authority projects.[2]

From the very beginning of our observations in camp, we realized that we could not utilize attitude surveys or questionnaires to get valid (or any) information from people whose recent experiences had led to an intense preoccupation with the real and imagined dangers of verbal commitments and to growing suspicions of the intentions of persons who asked them to commit themselves on even the most innocuous questions. We did, however, collect and exploit to the full data from surveys that emerged as administrative by-products (e.g., censuses by the Army and by the War Relocation Authority, the military registration questionnaire, segregation lists, results of voting on a number of issues, signatures to petitions of various sorts, and applications for renunciation of citizenship). In addition, the written documents of the highly literate people being studied were an important source (e.g., minutes of meetings, memoranda, manifestoes, bills of complaint, petitions and personal letters).[3]

Instead of sampling and surveying, either on a time or population basis, we had to depend on a day-by-day record, as complete as possible, of the maneuvers and reactions of an insecure, increasingly resentful people to policies imposed by government agencies and to incidents developing from the application of these policies. It was also apparent that the main part of the record of what was

---

[2] We have, in addition, observational records from four of the temporary assembly centers to which evacuees were moved pending establishment of War Relocation Authority projects.

[3] Minutes of most meetings were taken in both Japanese and English. In general, we have used the minutes taken by the so-called "English secretaries," without revision or editing of the "English" except in obscure passages where we have entered our own translation or interpretation in brackets. Petitions to the administration were in English, and we have quoted from them verbatim. Manifestoes, however, were usually in Japanese, and these we have translated ourselves, unless an English version was also circulating in camp. Wherever possible, we have obtained copies of both versions and have noted significant discrepancies between them.

going on inside the camps could be obtained only by "insiders," that is, by trained observers who were themselves participating in and reacting to the events under observation. Most of the staff observers were evacuees; at one time as many as twelve Japanese Americans were employed as technical or research assistants in the camps. Two of these remained in the camps for over three years. Eleven out of twelve of these assistants were bilingual so far as the spoken language was concerned and the two who remained longest were also highly skilled in written Japanese, having been educated both in Japan and in America.[4] All these observers had had university training in one or more of the social sciences, but only three of them had had any prior experience in field investigation.

In addition to the Japanese American staff observers, three "Caucasian" members of our staff resided for long periods in the camps we were studying. Two of these were graduate students in anthropology; one was a sociologist, with graduate training in political science.

Each staff observer built up a circle of participant informants[5] whose confidence he had obtained, and also made extensive records of acts and conversations of people who did not know they were under observation. As cleavages in the population became apparent and factions multiplied, efforts were made to extend the slate of observers and informants to cover all the divergent interest groups. Every staff observer kept a detailed journal, to which he appended all documents that he could obtain. These journals, which cover many thousands of pages, form the main body of material on which this volume is based. Excerpts from them are given footnote references as "Field Notes," with an indication of the date on which the observation was made.[6]

---

[4] Including the junior author of and one of the contributors to Volume I.

[5] One of the Caucasian observers—a contributor to this volume—obtained confidential reports from a group of determined "disloyals" with whom no Japanese American staff member could possibly have established contact.

[6] In some notes the information obtained or the attitude expressed postdated the event described by a considerable period, but the information was usually obtained very soon after the event. Postdated material is, in general, open to greater suspicion of its validity than is current material, but this device was necessary partly to fill in gaps which became apparent only after a lapse of time, partly because, in certain periods of crisis, some of our observers were unable to establish or continue normal contacts with informants.

Constant efforts had to be made to guard against betrayal of informants, and against divulging information even to friendly government agencies. In spite of the high regard accorded universities in general, and the University of California in particular, by evacuees it soon became apparent that the Japanese Americans on our staff could not operate openly as employees of the University. To their fellow evacuees, "research" was synonymous with "inquisition" and the distinction between "informant" and "informer" was not appreciated. Consequently every one of our evacuee staff members was stigmatized, or in danger of being stigmatized, as an *inu* (i.e., an "informer"; see Chapter X) by some of his fellow evacuees. The bases for the suspicions that led to this stigmatization were such acts as associating with the Caucasian personnel in the camps; taking notes in public meetings; using typewriters in their barracks; asking too-direct questions; receiving mail in envelopes marked "Evacuation and Resettlement Study"; and cashing university checks. Each of these acts raised suspicions that our staff members were operating as stool pigeons for the project administration or one of the governmental intelligence agencies, all of which, it was widely believed, employed operatives among the evacuees. Suspicion reached a maximum at the time of registration (see Chapter III), ebbed after segregation (see Chapter IV), recurred with every period of crisis in every camp (see, e.g., Chapter X), and was a factor that had to be considered from the inception until the closure of the camps. As a result, our evacuee staff members and collaborators had to exercise great ingenuity in establishing roles which would make it possible for them both to live as respected members of their own community and at the same time to carry on disinterested research for the study. Several of them were unable to resolve the conflict, and had to leave camp soon after the registration crisis.

Although most of the officials in charge of the program of evacuation and detention gave unstinted coöperation, conflicts inevitably arose with those members of the administration—camp, regional, and even national—who conformed to Leighton's definition of the "stereotype-minded."[7] Administrators of this sort tended to dis-

---

[7] "To the stereotype-minded staff members the evacuees were Japanese first and people secondarily . . . This conception of the evacuees varied a little from one staff member to another, some leaning more to hostility and suspicion than others, but for each individual it remained pretty constant no matter what kind

approve, on the one hand, of the "fraternization" through which
Caucasian observers obtained their information and, on the other
hand, of the refusal of all observers and of the director of the
study,[8] to divulge current information they had obtained in the
course of their research. Protection of the study's data in order that
sources would not be dried up, was a constant problem facing every
member of the staff.

The management of observation raised a number of serious problems. In the first place, the techniques of recording which we had to
use meant that, in the beginning, each observer had to make an
ad hoc selection of the events, words and acts that he considered
worth recording. After these early observations were assembled and
analyzed, the problems to be investigated became more sharply
focused, and more purposeful selection was possible.

In the second place, most of the observers were genuine participants in the events they were recording. Evacuee observers were,
like other evacuees, involuntarily detained in camps and their fate
was closely bound up with the course of events they were observing,
while Caucasian observers tended to develop an emotional identification with the group they were studying. The observers' subjective
reactions, under these tense conditions, were considered important
data in and of themselves, and were so recorded. One of our main
methodological problems was that of separating subjective ad hoc
interpretations from the more objective behaviorial records.

In the third place, the situation under observation involved two
cultures and two languages. This meant that we had to be on
constant guard against linguistic and cultural distortion both in
recording and in interpreting observations.

It must be apparent that no techniques could be devised to assure
complete success in overcoming all these methodological difficulties.
One safeguard was, of course, the competence, intellectual honesty,
self-control and self-correction of the observers themselves. Another

---

of evacuee he was dealing with."—Alexander H. Leighton, *The Governing of
Men,* Princeton University Press. 1945. p. 84.

Leighton, who, for a year, directed a sociological laboratory under the auspices
of the Office of Indian Affairs, at the Poston Relocation Project, made a pene-
trating analysis of conflict between the "people-minded" and "stereotype-
minded" administrators in this camp. The subject is outside the scope of our
investigation, but we were constantly, and often painfully, made aware of these
intrastaff conflicts in all the camps we were studying.

[8] The senior author of this volume.

safeguard was the interdisciplinary approach of the study (sociology, social psychology, anthropology, political science, economics) which resulted in a situation analogous to "differential diagnosis." A third was the bicultural composition of the evacuee staff (Issei, Kibei, Nisei). A fourth was the utilization, wherever possible, of administrative and particularly quantitative materials collected independently of the study for checking or revising the generalizations growing out of the materials of the study itself.

Of the safeguards listed above, the first three were established and reinforced by frequent conferences of observers and other staff members with the director of the study and its advisors. Because California was a "prohibited area," to our Japanese American staff members, these conferences could never be held at the University of California. They were, therefore, arranged every few months in Denver, Phoenix, Salt Lake City, or Chicago, and extended over a period of a week or more, during which each observer and staff member presented his problems and findings for the detailed criticism and appraisal of his colleagues. Interspersed between these general conferences were visits of the director and advisors of the study to the several camp "laboratories" and of both evacuee and Caucasian observers from one camp to another, as well as constant interchange of field notes and reports.

When the government program of resettling evacuees from the camps developed in early 1943, it became necessary to devise means of following up the experiences and adjustments of resettlers. Since the main area of resettlement was Chicago, part of the Japanese American staff was moved to that city where, through the courtesy of Dean Robert Redfield, an office was made available in the University of Chicago. Here, again, participant observation was used, primarily to obtain records of the associational life of the resettling evacuees. Files of the several agencies concerned were utilized to provide as complete a record as possible of the ecological aspects of resettlement. Beginning in April, 1943, a series of case histories of resettlers was undertaken. Eventually, more than sixty-five resettlers coöperated in this phase of the study and submitted to repeated interviews. Extensive life histories of these informants were built up and a wealth of detail bearing on their experiential and attitudinal developments for a period up to two years after leaving camp was obtained.

With the cessation of hostilities between Japan and America came the problem of organizing and analyzing the data collected over three and a half years and preparing volumes for publication.[9] Eventually the preparation of a two-volume work on the main problems raised by evacuation and resettlement was decided upon.[10] These problems were conceptualized in terms of the changing status of the Japanese minority in America, concomitant with evacuation, detention, dispersal, and return to the West Coast.

This, the first volume, analyzes the experiences of that part of the minority group whose status in America was impaired: those of the immigrant generation who returned, after the war, to defeated Japan; those of the second generation who relinquished American citizenship. It is, thus, concerned with the short-run "spoilage" resulting from evacuation and detention: the stigmatization as "disloyal" to the United States of one out of every six evacuees; the concentration and confinement of this group in the Tule Lake Center; the repressive measures undertaken by government agencies, including martial law, incarceration and internment; the successive protest movements of the group against these repressions, culminating in mass withdrawal from American citizenship. The scope of the volume is wide, and it is presented as what is believed to be a unique record and analysis of the continuing process of interaction between government and governed, through the point-by-point reproduction of stages in the process of attitude formation.

The second volume will include analysis of the short-run "salvage," i.e., the experiences of that part of the minority whose status in America was, at least temporarily, improved through dispersal and resettlement in the East and Middle West. This group includes one out of three[11] of the evacuees who left the camps to enter new areas as settlers, many participating directly in the war effort.

---

[9] We were bound, by various agreements, not to publish during the war.

[10] It is planned to publish at least two monographs concurrently with the two main volumes. One will deal with political and administrative aspects of evacuation and resettlement; the other with the ecology of "disloyalty."

[11] We limit the definition of "salvage" to those who resettled before the Army rescinded its exclusion orders in December, 1944. At that time, there were still more than 60,000 evacuees in War Relocation Authority camps, excluding Tule Lake. The bulk of them were young children (27 per cent) or middle aged and old adults (36 per cent). They resettled during 1945, following the War Relocation Authority's forcible closure of camps.

Not included in the present publication plans is analysis of the changing status of those evacuees who remained in camps until the relocation projects were liquidated and thereafter, for the most part, returned to the areas from which they had been evacuated. An analysis of this group should be made when it becomes possible to include an accounting of the residual, or long-run, effects of the forced mass migration of the Japanese minority. It is clear that these effects cannot be evaluated until after the passage of a considerable period of time. The "residue" of evacuation will include the net effects of short-run "spoilage" and "salvage" respectively; the extent to which those included in the former category who were able to remain in this country[12] become reabsorbed into the life of a more tolerant America; the extent to which the new foothold . obtained by the latter is a permanent gain, or whether with increasing unemployment, members of this minority group will be among the "first to be fired" and again displaced. The residue of evacuation will also include other net effects: the extent to which parts of the "spoilage" and of the "salvage," as well as the many evacuees who left camps only when they were forced out by the closure policy of 1945, reëstablish Japanese ghettos on the Pacific Coast and, correspondingly, the extent to which traditionally anti-Oriental pressure groups renew opposition to these minority concentrations.

The two volumes in this series, and its technical monographs, as well as the great mass of unpublished material in our files, will, we hope, provide the essential groundwork for study of the residue and for various other analyses. In this connection, we point out that our complete collection of original data bearing on the Japanese minority will be made available to other research workers. The University of California Library at Berkeley will be the repository for all of our unpublished material as soon as restrictions on parts now classified as confidential can be relaxed.[13]

---

[12] A large proportion (approximately one out of three) of the residents of Tule Lake either returned to Japan voluntarily during 1946 or are subject to involuntary deportation. This group represents long-run "spoilage."

[13] Other important collections have been or will be deposited in this Library. Among these are (1) county and city maps on the preëvacuation location of Japanese Americans in California, prepared under Governor Earl Warren's direction when he was State Attorney General; (2) Lieutenant Commander Alexander Leighton's files on Poston, covering the social history of the first year of this relocation project; (3) official documents, census schedules, IBM cards, segregation records, photographs, etc., prepared by the War Relocation Authority.

The staff of the Evacuation and Resettlement Study are indebted to a large number of individuals and organizations. The most significant data of the study could not have been obtained without the wholehearted coöperation of a great number of evacuees, most of whom must remain anonymous.[14]

The study was initiated and carried on during a national emergency. It is difficult to see how it could have progressed beyond the blueprint stage without the encouragement and active support of five persons: Charles Aikin, Robert T. Crane, Richard M. Neustadt, Robert G. Sproul, and Donald R. Young. Generous financial support was obtained from the funds of the University of California, from its Social Science Institute, from the Giannini Foundation, and from the Columbia and Rockefeller Foundations. The Rockefeller Foundation is, in addition, contributing to the costs of publication. Thanks are due especially to Joseph H. Willits of the Rockefeller Foundation, Mrs. Marjorie Elkus of the Columbia Foundation, and Harry R. Wellman of the Giannini Foundation.

The coöperation of agencies directly concerned with evacuation and resettlement is gratefully acknowledged. The study as a whole has benefited from unusually free access to unpublished documents and basic statistical data from the files of the War Relocation Authority. These were made available through the courtesy of Milton S. Eisenhower, Dillon S. Myer, Edward H. Spicer, Elmer L. Shirrell, Philip M. Glick, B. R. Stauber, Fern E. French, Evelyn M. Rose, Harvey M. Coverley, Robert B. Cozzens, and others. The War Department, through John J. McCloy and headquarters of the Western Defense Command and Fourth Army, have extended many courtesies. The latter, through Lieutenant Colonel David J. McFadden and Victor W. Nielsen of the Civil Affairs Division, has given access to various data, including the lists of pressure group members and of renunciants used in chapters XII and XIII. The Department of Justice has similarly made data available and thanks are due especially to Edward J. Ennis and John L. Burling. Ernest Besig of the American Civil Liberties Union has contributed important documentary material

[14] George Kuratomi and J. Y. Kurihara gave permission for the use of their names. Most of the other evacuees referred to in this volume are designated by pseudonyms. The appendix contains brief biographical notes on the evacuees referred to most frequently.

The authors of this volume are incalculably indebted to W. I. Thomas who has read and criticized the whole manuscript and made many suggestions for revisions. Our greatest hope is that his influence will be apparent. Finally, thanks are due Mrs. Mary Wilson for painstaking assistance in the preparation of the manuscript.

D. S. T.
R. S. N.

Berkeley, California.
April 1, 1946.

CONTENTS

[xvii]

CONTENTS

ILLUSTRATIONS

Chapter I

EVACUATION
Expulsion of a Minority Group

O̲N̲ ̲D̲E̲C̲E̲M̲B̲E̲R̲ 7, 1941, there were in the conti-
nental United States about 127,000 persons having common ancestry with the enemy that launched the Pearl Harbor attack.[1] Of
these, 113,000 lived in the four states of California, Washington,
Oregon, and Arizona, 94,000 being residents of California. A small
minority, they represented less than one tenth of one per cent of
the total American population, less than two per cent of the population in the state of their heaviest concentration (California).
Sociologically as well as numerically, they held minority status,
being biologically and culturally distinguishable from the white
majority and, at the same time, competing with them sharply in
economic activities.[2]

Some 47,000 of them had been born in Japan, and were known
as Issei, or first-generation immigrants. Ninety-eight per cent of
these had come to America prior to the Oriental Exclusion Act of

---

[1] Statistics cited in this chapter are, unless otherwise specified, from the Six-
teenth Census of the United States. The correct date of reference is, therefore,
April, 1940. No attempt has been made to adjust the statistics to December,
1941, since the rounded figures, as quoted, are sufficiently accurate for present
purposes.

Most of the census data on the Japanese American minority have been sum-
marized in a series of bulletins (Numbers 1–12) published by U. S. Army, Western
Defense Command and Fourth Army, Wartime Civil Control Administration,
Statistical Section, between March 17, 1942, and March 15, 1943. Other sum-
maries are included in U.S. Bureau of the Census. 16th Census of the United
States, 1940. Population. *Characteristics of the Nonwhite Population by Race.*
Washington, Government Printing Office, 1943.

[2] See Donald Young, *American Minority Peoples* (New York. Harper and
Brothers, 1932), for analysis of the social characteristics of American minority
groups.

[1]

1924, almost half of the total having arrived before 1910.[3] With numerically unimportant exceptions,[4] they were ineligible to American citizenship. In the states where they had settled in largest numbers, they were forbidden to own land.

Some 80,000 of them were born in America, the children (known as Nisei[5]) or the grandchildren (known as Sansei) of immigrant Japanese. By virtue of birth on American soil, they held American citizenship. Most of them had been educated in American schools[6] and, along with their classmates of the majority group (known on the West Coast as "Caucasians") had been indoctrinated in democratic principles. In only a few isolated communities had they been forced to attend segregated schools for nonwhites. Although, as citizens, they could own land, they, along with their parents, were subjected to many forms of discrimination in the western states. Residential choice was limited by covenants. Intermarriage with Caucasians was forbidden in most western states. Free access to certain places of public recreation (e.g., swimming pools and dance halls) was prohibited. Most severe in their effects were informal restrictions on entrance to occupations and professions for which their education had fitted them.

[3] Estimated from a 25 per cent sample of residents of three relocation projects (War Relocation Authority, manuscript tables).

[4] Aliens otherwise ineligible to citizenship were made eligible by an act of Congress (U.S. 49 Stat., 1935, 397–398) passed in June, 1935, if (a) they had served in the U.S. armed forces between April 6, 1917, and November 11, 1918, and been honorably discharged, and (b) they were permanent residents of the United States. A small number of Issei obtained citizenship under this act before the deadline, which was set at January 1, 1937.

[5] "Nisei" is used throughout these volumes as synonymous with "American-born" and, therefore, includes Sansei.

[6] The level of education attained by Nisei was extraordinarily high, and, for persons 25 years of age and older exceeded that of native whites of native parentage in the four western states. (See U.S. Army, Western Defense Command and Fourth Army. Wartime Civil Control Administration. Statistical Division. *Characteristics of the Japanese Population.* Bulletin 12, March 15, 1943, p. 21.) But because of the greater concentration of Nisei at younger ages than is true of other population groups, comparisons of this kind are not wholly reliable. Limiting comparison to white groups aged 25–34 in California (the state of heaviest settlement and of highest educational level in the western area), the generalization still holds for males: 57 per cent of the Nisei had completed at least four years of high school, compared with 53 per cent for native whites of native parentage and 48 per cent for native whites of foreign or mixed parentage. For Nisei females, the percentage was 53 per cent, compared with 59 per cent and 51 per cent for the two white population groups.

Most of the Nisei were bicultural, though their habits and attitudes conformed to the American pattern to a far greater extent than to the Japanese. Japanese was the language used between parents and children in the home but very rarely between siblings outside the home. Japanese festivals were celebrated, some Japanese food was eaten, marriages were often arranged through intermediaries, Buddhism was their religious faith more frequently than Christianity.[7] Most Nisei, unwilling though they were, had been required by their parents to attend, in their spare time, privately operated Japanese language schools. Some Nisei had been sent to Japan, and there they were cared for by their grandparents and other relatives, attended school, formed Japanese habits and were indoctrinated with Japanese ideologies. Returning to America these Nisei who were known as "Kibei"[8] most frequently found themselves handicapped linguistically and culturally and displaced among their America-oriented brothers and sisters. On the other hand, in the case of a certain number of individuals, usually economically and socially advantaged, the experience resulted in an often excellent integration of the two cultures.

[7] Results of a 25 per cent sample of evacuees in ten relocation projects in 1942 indicate that, of the American-born aged 14 and over, 50 per cent claimed Buddhism; 38 per cent Christianity; 10 per cent "no religion." Two per cent did not answer the question. (War Relocation Authority, manuscript tables.)

[8] "The literal meaning of 'Kibei' is 'returned to America.' . . . Therefore, the term could be taken to include any individual who has gone to Japan from America, for however short a time, and then returned to this country. For the term to be useful in defining a type of person, however, it must be narrowed. . . . Japanese Americans use the term Kibei to apply to those educated in whole or in part in Japan. Usage, however, among the second generation Japanese in America . . . has given a special meaning to the word 'Kibei.' It is applied to individuals not merely because they have been to school in Japan. It is reserved for those whose behavior is not like that of American youths; young men and women in the Japanese-American communities who spoke Japanese among themselves preferably to English and who otherwise behaved in what the Nisei regarded as a 'Japanesy' manner." (War Relocation Authority, Community Analysis Section, Community Analysis Report No. 8, January 28, 1944, mim.

In the report cited, analysis of a 25 per cent sample of American-born residents of ten relocation projects shows that 12.9 per cent of the total American-born had received some schooling in Japan. This analysis, however, takes no account of the age factor. Our own reworking of WRA statistics shows that only 2 per cent of Nisei under 15 years of age had resided in Japan for more than a year and that 93 per cent of them had never been in Japan. Of those over 15 years of age, however, 38 per cent had visited or resided in Japan, and approximately 20 per cent had attended schools there. Defined on this basis, then, one out of five Nisei 15 years of age or older in 1943 was a Kibei.

The Issei, like all immigrant groups in the American population in the 1940's, were old. Half of them were 50 years of age or older; 17 per cent had passed their sixtieth birthday; and only 8 per cent were under 35 years of age. In contrast, the Nisei were characterized by extreme youth, two thirds of them being under 20 years of age and less than 3 per cent having reached 35.

Occupationally, the West Coast group was split 45–55 between agricultural and nonagricultural pursuits. The bulk of the farmers operated as tenants,[9] or sharecroppers, but there were around 1,600 Japanese-owned farms with title vested in Nisei.

Truck farming predominated, and in this branch of activity Japanese American farmers had achieved importance far greater than the size of their group would suggest. In California, for example, they produced 30–35 per cent of all truck crops, and in some crops, e.g., fresh snap beans, celery, and strawberries, had a virtual monopoly.[10]

Of those in nonagricultural pursuits, two out of five were engaged in trade, and almost as great a proportion in personal and commercial services. Few were laborers in mechanical and manufacturing industries, and fewer still had attained status in the professions. As a whole the group belonged to the small entrepreneurial and service classes and was closely dependent upon agriculture, irrespective of occupational classification.

Demographically, they were indistinguishable from the majority group, with a high expectation of life and a low pattern of fertility.[11] Socially, the group was cohesive, with a high degree of family solidarity. Delinquency rates were low, and very few were found on relief rolls.

These were the people who were subject to increasingly severe restrictions from the outbreak of war until their forced mass migration, concentration, and detention in government-operated camps.

Most of the very early restrictions imposed on the Japanese mi-

---

[9] Of 6,170 Japanese-operated farms, 70 per cent were tenant-operated.

[10] See report by Lloyd H. Fisher, in U.S. Congress. House. Select Committee Investigating National Defense Migration. *National Defense Migration*, Hearings, 77th Congress, 2d Session. Pt. 31, Washington, Government Printing Office, 1942, pp. 11,815–11,832.

[11] See George Sabagh and Dorothy S. Thomas, "Changing Patterns of Fertility and Survival among the Japanese Americans on the Pacific Coast." *American Sociological Review*, October, 1945.

nority after the outbreak of the war applied only to the "enemy aliens" within the group. The only sense in which these restrictions were discriminatory was that almost all immigrants of Japanese origin were, because of their ineligibility to citizenship, automatically classified as "enemy aliens," a situation in sharp contrast with that facing immigrants from the two other enemy nations, Italy and Germany, a large proportion of whom had become naturalized American citizens and were thus exempt from the enemy-alien classification.

Presidential proclamations on December 7 and 8 made enemy aliens subject to apprehension and internment, restricted them in traveling, prohibited them from possessing a large number of contraband items, and designated them for possible exclusion from military zones. The Attorney General of the United States was charged with the execution of the terms of the proclamations.

The first official acts taken against enemy aliens occurred within a few hours after the Pearl Harbor attack, when agents of the Federal Bureau of Investigation began to round up those suspected of subversive activities. These arrests were based on lists previously compiled by various intelligence agencies. By nighttime hundreds of Japanese nationals had been taken into custody. In succeeding days arrests multiplied, and by February 16, 1942, 2,192 Japanese aliens had been placed under arrest in the United States, 1,266 of them from the Pacific Coast.[12] Because of the manner in which the attack had been launched by the enemy at Pearl Harbor, and because of wild stories (later proved to be entirely unfounded)[13] concerning a Japanese fifth column in Hawaii, Japanese nationals in the United States were apprehended and held on slighter evidence than were aliens of other enemy nationalities.[14]

---

[12] Department of Justice, Press Releases, December 8 and December 13, 1941; February 16, 1942.
[13] There was, for example, no act of sabotage committed by resident Japanese either in Hawaii or on the mainland, but even this fact was distorted to the disadvantage of the minority. The Commanding General of the Western Defense Command stated, "The very fact that no sabotage has taken place to date is a disturbing and confirming indication that such action will be taken." (U.S. Army, Western Defense Command and Fourth Army. *Final Report, Japanese Evacuation from the West Coast, 1942.* Washington, Government Printing Office, 1943, p. 34.)
[14] Extensive "spot" raids on Japanese Americans were later undertaken at the request of the Western Defense Command by agents of the FBI, accompanied by

Following quickly upon the initial arrests and incarcerations of aliens of enemy nationality, instructions were issued to all transportation companies prohibiting travel of "Japanese individuals" by train, plane, bus or vessel. The Treasury Department froze assets and credits, and business enterprises operated by enemy aliens were ordered closed.[15]

It soon became apparent that both official and popular classifications of members of the Japanese minority failed to make any differentiation on the basis of citizenship. As early as December 8, the status of Nisei[16] as American citizens was disregarded in favor of their status as descendants of the Japanese enemy. Thus the restriction on travel referred to "Japanese individuals" and was interpreted as applying both to aliens and citizens.[17] This confusion of citizens with aliens became especially marked on the West Coast where about 90 per cent of all persons of Japanese ancestry resided. In this area strategic points on highways were watched, and Japanese Americans, aliens and citizens alike, were stopped and questioned; many were held for days by local law-enforcement officers, no charges being filed against them. Many Japanese Americans were dismissed from private employment; others were evicted from their residences. Grocery stores and other business firms refused to sell them goods, and extensive economic and social boycotts developed against them. By the first week in February, confusion of alien ancestry with alien status had reached a point where the California State Personnel Board voted unanimously to bar from future civil service positions all "descendants of nationals with whom the

local and state law-enforcement officers. The most important positions involved were the large Japanese settlement on Terminal Island in the Los Angeles Harbor area; the Japanese area on Bainbridge Island, near the Bremerton Navy Yard (Washington); the town of Vallejo, California, near the Mare Island Navy Yard; the Palos Verdes area in Los Angeles County, and the California coastal counties of Monterey and Santa Cruz. Searches of Japanese-occupied homes and apprehension of Japanese nationals recurred at frequent intervals. For example, it was reported that the FBI arrested 119 Japanese aliens in northern California on February 21 (*San Francisco Examiner*, February 22, 1942); 93 in the same area on March 6 (*Oakland Tribune*, March 7, 1942); about 200 in southern California on March 13 (*Nichi Bei*, March 15, 1942); about 100 in central California on March 26 (*Nichi Bei*, March 28, 1942).

[15] Some of these restrictions were relaxed or rescinded within a short period.
[16] Sixty-four per cent of the total Japanese group in the western states were Nisei; of those 21 years of age or older, 36 per cent were Nisei.
[17] This restriction was modified within a few days to exempt Nisei.

United States is at war."[18] Though technically covering "descendants" of Germans, Italians, and Japanese alike, the order was applied only against Nisei.

Meanwhile, John L. DeWitt, Commanding General of the Western Defense Command, was urging a program of tightened control, asking specifically for the delineation of "zones" to be prohibited to aliens of enemy nationality and "areas" within which their activities could be more radically restricted.

In line with these recommendations, Attorney General Biddle announced, on January 29, two prohibited zones, one on the San Francisco waterfront and one around the Municipal Airport of Los Angeles. German, Italian, and Japanese aliens were instructed to evacuate these areas before February 24.[19] Between January 31 and February 7, the Attorney General delimited 133 additional prohibited zones in the vicinity of airports, hydroelectric dams and power plants, gas and electric plants, airfields, pumping stations, harbor areas, and military installations. The majority of zones were small, usually circles of 1,000 feet radii or rectangles of several city blocks.[20] On February 4, twelve "restricted areas" were defined, eleven being small zones surrounding hydroelectric plants in California, but the twelfth encompassing the entire coastal strip from the Oregon border south to a point approximately 50 miles north of Los Angeles and extending inland for distances varying from 30 to 150 miles. Regulations for these areas required that enemy aliens remain within their places of residence between the hours of 9 P.M. and 6 A.M.; (2) that at all other times during the day they be found only at their place of residence or employment or traveling between those two places, or within a distance of not more than five miles from their place of residence; (3) that if found disobeying the regulations they be subject to immediate apprehension and internment.[21]

The problem of the removal and resettlement of aliens of enemy nationalities and their families from prohibited zones was placed on a voluntary basis. A deadline had to be met, but the evacuees

---

[18] Minutes of the Meeting of the California State Personnel Board, January 27 and 28, 1942.

[19] Department of Justice, Press Release, January 29, 1942.

[20] *Ibid.*, January 31, February 2, February 4 and February 7, 1942.

[21] *Ibid.*, February 4, 1942.

were free to choose any residence outside the prohibited zones. At the same time a social assistance program was developed to implement their resettlement, and the principal responsibility for developing this program was vested in the Federal Security Agency. Simultaneously, Tom C. Clark, a representative of the Department of Justice, was made coördinator of the control program with the Western Defense Command.

Many of the dispossessed found refuge in the homes of relatives and neighbors just outside the prohibited zones. The hostility of public opinion, which will be described later, made further extensive movements most difficult. Housing and employment were almost impossible to find, and the government had, up to this time, made no arrangement for custodianship of the property of evacuees, who could, according to one of the high-ranking officials in charge of the program, do no more than "either turn over their business to their creditors at great loss or abandon it entirely" while "the commercial buzzards" were "taking great advantage of this hardship, making offers way below even inventory cost, and very much below real value."[22]

Approximately 10,000 aliens of enemy nationality resided in prohibited zones that were to be evacuated by February 24. Before the movement could be completed, DeWitt recommended that piece-meal voluntary evacuation of enemy aliens from small zones under the auspices of the Department of Justice be superseded by forced mass evacuation from large areas, under War Department auspices, of not only enemy aliens but also of "all Japanese" and any other classes or persons who might be specified. Alien enemies would be evacuated and interned under guard, while Japanese American citizens would be offered an opportunity to accept voluntary internment and those who declined would "be excluded from military areas, and left to their own resources, or, in the alternative, be encouraged to accept resettlement outside of such military areas with such assistance as the state governments concerned or the Federal Security Agency may be by that time prepared to offer."[23]

---

[22] Field Notes (based on a manuscript by this official), February 18, 1942.

[23] DeWitt to Secretary of War, "Final Recommendations of the Commanding General, Western Defense Command and Fourth Army, February 14, 1942." U.S. Army. Western Defense Command and Fourth Army. *Final Report, Japanese Evacuation from the West Coast, 1942.* Washington, Government Printing Office, 1943, p. 37.

DeWitt's recommendations were quickly acted upon, but without specification of the groups to be evacuated or the Military Commander who should order evacuation. On February 19 President Roosevelt issued Executive Order 9066, authorizing

the Secretary of War, and the Military Commanders whom he may from time to time designate . . . to prescribe military areas . . . from which any or all persons may be excluded, and with respect to which, the right of any person to enter, remain in, or leave shall be subject to whatever restriction the Secretary of War or the appropriate Military Commander may impose in his discretion.

And the Secretary of War, on February 20, delegated to General DeWitt the authority

to carry out the duties and responsibilities imposed by said Executive Order for that portion of the United States embraced in the Western Defense Command, including such changes in the prohibited and restricted areas heretofore designated by the Attorney General as you deem proper to prescribe.[24]

General DeWitt promptly prescribed "military areas" and defined classes of persons who should be excluded from these areas. On March 2 he issued "Public Proclamation Number One," designating the western third of Washington and Oregon, the western half of California and the southern quarter of Arizona as Military Area No. 1—an area from which, he announced, all persons of Japanese ancestry as well as German and Italian aliens would be excluded. The remainder of the four states was called Military Area No. 2, within which there were a number of small "prohibited zones," but which was otherwise unrestricted. Although Proclamation Number One had referred to aliens of all enemy nationalities as well as to all persons of Japanese ancestry, no mass action was ever taken with regard to Germans and Italians. A press release accompanying the proclamation stated that orders would be issued "requiring all Japanese, including those who are American born, to vacate all of Military Area No. 1." Such persons "will be required by future orders to leave certain critical points within the military areas first. These areas will be defined and announced shortly." Following this, "a gradual program of exclusion from the remainder of Military Area No. 1 will be developed."[25]

[24] Secretary of War to DeWitt, February 20, 1942, *ibid.,* p. 25.
[25] Western Defense Command and Fourth Army, Press Release, March 3, 1942.

Simultaneously, restrictions previously imposed on enemy aliens were extended to American citizens of Japanese ancestry. Proclamation No. 1 required Nisei to execute "change of address" notices. And Proclamation No. 3, on March 24, established a curfew, prohibited traveling "more than five miles from their place of residence," and imposed contraband regulations.

Up to this point, plans of the Western Defense Command called for exclusion but not detention. The Command was interested in removing, as a matter of "military necessity,"[26a] the whole Japanese minority (which it regarded as "potential enemies"[26b]) from strategic areas on the West Coast. It had no interest in the process of resettlement, provided this resettlement was outside the areas marked for exclusion. As will be described in Chapter II, the War Relocation Authority, a nonmilitary organization, was created to implement resettlement, although its program was later diverted to one of detention. Meantime, in order to facilitate evacuation, DeWitt, on March 14,[27] formed the Wartime Civil Control Administration, which in turn established 48 offices in centers of Japanese population. Because it was realized that some evacuees might not, for physical or economic reasons, be able to find homes and jobs in other areas and thus meet evacuation deadlines, construction of two "reception centers," one at Manzanar, California, and the other near Parker, Arizona, was rushed to accommodate them temporarily.

Evacuation by individual initiative, however, met many obstacles due primarily to public hostility in the receiving areas.[28] The protest against the influx of Japanese Americans was especially vehement in the interior counties of California. Persons of Japanese lineage "considered too dangerous to remain on the West

---

[26a] DeWitt to Chief of Staff, U.S. Army. Letter of transmittal June 5, 1943. U.S. Army. Western Defense Command and Fourth Army. *Final Report, Japanese Evacuation from the West Coast, 1942.* Washington, Government Printing Office, 1943, p. vii. Also DeWitt to Secretary of War, "Final Recommendations of the Commanding General, Western Defense Command and Fourth Army, February 14, 1942." *Ibid.,* pp. 33–34.

[26b] *Ibid.,* p. 34

[27] Wartime Civil Control Administration, Press Release, March 14, 1942. In the U.S. Army Fnal Report *(op. cit.)* it is stated on p. 41 and p. 66 that WCCA was established on March 11; on p. 106 and elsewhere the date is given as March 12.

[28] See pp. 24–25.

Coast [were] similarly regarded by state and local authorities, and by the population of the interior."[29]

There was general agreement that voluntary migration of evacuees should cease,[30] and on March 27 General DeWitt issued Public Proclamation Number Four, "freezing" all persons of Japanese ancestry in Military Area No. 1 as of midnight, March 29. From that date, voluntary movement ceased, and plans were developed both for controlled mass evacuation and for detention of the evacuees until the War Relocation Authority could assume control. It became apparent that the plan for two "reception centers" was inadequate. Sites for a number of detention camps had to be found quickly within the exclusion area. In all, fifteen such camps—called "Assembly Centers"—were established, for the most part at large fairgrounds and race tracks. The acquisition of the first of this type of center, the Santa Anita race track near Los Angeles, was announced on March 19,[31] and the Manzanar Reception Center was also used for this purpose.[32]

Evacuation was accomplished by a series of Civilian Exclusion Orders, each of which covered a defined area within the total Prohibited Zone. Civilian Exclusion Order No. 1 was issued on March 24, and led to the mass evacuation five days later of 258 persons of Japanese ancestry from Bainbridge Island, Washington, to Manzanar.[33] The second forced migration from the coastal area in Los Angeles County to Santa Anita involving some 2,500 Japanese Americans, took place on April 5. Civilian Exclusion Order No. 99, defining a small area near Sacramento, cleared the last of the evacuees from Military Area No. 1 (June 6, 1942). In all, 100,313 persons of Japanese ancestry were evacuated, by virtue of Civilian Exclusion Orders Nos. 1–99, from Military Area No. 1, 90,307 of

[29] U.S. Army. Western Defense Command and Fourth Army, *Final Report, Japanese Evacuation from the West Coast, 1942.* Washington, Government Printing Office, 1943, p. 43.

[30] *Ibid.*, p. 106. See p. 25 for recommendations by Director of the War Relocation Authority.

[31] Wartime Civil Control Administration, Press Release, March 19, 1942.

[32] Parker was never used as an assembly center. It became a relocation project operated by the Indian Service under WRA control and was renamed Poston. See pp. 27–28.

[33] There was a voluntary mass movement of some 2,100 persons from Los Angeles to the Manzanar Reception Center, which was then still in the process of construction, beginning on March 21, 1942.

them moving to assembly centers, the remainder directly to relocation projects.[34] (See Chapter II.)

In announcing the first evacuations, the Western Defense Command had designated roughly the eastern two thirds of Washington
and Oregon, the eastern half of California, and the northern three
quarters of Arizona as "Military Area No. 2." Although this area
contained a number of small prohibited zones, it soon became
known as the "Free Zone" or "White Zone," the natural destination of voluntary migrants who sought to establish homes and businesses as near as possible to the area from which they were being
evacuated. In this, they were encouraged explicitly by various government agencies. Proclamation Number One by General DeWitt
had assured them that "the designation of Military Area No. 2 as
such does not contemplate any prohibition or regulation or restriction except with respect to the [prohibited] zones established
therein." Tom C. Clark further urged voluntary evacuees to "save
themselves unnecessary trouble, hardship and expense by moving
at least *beyond* the confines of Military Area No. 1 and also *outside*
the smaller 'prohibited' zones in Military Area No. 2."[35] At no time
was official warning given evacuees against settling in the unrestricted territory of Military Area No. 2. Before the freezing orders
were enforced, more than 4,000 evacuees, almost one half of the
total group of voluntary migrants,[36] moved to the California portion of Military Area No. 2, with travel permits and in some cases
traveling funds provided by the military authorities. Suddenly, on
June 2, 1942, the Commanding General of the Western Defense
Command and Fourth Army issued Public Proclamation Number
Six, prohibiting all persons of Japanese ancestry from leaving the
California[37] portion of Military Area No. 2, establishing a curfew
for them and announcing that they would be excluded "from said

[34] U.S. Army, *op. cit.*, pp. 357 and 375.

[35] Western Defense Command and Fourth Army, Press Release, March 7, 1942.
Italics theirs.

[36] "Approximately 9,000 persons of Japanese ancestry voluntarily [migrated]
from Military Area No. 1 to interior points." U.S. Army. Western Defense Command and Fourth Army. *Final Report, Japanese Evacuation from the West
Coast, 1942.* Washington, Government Printing Office, 1943, p. 43.

[37] It is significant, in consideration of the public and political pressures, that
only the California portion of Military Area No. 2 was covered by these later
evacuation orders. Corresponding portions of Washington, Oregon, and Arizona
were not designated in the orders and were never evacuated.

California portion of Military Area No. 2 by future orders or proclamations." The first Civilian Exclusion Order for this area was issued on June 27, and by August 8 all persons of Japanese ancestry, aliens and citizens alike, had been removed from the eastern part of California. In all, 9,337 evacuees were encompassed in Civilian Exclusion Orders 100–108,[38] almost half of whom were experiencing a second uprooting in less than six months. When this movement was completed, the total number of persons forcibly removed from the Western States was 109,650.[39]

The mechanics of forced evacuation operated with extraordinary speed and precision. The Wartime Civil Control Administration had set forth six principles to guide the movement:

First, it was determined that the areas to be evacuated would be handled so far as possible in the order of their relative military importance. . . .

Second, it was determined that the evacuation would not split family units or communities where this could be avoided. . . . The basic principle of maintaining communities was adopted to maintain a natural community and economic balance and to preserve desirable institutions by moving each family with its relatives and friends.

Third, it was determined that the program should entail a minimum of financial loss to the evacuees; that all possible advice and assistance be available to (but not forced upon) evacuees. . . .

Fourth, it was desired that a minimum of active military units and other military personnel be used in the program; that, instead, the evacuation should be accomplished as far as practicable by civilian personnel, making full use of Federal and State civilian agency facilities. . . .

Fifth, it was desired that the evacuated population not only be removed to areas outside of the critical military area as rapidly as practicable, but also to locations where the evacuees could be relatively self-supporting for the duration. . . .

Sixth, it was concluded that evacuation and relocation [resettlement] could not be accomplished simultaneously. This was the heart of the plan. It entailed provision for a transitory phase. It called for the establishment of Assembly Centers at or near each center of evacuee population. These Centers were to be designed to provide shelter and messing facilities and the minimum essentials for the maintenance of health and morale.[40]

In each area covered by a Civilian Exclusion Order, a civil control station, staffed with representatives of the Federal Reserve Bank, the Farm Security Administration, and the associated agen-

---

[38] U.S. Army. Western Defense Command and Fourth Army. *Final Report, Japanese Evacuation from the West Coast, 1942*. Washington, Government Printing Office, 1943, p. 357.

[39] *Ibid.*   [40] *Ibid.*, pp. 77–78.

cies of the Federal Security Agency, was set up. The head of each evacuee family was required to report at the station, at a specified time, for instructions and registration.

The control station was so set up that evacuees could be "processed" with a minimum of time and confusion. During the processing, the evacuee was told of services offered by the Farm Security Administration and the Federal Reserve Bank for property protection. His needs with respect to food, shelter, and clothing in the interim before the date of moving were ascertained, and disbursal vouchers were issued where necessary.[41]

Evacuees were instructed to carry with them on departure bedding and linen, toilet articles, extra clothes, tableware, and "essential personal effects." The size and amount of goods to be taken was "limited to that which can be carried by the individual or the family group."[42] No provision was made for shipping of household goods to the assembly centers.

Failure to protect the property of aliens leaving the first "prohibited zones" designated by the Department of Justice had resulted in widespread distress. The mass evacuation of citizens as well as aliens, under the Army program, made provision for property protection even more urgent, and the War Department had finally requested the assistance of the Treasury Department.

The Federal Reserve Bank of San Francisco had been designated by the Secretary of the Treasury as the authority to undertake the property conservation program.[43] A special delegation of power had been made by the Secretary of the Treasury to the Secretary of Agriculture who, in turn, had designated the Farm Security Administration as the agency to administer the farm property program. Though there were some borderline cases, the division of responsibility between the Federal Reserve Bank and the Farm Security Administration was clear; the former agency handled personal property and household goods, motor vehicles, and non-agricultural businesses; the latter was charged with responsibility over farms and farm equipment.

[41] Only a small number of evacuees asked for or received such aid.

[42] Actually, no great restrictions were placed in practice on the amount of hand luggage taken to Assembly Centers. Packages which the family was unable to carry were usually transported by baggage cars or trucks.

[43] See Joint Statement of Alien Property Custodian and Secretary of the Treasury, Treasury Department, Press Release, March 12, 1942.

To protect the evacuees from forced sales, both the Federal Reserve Bank and the Farm Security Administration were given authority to "freeze" transactions involving the property of evacuees. Evacuees were also informed that

no Japanese need sacrifice any personal property of value. If he cannot dispose of it at a fair price, he will have opportunity to store it prior to the time he is forced to evacuate by Exclusion Order. Persons who attempt to take advantage of Japanese evacuees by trying to obtain property at sacrifice prices are un-American, unfair, and are deserving only of the severest censure.[44]

The important safeguard of "freezing" was never used by the Federal Reserve Bank and in only a single instance by the Farm Security Administration. The opportunity for voluntarily storing personal property was qualified by the fact that evacuees had to agree that property delivered to the Federal Reserve Bank would be "at the sole risk" of the owner and, consequently, very few evacuees took advantage of the facilities offered. The property form which evacuees were required to sign stated:

It is agreed that no liability or responsibility shall be assumed by the Federal Reserve Bank . . . for any act or omission in connection with its [the property's] disposition. It is understood that no insurance will be provided on this property.[45]

The Bank undertook a definite policy of encouraging liquidation and by far the greatest number of evacuees sold their property at distress prices, gave it away, or stored it at their own expense and risk.

As a whole, Japanese American merchants and businessmen were faced with problems that made equitable settlement impossible. In the space of a few weeks they were required to sell or liquidate their business interests and their business properties. The compulsory nature of the movement placed them under every conceivable commercial disadvantage. Buyers as a rule were unwilling to pay reasonable prices when fully aware of the fact that a sale would have to be made, whatever the price, if the owner were to salvage anything from his enterprise. The shortness of time and the fact that there were many evacuees in the same predicament gave every

---

[44] Wartime Civil Control Administration, Press Release, March 29, 1942.
[45] Personal Property Form, Wartime Civil Control Administration, Form FRB-2.

advantage to even the honest buyer. For the dishonest, the confusion and fears of the evacuees made fraud and cheating easy. Many cases of forced sales were put on the record.

This resulted in something close to disaster for virtually every Japanese American businessman. Precise data on losses are difficult to obtain, but it may safely be concluded that every evacuee incurred some loss, that many of them suffered severe and irreparable losses, both tangible and intangible, and that the burden fell more heavily upon the small owner than the large.

The Farm Security Administration arranged for transfer of farm properties to Caucasian tenants and corporations and, in many cases, provided loans for the latter. It had two functions: (1) insuring the continuation of full farm production, and (2) protecting the evacuated farmer from unfair and inequitable transfers. In practice, these ends were frequently incompatible. However clear the twofold emphasis was in the abstract, the practical policy of the Wartime Civil Control Administration and the Farm Security Administration was geared principally to insuring farm production and only secondarily to minimizing evacuee losses.

Evacuee farmers were in the worst bargaining position possible. The evacuation came during late spring and summer months, after planting and fertilizing but before harvesting. The authorities urged Japanese Americans to continue their farming activities and warned them that destruction of crops was sabotage and would be punished as such. The Tolan Committee, which investigated the problems of evacuation, stated that "while supporting the exhortation of the Wartime Civil Control Administration to the evacuees to continue farming operations up to the time of evacuation as a demonstration of loyalty," it felt "nevertheless constrained to point out that this policy has frequently worked to the economic disadvantage of the evacuees or has proved beyond their economic means to carry out."[46] The continuation of farming operations required, for example, the utilization of farm implements to the very last moment, thus making it more difficult to find acceptable offers for the equipment when the evacuation order finally came. Again,

[46] U.S. Congress. House. Select Committee Investigating National Defense Migration. *National Defense Migration, Fourth Interim Report.* 77th Congress, 2d Session. Findings and Recommendations on Evacuation of Enemy Aliens and Others from Prohibited Military Zones. Washington, Government Printing Office, 1942, p. 15.

continued farming operations required payment for sprays, fer-
tilizers, labor, and other farm necessities which were a drain upon
the farmer's resources. A farmer who obeyed the dictates of the
Wartime Civil Control Administration found himself in the position of having a substantial portion of his total resources involved
in growing field crops. Since evacuation made it impossible for him
to harvest this crop, it was necessary for him to accept the best offer
available.

Instances were soon encountered where the interests of landlords, creditors and potential purchasers of crops and farm assets came into conflict,
not only with the interests of Japanese farmers, but also with those of
each other. Landlords, because of the presence of non-assignability clauses
in leases, sought to deprive Japanese farm operators of their crops and
leasehold interests. Conditional contract sellers were ready to exercise for-
feitures based upon breaches which would be necessitated by the enforced
evacuation. Landlords, creditors, and prospective purchasers were ready to
take advantage in other ways of the adverse bargaining position of Japanese evacuees, even at the cost of serious loss of agricultural production.[47]

Before and during the period when evacuees were desperately
trying to safeguard their economic interests, attitudes were being
built up which transformed many members of a traditionally law-
abiding, coöperative minority group into factions collectively protesting and rebelling against both the Caucasian majority which
was pressing to dispossess, evacuate and incarcerate them and persons of their own racial group who collaborated with government
agencies.

The conviction was growing that they were an unwanted people,
rejected by a hostile and prejudiced American public. Their definition of public hostility was formed, in the main, by radio and
press. For example, John B. Hughes, a Los Angeles news commentator for the Mutual Broadcasting Company, initiated a one-man
campaign against the resident Japanese Americans on January 5
and for almost a month thereafter devoted some or all of his broadcasting time to arousing public opinion in favor of "drastic action."
The local press, in spite of some editorial pleas for tolerance,[48]

---

[47] U.S. Army. Western Defense Command and Fourth Army. *Final Report,
Japanese Evacuation from the West Coast, 1942.* Washington, Government Printing Office, 1943, p. 138.

[48] E.g., the *San Francisco Chronicle* of December 9, 1941:
The roundup of Japanese citizens in various parts of the country . . . is not a

printed, day after day, news stories slanted in such a way as to cast suspicion upon the minority group and to arouse fear among its members. In December, for example, the following, among other, items were reported: Chinese were said to be preparing to wear "anti-Jap" badges;[49] a barber shop was offering "free shaves for Japs" but was "not responsible for accidents";[50] a funeral parlor was advertising "I'd rather do business with a Jap than with an American";[51] armed Japanese in Lower California were said to be ready to cross the border;[52] a naval sentry had seen flashing lights (presumably signals) in a Los Angeles Japanese waterfront colony;[53] in connection with the suicide of a Japanese-American doctor, a "spy ring" in the Los Angeles district was said to have been revealed;[54] "the Fifth Column character" of Japanese language schools was "exposed";[55] several arrested Japanese Americans were said to have been discovered with revolvers, signal flares, rifle bullets, a telescope sight and a short-wave radio set;[56] riots were feared in Stockton, California, where Filipinos had already killed one Japanese American.[57] Slanted news items of this sort occurred with increasing frequency during the months that followed.

Nationally known writers "uncovered" dangers and presented "solutions" in their syndicated columns. Henry McLemore in the *San Francisco Examiner* and other papers of January 29, 1942, argued for the removal of every Japanese American on the West Coast "to a point deep in the interior." He didn't mean, he pointed out, a "nice part of the interior either":

Herd 'em up, pack 'em off and give 'em the inside room in the badlands. Let 'em be pinched, hurt, hungry and dead up against it. . . . let us have

---

call for volunteer spy hunters to go into action. Neither is it a reason to lift an eyebrow at a Japanese, whether American-born or not. . . .

There is no excuse to wound the sensibilities of any persons in America by showing suspicion or prejudice. That, if anything, is a help to fifth column spirit. An American-born Nazi would like nothing better than to set the dogs of prejudice on a first-class American Japanese.

[49] *Los Angeles Examiner*, December 16, 1941.
[50] *Los Angeles Times*, December 19, 1941.
[51] *Ibid.*
[52] *Los Angeles Examiner*, December 11, 1941.
[53] *Sacramento Bee*, December 17, 1941; *Los Angeles Times*, December 18, 1941.
[54] *Los Angeles Times*, December 19, 1941.
[55] *Los Angeles Examiner*, December 20, 1941.
[56] *Ibid.*, January 4, 1942; see also *Sacramento Bee*, December 11, 1941.
[57] *San Francisco Examiner*, December 27, 1941.

no patience with the enemy or with anyone whose veins carry his blood . . . Personally, I hate the Japanese. And that goes for all of them,

while Westbrook Pegler urged that "the Japanese in California should be under armed guard to the last man and woman right now and to hell with habeas corpus until the danger is over."[58]

Through the newspapers also, Japanese Americans were made aware of demands by West Coast politicians for their evacuation and internment and of resolutions to the same end passed by a multitude of local political, economic, and social organizations. Among political leaders thus quoted were Attorney General Warren of California; many of the West Coast congressmen, particularly Leland Ford and A. J. Elliott of California; mayors of many large and small cities, particularly Mayor Bowron of Los Angeles and Mayor Riley of Portland. Resolutions were passed by local American Legion and other veterans' groups; by county boards of supervisors; by civilian defense councils; by Townsend Clubs; by farm groups, labor unions, business men's associations, and even by mothers' clubs. At the same time, such traditionally anti-Oriental organizations as the California Joint Immigration Committee and the Native Sons and Daughters of the Golden West released an almost constant stream of propaganda against the resident Japanese Americans.

Lost in the ever-increasing cries of approval of the Army's action and demands for even more stringent means of control, were the voices of organizations and individuals who urged tolerance and fair play and raised questions about the justice of some aspects of the procedures that were being undertaken.[59]

To many of the Japanese Americans, the apparent general public hostility and the widely reported activities of anti-Japanese pressure groups were taken as convincing evidence that the evacuation orders were motivated more by racial prejudice than by the Army's stated regard for military necessity. Much later this belief was confirmed in the minds of the evacuees when General DeWitt was reported in the public press as saying

[58] "Fair Enough," February 16, 1942. In *Los Angeles Times* and other papers.

[59] For example, the Pacific Coast Committee on National Security and Fair Play, the American Civil Liberties Union, the International Institute, various church, educational and social welfare groups, and such prominent individuals as the President and the Provost of the University of California, the President of Stanford University, the political commentator of the *San Francisco Chronicle*.

A Jap's a Jap. . . . It makes no difference whether he is an American citizen or not. . . . I don't want any of them . . . They are a dangerous element . . . There is no way to determine their loyalty.[60]

In the months that followed, this statement was quoted by many Japanese Americans as incontrovertible evidence of the prejudice that had motived the evacuation. (See chapters IV and XIII.)

While attitudes were thus being formed about the prejudice and hostility of the American people and their government (by definition, the Army), resentment was being built up against Japanese Americans who collaborated with the prejudiced and hostile majority. Members of one organization—the Japanese American Citizens League—fell under especial suspicion. This, an all-Nisei organization, had taken over the community leadership lost by the interned Issei[61] in the days immediately following Pearl Harbor. At the outbreak of the war it already had a chapter in every urban and rural center of Japanese settlement, and national headquarters, as well as many of the local chapters, immediately sent President Roosevelt pledges of allegiance to the United States. They offered wholehearted coöperation with government agencies, and were soon recognized as the official liaison group. They endeavored to maintain good public relations. They coöperated with the FBI in the apprehension of suspected subversives and in the investigation of alleged acts and utterances of disloyalty by members of the Japa-

[60] *Los Angeles Times,* April 14, 1943, and various other West Coast newspapers. The official transcript of the hearings, thus quoted in the newspaper, records the General as saying, less colloquially:

I don't want any of them here. They are a dangerous element. There is no way to determine their loyalty. . . . It makes no difference whether he is an American citizen, he is still a Japanese. American citizenship does not necessarily determine loyalty. (U.S. Congress. House. Committee on Naval Affairs. *Investigation of Congested Areas.* Hearings before a Subcommittee. 78th Congress, 1st Session, Washington, Government Printing Office, 1943, pp. 739–740.)

There are many similar statements by General DeWitt on record, e.g., "The Japanese race is an enemy race and while many second and third generation Japanese born on United States soil, possessed of United States citizenship, have become 'Americanized,' the racial strains are undiluted." (U.S. Army, Western Defense Command and Fourth Army, *Final Report, Japanese Evacuation from the West Coast, 1942.* Washington, Government Printing Office, 1943, p. 34.)

[61] Many of those taken into custody in the FBI roundups were Issei community leaders, including officers of Japanese American organizations, vernacular newspaper publishers, language school teachers, Shinto and Buddhist priests. The fear resulting from these arrests made other Issei, many of whom had occupied positions in social, political, and economic activities subordinate to the internees, hesitant to assume leadership.

nese communities. These activities soon earned for the Nisei leaders the reputation of being *inu* (informers; literally "dogs"), and of betraying the parent generation. They became the target of social censure in Japanese American communities, for the accepted code of the Japanese immigrants had been that no detrimental information would be divulged outside the racial group.[62]

The JACL leaders had also made strenuous efforts to have Nisei exempted from evacuation orders. Upon the promulgation of the mass evacuation policy, however, they continued to offer wholehearted coöperation to the Army and all other branches of the federal government. The national president of the JACL was reported as saying:

> Never in the thousands of years of human history has a group of citizens been branded on so wholesale a scale as being treacherous to the land in which they live.
> We question the motives and patriotism of men and leaders who intentionally fan racial animosity and hatred ...
> [But] we are going into exile as our duty to our country because the President and the military commander of this area have deemed it a necessity. We are gladly coöperating because this is one way of showing that our protestations of loyalty are sincere.[63]

And another JACL leader wrote, "We can turn the tragedy of evacuation into a display of loyalty."[64]

The readiness of the JACL to identify itself as an adherent and supporter of the Army policy widened the normal generational and cultural cleavages in the Japanese American group. The older Nisei, in particular, were blamed for their attempt to save themselves from evacuation at the expense of Issei.

The collaborationist activities of the JACL continued after the evacuees had entered assembly centers. Since the use of the Japanese language was forbidden, both in public meetings and in the center newspapers, leadership remained largely within the Nisei group in general, and the JACL organization in particular. The status of JACL as a liaison group was thereby strengthened and its

---

[62] *Inu* branding dated back to the late 1920's and early 1930's when extensive searches by immigration officials for Japanese nationals who had entered the United States illegally led to the belief that some Japanese had turned in others for personal revenge or from mercenary motives.

[63] *Oakland Tribune*, March 9, 1942.

[64] President of the Pasadena Chapter to the national secretary, February 28, 1942. From official JACL files.

members appropriated many of the positions of prestige in the centers. At the same time, their *inu* status within their own racial group was confirmed in the minds of many of their fellow evacuees, and they were even blamed for the evacuation itself.[65] There were, however, no outbreaks against them in the assembly centers, although accumulated resentments later led to acts of violence in relocation projects. (See chapters II and III.)

Assembly centers had been planned for use for very short periods. Their sole purpose was to serve as points of concentration and confinement until the War Relocation Authority could take over. (See Chapter II.) But owing to wartime difficulties in construction and transportation, the period of assembly-center operation extended through 224 days. The largest center, at the Santa Anita race track "had the longest period of occupancy: 215 days, with an average population of 12,919 for this entire period. During most of the period, the population of Santa Anita was more than 18,000."[66] Here, as in other assembly centers, life in converted horse stalls and hastily constructed barracks presented many difficulties. As the Army report states: "For extended occupancy by men, women and children whose movements were necessarily restricted, the use of facilities of this character is not highly desirable."[67]

Up to this point, while the evacuees had been subjected to an extraordinarily tortuous experience they had manifested no overt mass resistance to authority. In many centers a nebulous protest movement developed but in only one (Santa Anita) was there a disturbance of serious proportions. This and the latent protests are significant as setting the pattern later to be repeated with variations in one relocation project after another.

---

[65] As the suspicion of the JACL leaders' *inu* status grew, many evacuees forgot the nonpolitical activities of this organization. There is abundant evidence that its members had worked unceasingly to alleviate the distress of Japanese Americans "on the verge of being evicted because they could not pay their rent ... travelers caught short; bachelors with no place to stay or eat; families whose heads had been interned"—and to channel information about the ever-changing regulations to which they were subjected to "the first generation group which could not read the daily [American] newspapers." (Final Report of the National Secretary to the National Board of the JACL, manuscript, April 22, 1944. From official JACL files.)

[66] U.S. Army. Western Defense Command and Fourth Army. *Final Report, Japanese Evacuation from the West Coast, 1942.* Washington, Government Printing Office, 1943, p. 227.

[67] *Ibid.,* p. 152.

The Santa Anita incident is described in the Army report as follows:

At Santa Anita on August 4, 1942, a routine search for various articles of contraband was started immediately after the morning meal. A few of the interior security police became over-zealous in their search and somewhat overbearing in their manner of approach to evacuees in two of the Center's seven districts. Added to this was an order from the Center Manager[68] to pick up, without advance notice, electric hot plates which had previously been allowed on written individual authorization of the Center Management staff to families who needed them for the preparation of infant formulas and food for the sick. . . .

Poor liaison, or rather the complete lack of liaison in this incident, between the Center Management and the heads of the interior security police resulted in the failure of reports of complaints to reach the chief of interior security police until mid-afternoon. Those complaints, based to a certain extent on solid ground grew in the intervening four or five hours to rumors of all kinds of violations on the part of the police. When finally the complaints reached the chief of interior police, the search was promptly postponed just as the crowds were beginning to gather.

Two mobs and one crowd of women evacuees formed. One evacuee who had long been suspected by the disorderly elements among the population of giving information to the police was set upon and severely beaten though not seriously injured. The interior security police were harassed but none were injured.

This is the single instance . . . in which the military police were called into [an assembly center]. . . . No further disturbance occurred after the military police entered. The crowds dispersed, and no further threats of violence were circulated and no actual attempts at violence occurred. This disturbance was spontaneous and not the result of subversive planning. . . .

Center Management and Interior Security staff officials responsible for the lack of liaison which had allowed the all too evident signs of brewing trouble to reach the boiling point without action were removed from the Center.[69]

----

[68] "The Assembly Centers were largely staffed by personnel 'borrowed' from the Work Projects Administration." *Ibid.,* p. 222.

[69] *Ibid.,* pp. 218–219. Accounts by participant observers do not deviate greatly from this revealing official report. They emphasize cumulative resentments over repressive measures during the month preceding the "incident," e.g., curtailment on reading and possessing Japanese language literature on July 9; and a ban on Japanese phonograph records on July 28. They indicate that suspicion of alleged *inu* was widespread among the population and was not limited to the "disorderly elements." (Field Notes, August, 1942.)

Јᒪᒪᒪᒪᒪᒪᒪᒪᒪᒪᒪᒪᒪᒪᒪᒪᒪᒪᒪᒪᒪᒪᒪᒪᒪᒪᒪᒪᒪᒪᒪᒪ

Chapter II

DETENTION
Confinement Behind Barbed Wire

THE WAR RELOCATION AUTHORITY was created
by executive order in March, 1942, and Milton S. Eisenhower of
the Department of Agriculture was appointed as director. Its functions were defined as supervision of, provision of employment for,
and resettlement of the displaced evacuees. In performing these
functions, it was given broad discretionary powers, subject only to
two limitations: (1) it could not initiate further evacuation; and
(2) it had no power to return evacuees to the areas from which
military authorities had excluded them.

Policies formulated in Washington early in March had been
intended merely to implement the War Department's plan of
encouraging voluntary migration of evacuees to inland areas. WRA
never had an opportunity to put these policies into effect, for, as
described in Chapter I, appreciable numbers of the 9,000 evacuees
who had moved, with Army encouragement, to inland areas were
met with general hostility and physical violence. Governors in the
intermountain states had, with one notable exception,[1] unanimously opposed further influx. They had refused to coöperate in
a program which they interpreted as an attempt on the part of
California to dump upon them its "undesirable enemy aliens" and
"potential saboteurs." They had expressed willingness to accept the
migrants only if they were placed in "concentration camps," and
if a labor program were worked out with local labor on a non-
competitive basis and with the work force under armed guards.
The press and various local organizations had joined vigorously
in the opposition. Many Japanese American leaders, both on the

---

[1] Governor Ralph Carr of Colorado.

[24]

West Coast and in inland areas, and many officials concerned with the evacuation, discouraged by the reception the voluntary evacuees were meeting, advised that the movement stop. On March 24, Mr. Eisenhower formally recommended cessation of voluntary evacuation. Three days later, military orders confirmed this recommendation and, as described in Chapter I, "froze" evacuees in Military Area No. 1, and led to the detention of the bulk of them in assembly centers.

Planning on a new level was immediately required, for, whereas it had previously been hoped that most of the evacuees would resettle on their own initiative, it was now clear that almost the entire group would have to be cared for by WRA. Projects capable of housing and providing work opportunities for more than 100,000 people had to be found and developed, and procedures for moving the evacuees rapidly from assembly centers or direct from their homes into these projects had to be devised. The War Relocation Authority

... had in mind what might be thought of as a five point program. We planned for relocation centers in such places that there would always be public works to do, such as conservation, subjugation of land, and so on.

Second, there would be opportunities for producing agricultural crops.

Third, we would establish some small industries. ...

Fourth, if there developed definite labor shortages in the Western States ... we have hoped from the first that conditions could be worked out so that it would be possible for the evacuees to engage in private employment during portions of the year particularly in agricultural work.

And, fifth ... we hoped it would be possible for many of the evacuees to establish their own communities and to be entirely self supporting.[2]

This program was noteworthy for its dual aspect: it called for extensive public works, agriculture, and manufacturing, within the centers, and it also provided for employment outside the centers. This latter aspect of planning reflected the continued hope of WRA officials that the reintroduction of Japanese Americans into normal American life was still possible, despite the public hostility that had halted voluntary evacuation.

These plans, too, were defeated shortly after their formation by the pressure of public officials and of representatives of political organizations in the inland states, in spite of the desire of certain of the farm interests to facilitate the importation of evacuee labor.

[2] WRA, *First Quarterly Report*, March 18 to June 30, 1942.

This second failure meant further drastic revision in WRA plans, which were accordingly contracted to exclude both individual resettlement and the setting up of independent, self-sufficient Japanese American communities. What remained was a program of public works, agriculture, and industry within large centers, each a military zone, and each guarded by Army troops. The economic and community life of Japanese Americans was to be confined to these centers.

Public and political pressure thus determined the form of the entire program. The original evacuation had not been intended to limit the free movement of evacuees in any way once they were outside the narrow coastal strip of the Prohibited Zone. The reaction of the inland areas, however, resulted in evacuation becoming detention; and in the plan of domicile at temporary refuges becoming a plan for confinement in centers designed to last for the duration of the war.

Selection of sites for what were now known euphemistically as "relocation centers" or "relocation projects" was the first step in the newly revised program. It was required that these sites be on public land, where improvements would become public assets; that they be large enough to accommodate minimum populations of 5,000 each; that they be suitable for work projects throughout the year; that they be located "at a safe distance from strategic points"; and that transportation, power, water supply, etc., be satisfactory.[3]

While sites for relocation centers were being sought, the relationships between the War Department and the War Relocation Authority were defined. In a memorandum of April 17 it was agreed that the War Department would procure and supply the initial equipment, including kitchen, barrack, and hospital supplies and an initial store of nonperishable food. After the center was opened, supply became the responsibility of WRA, which could, however, "effect its procurement through the War Department Agencies."[4] The agreement also provided that relocation centers would be designated as prohibited zones and military areas. This meant that

---

[3] WRA, Press Release, April 13, 1942.

[4] This provision was necessary because only the Army Quartermaster Corps controlled food supplies in quantities sufficient for WRA's purposes. Throughout the history of WRA, virtually all food, except that grown on the projects, was procured through Army channels. See WRA *Administrative Instruction No. 21*, August 12, 1942, and subsequent revisions.

evacuees could be prevented from leaving the projects in accordance with the criminal sanctions of Public Law 503.[5]

Military Police units were to be assigned to each relocation project. Their principal duties included: (1) controlling traffic into the relocation project; (2) preventing visitors from entering or leaving the area without authority from the project director; (3) preventing, by force if necessary, evacuees from leaving the project without permission; (4) maintaining (in Western Defense Command Projects) an inspection of parcels coming to evacuees, for the purpose of confiscating contraband as defined by orders of the Western Defense Command. At all times, except when called upon by the project director to enter the community itself, the functions of the Military Police were to be concerned solely with external guarding. They were to have no interior police functions and to interfere in no way with the internal management of the center. The project directors were to have full charge of the communities and to be solely responsible as well for issuing passes to persons entering and leaving the areas. When called into the community to meet an emergency, however, the Commanding Officer of the Military Police unit was to assume full charge of the center, until the emergency ended.[6]

By the second week in June, eleven centers, with a combined capacity of some 130,000 people, had been selected and received Army approval. The following ten were utilized:

Name	Location	Capacity
Manzanar	California	10,000
Tule Lake	California	16,000
Poston[7]	Arizona	20,000
Gila River	Arizona	15,000
Minidoka	Idaho	10,000
Heart Mountain	Wyoming	10,000
Granada	Colorado	8,000
Topaz[8]	Utah	10,000
Rohwer	Arkansas	10,000
Jerome	Arkansas	10,000
	Total	119,000

[5] This law provided maximum penalties of $5,000 fine or imprisonment for one year or both for persons entering, remaining in, or leaving prescribed military areas contrary to the restrictions applicable to such areas.

[6] The basic agreement was contained in Memorandum of Understanding as to

[For footnotes 7 and 8, see p. 28]

The relocation sites varied in size from 6,000 acres at Manzanar to 72,000 acres at Poston. All were situated on essentially undeveloped land, with the exception of certain limited acres at Tule Lake, Gila and Granada which were ready for planting. Tule Lake and Gila were the most favorably situated for agricultural pursuits, the former area lying on a fertile lake bottom in a rich potato-growing section of northern California, the latter being situated in a district famous for winter vegetable production. Soil or water conditions were deterring factors for agricultural production at other centers. For example, Manzanar was handicapped by a porous soil and relatively expensive water charges; Poston land was completely undeveloped and covered with brush; Minidoka's "68,000 acres [were] covered with lava outcroppings in such a way that only about 25 per cent of this land [was] suitable for cultivation."[9]

Each of the ten sites was relatively isolated. The six western projects were wind and dust swept. Tule Lake, Minidoka, and Heart Mountain were subject to severe winters. Poston and Gila, both in the Arizona desert, had temperatures well above 100 degrees for lengthy periods, and Rohwer and Jerome experienced the excessive humidity and mosquito infestations of swampy delta land.

The physical layout of relocation projects can be exemplified by a description of Tule Lake.[10] Although the Tule Lake project covered 32,000 acres of land, its residents were, for the most part, confined to an area of about one-and-a-quarter square miles, encircled by a barbed-wire fence and guarded by military police in watchtowers placed at intervals near the fence. No one could pass through the gate to the farm, which lay across the highway, without a work permit.

Within the narrow confines of the barbed wire was a further restricted area, a fenced-off corner where the military police had their

Functions of Military Police at the Relocation Centers and Areas Administered by the War Relocation Authority, July 3 and July 8, 1942.

[7] Also known as the Colorado River Project; formerly designated "Parker."

[8] Also known as the Central Utah Project.

[9] See WRA, *First Quarterly Report,* pp. 8–12.

[10] The general layout of the projects did not vary greatly from one to the other. In some, e.g., Gila, the outward appearance was improved by light-colored barracks with red-tile roofs in contrast to the black tar-paper covering used in most projects. In Arkansas it was possible to develop attractive gardens, which deficiently irrigated or alkali soil in most other projects made impossible. In the more easterly projects the military paraphernalia was kept at a minimum.

living quarters and recreation field. The rest of the project was roughly divided into four areas: the administrative section, the warehouse and factory section, the hospital section, and the residence area. Immediately inside the gateway was the Provost Marshal's office where all incoming and outgoing traffic had to register. Just beyond this office were the administration buildings and the living quarters of the administrative personnel. The industrial section, factories and warehouses, and the hospital were placed close to the administration section. Separated from all these by a wide firebreak and occupying one large unit of space were the sixty-four blocks of evacuee living quarters, the section which was commonly called the "colony" by the administration.

The block, composed of fourteen barracks, was the basic unit of the evacuee community. Nine blocks were usually grouped together to form a ward, and each of the wards was separated from the others by firebreaks of two hundred feet width.

Food and general merchandise canteens were established in three of the wards, as well as near the administrative personnel quarters. There was also a centrally located dry goods canteen, a shoe repair shop, a barber shop, a beauty parlor, a newspaper stand, and a bank. Schoolrooms were set up in barracks throughout the project, and, after some months, a high school was built in the firebreak.

Each block was designed to house 250 evacuees. Barracks were divided into individual apartments, intended primarily for sleeping quarters; no kitchen, water faucet, shower, or toilet was attached to an apartment. For most needs, communal facilities were provided. Each block had a mess hall, a recreation hall, public toilets and shower rooms for men and for women, a laundry room, and an ironing room.

The type of construction used for the evacuee living quarters was a modification of the Army "theater of operations" construction. The barracks were 20 by 100 feet and they were divided into apartments of either 20 by 25 or 16 by 20 feet to provide for different-sized families. The exterior walls and roofs of the barracks were shiplap covered with tar paper. No inside walls or ceilings were originally planned, but it was later decided that protection against the severe winter in the district was inadequate and evacuee construction crews put in firboard ceilings and sheetrock walls. Crude floors of shiplap were used, and the green lumber soon dried and

buckled, leaving wide gaps in the floor. A single family was assigned
to one apartment, but the unpartitioned apartment offered little
privacy, especially for the large families. No furnishings were provided by WRA except a stove, which was set in the center of every
apartment, and cots, mattresses, and blankets for each resident.
Each apartment had not less than three windows which gave adequate sunlight and ventilation.

In each block, one apartment was converted into an office for the
block manager. As a focal point of block activity, this office was
generally provided with tables and benches to permit lounging and
gathering. Another barrack in each block was assigned for use as
a recreation hall for the block people, but because of the lack of
office space, many of these were appropriated for administrative
offices. Since most of those not so used were unequipped for recreational purposes, social activities tended to center in the block mess
halls, the block manager's offices, the laundry rooms, the ironing
rooms, or the washrooms. Both the mess halls and recreation halls
were at the extreme end of each block, but the latrine facilities
were in buildings at the center.

The project was practically devoid of vegetation to hold down
the soil, except for stubble of desert grass, and a breeze of any
strength would raise clouds of dust and sand that would seep into
the apartments through the slightest cracks. While the surrounding
countryside was not unattractive, there was little beauty in the center itself to set off the background scenery. The monotonously
uniform rows of black tar-papered barracks made the country seem
colorless and somber.

The peopling of the projects, the movement of almost 110,000
persons from assembly centers, from institutions and from home
communities began on March 21 and was not completed until
October 27.[11] The first major movements were direct to Manzanar
and Poston from home communities; then came the extensive transfers from assembly centers, the first being to Tule Lake and Poston;
the last to the Arkansas projects. Chart I shows the age-sex composition of the projects when the movements had been completed.

[11] Home communities had been cleared by August 8. All subsequent movements were from assembly centers or institutions. See U.S. Army, Western
Defense Command and Fourth Army. *Final Report, Japanese Evacuation from
the West Coast, 1942.* Washington, Government Printing Office, 1943.

Preceding the systematic intake of evacuees, a crew of evacuee volunteers from assembly center or home community arrived on the project. "This advance detachment consisted of the key evacuee personnel necessary to receive, feed, house and provide medical service for the evacuees of the main body as they arrived."[12] The intake process at Poston is described vividly by Leighton:

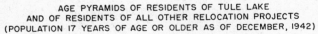

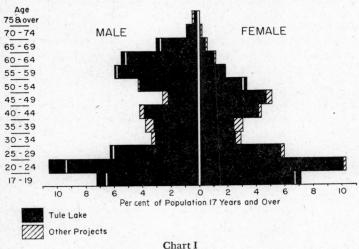

Chart I

In May the physical shell of Poston began to fill with its human occupants. First came the volunteers and then a swelling stream of evacuees until the city of barracks had become alive. . . .

[The] first volunteers were soon followed by others until a total of 251 turned to in the growing heat and cleaned up the barracks for the 7,450 evacuees who arrived during the succeeding three weeks. The volunteers worked at the receiving stations interviewing, registering, housing and explaining to the travel-weary newcomers what they must do and where they must go. . . .

The new arrivals, coming in a steady stream, were poured into empty blocks one after another, as into a series of bottles. The reception procedure became known as "intake" and it left a lasting impression on all who witnessed or took part in it.

Picture the brightness of morning and a sun that heats the earth and

[12] *Ibid.,* p. 287.

beats down on rubbish piles and row after row of even, black tar-papered barracks. There is the sound of hammers and the hum of motors in trucks, cars, bulldozers, tractors, pumps and graders. In the single wooden building that houses the administrative offices, desks are jammed together and the members of the departments of law, housing, supply and transportation, bump into each other as they go about their business and try to shout above each other's noise. . . .

Clerks, stenographers, interviewers, guides and baggage carriers collect at the mess hall that will serve as the scene of "intake" and a crowd gathers to watch.

It is almost 6 when someone shouts that the first bus is coming, and it can be seen plowing through the dust. . . .

When the bus stops, its forty occupants quietly peer out to see what Poston is like. A friend is recognized and hands wave. The bus is large and comfortable, but the people look tired and wilted, with perspiration running off their noses. They have been on the train for twenty-four hours and have been hot since they crossed the Sierras, with long waits at desert stations. Nevertheless, there are remnants of daintiness among the women, and all are smiling. . . .

They begin to file out of the bus, clutching tightly to children and bundles. Military Police escorts anxiously help and guides direct them in English and Japanese.

They are sent into the mess halls where girls hand them ice water, salt tablets and wet towels. In the back are cots where those who faint can be stretched out, and the cots are usually occupied. At long tables sit interviewers suggesting enlistment in the War Relocation Work Corps. . . .

Men and women, still sweating, holding on to children and bundles try to think.

A whirlwind comes and throws clouds of dust into the mess hall, into the water and into the faces of the people while papers fly in all directions. . . .

Interviewers ask some questions about former occupations so that cooks and other types of workers much needed in the camp can be quickly secured. Finally, fingerprints are made and the evacuees troop out across an open space and into another hall for housing allotment, registration and a cursory physical examination. . . .

In the end, the evacuees are loaded on to trucks along with their hand baggage and driven to their new quarters; there each group who will live together is left to survey a room 20 by 25 feet with bare boards, knotholes through the floor and into the next apartment, heaps of dust, and for each person an army cot, a blanket and a sack which can be filled with straw to make a mattress. There is nothing else. No shelves, closets, chairs, tables or screens. In this space 5 to 7 people, and in a few cases 8, men, women and their children, are to live indefinitely.

"Intake" was a focus of interest and solicitude on the part of the administrative staff. The Project Director said it was one of the things he would remember longest out of the whole experience at Poston. He thought the people looked lost, not knowing what to do or what to think. He once found a woman standing, holding her 4-day-old baby and sent her to rest in his room. The Associate Project Director said that one of the pictures which would always stay in his mind was one he saw in an "apartment" where people had just arrived. An elderly mother who had been in a hospital some years sat propped on her baggage gasping and being fanned by two daughters, while her son went around trying to get a bed set up for her. The old lady later died.[13]

Committed to a policy of detention, even before the projects were established, WRA began making plans to assure evacuees "for the duration of the war and as nearly as wartime exigencies permit, an equitable substitute for the life, work, and homes given up, and to facilitate participation in the productive life of America both during and after the war."[14] The agency's responsibility was defined as providing the minimum essentials of living—shelter, medical care, and mess and sanitary facilities—and opportunities for self-support. Every able-bodied evacuee was to be given an opportunity for productive work and for participation in well-rounded community life. Projects were to be made self-supporting. Evacuees would, in the course of time, organize and administer local self-government; meantime, temporary advisory councils would be formed.

One of the first problems faced by WRA was the determination of a wage scale. In March, 1942, an unauthorized statement by a project official to the effect that wages would follow Work Projects Administration procedures, brought a storm of public protest. Again, WRA yielded to political pressure and decided that "purely from a public-relations standpoint, it seemed unwise to pay evacuees . . . a higher wage than the minimum wage of the American soldier."[15] It was decided to advance workers a small cash allowance, to maintain a set of project records of all expenditures and all income, and to distribute profits to the workers at stated intervals. "Miserably low cash advances of $12, $16, and $19"[16] monthly, were set, unskilled workers receiving $12, professional and highly skilled workers qualifying for the $19 stipend, others receiving $16.

Recognizing the severity of this wage policy, WRA sought to

---

[13] Alexander H. Leighton, *The Governing of Men*, Princeton University Press, 1945, pp. 61–66.
[14] WRA, "Tentative Policy Statement" (mimeographed), May 29, 1942.
[15] WRA, *First Quarterly Report*, p. 17.
[16] Eisenhower to Budget Director Smith, May 11, 1942.

develop a plan whereby surpluses might be accumulated for the evacuee workers. A corps was to be organized to "undertake all essential work on the projects, including development of natural resources, production of food, manufacture of needed articles, and operation of community services."[17] All employable evacuees over 16 years of age, irrespective of sex or citizenship, were eligible for enlistment in the Work Corps. Obligations incurred through enlistment included: service until fourteen days after the end of the war; performance of any and all tasks assigned and acceptance in full payment for services of such cash or other allowances as WRA might determine; agreement to transfer from one Relocation Project to another at the will of WRA; agreement to make no claims against the United States government for injuries incurred while a member of the corps; willingness to swear loyalty to the United States "in thought, word, and deed."

At the same time, a definite promise of financial profit to enlistees was held forth. Each relocation center would function "as a type of coöperative." Careful accounts would be kept of all costs; profits would accrue and be distributed, perhaps "in the form of increased monthly 'cash advances.' . . . Food raised on the project will reduce project costs, which in turn will enhance the opportunity for profit."[18]

In June, 1942, Eisenhower resigned and Dillon S. Myer, also of the Department of Agriculture, replaced him as Director. Even before Myer's assumption of responsibility, the Work Corps plan had proved unfeasible. When, in the latter part of May, enlistment in the corps was made prerequisite to furlough work in the Oregon beet fields, evacuees refused to enlist because of the "blank checks" in the Work Corps agreement. They were unwilling to enlist when WRA could not specify the work they were to do or the precise income they would receive. They objected to enlisting for the duration "and 14 days thereafter" without some provision for withdrawing; they objected to the blanket agreement about transfer from one project to another, fearing they might be separated from their families; they objected to a vague statement about "trial and suitable punishment" for infraction of unspecified "rules and regu-

[17] WRA, Press Release, May 15, 1942.
[18] WRA, Regional Office, Questions and Answers for Evacuees, undated pamphlet distributed to evacuees in assembly centers.

lations." Significantly, however, objections were not raised at this time to the loyalty pledge.[19] By June, the Work Corps requirements had been dropped as prerequisites for furlough work and when, on September 1, 1942, a general instruction on Emloyment and Compensation was issued, it simply provided that each evacuee "upon first being assigned to a job" at a relocation center would "become thereby enlisted in the War Relocation Work Corps."

Producers' coöperatives, too, were an early casualty, abandoned without trial when it was discovered that certain relocation projects were potentially more profitable than others, that over-all profit was improbable on a short-term basis, and that no agreement could be reached as to what expenses should be charged off against income. Until the middle of September, however, promises of the development of this plan were still held out to the evacuees.

By September monthly payments were generally called "wages," rather than "cash advances." The $12 rate was restricted to apprentices, and later dropped; the $16 rate was made general; and the $19 rate was expanded to include not only professional people (doctors, lawyers, engineers, etc.) and managerial personnel, but also those making "an exceptional contribution to project operation, entailing extremely hard work essential to the welfare and morale of large numbers of people, or which involve exceptional skill."[20] A full 48-hour week was expected of workers. The involuntarily unemployed were entitled to unemployment compensation at rates of $4.25 to $4.75 monthly.[21] Supplementary clothing allowances, to be paid in cash and varying with the age of the recipient and the climate of the center, were to be granted to workers and involuntarily unemployed workers and their families. In the coldest centers, maximum payments were $3.75 monthly for adults and $2.25 monthly for children under eight years of age.

Ambitious plans for extensive agricultural and industrial developments within the projects were formulated with three objectives: (1) reduction of project operating expenses by producing for project needs; (2) production for war needs, and (3) establishing a source of income for evacuees. It soon became apparent that agricultural

---

[19] See Chapter III for resistances that developed later to a pledge of loyalty.
[20] WRA, *Administrative Instruction No. 27*, September 1, 1942, p. 3.
[21] Dependent children of the unemployed received $1.50 to $2.50. The rate for unemployed adults was later raised to 60 per cent of the monthly wage, i.e., $7.20 to $11.40.

enterprises could fulfill only the first of these objectives, but efforts were made for many months to develop industries in accordance with all three objectives. Industrial enterprises were authorized for operation by the War Relocation Authority itself, by evacuee coöperatives, or by Caucasian individuals or firms. The second and third of these categories could use evacuees only if prevailing wages were paid and other special conditions of employment deemed necessary by WRA and Federal and State regulations were met. Wages received were not, however, to be retained by individual workers unless the community government so recommended. Otherwise, the difference between actual wages and the sum of cash compensation and clothing allowances they would have received if employed by WRA would be placed in a "community trust fund," to be held for distribution among all employed persons in the community. Other methods of distribution would be considered, if recommended by the community government.

The industrial program was never fully developed. The only industry in actual operation on June 30 was a camouflage-net factory at Manzanar where nearly 500 evacuees were employed at WRA wage rates. Later, similar camouflage-net projects were established by contract, with prevailing wages paid, at Poston and Gila. Other industrial developments were on a minor scale.

WRA policy specifically provided that "private enterprises for the sale of goods and services directly to residents of centers may not be located in the relocation area."[21a] Under the guidance of trained leaders at each center and a national director of coöperatives in Washington, consumer coöperative organizations were developed to operate retail establishments of all kinds—grocery stores, shoes, radio repair shops, barber and beauty shops, and various specialty and refreshment stores. An Administrative Instruction provided that the coöperatives might operate center newspapers under conditions of "maximum freedom of expression short of libel, personal attack, and other utterances contrary to the general welfare."[22]

Instructions for the establishment of local self-government were issued on June 5, 1942. These provided for the election of temporary community councils, whose functions would be advisory. The block was designated as the unit of representation; all persons over

[21a] WRA, "Tentative Policy Statement" (mimeographed), May 29, 1942.
[22] WRA, *Administrative Instruction No. 8,* Supplement 4, October 15, 1942.

16 years of age, irrespective of citizenship, were eligible to vote, but aliens were declared ineligible for office holding.

The ban on aliens was retained in an instruction of August 24 providing for the selection of a commission to prepare a permanent plan of government, to become effective when approved by a majority of qualified voters, and the age for qualification was raised to 18 years. The functions of the permanent council were defined as prescription of regulations and provision of penalties on all matters (except felonies) affecting the internal peace and order of the project and the welfare of the residents "insofar as such regulations are not in conflict with any federal law, military proclamation, law of the state in which the project is located, or any order issued by an appropriate officer of the War Relocation Authority."[23] These functions were, however, specified as being in addition to and not substitute for the functions and responsibilities of the Project Director, who would review and could veto all actions of the council. It was also stipulated that the plan of government should provide for a Judicial Commission and an Arbitration Commission.

Schools were planned to follow the precepts of progressive education.[24] It was hoped they would become "in a measure often dreamed of by educators but seldom realized, an effective instrument of community building . . . [through participation] in every phase of community life."[24a] Every effort was to be made to make this community-building an Americanizing factor.

The center schools were designed to meet state elementary and high school requirements and provide courses necessary for admission to state colleges and universities. The language of instruction in all schools was to be English. It was specifically provided that "Japanese language schools shall not be permitted to operate in any center." Vocational training classes were to be organized for high school graduates and a full night school Adult Education Program provided.

[23] WRA, *Administrative Instruction No. 34*, August 24, 1942, pp. 2–3.

[24] The blueprint for community schools was worked out by WRA in coöperation with Stanford University. See *Proposed Curriculum Procedures for Japanese Relocation Centers*, prepared by summer session students of Curriculum Development, Stanford University, 1942.

[24a] Lester K. Ade, "The Educational Program for Evacuees at Ten War Relocation Centers" (manuscript, undated). Dr. Ade was Education Consultant, later Chief of School Systems, for WRA.

The evacuees had, in the main, entered the relocation projects with attitudes either of optimism or of dogged determination to make the best possible adjustment in building up communities in which they would have to live for the duration of the war. Director Eisenhower testified before the House Subcommittee on Finance, on May 15, 1942: "I just cannot say things too favorable about the way they have coöperated under the most adverse circumstances." His successor, Myer, wrote to the Secretary of War on June 8 of the "high degree of coöperation and helpfulness on the part of the evacuees."

These initial reactions are in part to be attributed to the hope and belief prevalent among WRA personnel that a "good life" could be built up in these wartime communities; in part to the relief of the evacuees in achieving duration security after the uprooting of evacuation and the instability of life in temporary assembly centers. The course of this initial adjustment can best be traced by exemplification, and again Tule Lake is used for this purpose.

The first evacuees to reach Tule Lake on May 26, 1942, were volunteers from the Portland and Puyallup Assembly Centers. Although they were disappointed by the dull barrenness of the countryside, the nonexistence of the much-talked-of lake, and the presence of barbed-wire fence and armed guards, this initial disappointment was soon followed by enthusiasm over their reception by the Caucasian personnel, under the leadership of Acting Project Director Elmer Shirrell,[25] a man of great energy and good will.

Between June 2 and 6, about 1,500 people arrived by direct evacuation from their homes in Washington and Oregon and a few from the Free Zone in California. They devoted themselves for several weeks to making livable homes and finding suitable employment. WRA had provided no lumber for furnishings, but huge piles of scrap lumber dumped by the contractors were available. The minimum requirement of each family was a table, benches, and poles for clothes lines, and these were readily and quickly constructed. To give added comfort, many of the men built closets,

---

[25] Shirrell was replaced as Project Director by Harvey Coverley in December, 1942. Coverley functioned during the registration crisis, described in Chapter III, and was, in turn, replaced by Raymond Best just before the initiation of the segregation program described in Chapter IV. Best remained as Project Director throughout the whole history of the Tule Lake Segregation Center, described in Chapter V and subsequent chapters.

lined their walls, set up partitions in the apartments and constructed porches outside the barracks, while the women made curtains and rugs. Jobs, too, were not only plentiful but in many cases interesting. Many Nisei trained as stenographers, clerks, architects, and engineers found for the first time in their lives an opportunity to practice their professions. Issei, however, had greater difficulties in job placement, partly because of linguistic handicap, partly because their preëvacuation experience had been in the main of the small entrepreneurial sort. Many of them were forced by circumstances to take the more disagreeable jobs: construction work, labor on the farm, cooking or dishwashing in the mess halls, and janitorial operations. Others became dependent on their children.

To the younger Nisei, the chance for unlimited social activities was attractive; baseball and dances especially flourished. Issei women found pleasure in the new leisure, freedom from the burdens of cooking and the worries of providing for a family, and they spent much time at knitting, sewing, handicraft, and English classes, while Issei men indulged in typical Japanese forms of recreation: *goh, shogi, hana,* etc. The Christian churches organized multifarious activities for young and old alike. Owing to temporary oversupply in the warehouses, food was abundant and meals sometimes approached lavishness.

In all projects, in spite of physical hardships,[26] the initial adjust-

---

[26] The physical conditions in Tule Lake, at the time of intake, were distinctly superior to those in certain other projects. In Manzanar, for example, equipment for sixteen of thirty-six mess halls was still lacking three months after the project was opened, and the ones operating were grossly overcrowded. The Assistant Regional Director of WRA reported, on June 17 (letter to Fryer, Regional Director of WRA) that "at one time, while meals were being served and the line was moving, I counted 300 people standing in line outside the mess hall." And Congressman Leland Ford said of the barracks that "on dusty days, one might just as well be outside as inside." ("Report on Visit to Japanese Evacuation Camps," undated.)

At Gila, evacuees were moved in at the rate of 500 daily at a time when there were no hospital facilities, gas connections were incomplete, and only a skeleton project staff was available. By August 20 there were 7,700 people crowded into space designed for 5,000. They were housed in mess halls, recreation halls, and even latrines. As many as 25 persons lived in a space intended for 4. Heat in the desert ranged above 100 degrees. There were maggots in the food, epidemic dysentery, heat rash, and sunstroke. The sewage disposal system broke down, and sewage was dumped into open pits as close as 200 feet to the barracks. Stench from the pits invaded the whole camp, and flies had ready access to the unscreened mess halls.

ment to "pioneer life" was favorable. As the projects became filled, however, intergroup antagonisms flared up and faith in the good intentions of the administration declined. Evacuees soon realized that the developing WRA practices were not correspondent with the early promises made to them. Wage payments were weeks behind schedule. Promised clothing allowances were not forthcoming. Work clothes were not, as had been agreed, given to those workers who had to perform dirty and arduous tasks, and their own clothes were rapidly wearing out. Agricultural and industrial planning was drastically revised downward. WRA had promised that one of its first jobs would be to build schools and to furnish school equipment, but priorities were often given instead to the improvement of housing for the Caucasian personnel. The education system fell far below the publicized plans for community schools. Evacuees had been promised that "as soon as you move to your war-duration home . . . the War Relocation Authority will have [household] goods brought to you."[27] But war transportation complications were added to technical administrative difficulties of filtering the desired proportion of the given person's furniture to the right project and months after the last evacuees arrived at the relocation projects no household goods had been received.

In Tule Lake, the interlude of optimism and enthusiasm came to an abrupt end with the transfer of 4,000 additional evacuees from the Walerga Assembly Center (Sacramento) between June 16 and 26. These people almost immediately felt themselves at a disadvantage as compared with the earlier arrivals. Scrap lumber had become scarce, and desirable jobs were less plentiful. Sectional conflicts broke out among the Nisei elements from California and from the Northwest, largely on the basis of competition for jobs.

Censorship of mail, suddenly instituted by the military police on June 29, caused a flare-up of resentment against the administration, for it was not generally known that the WRA personnel had strenuously opposed the measure.

The quantity and quality of food began to deteriorate, and a local mess-hall strike took place on July 6. After the arrival of another large contingent of evacuees from the Pinedale Assembly Center in late July, shortages of kitchen equipment developed and

---

[27] WRA, Regional Office, "Questions and Answers for Evacuees," undated pamphlet distributed to evacuees in assembly centers.

a rumor spread that WRA food warehouses were rapidly being depleted. A rush on the canteens ensued, and people began to hoard rice and canned goods. The rumor was later elaborated that WRA personnel were diverting food intended for the mess halls to the canteens, and profiting from the evacuees' purchases.

Procurement difficulties led to deficiencies in hospital supplies, and tension developed between evacuee doctors and the Caucasian Chief Medical Officer.

The administration attempted to introduce an efficient timekeeping system, and evacuees resisted the effort to make them work a full day for $16 a month compensation. In August they began a campaign for higher wages, free haircuts and free shoe repairs. Resistance developed against the opening of new canteens, for the Issei in particular were beginning to worry about the extent to which savings were being spent for things they felt WRA should have provided for them.

Conflicts between Issei and Nisei broke out in the recreation department because of the different forms of recreation desired by the two generations. On August 5, some Issei held a special entertainment during the absence of Caucasian personnel, in which, it was reported, Japanese nationalistic expressions had been heard. When news of this event reached the administration, popular suspicion of *inu* arose.

In early August the growing discontent of the residents was manifested by strikes in two of the largest work units: the farm workers and the construction crews. Each of these crews had grievances because of the seasonal nature of the work, the administrative pressure applied for production, and the manual character of its work which required more than the usual amount of food, clothing, and shoe repair.

The grievances culminating in the farm strike on August 15 had been accumulating since the opening of the project. Planting had to be speeded up to ensure harvesting before the frosts, which come early in this area. The first evacuee contingents were slow in accepting farm work and on July 19 an appeal to save the valuable potato seed was made through the *Tulean Dispatch,* with a statement, attributed to the Project Director, that "the failure of the crop will be placed on the shoulders of the unwilling or uncoöperative colonists." Some people accepted the responsibility willingly and a shortage was averted. Many others, however, resented being held responsible for the success of a farm which was not their own and being pressed by the Caucasians to speed up their work for a wage of $16 a month. Experienced Issei farmers on the crew developed antagonisms toward less experienced Caucasians in charge of the program. June and July wages had not been paid by the first of August, nor had promised work clothes been issued. Meals, particularly the light breakfast served on the project, were considered an inadequate basis for the hard work required.

On the morning of August 15, the farm crew gathered as usual at the dispatching station to be transported by truck to the farm. As the men gathered, a group from Block 6 refused to board the trucks because of the meager breakfast (said to have been little more than tea and toast) served that morning. Others took up the cry of inadequate food, and self-appointed leaders circulated among the men urging a strike over the food question. Trucks that were loaded and ready to leave were restrained from starting. A committee was formed and representatives notified the farm supervisor of the workers' decision to strike. Small groups gathered to discuss the situation, and the cry arose that this was a community problem and should be presented at a mass meeting of all the residents. At 2 P.M. a meeting was called of the construction and farm foremen, cooks, and other selected delegates to formulate grievances. The food problem was emphasized, and the Caucasian assistant mess supervisor was blamed for curtailing distribution. At a meeting with representatives of the administration assurance was obtained that the food situation would be improved and the crew was advised to call off the strike on Monday (August 17). On the evening of the 16th, however, a spontaneous mass meeting, dominated by Issei, gathered around an outdoor platform in the firebreak. In spite of the tense atmosphere, the meeting proved a debacle for those who had hoped that a general strike would be called and that the community as a whole would back the farm workers. The chief difficulty in carrying out this program was fear on the part of many evacuees of speaking publicly in favor of a continuation of the strike, since rumors were prevalent that *inu* were present and would repeat their utterances to the FBI.

On Monday morning a heavy breakfast was served in all mess halls, and the crews returned to work without further concrete

TULE LAKE SEGREGATION CENTER

evidence of administrative provision for their basic needs. Some improvements were immediately initiated, but complaints continued to be heard among the thoroughly disaffected workers.

Shortly after the strike, several instances of violence occurred, including the beating of an alleged *inu*.

By the end of August, the improvement in food, which was the only concession gained by the farm strike, failed to quiet the underlying discontent of the residents. Their demands for clothing allowance and payment of back wages had not been met. Talk of strikes was heard among various crews and several minor work stoppages developed, but these were quickly settled. On September 3 a major strike was called by the construction workers, the immediate causes being (1) a layoff of sixty workers for ten days without pay, and (2) a rumor of a planned reduction of the evacuee crew by 50 per cent while continuing employment of all Caucasian carpenters at "prevailing wages." In addition, the matters of delayed wage payments and lack of clothing were raised. While negotiations regarding resumption of work were proceeding, work clothes were received and distributed and an announcement was made of the initiation of a new system of wage payments, which would avoid delays. Although the other grievances were not solved, the crew was persuaded to return to work on September 5.

In October, dissatisfaction about food distribution and mess-hall conditions led to the circulation of a petition demanding the removal of the unpopular Caucasian assistant mess supervisor and improvement of food served in the mess halls. The petition carried 9,000 signatures and its circulation was followed, on October 12, by a general "slow down" strike in the mess halls, where meals were served at irregular and unannounced intervals. The result was equivalent to a general strike, for few people were willing to risk missing meals by going to their jobs. The administration yielded on the following day by terminating the employment of the assistant supervisor.

During this period of unrest the temporary Community Council had attempted to act as a "sounding board" of the community for the administration and as a liaison body between administration and evacuees. This council had been established within a few weeks after the arrival of the first evacuees, and consisted of one representative from each block. At the elections in the first populated ward, the ban on aliens had not been announced and a few Issei were elected. By the time other wards held elections, it was understood that only citizens were eligible and the temporary council was not only overwhelmingly Nisei in composition but several of its leaders were from the proadministration JACL element.

From its first meeting, the practice was established of having each councilman review council activities before the residents of his own block. This practice soon led to a conflict for control between the older and younger generations, for while the council was dominated by Nisei, block meetings were controlled by Issei. Deprived of direct political expression through the ban on holding office on the council, Issei soon adapted block meetings to this purpose. One important issue after another was approved by the councilmen, only to be reversed in a referendum forced by dissent from the block meetings. Late in September, for example, the council sponsored a proposal by OWI to have the residents participate in shortwave broadcasts to Japan. It was proposed that evacuees describe "actual conditions" in camp as a means of combating the Japanese government's claims that mistreatment of Americans interned in the Orient was a justified reprisal for the mistreatment of persons of Japanese ancestry in the United States. Following precedent, the council referred the plan to an Issei-dominated assembly of block representatives at which the plan was overwhelmingly rejected, to the dismay of many council members, who insisted that the matter be reconsidered. At a second assembly, the plan was again defeated, and the council was forced to accept this decision. A few days later, another important decision of the council was reversed. The administration had purchased lumber to build a community theater from canteen profits. The plan was destined to meet popular opposition, since WRA had earlier promised that these profits would not be used without consulting the residents. The administration justified its act on grounds that lumber was about to be "frozen" by government order and that speed was essential. The plan was also opposed because of Issei fear that the proposed admission charges would be a further drain on evacuee savings. In spite of the council's approval of the plan, it was overwhelmingly defeated in a popular referendum. This defeat was followed by wholesale resignations of council members, but a skeleton organization was maintained for the next month until a plan for a permanent community govern-

ment could be ratified. By this time there was so little enthusiasm
for the sanctioned forms of "self-government" that the charter was
ratified, on November 16, by a margin of only 441 votes out of a
total of 6,619. When elections for new councilmen were held, the
outstanding JACL leader was not reëlected.

Meantime, two Issei-dominated organizations had sprung up
which tended to diminish Nisei influence in the community even
further. One was a Planning Board, consisting of an Issei representative from each of the seven wards. In many ways it acted as
a second council. The other was the Coöperative Enterprises, which,
through its control of so many important aspects of the economic
life of the project, exercised an important influence on the trend
of community affairs.

The pattern of adjustment to detention described for Tule Lake
was followed, with minor variations, in all the relocation projects
from the period of intake to the crisis period described in the next
chapter. The pattern shows an initial coöperative and surprisingly
unprotesting acceptance of a new situation by the evacuees followed
by unrest and distrust directed toward both the administration and
fellow evacuees, with periods of protest and manifestations of revolt
against the administration and cleavages among the residents.

In two projects, Poston and Manzanar, the revolt aspect assumed
major proportions. In the former, the revolt was handled by negotiation and was followed by a superior adjustment between evacuees and administration. In the latter, the revolt was met with
repressive tactics, including the calling in of soldiers, the removal
of alleged agitators and troublemakers to an isolation camp and
the hasty withdrawal and resettlement of a number of JACL leaders
and other collaborators with the administration. The repercussions
of both incidents had lasting effects, not only upon the evacuees but
also upon the agencies administering the detention program.

In Poston, suspicion that fellow-evacuees were acting as informers to the
FBI led to two severe beatings on October 17 and November 14, 1942. On
November 15 two Kibei, Nobuo Yamada[28] and Frank Numata were suddenly arrested in Camp I[29] and placed in the project jail for alleged complicity in the beatings. Delegations, predominantly Issei, called on the

[28] Yamada's role in postsegregation Tule Lake is described in later chapters in
this volume.
[29] Poston was divided into three separate residential areas, known as Camps I
II, and III.

administrators[30] and requested the release of the young men, claiming they were innocent. They were informed that the disposition of the case was in the hands of the FBI.

A rumor had spread that the FBI was coming on Wednesday morning, November 18, and someone sent a message to the subjugation (land reclamation) and warehouse crews to quit work and picket the police station. Meanwhile three to four hundred residents from interested blocks gathered in front of the police station to prevent the FBI from taking the prisoners. About 10:30 A.M. the chairman of the Issei Advisory Board proposed the framing of a resolution to the Project Director requesting the immediate release of the two boys. One of the leaders in the crowd also instructed the driver of the block managers' supply truck to go to each block manager's office and order him to close his office and send the block residents to the police station. By noon a crowd of some 2,500 had assembled and the following resolution in Japanese was read to them:

"We, residents who number 5,000 have assembled here to request the immediate and unconditional release of two coresidents."

The crowd increased after lunch. People gathered in small groups and talked in whispers. They were Issei and Kibei with a sprinkling of Nisei.

At two o'clock the acting project director appeared to address the group over a public address system set up at the entrance of the police station. The gist of his speech was as follows:

"The administration guarantees that justice will be carried out. If these persons are guilty I know that you want them punished. If they are innocent the authorities will release them without delay. The administration pledges that justice will be meted out, so please have faith in us. This is not the conduct of people in a civilized world. Let's go back to the course of normal life where we can be of greater service. This is not the thing to do, go back."

When an interpreter began to translate the speech into Japanese, someone pulled the plug out of the public address system so that the last part of the speech was lost.

Later someone suggested that half of them stage a demonstration near the hospital, where the council was now meeting with the administration. The council had drafted a resolution, in accordance with the wishes the residents had expressed, asking for release of the young men. When this was refused, they immediately resigned, as did the Issei Advisory Board. In the evening a mass meeting was held and emergency delegates were selected from each block. These delegates immediately decided on a general strike the next morning, exempting, however, those employed in the mess halls, garages, maintenance department, hospital, schools, canteen warehouse, garbage department, fire department, and the personnel kitchen. (The personnel kitchen was placed in the list of exemptions because a large number of teachers ate there, but none of the evacuee staff

[30] The Project Director, W. Wade Head, left on Wednesday morning to attend a WRA meeting in Salt Lake City. An acting project director was the chief administrative negotiator during most of the strike period.

appeared next morning and the Caucasians were compelled to prepare their own breakfast.) Meanwhile, all the block managers resigned.

The first clearcut demarcation of picketing by blocks occurred on the morning of November 19. Each block built a separate camp fire and constructed a cardboard sign bearing the block's number in black crayon. Picketing by shifts also began on this day. The regulation of shifts was not uniform throughout the picket line since each block had been instructed to determine its own shifts. Some blocks had three shifts of eight hours each; some had four-hour shifts for older men and a six-hour shift for younger men; some had special hours designated for certain people, e.g., the period from 6 P.M. to 1 A.M. was restricted to young married men, 1 to 6 A.M. to older men, and 6 A.M. to 6 P.M. to all others. Still others had four-hour shifts divided between the eastern and western sections of the block. The subjugation crew, aided by enthusiastic volunteers, supplied the wood for the camp fires.

Toward afternoon the people became worried about subsistence. Rumors began to fly that the administration was planning to cut off the food supply for the duration of the strike. A few Issei Advisory Board members therefore contacted the Chief Steward and received assurance from him that as long as he had the crew to transport provisions, the food supply would remain as usual.

On the same afternoon, the FBI withdrew from the case and the administration decided to release Numata and to turn Yamada over to the Yuma County authorities on the charge of assault with a deadly weapon. Numata, however, refused to leave the jail until Yamada's unconditional release.

By afternoon the cardboard signs designating blocks were replaced by more substantial banners. At first these were usually white strips of cloth with a red circle around the block number. As the evening progressed the banners became larger and began more and more to resemble the Japanese flag. More Nisei began to appear on the scene, giving the superficial impression that the Issei and Nisei were united for once. But it soon became evident that most of them were there simply out of curiosity or because of intimidation or pressure from the Issei. In a number of blocks it had been announced at breakfast that anyone who refused to picket the police station would be branded as *inu* and treated as such. In other blocks the intimidation was more subtle.

That same morning the council and block managers of Camp II had met in an emergency session with the council and advisors from Camp III to hear three representatives from Camp I state their grievances. The spokesman for the strikers informed them that since the council and block managers in Camp I had resigned the day before they had no organized or recognized body to carry on negotiations with the administration and therefore were calling upon them for help. The assembled group then selected a committee of twelve consisting of two block managers, two councilmen, and two advisors from the two units (Camps II and III). They immediately began negotiating with the administration.

At sunrise on November 20 the pickets who had been huddled before the camp fires stood up and facing east shouted in unison, *"Dai Nippon Teikoku Banzai!"* (Banzai to the great Japanese Empire!)

Warnings to *inu* (in this case possible informers to FBI) became conspicuous. Having reference to the fact that the word *inu* means literally "dog" a dog-faced man appeared on the post, which bore the block 22 flag; a cartoon of a dog, and a real dog-bone bearing the message, "This is for dogs" on the police station wall; a dog with a wienie suspended in front of it on the block 19 post, and a Japanese boy chasing a dog on the block 35 banner. The anxious voice of parents admonishing their teen-age sons not to become *inu* could be heard near the camp fires. At all hours of the day and night the pickets were entertained with Japanese music from records played by a Kibei about fifteen years of age. An American record had been played sometime Thursday afternoon but was hooted down. American music did not reappear on the program until late Saturday afternoon (November 21).

About this time some Issei began to question whether the demonstrations were not going too far. Some said, "Something must be done about those flags and banzais," and others, "This kind of thing is okay for bachelors and childless people but not for us with families." This was the beginning of the sentiment that the strike must be settled quickly.

The Emergency Council had in its meeting on November 19 selected an Executive Committee of nine members. This committee was, on November 20, called upon to consider a compromise plan to settle the strike, introduced by the intermediaries from Camps II and III, and approved by the administration. This plan proposed that Yamada be released immediately and tried by an evacuee jury at Poston upon charges instituted by the Chief of Internal Security. However, neither this committee nor the larger Emergency Council was willing to decide the matter, and it was referred to the blocks.

On the evening of November 20 each block of Camp I held a meeting to decide on one of two proposals: (1) to continue the demonstration until Yamada was unconditionally released or (2) to accept the Camp II plan.

The plebiscite resulted in an almost equal division of the camp—half of the blocks favoring the continuation of the demonstration, the other half demanding a trial.

Since the results of the plebiscite were so close, the Emergency Council was afraid to take any decisive steps toward the adoption of the compromise plan, although many of them seemed to favor it. The Executive Committee thereupon resumed direct negotiations.

On the morning of November 22, when the Executive Committee approached the Project Director (who had returned from Salt Lake City) for an audience, the request was refused on the ground that he was busy and could see them at the earliest on Monday (November 23).

When the Executive Committee arrived for their conference with the Project Director, he agreed to the release of Yamada pending trial by an evacuee jury in Poston, but at the same time demanded a guarantee of a better community in the future. The delegates returned home to work upon plans toward this end to be presented to the Project Director on November 24.

At this meeting they presented the following three proposals to the Project Director:

1. To establish a public relations committee to mediate with and settle all problems affecting personal reputations and damages out of court.

2. To give Poston residents the right to select and appoint all evacuee personnel in the administration and important positions.

3. To establish a City Planning Board based upon the present Emergency Council, within the framework of the WRA, which should create the necessary administrative, legislative, and economic organizations.

The Executive Committee then met the delegation from the administration and details of procedure were worked out. In the evening the Project Director spoke before the assembled residents. He began informally: "Hello, folks. I see that you are in a better mood tonight." He then proceeded to explain that the community was not to blame for the unfortunate incident and that he wished to see Poston become the best community in the entire United States.

After warmly applauding the Project Director the crowd dispersed at about 11:00 P.M. and the strike was over.[31]

The Manzanar riot had a more bitter, violent and moblike character and resulted in numerous injuries and two deaths.

On the evening of Saturday, December 5, 1942, Frank Masuda, a Nisei, formerly a Los Angeles restaurant owner and chairman of the Southern District JACL was beaten up by a gang and severely injured.

Early on the morning of December 6 several persons suspected by Masuda of being involved in his beating were ordered arrested. Among these was Dick Miwa, a Kibei junior cook, who for some time had been trying to organize the mess-hall workers and had publicly accused the Assistant Project Director and the Caucasian Chief Steward of theft of sugar and meat from evacuee warehouses. Reports of these charges were widely circulated and generally believed by the residents.

It is not plain that Masuda recognized positively any of his assailants but the bitter and contemptuous opposition of Miwa to the administration and its alliance with the hated JACL made him a natural suspect. Furthermore he could not account for his movements on the previous night. He was therefore taken to the county jail at Independence, California, while the other suspects were lodged in the project jail.

Popular resentment and reaction were immediate. By 1 P.M. a crowd had gathered near Miwa's former residence. A public address system had been set up, and J. Y. Kurihara,[32] among others, made demands (1) for the unconditional release of Miwa, (2) for an investigation by the Spanish

---

[31] Based on a report prepared for this study by Tamie Tsuchiyama.
[32] See Appendix for his life history.

Consul[33] of conditions at Manzanar, (3) for further action against Masuda and other *inu* in camp.

In the course of the meeting, "death lists" and "black lists" of alleged *inu,* most of whom were JACL collaborators with the administration, were read off. In addition to Masuda, individuals so listed included Tokutaro Slocum, a World War I veteran who had attained American citizenship (under the act of 1935[34]), and who had openly boasted of his connections with the FBI and other intelligence agencies, and Togo Tanaka and Joe Masaoka, former JACL leaders who, serving as "documentary historians" for the WRA Reports Office, were under suspicion of informing on fellow evacuees.

An Issei informant reported, concerning this afternoon meeting, that "the majority sentiment is that they want Mr. Miwa released from jail; they are convinced he was framed and wrongly accused by Mr. Masuda, whose accusation [that Miwa beat him up] is believed to be only another of a list of bad things he has done against the Japanese. Some speakers even said they would 'do a lot of killing tonight unless Miwa was released.'" Another Issei reported: "The meeting served to fire up the men with great zeal. Many speakers said that Miwa was being made a scapegoat by the administration because he had exposed the sugar fraud and had sacrificed himself for the people. They said that Masuda was in on the plot. It was decided that unless the administration released Miwa that night, the mess-hall workers would all go on strike the next day."

According to official reports Project Director Ralph Merritt met with evacuee representatives shortly after the noon assembly. Meantime he had requested military police to be in readiness to intervene, and they had lined up at the police station inside the project area. Merritt agreed to bring Miwa back to the project, but insisted that he be confined in the Manzanar jail.

Dissatisfied with this compromise, evacuees assembled again at 6 p.m. The second Issei quoted above reported: "The evening meeting was much worse. They're going out to get about ten or eleven *inu,* I can't remember all the men whose names were read off several times over the microphone. I don't know the man's name who made the speech and began calling off the names, but he was terribly excited. The first name called off to be killed was Mr. Masuda. They said that the hospital should be invaded and Mr. Masuda killed because the administration had refused to release Mr. Miwa, and that the Negotiating Committee had gotten no place at all with Mr. Merritt. The speakers were also excited about the soldiers who had been drawn up by the police station and said that as true Japanese 'we should not be afraid to die in this cause as our brothers are dying for justice and permanent peace and the new order in Asia.' Most of the talk though was about the *inu* activities of the men on the 'death list.'"

The assembled crowd split into two parts, one heading for the hospital

---

[33] The Spanish Government represented Japanese nationals in the United States during most of the war period.

[34] See footnote 4, p. 2.

to "get" Masuda, the other moving toward the project jail where Miwa was, by this time, confined. When Masuda could not be found (he had been hidden under a movable hospital bed), the part of the crowd that had headed for the hospital moved toward the barracks of half-a-dozen other alleged *inu* on the death list but, failing to locate the intended victims, joined up with the larger crowd and pushed toward the police station.

The Project Director called on the commanding officer of the military police, and authorized him to declare martial law. A detachment of soldiers shortly appeared, and forced the crowd away from the police station. The Assistant Project Director at this point called the FBI in Los Angeles requesting agents to come into the center and "get at the bottom of this thing." Evacuee spokesmen demanded audience with the Project Director and pressed the commanding officer for release of Miwa. They were refused. The soldiers, who had managed to push the crowd completely away from the police station, now lined up, armed with submachine guns, shotguns, and rifles. Evacuees jeered and made insulting gestures. The soldiers thereupon donned gas masks and threw a number of tear gas bombs into the crowd. The evacuees fled blindly in every direction and some were piled up against a telephone pole, covering it with blood. The crowd re-formed and the soldiers fired, without orders. Within two minutes after the gas bombs had been thrown, no evacuee was in sight except the wounded lying in the street. A short time later a small crowd re-formed and started a parked automobile, aiming the car at a machine gun emplacement. The car curved away from the machine gun, crashing through the northwest corner of the police station and finally stopped against one of the army trucks parked west of the police station. Several bursts were fired by the machine gunner at the car as it swung across the road. The empty car was hit several times, one of the bullets ricocheting and wounding a corporal of the military police.

In all, ten evacuees were treated for gunshot wounds and it was believed that several others were hurt but did not ask for treatment, from fear of implication in the affair. One evacuee died almost immediately. He was a young Nisei, one of whose brothers was then serving in the United States Army. A second evacuee, nineteen years old, died on December 11 from complications resulting from his wounds. Throughout the night military police, augmented by State Guardsmen, patroled the interior of the camp. Among the evacuees, shifts were arranged at each mess hall, and the bells tolled loudly and continuously throughout the entire night and late into the morning. Small crowds assembled outside the barracks occupied by the Slocums, the Tanakas and the Masudas. The families were intimidated, but the men who were being sought escaped. Within twenty-four hours all the family members of the alleged *inu* were taken to military police barracks for safety.

On the next day block managers distributed black arm bands, instructing residents to wear them until the funeral of the first youth killed. It was estimated that between two-thirds and three-quarters of the residents wore some symbol of mourning for several days. Many Nisei voluntarily wore their mourning stripes; others were openly coerced, mothers being told that their children would be treated as *inu* unless they conformed.

On Sunday morning (December 13), Masuda, Slocum, Masaoka, Tanaka and some twenty others on the death lists and black lists were, with their families, removed from Manzanar and taken to an abandoned CCC camp in Death Valley, from which two months later they were permanently resettled. Miwa, Kurihara, and others suspected of implication in the "riot" had been sent to the County Jail, and later moved to a Department of Justice Internment Camp (if aliens) or to a WRA Isolation camp at Moab, Utah (if citizens). Following the riot there were no work activities for a period, but relatively normal conditions prevailed in about a month.

Opposition to JACL leadership was undoubtedly the underlying factor in the Manzanar incident, aggravated by the encouragement the government agencies (particularly WCCA) gave the JACL organization. When Washington directives announced that the temporary government, comprised largely of Issei, would be supplanted by an all-citizen council, JACL was blamed. When Masuda and other JACL leaders formed a patriotic "Manzanar Citizens Federation," the attempt met intense opposition. When Tanaka (another JACL leader) assumed chairmanship of a commission on Self-Government, an anonymous "Blood Brothers' Organization" sent threatening letters to all the commissioners and posted signs accusing them of being *inu*. When Masuda attended the JACL convention in Salt Lake City in mid-November and was reported to have given support to a resolution pledging Nisei to volunteer for the armed forces, *inu* accusations became more frequent and intense, and when, shortly thereafter, volunteers were sought by the Army for one of its language schools, acts of violence against the first volunteer (who had been associated with Masuda's activities in Manzanar) were reported.

Furthermore, the resentment against Masuda and the JACL reached back into a period antedating the war. The residents of Manzanar were, in the main, from Los Angeles, and it was known to them or believed by them that at the time Masuda was Chairman of the Southern District of the JACL in Los Angeles he and the JACL had been in active collaboration with American intelligence agencies, in anticipation of war. Specifically, several months before the outbreak of war, the Southern District JACL had organized a Coördinating Committee for Defense. Among other duties, this body was charged with gathering information to be turned over directly to Naval Intelligence. As a result, frequent *inu* accusations were already being applied to some JACL leaders in "Little Tokio," Los Angeles, as early as August and September, 1941.[35]

---

[35] Based on a report prepared for this study by Togo Tanaka.

Chapter III

REGISTRATION

Administrative Determination of "Loyalty" and "Disloyalty"

THE WAR RELOCATION AUTHORITY had been established in March, 1942. Not until November of that year were all involuntary evacuees settled in relocation projects under its jurisdiction. By this time officials of the Authority had embarked on a program for facilitating resettlement in the "outside world" by the evacuees under their control, with a view toward the eventual liquidation of the relocation projects. The implementation of this program resulted in an unanticipated, almost fortuitous, administrative determination of evacuee "loyalty" and "disloyalty" and the segregation of the "disloyal" into a center from which access to the outside world was strictly prohibited.

Detention of evacuees for the duration of the war in ideally planned communities had been the program formulated by Eisenhower in April, 1942. "A genuinely satisfactory relocation of the evacuees into American life" would have to wait until the end of the war "when the prevailing [popular] attitudes of increasing bitterness have been replaced by tolerance and understanding."[1]

Exceptions to the nonresettlement policy were few in the early days and were limited to (1) mixed bloods and the female spouse in mixed marriages, most of whom had been released by the Army; (2) those who had made previous arrangements to evacuate voluntarily but were unavoidably prevented from meeting the Army deadline; (3) tubercular cases; and (4) college students who wanted to continue their studies outside the prohibited areas. Only the last

---

[1] Eisenhower to President Roosevelt, June 18, 1942.

[53]

of these four classes became numerically important. A plan for federal subsidies for such students, proposed by President Sproul of the University of California, did not materialize; but it led, with the approval of the War Department, to the formation of the privately organized National Student Relocation Council under the auspices of the American Friends Service Committee, which, in the course of time, placed several thousand evacuee students in eastern colleges and communities.

Seasonal furloughs for agricultural work were encouraged from the early spring of 1942, but evacuee workers on furlough were still considered to be "in the constructive military custody of the Western Defense Command," and violation of furlough regulations made them subject to the penalties of Public Law 503.[2] Under these regulations, more than 1,500 evacuees worked in the fields of eastern Oregon and the intermountain states during the spring and summer of 1942.

Members of the WRA employment division soon felt that a seasonal employment program was not enough and that efforts should be reinstituted for a more vigorous plan of resettlement. By the time Myer assumed office as Director, they had developed proposals for his consideration. By the end of July a cautious policy had been worked out limiting nonseasonal leaves from relocation projects to American citizens who had never at any time resided in Japan. An applicant for such leave was required to give proof that he had had a valid job offer, and that he had made adequate arrangements for the care of his dependents. A detailed report on his behavior in the relocation project and a formal investigation of his "loyalty" was required from the Project Director. A check with FBI records was organized under the auspices of the Regional Director, while the National Director, charged with final approval of the application, might require additional investigation and impose other conditions, such as evidence of sponsorship in the community of destination. Failure to observe any conditions set up by the National Director made the individual concerned also subject to the penalties of Public Law 503, and the leave permit was revocable at the will of the National Director.

Not even a moderate number of evacuees was resettled under this program, and new restrictions were hampering the already clumsy

---

[2] See p. 27.

procedure. The FBI check on the individual was augmented by checks by other intelligence agencies. For a period, each prospective employer, as well as the applicant for leave clearance, was checked. But this requirement was dropped after a short trial period in August.

Meantime, student relocation was showing some progress in spite of restrictions by the Army and Navy on entry of evacuees to most of the leading colleges and universities of the country,[3] and seasonal work had become so popular that, at the peak of the harvest season, some 9,000 evacuees were working in temporary jobs in agriculture in eight western states.

Determined to liberalize the policy, Myer, in late September, obtained the approval of the Justice and War departments to extend the leave program to all evacuees rather than a limited segment of the citizen group, and to drop the "constructive military custody" feature. New instructions were issued early in November,[4] providing for limited short-term and work-group leaves in addition to indefinite leaves for permanent resettlement. Liberalization did not, however, extend to the matter of investigation of applicants. Investigation of the individual's character and "loyalty" became, in fact, even more elaborate.

Having decided to go all out for resettlement, Myer instructed project directors, at a meeting in Salt Lake City late in November, to make this their major point of emphasis, and an extensive propaganda program was thereupon initiated. It was, however, still taking about three months to clear an individual record through the FBI. Even under the most favorable circumstances, in cases given special handling, a period of weeks was necessary to complete the filing of forms and recommendations, the final investigation, and the transmission of papers from the projects to Washington and back to the projects again. Jobs promised the evacuees were frequently lost as a result of these delays. WRA, therefore, decided to attempt a blanket determination of persons eligible for indefinite leave, irrespective of whether or not these persons had yet indicated a desire to resettle.

The chance to build up a file of persons eligible for leave clear-

---

[3] In general, any college or university carrying on a "classified" program sponsored by the Army or the Navy could not accept Nisei students from camps.

[4] WRA, *Administrative Instruction No. 22* (Revised), November 6, 1942.

ance was suddenly offered WRA as a by-product of a decision of the War Department to have all male citizens of Japanese ancestry, of appropriate ages, execute "loyalty" questionnaires as a preliminary to the formation of a combat team of Japanese American volunteers. This action of the War Department was in part the result of some prodding by WRA officials, who felt that their public relations program for resettlement was greatly hampered by nonparticipation of the Japanese minority in the armed forces and who had also been led to believe[5] that the observed decline in evacuee morale was directly attributable to relegation of Nisei to the status of "second class citizens," ineligible for military service, and they, therefore, urged reinstitution of selective service procedures for this group on the same basis as for other American citizens.[6]

This recommendation was not acceptable to the War Department at this time, but an alternative plan for voluntary induction in a separate combat unit was approved and announced by Secretary Stimson on January 28, 1943, with the statement that "it is the inherent right of every faithful citizen, regardless of ancestry, to bear arms in the Nation's battle." President Roosevelt reiterated this standpoint in a message to Stimson, which was released to the press on February 3, saying that "no loyal citizen of the United States should be denied the democratic right to exercise the responsibilities of his citizenship, regardless of his ancestry," and Dillon Myer found "deep satisfaction in the announcement ... [which makes] January 28, 1943, the most significant date of the last ten months for persons of Japanese ancestry."[7]

The Army program of "processing" citizens prior to enlistment immediately became tied in with a hastily devised WRA program of "processing" the whole adult population prior to resettlement, and a joint agreement for the registration of all persons 17 years of age or older was reached. WRA planned thereby to capitalize for publicity purposes on what it believed would be a successful pro-

[5] By JACL leaders and other highly articulate Americanized Nisei.

[6] Many Nisei, inducted before Pearl Harbor, had been given honorable discharges, after the war began, with no specification of cause of dismissal. In March, 1942, potential Nisei inductees were arbitrarily assigned to IV-F, the category previously reserved for persons ineligible for service because of physical defects: and on September 1, 1942, this classification had been changed to IV-C, the category ordinarily used for enemy aliens.

[7] WRA, Press Release, January 28, 1943.

gram of Army enlistment and to break the existing bottleneck in its leave-clearance program. Together, the two agencies worked out a plan for the implementation of the entire program, to begin only ten days after the announcement of January 28.

The War Department organized ten teams, each consisting of a commissioned officer, two sergeants, and one Japanese American technician or sergeant to conduct the Army registration and accept volunteers. The personnel of these teams was assembled in Washington and given a short training course before proceeding to the projects. At the same time representatives of each of the relocation centers came to Washington for conferences on registration. Other project officials were told of the program by the national director at meetings scheduled for general policy discussion, in Denver and elsewhere. The conclusion reached at the Washington meetings was to leave detailed planning and execution of registration as the joint responsibility of each project director and the captain of the Army team.

Two registration forms were prepared in Washington, one for male citizens of Japanese ancestry (17 years of age and over) with the seal "Selective Service System" at the top, and headed "Statement of United States Citizens of Japanese Ancestry," the other for female citizens and for Issei males and females. The latter form was headed "War Relocation Authority Application for Leave Clearance." The questionnaires were complicated and lengthy, including some thirty questions. Most of the questions covered the individual's sociodemographic history and status, with, however, additional questions of a somewhat unusual nature—whether close relatives resided in Japan; details regarding foreign travel and foreign investments; membership in and contributions to societies, organizations, and clubs; magazines and newspapers customarily read; possession of dual citizenship, etc. The crucial questions were numbers 27 and 28. On the form for male citizens these read:

Question 27: Are you willing to serve in the armed forces of the United States on combat duty, wherever ordered?

Question 28: Will you swear unqualified allegiance to the United States of America and faithfully defend the United States from any or all attack by foreign or domestic forces, and forswear any form of allegiance or obedience to the Japanese emperor, or any other foreign government, power, or organization?

On the form for female citizens and aliens of both sexes,[8] the questions were formulated as follows:

Question 27: If the opportunity presents itself and you are found qualified, would you be willing to volunteer for the Army Nurse Corps or the WAAC?

Question 28: Will you swear unqualified allegiance to the United States of America and forswear any form of allegiance or obedience to the Japanese emperor, or any other foreign government, power, or organization?

Formal WRA instructions provided simply for the registration of male citizens over 17 years of age, who were to fill in not only the "Statement of United States Citizens of Japanese Ancestry," but also an abbreviated version of the regular WRA leave-clearance form. The two forms were to be processed as an application for leave clearance. Questions on the selective service questionnaire were, in general, to be answered before WRA interviewers, but questions 27 and 28 had to be answered in the presence of an Army representative.[9]

In a letter accompanying these instructions, the Acting National Director (Rowalt) pointed out that the War Department acceptance of Nisei was "readily the most important development since the evacuation and relocation program was ordered almost a year ago." Registration would become the "No. 1 priority" on the projects. In this letter, the registration of adults other than male citizens was covered merely by a statement that the instructions were to be used also in "registering all other persons, male and female, regardless of citizenship, who have also attained age 17." The registration was to be compulsory "except in the case of those who have requested repatriation."[10] The letter contained also a sentence of warning, as follows.

---

[8] See p. 61.

[9] WRA, *Administrative Instruction No. 22* (Revised), Supplement 3, January 30, 1943. The Selective Service Form was DSS Form 304a; the abbreviated form for leave clearance, WRA Form 126a.

[10] Repatriation procedures had been initiated by the State Department on June 1, 1942, when the first list of "eligibles" designated by the Japanese government was submitted to the Wartime Civil Control Administration. By the middle of July, evacuee-initiated applications for repatriation (of aliens) and expatriation (of American citizens) were made possible, though no assurance of the acceptance of such applications could be given. By October 21, 1942, some 2,800 evacuees (including their minor children) had applied for repatriation or expatriation, but less than 6 per cent of these were on the Japanese government's

Please make it clear that we are not going to force people to relocate when they do not want to be relocated.[11]

War Department officials were aware of the fact that their program of recruiting volunteers might not be received with enthusiasm by the camp residents. They had, therefore, prepared a skillfully worded document, which was to be read by a member of the Army team to evacuee groups at each project.[12] The document started with an assurance that the program

... is not an experiment but marks the radical extension and broadening of a policy which has always intended that ways should be found to return you to a normal way of life ... its fundamental purpose is to put your situation on a plane which is consistent with the dignity of American citizenship.

It anticipated objections that life in camp "is not freedom":

The circumstances were not of your own choosing, though it is true that the majority of you and of your families accepted the restrictions placed upon your life with little complaint and without deviating from loyalty to the United States.

It pointed out that there are "millions of Americans who agree with your point of view." The hardships of evacuation were admitted, but were justified as a temporary sacrifice of the "best interests of the few . . . for what seems the good of the many." The obligation to "protect this nation from the acts of those who are not loyal" meant the temporary sacrifice of "the loyal citizen who wishes only to serve this country."

It was hoped "that ways shall be found to restore you as quickly as may be to your normal and rightful share in the present life and

---

list. Applications increased during the registration program, the total number of requests reaching 6,400 by July 1, 1943; and pyramided in the postsegregation period (see chapters IV ff.), the total exceeding 8,000 by December 1, 1943; 10,000 by April 1, 1944; 15,000 by July 1, 1944; and 19,000 by October 15, 1944. (See U.S. Army. Western Defense Command and Fourth Army. *Final Report, Japanese Evacuation from the West Coast, 1942.* Washington, Government Printing Office, 1943, Chap. XXIV; and War Relocation Authority, Community Analysis Section, "An Analysis of Requests for Repatriation and Expatriation," manuscript, November 18, 1944.)

[11] E. M. Rowalt to Project Directors, January 30, 1943.

[12] An official Japanese translation of the speech reached most projects too late to be useful. In at least two projects it was not used on the ground that it failed to convey the meaning of the English version. Thus, many Issei were not exposed to the propagandic effects of the speech.

work of the people of the United States"—a life that would not be without hardships, but that would involve "the same hardships which are now being experienced by other American families."

The "willing . . . and loyal" of military age were asked to volunteer. The loyal not qualified for service "will be given the opportunity to support the war effort by work upon the home front." Individuals "whose ties with the Japanese Empire are such as to disqualify them for positions of trust in this country" were not wanted. They would, however, "be treated humanely." The questionnaire was to be the means of differentiating between this group and the loyal.

Those failing to volunteer "will probably be taken into the military service in due time" via selective service. The combat team would be composed exclusively of "Americans of Japanese blood." This was justified on a public relations basis, for the record made by this team "would be a living reproach to those who have been prejudiced against you because of your Japanese blood."

WRA officials had prepared no such propagandic approach to their program of registration for leave clearance. They had evidently assumed that registration would be taken as a matter of course by the evacuees and that affirmative answers to questions 27 and 28 would likewise be given as a matter of course. This assumption was apparently so strong that they had not even attempted to adapt the wording of the Army questionnaire for citizens of military age to the far different outlook and problems of the alien group. Thus no explanation was made of the obvious absurdity of asking elderly aliens, especially males, whether they would be willing to enlist in the Army Nurse Corps or the Women's Army Auxiliary Corps (question 27 for aliens; see p. 58).[13] The inference of forced resettlement that might be drawn from the heading, "Application for Leave Clearance," used on forms for aliens, although anticipated, was not elaborated upon. Finally, the implications of asking aliens ineligible for American citizenship to "forswear any form of allegiance or obedience to the Japanese emperor" were not recognized. This last point was appreciated belatedly, and a few days after registration began, a substitute question was formulated, which would avoid the technical assumption of status as "stateless persons" by aliens who could not become

---

[13] In some relocation projects aliens were not required to answer this question.

citizens of the country to which they had been asked to swear allegiance. This substitute question 28 read:

Will you swear to abide by the laws of the United States and to take no action which would in any way interfere with the war effort of the United States?

How far results were from anticipations, both of the War Department and of WRA, is shown by a brief summary of the registration results.

(1) It had been hoped to recruit at least 3,500 volunteers. The number recruited was approximately 1,200.

(2) It had been expected that registration would be taken as a matter of course. There was an immediate and widespread resistance to registering in several projects, and in one—Tule Lake—the opposition was never overcome. When the registration period ended, 30 per cent of the eligible adults still remained unregistered at that project.

(3) It had been expected that affirmative answers, particularly to question 28, would be made as a matter of course. Instead, a marked tendency to negative replies developed, especially among American citizen males, some 28 per cent of whom refused to "swear unqualified allegiance to the United States" or to "forswear any form of allegiance or obedience to the Japanese emperor." The comparable proportion for female citizens was 18 per cent. Aliens, most of whom were permitted to answer the substitute question 28, gave negative answers or refused to register in 10 per cent of the cases of males, 7 per cent of females.

There were the widest variations in responses among residents of different relocation projects. In Tule Lake 42 per cent of all eligible persons either refused to register or answered question 28 in the negative; and in Manzanar and Jerome, while all registered, 26 per cent replied in the negative. At the other extreme was Granada, with only about 2 per cent giving a technically "disloyal" reply.

Chart II shows the "loyalty" pattern, as determined by registration results, for the ten relocation projects and indicates, strikingly, the contrast between Tule Lake and all other projects. And Chart III shows the peculiarities of the alien-citizen contrasts among males, for selected projects. The reasons for these peculiarities will become clear in the accounts which follow on pages 64 to 82 of the course of registration at several of the projects.

The strong alien-citizen contrast, and the extreme variation among relocation projects soon made it apparent that negative answers to questions devised to test "loyalty" were motivated by many other factors in addition to political allegiance. The ques-

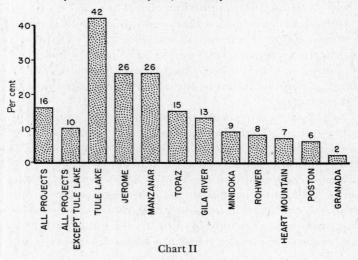

Per cents of Total Population 17 Years of Age or Older Giving Nonaffirmative Replies to Question 28 or Refusing to Register, by Relocation Projects, February – March 1943

Chart II

tions, and their method of presentation, aroused a strong protest reaction among Nisei, who, having had almost all their rights as citizens abrogated through evacuation and forcible confinement, questioned the justice of the restoration of just the one "right" of serving in the armed forces. They aroused fear and resistance among Issei who, stripped of all other possessions, used every means at their disposal to hold their families intact and to avoid what they conceived to be the certainty of the loss of their sons in combat,[14] and who, having acceded to a forced evacuation from their homes

[14] Among the Japanese, it is assumed that if a boy enters the Army he will be killed in combat. This fatalistic view of Army service is found almost universally among the Issei and, to a surprising extent, is shared by many Nisei.

to camps, were now determined to avoid a threatened second evacuation from camps to an "outside world" that they had every reason
to believe would regard them with hostility. These protest and
fear reactions were fortified by administrative procedures which
inadvertently attached penalties to affirmative answers and rewards

Per cent of Male Citizen and of Male Alien Population
17 Years of Age or Older Giving Nonaffirmative Replies
to Question 28 or Refusing to Register,
by Selected Relocation Projects, February–March 1943

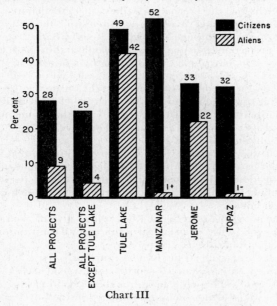

Chart III

to negative answers, and by sudden and incompletely understood
changes in policies. In several relocation projects, the mechanics of
registration were handled skillfully and, as a consequence, no overt
resistance developed. This was especially true in Minidoka. In
Poston also the mechanics of the program proceeded smoothly, but
the overt responses of the residents were far different from those in
Minidoka. The progress of registration at Gila, Manzanar, and
Jerome followed a more turbulent course. The following partial
accounts of the course of registration in these projects illustrate the
varying reactions.

TOPAZ

The nature of the Nisei protest can best be exemplified by a petition, drawn up at Topaz and sent to the War Department, asking full restoration of civil rights and assurance of protection for their families as a prerequisite to proceeding with the registration. This resolution was printed in the Topaz Times of February 15 and was widely used as propaganda against registration or for negative answers by Nisei and Kibei groups at other projects.

The preliminaries to the resolution pointed out the acceptance and full coöperation by the Nisei "of the extraordinary orders of the United States Army," including the evacuation orders; their temporary surrender of "many of the rights and privileges of citizenship"; the failure of the government, operating through the Federal Reserve Bank, to give its promised "full protection from unscrupulous people at the time of evacuation"; the "losses of homes, properties, work, freedom of movement, separation from friends" which had been "suffered . . . without protest." They stated further their earnest desire "to prevent in the future the mass evacuation or confining of citizens without trial," their belief "that there is only one class of citizenship in the United States" and that "some of the things mentioned above constitute a violation of our civil rights."

The resolution read:

"1. That we ask Secretary of War Henry L. Stimson that after a thorough investigation by the Military Intelligence and the Federal Bureau of Investigation and other Federal authorities, that persons that are cleared should have absolute freedom of movement and a choice of returning to their homes.

"2. That we request President Roosevelt to give us assurance that he will use his good Office in an endeavor to secure all constitutional and civil rights as American citizens.

"3. That the security for the Issei be assured.

"4. That we ask President Roosevelt to use his good Office to bring favorable impression to the public regarding the loyal citizens.

"5. That we ask that those Issei considered by the Government as being not disloyal to this Government be classified as friendly aliens.

"6. That we have the Government note the advantages of the good publicity to be gained by disbursing [dispersing] Nisei soldiers into the Army at large, rather than by forming a separate Combat Team; and that the Government further note that the education of Caucasian soldiers can be made through deep comradeship that grows between soldiers facing a common task, and thereby educate the American public.

"7. That the Government, recognizing that we are fighting for the Four Freedoms as embodied in the Atlantic Charter, should apply these democratic principles to us here at home.

"8. That we believe that if satisfactory answers can be given by a Government spokesman, preferably the President of the United States, to these questions, we can go and fight for this our country without fear or qualms concerning the security of our future rights.

"And be it further resolved that we respectfully ask for immediate answers to the questions in this resolution."[15]

The overt Nisei protest at Topaz centered around the problems of restoration of what they conceived to be their abrogated civil rights, failure of government agencies to assure protection of their Issei parents, and the segregated, discriminatory basis on which they were being asked to serve in the armed forces. Underlying this protest was also a general reluctance to be inducted into the Army from behind barbed wire. Dillon Myer answered the resolution on February 16 by pointing out that the War Department announcement and President Roosevelt's statement had been made "in good faith," that the response would be a "crucial test" for the evacuees, and that it was not the time "to quibble or bargain."[16] Three days later, an official War Department message reiterated these points, emphasizing that "it is only by mutual confidence and coöperation that the loyal Japanese Americans can be restored to their civil rights."[17]

The Topaz committee which had drawn up the resolution immediately issued a statement accepting "this registration as an indication of the government's good faith." The strength and persistence of the underlying doubts and resentments are, however, indicated by the fact that 32 per cent of the male citizens answered question 28 in the negative.

MINIDOKA

The registration program placed emphasis upon volunteering for the Army as a patriotic duty and a wise course. Little attention was paid to other aspects of the program. Evacuee leaders, particularly Issei, were involved in planning and procedures at all stages. Five days of intensive discussion preceded the arrival of the Army team on February 6. Propaganda was developed by the administration to convince the residents that upon the success of the volunteering program depended, in large part, the future of the Japanese minority in America. Evacuee leaders emphasized the same points and, in addition, made much of the moral obligation of citizens and of aliens who intended to stay in this country to participate actively in the war effort. Reaction of the residents was mixed. There were frequent references to the injustice of the sacrifice demanded of Issei in giving up their sons, but the protest was an individual matter and was driven underground during this period. At the initial meeting with Army representatives, doubts revolved around the following points:

1. How will we be treated in the Army? Will we be treated fairly?
2. How much discrimination are we going to meet after the war even though we volunteer?
3. What is going to become of my family? Will they be secure?
4. What benefits will we get by volunteering?
5. What will be the consequences of not volunteering?

---

[15] *Topaz Times,* February 15, 1943.
[16] *Ibid.,* February 16, 1943.
[17] *Ibid.,* February 19, 1943.

Efforts were made by the administration to reward the "loyal." A War Department plan to man and equip the hitherto unused watchtowers was forestalled. The Washington office was asked to take steps to improve the status and facilitate the release of Department of Justice internees whose sons volunteered for induction. Finally, it was officially stated that

"Army volunteers and others who leave dependents in the center may rest assured that they will be cared for as long as they wish to remain in this center."[18]

Registration proceeded in an orderly manner from block to block. After male citizens completed the WRA form, they were taken immediately in trucks to the administrative area and, if their answers to question 28 had been in the affirmative, they were asked to volunteer for the combat team. Reinstatement of selective service procedures for Nisei was presented as a necessary basis for restoration of other citizenship rights and was further described as dependent upon the success of the program of voluntary induction. The approach made by the Army team made it difficult not to volunteer. The young men were first asked how they would answer question 27, and the answers were often "yes." Next they were asked how they would answer question 28, and the answers were again "yes." They were then asked to sign the voluntary induction form. If they did not sign it, they were told that they could not answer "yes" to both questions 27 and 28. As a result many of the boys answered "no" to question 27 rather than to sign for voluntary induction. A qualified answer to question 27, such as "yes, if drafted" evidently was not allowed during the early days of registration. Some of the young men felt that they could not refuse to volunteer even though they had not intended to.

An editorial in the project newspaper emphasized the official standpoint: "There can be no more holding back with 'Yes, but' rationalizations.

"And if it should be charged that we are being forced to volunteer, let it be remembered first that compulsion arises only from our own dilemma. ... The hard, unrelenting fact is that the fix we are in—and the extent and importance of all that is at stake—does not permit petty quibbling and squirting of hypersensitive criticism at the one great chance we have. For the burden we bear is that we are to decide in no small measure, whether the generations to follow us will walk the main streets of America as equal citizens, or seek the side-streets as despised pariahs. ..."[19]

By February 25 the registration was complete. Only 9 per cent negative answers were recorded for citizen males. During registration and in succeeding weeks, over 300 young men (21 per cent of the total eligible) volunteered for induction. With less than 7 per cent of the total male citizen population in relocation projects, Minidoka accounted for 25 per cent of all Army volunteers.

---

[18] *Minidoka Irrigator*, March 13, 1943. This administrative promise was abrogated when all relocation projects were closed in the fall of 1945.

[19] *Minidoka Irrigator*, February 13, 1943.

POSTON[20]

In general, registrants appeared for their interviews at the appointed hour and there were no refusals to register. In this project registration of all male citizens was completed before similar proceedings were initiated for female citizens and for aliens. Discussions of procedures were held in frequent meetings before registration began, and no organized attempts to intimidate or influence decisions were reported.[21] An appreciable proportion (18 per cent) of the male citizens, however, answered question 28 in the negative. It was reported at the time that "those who answered 'no' are secretive. They meant what they said and are willing to take the consequences." The extent of the underlying tensions is suggested by the following description of a mass meeting on February 17 in Camp I.

The crowd kept respectfully quiet while Lieutenant Bolton read the prepared army message. When the questioning began it soon became obvious that the people were out to heckle the army team. The type of inquiries they made mirrored their resentment and distrust of the U. S. government. They wanted definite commitments in return for volunteering. If any enthusiasm toward joining the army was present it was cautiously camouflaged. When Lieutenant Bolton in the course of his speech announced that he had just received authority from Washington to accept loyal Issei who wished to serve in the U. S. Army, the crowd broke into a wild derisive laughter and hooted: "Try and get one!" People were also commenting that if the army team had brought along two or three Nisei captains instead of a single Nisei sergeant, it could probably whip up greater enthusiasm to serve its purpose. The lone Nisei sergeant was to them a symbol of racial discrimination in the U. S. Army.

An idea of the type of heckling indulged in by the audience is shown by the following selection of the more extreme questions asked of the army team:

1. Why are the loyal Japanese Americans not allowed to go back to California?

2. My two brothers in Camp Savage and Camp Hare have been denied permission to visit our sick father in the Los Angeles County Hospital. Why can't they, who are in the uniform of the U. S. Army, visit their dying father when Caucausians in army uniforms may do so?

3. What is the reason for giving some of us IV-C classification? We are without a country now.

4. Why were Nisei draftees kicked out of the army after December 7?

5. Why can't Nisei soldiers visit this camp? Are you afraid that they will see how bad conditions are in camp?

6. Why were Nisei changed from combat duty to menial tasks after Pearl Harbor?

---

[20] Based on report prepared for this study by Tamie Tsuchiyama.

[21] In a preregistration flare-up in Camp II, the JACL National President was beaten up by eight Kibei for his alleged sponsorship of reinstitution of selective service procedures. The matter was turned over to the FBI, who picked up a

7. Why are Nisei not accepted in the Navy?

8. Why the Jim Crow decision?

9. Why were the Nisei stripped of their ranks after Pearl Harbor?

10. Why were veterans of the last war put in camps when they proved their loyalty then?

11. If we volunteer, will our interned parents be returned to our families?

12. My brother is a pre-med student. Will he be given an opportunity to finish his medical training if he volunteers? I feel that since he is Japanese he will not be given the same consideration as a Caucasian soldier.

13. May a Nisei apply for appointment at West Point?

14. Why were Italian aliens in internment camps released while we were not released?

GILA[22]

The Army registration team arrived on February 8. Prior to its arrival, the project newspaper and other sources of communication had been devoted to extensive propaganda favoring enlistment, and, at the first meeting of the team with evacuee leaders (councilmen, block managers, etc.) the whole emphasis was put on this aspect of the program. Captain Thompson, who was in charge, read the prepared Army statement, and added that a quota of some 300 to 350 volunteers was expected from Gila. This statement aroused intense resentment among the evacuee leaders, who pointed out that the Japanese Americans had already shown their patriotism by coöperating in the government plan for evacuation, that their present situation represented a denial of all their rights, and that enlistment in the Army, under these conditions, was not a privilege but an unbearable sacrifice.

When Captain Thompson stated that those families who had a son in the service would be given preference in the matter of relocation, a hiss of protest went up throughout the audience. It was pointed out to him that he apparently did not realize that the average modal age of Issei was 56, of Nisei 21. The Nisei was the breadwinner of the family, and if he were drafted the family hope of resettlement would be gone.

The questions raised most persistently were those concerned with democratic principles and those which expressed a fear of the disuniting of families. Answers to the effect that family disunification had occurred throughout the world and was happening to many Caucasian American families were not considered satisfactory by the evacuees.

At this first meeting, the subject of loyalty to the United States did not arise. Loyalty became an issue later and was brought up, not by the evacuees, but by the administration.

---

number of antiadministration "agitators" and interned them at Santa Fe. Among them was Yamashita, who was later to play an important role in developments at the Tule Lake Segregation Center. (See chapters VII, XI, and XII.)

[22] Based on a report prepared for this study by Robert F. Spencer.

Pressures against enlistment were followed by pressures against registration. These pressures seemed to center in the Issei group and in the Kibei organizations of both camps.[23]

On Tuesday, February 9, a meeting, sponsored by the JACL was held in Butte Camp for a Nisei audience. On the next evening meetings were held simultaneously in Canal and Butte, both directed primarily toward the Issei, in an attempt to convince them of the necessity of allowing their sons to enter the armed forces. Captain Thompson presided at the Canal meeting and met with little enthusiasm. The Nisei sergeant who presided in Butte was greeted with howls of derision and was not allowed to present his prepared speech.

On Thursday night, February 11, a meeting with the well-organized Kibei Club in Butte was arranged. Its leader, George Wakida, who had been outspoken in opposition to the registration program, had been called into the Project Director's office earlier in the day and told that if his group failed to coöperate with Captain Thompson he would be held personally responsible and might be indicted under the Espionage Act. The meeting of the Army officers with the Kibei proceeded quietly. There was no demonstration and few controversial questions were raised. After the open meeting, however, the Kibei Club held a closed meeting for its own members and was said to have advocated pressure tactics to bring about negative answers to the loyalty question.

During the first two days of registration (February 11 and 12), more than half of those registering were reported to be giving negative answers. The administrators thereupon called in evacuee leaders and read the Espionage Act to them. This put an end to organized pressure against registration, but did not prevent outspoken expressions, particularly from Kibei leaders, and it soon became obvious from the continuing large number of negative answers that opposition to the questions was still powerful.

The administration decided to take more drastic steps against the elements of opposition. A list of alleged subversive leaders was, therefore, turned over to the FBI, who moved into the project in six cars with protection from jeep patrols on the afternoon of February 16 and apprehended some twenty-eight Issei and Kibei suspects, who were later removed to the Lordsburg internment camp for enemy aliens and the WRA Isolation Camp at Moab, Utah, respectively. Following the roundup all demonstration died down, the leaders were gone, and pressures against registration became an individual family affair. The net result of the registration at Gila was negative answers for some 37 per cent of the male citizens, but almost 100 per cent affirmative response among aliens.

---

[23] The Gila project consisted of two camps, Butte and Canal.

MANZANAR[24]

It was in this charged atmosphere [that which followed the December "riot"] and while these many wounds [connected with evacuation] still smarted that registration began in February. Issei, who were painfully and doubtfully considering how they might pick up the threads of their lives in America after the war, were appalled to see that the questionnaire submitted to them was for the purpose of leave clearance. They envisaged themselves forced out of the center at a time when they were poor and discouraged and in the face of hostile public opinion. Those who had depended upon a Japanese community economically and socially, were dismayed at the program for thin dispersal in unfamiliar regions.

But their most decided reaction was to question 28, the "loyalty" question submitted to them. It called upon them, in effect, to renounce their Japanese citizenship, something that enemy aliens, ineligible to American citizenship could hardly be expected to accept without protest. The majority of them determined to say "no." They assumed that this "no" would mean further restrictions upon their liberty and ultimate deportaion to Japan. Many of them resolved to anticipate their "liquidation in America" and to cast the die without further delay. A movement to sign repatriation forms began that almost grew to stampede proportions. The authorities, realizing that a wave of hysteria on the subject had set in, closed the door to repatriation requests until after registration was completed.

In the meantime, government officials had recognized the doubtful legality of the original alien question 28. Those who were in charge at Manzanar understood that they were authorized to offer a substitute question. However, in their desire to stay reasonably close to the Washington version and because of a misunderstanding that arose in translating a word from English into Japanese (where the nearest Japanese equivalent has a much stronger and more military connotation) the Manzanar revision was still not acceptable to many Issei. [The English version was: "Are you sympathetic to the United States and do you agree faithfully to defend the United States from any and all attack by foreign or domestic forces?"] Besides, by this time a negative attitude had swept the camp which would have made a receptive state of mind toward *any* question impossible at that time.

It was at this time that the aliens turned to counsel and instruct their children. Those who had decided that there was no longer a place for them in America were determined that this country would not "rob" them of their children as it had taken their possessions. There began a campaign to prevail upon the children 17 years of age and over to say "no" to their loyalty question. The friction that was generated in homes over this issue is almost unbelievable. . . . Many children, knowing what the parents had lost and suffered, were unwilling to cause them further grief and anxiety and agreed to comply with their wishes.

[24] The description of the situation at Manzanar is quoted from a manuscript ("Studies of Segregants at Manzanar") prepared by Morris Opler for the Community Analysis Section of WRA.

Moreover, the Nisei had many complaints of their own. They were anything but pleased with the question 28 submitted to citizens. This was especially true of those who did not possess dual citizenship, for the question called upon them to forswear allegiance to the Japanese emperor. It read more like a naturalization oath than something prepared for American citizens. Question 27, the answers to which were to be used as the basis for organizing a volunteer Nisei army combat team, was viewed with great suspicion, too.

Out of the turmoil and confusion came family decisions. Though there were some families that split on the issue, in the main the problem was threshed out in the family circle and parents and children answered in much the same vein. In view of the rumors and fears, the suspicion and irritation, the setting and the intimidation, it is remarkable that so many did hold to a "yes" answer. [52 per cent of the male citizens answered question 28 negatively, the largest proportion in any project. About half of these, however, later changed their answers to the affirmative.]

In April still another substitute question 28 was submitted to the aliens. It was a mild and innocuous question which simply called upon the person to obey the laws of this country as long as he resided here and to do nothing to impede America's war effort. Approximately 98 per cent of the aliens found no difficulty in answering this in the affirmative [59 per cent had answered nonaffirmatively to the Manzanar revision]. It did not jeopardize their Japanese citizenship, it did not commit them to plans for the future (they had declared that Japan would never receive them if they agreed to the original question) and they had no hesitation in affirming that they would be law-abiding residents. The justification for putting this revised question before the aliens was that it had become the official Washington version (too late, however, to be submitted at Manzanar in February) which had been asked at every other center. The favorable response to this question put most of the aliens of Manzanar in the "yes" ("loyal") column. It left their citizen children, who had in most instances answered in the negative to conform to parental wishes and practice, uncomfortably isolated in the "no" ("disloyal") column.

JEROME

The Jerome project in Arkansas[25] showed deviation from the general pattern in one important respect: although registration had begun, as scheduled, on February 9, it was allowed to proceed in a desultory way, with no mention of compulsion, until March 6, when an announcement from Dillon Myer was submitted to the residents informing them that failure to register was a violation of WRA regulations and offenders were subject to 90 days' imprisonment. On that day some 500 men, mostly Nisei and Kibei, had assembled at the Administration Building and selected representatives to consult with the Project Director. Among these representatives were Abe, Kuratomi, Aramaki and Kodama, who were later to play

[25] Details regarding registration in Jerome were furnished by George Kuratomi.

important roles in the Tule Lake Segregation Center. When informed that registration was compulsory, they indicated their desire to apply for expatriation and presented a petition to that effect to the Project Director. The Project Director in a signed statement assured the petitioners that they would not be "arrested for refusal to register unless I am specifically directed by the Washington office of the War Relocation Authority. In case Washington directs the arrest of such persons, I will notify each individual at least 24 hours before any arrests are made." The registration deadline was extended and all those eligible to register complied with the requirement, although many of the original petitioners merely marked questions 27 and 28 as "Repatriate" or "Expatriate" instead of giving an unequivocal "no" answer. Including these, 33 per cent of the male citizens were recorded as giving nonaffirmative answers; and because of this peculiar administrative policy, 22 per cent of the alien males likewise appeared in the records as nonaffirmatives—a result quite out of line with the average of other relocation projects. (See Chart III.)

Doubt and fear accompanied registration in all relocation projects. Only in Tule Lake, however, were the unfavorable predispositions of the residents channeled into a persistent collective movement of noncoöperation and resistance—a movement that eventually stigmatized its residents as "disloyal" in the eyes of the American public and within a few months led to the designation of this relocation project as a segregation center for evacuees whose loyalties were thought to lie with Japan. Resistance at Tule Lake was fostered by defective coördination between evacuee and administrative organizations; by the breakdown in communications between national and local representatives of the several branches of government responsible for registration; by the consequent inability of project officials to clarify issues, procedures, and penalties for the evacuees; by the speeding up of the program to meet a predetermined deadline in spite of this lack of clarification; by errors in the administrative definition of penalties for noncoöperation; and by use of force in the application of these penalties. Because of the far-reaching consequences of the Tule Lake program, its course will be described in detail.

News of the proposed registration reached Tule Lake residents through the War Department release to the public press on January 29, 1943. Not until February 4 was the fact that registration for recruitment would be correlated with general registration "for leave clearance" made known through the *Tulean Dispatch*. At the same time it was stated that registration would not be necessary for persons who had applied for repatriation to Japan.

Repeated efforts by the Community Council and Planning Board representatives to obtain authentic information in the interim met with no success. The Project Director, Coverley, put off all questions with promises of clarification by Hayes, the Assistant Project Director, who had gone to Washington for detailed instructions. When Hayes returned on February 2, however, he stated that he could add no details to the press releases, and was quoted in the *Tulean Dispatch* of February 4 as saying that "further clarification of recruitment will be announced by the Army team arriving on the project, February 6." The Army team did not arrive on February 6, as promised, but came on February 9, and registration had, meantime, been scheduled to begin on the morning of February 10.

Left in a state of uncertainty about what they were to register for, why they had to register, and how registration was to proceed, from January 29 to February 9, evacuees made their own definitions of issues and procedures. Formal and informal discussions centered on the injustice of instituting military service, on the discriminatory aspects of the proposed segregated combat unit, on the probability of forced resettlement as inherent in the program and on the dubious prospects of favorable employment opportunities on the outside. With official definitions still unclarified, when the JACL held a meeting on February 3, and its leaders advocated voluntary enlistment, reinstitution of selective service, and resettlement to work in war industries, rumors immediately arose to the effect that JACL and its Tule Lake leaders were responsible for the registration policies.[26]

Members of the Army team and WRA officials finally met with various evacuee groups during the day and evening of February 9. At these meetings the prepared War Department statement was read. In very few meetings were questions accepted from the floor, and even accepted questions were left unanswered unless they conformed to a standardized series of anticipated questions to which equally standardized answers had been prepared. The people approached the first day of registration in an uneasy frame of mind

---

[26] Resentment against the JACL had been widespread in Tule Lake since its inception, owing partly to the control JACL leaders had exercised in the Walerga and Puyallup Assembly Centers, from which Tuleans were recruited, and partly to the prominence they achieved in politics in the Tule Lake Center itself.

and with profound doubts of the meaning of the whole procedure. It had been determined that registration would proceed simultaneously in all blocks for all classes of the population. Two teachers, one Nisei and one Caucasian, appeared at each block manager's office shortly after breakfast to serve as registrars, while Army officers opened special offices to enlist male citizens for military service. Block managers had instructed all people over 17 years of age in the first barrack of each block to register that morning, but the instructions had often lacked definiteness and conviction. Very few answered the summons. Reports began to circulate that many Nisei and Kibei were tearing up their birth certificates—a symbolic repudiation of their citizenship—when they learned that they were being asked to serve in the Army after having been subjected to the indignity of evacuation, confinement behind barbed wire, and the insults of the American press.

On the evening of the 10th, meetings were held in every block and hundreds of questions were gathered, classified, assembled and submitted to the Project Director. One series of questions related to the fact that Issei became stateless persons if they answered question 28 affirmatively.[27] A more difficult set of questions related to the interpretations which could be given to question 28 for citizens, particularly the relation of "yes" and "no" answers, respectively, to the eventual application of selective service procedures; the effect on remaining citizenship rights and other possible penalties of a negative answer; whether there would be immediate rewards for answering "yes," e.g., return to the West Coast, the removal of discriminatory practices against minorities in the armed forces, free access of inductees to relocation projects where their families resided, assurance of support of dependents of inductees and, by inference, assurance that such dependents would not be forcibly resettled. Other questions attempted to clarify the definition of "loyalty," and to assess the relevance of questions 27 and 28 to such a definition. Still others were of a rhetorical sort and had little to do with immediate issues, but reflected protests against past injustices.

By the third day of registration, only an insignificant number had complied with the requirements. In some blocks general agreements, binding residents not to register, were being made. Individ-

---

[27] The substitute question for aliens (see p. 61) had not yet reached the project.

uals and families in other blocks failed to appear at the registrar's office at the appointed time. Some persons who had registered in the first two days were now asking to have their papers withdrawn. A stalemate existed. The desire to avoid commitment of any kind had become crystallized.

Scapegoats were sought, and resentment against registration was turned against the vociferous, pro-America, JACL leaders, who had long been objectionable to most evacuees because of their consistently collaborationist policy in relations with the Army, WCCA, and WRA. Three of the leaders received anonymous, threatening notes, and one of them was hurriedly removed from the project on February 11.

On February 14 the first of a number of petitions against compliance with registration orders began to be circulated. On February 15 officials met evacuee representatives (Council, Planning Board, and block managers) to answer the voluminous questions submitted on February 10. Prepared answers to some sixty questions were read, but the replies were considered vague and indefinite by most of the evacuees. At this meeting officials stated that interference with registration was punishable under the Espionage Act by maximum penalties of $10,000 fine or 20 years imprisonment or both.

The questions and prepared answers of February 15 were presented to the residents in mimeographed form at block meetings on February 16 and 17. Meantime, little progress had been made in the mechanics of registration. The majority was still opposed to compliance, and even those who favored registration waited for a change in community sentiment and a more propitious atmosphere before submitting themselves to registration. On February 17 the administration announced a new set of registration rules transferring registration from the blocks to the administrative area, with separate locales for the registration of male citizens, female citizens and aliens. On the same day, an administrative notice appeared in the *Tulean Dispatch,* reiterating the compulsory aspect of registration and emphasizing the penalties for "seditious" opposition. Blocks from which compulsory registrations would be made on the following day were listed, including block 42 for male citizens. (See Chart IV, p. 105, for location of blocks and proportions "disloyal.") Tension mounted in these blocks during the day, and in block 42 an overwhelming vote to refuse to register was reported from male citizens, who thereupon, in small groups, intruded themselves in other block meetings, demanded expressions of opinion, and urged that representatives meet together to draw up a plan in opposition to registration. On the next morning, registration proceeded at a slow pace, less than a hundred of the required 250 male citizens complying with the order to report. Simultaneously, Nisei and Kibei, and later many Issei, began lining up outside the Internal Security office to apply for repatriation. This rush represented a belated comprehension of the possibilities of the administrative statement that "registration is compulsory except for those who had requested repatriation."

On the evening of the eighteenth, the *Tulean Dispatch* carried an announcement from an Army representative to the effect that it was a "mistaken idea" to suppose "that if male citizens obtain repatriation blanks, they do not have to register." This was a direct contradiction of previous assurances, and a crowd of about fifty angry youths pushed into the administration building demanding application blanks, but were refused.

On the same day a Planning Board representative from Block 45 was arrested on suspicion of encouraging opposition to registration. By this time, project officials were convinced that the resistance to registration was traceable to "pro-Japanese agitators" and they embarked on a policy of identifying, arresting, and removing the disruptive elements.

Meanwhile, the Planning Board, making an attempt to stem the antiregistration tide, had prepared a statement urging "careful thought" of the registration situation, particularly by those "who wish to remain in the United States of America." The Project Director, however, withheld approval of distribution of the statement because of his objection to the following sentence: "We feel that the parents should act as consultants to their children." The view of the administration was that parents would have a detrimental influence on the Nisei. Thereupon the Planning Board prepared another statement, instructing its representatives not to participate in any action favoring group decisions against registration and emphasizing the standpoint that "registration is a matter of individual judgment and the final decision should be left up to each person." This, too, was rejected by the Project Director on the ground that "registration is not a matter of individual judgment." Thus what might have been important evacuee efforts to forestall group resistance were completely frustrated.

Block 42 residents continued their resistance. Only about a third of those scheduled appeared at the registrar's offices during the whole day of February 18, and this in spite of the fact that Army and Internal Security officers had appeared at the mess hall at lunch time, read off the names of those required to register and stated the sedition penalties for failure to register. The same performance was repeated during the noon meal of February 19, and an announcement was made that trucks would appear to convey the unregistered to the registrar's offices at 1 o'clock. When the trucks arrived, no one boarded them, and they returned empty. The block residents met to discuss further steps, and at about 2:30 that afternoon a delegation of thirty-four youths, followed by a large crowd, approached the administration building to demand the right of expatriation in lieu of registration. The project officials refused to accept their applications and made further efforts to persuade the young men to register. Failing in these efforts, the Project Director called in the military police on February 21, and at about 5 P.M. a caravan of cars bearing WRA officials followed by jeeps and trucks carrying M.P.'s armed with machine guns and bayonets, moved into the block, picked up the boys (who were waiting with packed suitcases), and took them off to the county jails. An angry crowd had gathered and threats were shouted at the departing soldiers.

The Block 42 incident had immediate repercussions. Signs of panic among previous opponents of registration appeared, and numbers of them reached a decision to register. For others, however, there was a strengthening of the determination not to register. Block meetings were held throughout Ward V and agreement was reached in most blocks in this ward that there would be no coöperation with the administration until the young men who had been arrested were released. In Block 44, where there were close friends and relatives of the arrested boys, it was agreed that (1) no one should register; (2) a petition signifying this stand should be circulated throughout the community; and (3) a general strike of block residents would be declared and a similar stand urged on the community at large.

At an emergency meeting of the Planning Board and Council, held that evening, the proposal for a general strike was tabled on the ground that it would disrupt the whole community. A delegation was appointed, however, to approach the administration and ask for immediate release of the boys and to propose a new plan of registration. Early on the morning of February 22, some evacuees set off the fire siren, a prearranged signal for the emergency closing of high schools, and mess-hall gongs began to ring to call the residents to early block meetings. Petitions for refusal to register were widely circulated, under conditions of maximum social pressure, e.g., at meal time when all residents were assembled and nonsigners could be readily identified. Meantime, the delegates conferring with the Project Director were meeting with little success. They asked the unconditional return of the arrested boys and were forthwith refused. They asked guarantees that no further arrests would be made and were likewise refused. Proposals to submit registration questionnaires by mail, to suspend registration until tension had diminished, to instruct Caucasian and Nisei teachers to cease exerting pressure on registrants to change "no" answers to "yes" were all turned down. Faced with the unwillingness of the administration to make any concession whatsoever, Planning Board and Council members resigned en masse.

The same evening, a group of Kibei held a mass meeting in Block 4 and drew up a petition demanding (1) that they be treated as Japanese nationals; (2) that they be taken from the project "at bayonet point" as the Block 42 boys had been taken; and reaffirming their "absolute refusal" to register. Members of this group entered various block meetings and demanded that signatures be affixed to the petition before the meetings broke up. At the same time they threatened to beat up *inu* who, by this time were defined as people willing to collaborate with the administration by registering. On the assumption that the petition would meet with a favorable response from the community, the group developed plans for a mass meeting on the following morning, after which the participants would march on the administration building and present the petitions to the Project Director and the Army representative.

Residents who indicated willingness to take an overt stand in favor of registration by refusing to sign the petition, immediately met intense hostility, ostracism and threats of physical violence. In Ward V they were isolated in the mess halls at special *inu* tables, other block residents would not speak to them, they received anonymous written threats, and children making barking noises followed them along the streets. That evening two of the alleged *inu,* a Christian Issei minister and the Kibei translator for the *Tulean Dispatch,* were severely beaten. Attempts to beat another Christian minister, a prominent JACL leader, and the former chairman of the Community Council, were frustrated in the first case by the skill of the minister in talking to the boys; in the second case by barring the door; in the third, by the temporary absence of the councilman from his apartment. The JACL leader was immediately removed from the project for safety.

The next day rumors of the number of beatings reached fantastic proportions. Many people felt that the beatings and the alleged beatings were just acts of retribution; but others, particularly members of the churches of the beaten and threatened ministers, were deeply shocked at the outbreak of violence.

The demonstration and march on the administration building, which had been planned for the morning of February 23, failed to materialize. The response to the petition had not been as great as expected, except in wards V and I, for, although few people had been willing to take a stand of overt opposition, techniques of avoidance of committing themselves had developed among many. Furthermore, in spite of the defiant attitudes manifested in the petition, not many members of the Kibei group were willing to risk criminal charges. Few parents desired to see their sons arrested at "bayonet point" and family pressure was exerted to withdraw them from the more extreme standpoint.

Individuals continued to press the administration for release of the arrested boys, without result, for WRA had by this time turned the matter over to the FBI. The reorganized Planning Board was stalemated because of widening schisms within the organization. There were, however, increasing signs among large sections of the community of a desire to find some compromise that would break the deadlock.

On February 23, Major Marshall, the Army representative, posted in all mess halls a mimeographed statement regarding the meaning of "no" and "yes" answers, respectively. This significant document read, in part:

Nisei and Kibei who answer "No" to questions No. 27 and 28, and who persist in that answer, *cannot anticipate that the Army of the United States will ever ask for their services* or that they will be inducted into the armed forces by Selective Service.

A "No" answer on question 27, accompanied by a "Yes" answer on question 28, *is not regarded by the War Department as a proof of disloyalty* in the individual, or as bearing on that question . . . [but] these men have the minimum chance of being called into the military service.

The "Yes" answer to both questions speaks for itself. . . . In case it is so filled, then *they are liable to induction* for general service elsewhere throughout the Army of the United States, in the same manner as any other inductee within the country.[28]

This official statement suddenly and completely provided a means of breaking the deadlock, for it gave an official assurance of exemption from military service to persons answering questions 27 and 28 in the negative. Protest could now be expressed by No-No answers rather than refusal to answer questions 27 and 28 and would bring reward rather than punishment. At the same time, fence-sitting or failure to commit oneself irrevocably was encouraged by the statement that No-Yes answers would probably lead to exemption from military service without the stigma of disloyalty to America. For many of the citizens behind barbed wire and their dispossessed alien parents, the attraction of a No-No or a No-Yes answer over that of a Yes-Yes answer for males of military age was obvious.

One by one, blocks in the resisting wards released their residents from agreements not to register, although in many cases this release was accompanied by a directive to answer questions 27 and 28 in the negative. Minorities were, however, still active in opposing registration throughout the last week of February. One of these was the remnants of the Kibei organization, members of which posted a mimeographed statement in all latrines on February 25, informing residents "Why You Should Not Register." This bulletin warned of the dangers of any commitment in writing and pointed out that "written statements of your 'Yes's' and 'No's' will be used against you." Dangers of negative answers were that Congress and the Army "could define all of us disloyal, they could cancel our citizenships, making us enemy aliens . . . [and thus] confiscate legally our properties." Such laws could not be enacted without the written evidence which would accrue with registration;

---

[28] Statement by Major S. A. L. Marshall, War Department, to Tule Lake evacuees, February 23, 1943. Italics ours.

therefore "beware of your written statements." Another minority still opposing registration was comprised of friends and neighbors of the arrested boys from Block 42. These people felt and urged that resistance should not be discontinued until the boys were released.

Meantime, the administration found itself in an embarrassing situation in connection with the Block-42 boys who had been arrested without specific charges. While preparing charges of failure to comply with selective service regulations, maximum penalties for which were 20 years in jail, or $10,000 fine or both, the Project Attorney was informed by FBI agents that mere refusal to fill in the questionnaire was not a violation of the Selective Service Act.

When the Project Director queried Dillon Myer, the National Director, about this matter, he in turn queried the War Department on February 26 and discovered that the filling in of questionnaires by male citizens of military age had not been made compulsory by the latter agency. The threats of 20 years' imprisonment to which the evacuees had been subjected were, therefore, totally invalid. No announcement of this fact, however, was made to the evacuees, who were allowed to continue in the belief that they were violating the Espionage Act by failing to register. Instead, WRA embarked upon a policy of further arrests and sought legal refuge in the fact that nonregistrants were disobeying WRA administrative instructions, and could therefore be punished by a maximum of 90 days' confinement in jail or suspension of certain compensation privileges or both.

Registration of citizens had been scheduled to end on March 2. In spite of the rising tide of registration after Major Marshall's announcement, only one third of the male citizens and one half of the female citizens had appeared at the registrar's office by that date. To break the remaining resistance, the Project Director decided to extend the deadline for citizen registrants until March 10. At the same time, he began issuing peremptory orders to all non-registered Kibei bachelors to appear for registration. When they disobeyed these orders, they were promptly isolated in a near-by abandoned CCC camp. To the Nisei, in general, the Project Director issued a bulletin stating that those who did not meet the March 10 deadline "will be considered as having violated the orders of the

War Department and the War Relocation Authority and subject to such penalties as may be imposed."[29]

By the close of the registration, approximately 100 Kibei had been removed to the CCC camp. In addition to these, some 500 Nisei and Kibei male citizens had failed to register; and the unregistered female citizens totaled over 500.

Alien registration, which, under the new policies, had been postponed to March 3, continued in a desultory manner until March 25. Although the National Office of WRA had decided on February 27 that registration of aliens of both sexes and of female citizens was not compulsory, no announcement to this effect was ever made to the evacuees on the project. In spite of the fact that aliens were led to believe they might be subject to penalties for nonregistration, their profound distrust of the intentions of the government, in respect particularly to forced resettlement, resulted in 41 per cent of the males and 30 per cent of the females remaining unregistered.

The CCC isolation camp was operated for several weeks by WRA, with Army coöperation. Severe discipline was maintained and on March 9 the WRA Internal Security division instituted complete censorship of all incoming and outgoing mail. In the course of time, public hearings were held for all those who had been confined. Some of them, including Suzukawa, an evacuee warden on the police force, registered and were returned to the project. They immediately came under suspicion of having informed on their fellow prisoners as a price of their freedom.[30] Others who persisted in their stand of noncoöperation were removed to the isolation center at Moab, Utah, which had been established after the December (1942) trouble at Manzanar, and later to its successor at Leupp, Arizona. A number of them were returned to Tule Lake in December, 1943, after it had become a segregation center.

It is clear that the strong contrasts among relocation projects reflected, in large measure, administrative variations in the handling of the program and conflicting evacuee-administrative definitions of the issues involved. Within a given relocation project

---

[29] *Tulean Dispatch*, March 2, 1943. The project administration had, of course, known since February 26 that the War Department would impose no penalties for failure to register and that the authority of WRA to punish was limited.

[30] Many *inu* suspicions persisted after segregation. See p. 276 for a discussion of Suzukawa's fate as *inu*.

there was also a systematic relationship between "disloyalty" and various factors in the background of the groups of evacuees concerned. And, within these groups, the train of individual experience played an important role in motivating negative answers to questions 27 and 28. These aspects of the problem will be discussed in the following chapter.

Chapter IV

SEGREGATION

Separation of the "Loyal" and "Disloyal"

R<small>EGISTRATION HAD SPLIT</small> the evacuee population in each of the ten relocation projects into two groups: (1) A majority of the adults in each camp—an overwhelming majority in most, a bare majority in several—who had committed themselves, if citizens, as holding no allegiance to any country other than the United States and willing to serve in its armed forces, or, if aliens, as willing to abide by its laws and to do nothing to hamper its war effort. Having answered the registration questions affirmatively, persons in this group became known as Yes-Yeses. (2) A minority in each camp—a small minority in most but a very large minority in several—who had either refused to answer the registration questions or had answered them in the negative. They became known as No-Noes.

The latter group became stigmatized as politically disloyal to the United States and potentially dangerous to its war effort, and pressures developed in Congress, in the War Department, and through the press and radio, to segregate and intern the disloyal for the duration of the war. These pressures culminated in a Senate resolution requesting WRA "to take such steps as may be necessary for the purpose of segregating persons of Japanese ancestry in relocation centers whose loyalty to the United States is questionable or who are known to be disloyal . . . for the purpose of establishing additional safeguard against sabotage by such persons."[1]

In conformity with this action, WRA issued an Administrative

---

[1] 78th Congress, 1st Session, S. Res. 166, introduced July 2, approved July 6, 1943.

[84]

Instruction on July 15, 1943,[2] whereby the Tule Lake Relocation Center was selected for the segregation of "those persons of Japanese ancestry residing in relocation centers who by their acts have indicated that their loyalties lie with Japan during the present hostilities." The plan involved the transfer of "loyal" Tuleans to other projects, and of the "disloyal" from the other nine relocation projects to Tule Lake. Or in the case of the "loyal" it was possible to obtain leave clearance from the administration and resettle (take up residence) at will in any unprohibited locality in lieu of transfer to another project.

Preliminary to segregation, the population of each project was to be classified into four categories. The following three were subject to segregation:

I. All persons who had formally asked for repatriation or expatriation before July 1, 1943, and did not retract their applications before that date.

II. All persons who, during the February and March registration (a) answered question 28 in the negative, or (b) failed or refused to answer it, or (c) failed or refused to register at all and (d) had not changed their answers or registered affirmatively prior to July 15, 1943, and (e) were, in the opinion of the Project Director, loyal to Japan, and not loyal to the United States.

III. All persons who were denied leave clearance after appropriate hearings. This category included (a) persons about whom there was an adverse report by a Federal intelligence agency; (b) persons who had answered 28 negatively and who changed their answers prior to July 15; (c) persons who answered question 28 with a qualification; (d) persons who had requested repatriation or expatriation and who had retracted such requests prior to July 1, 1943, and persons who had requested repatriation or expatriation subsequent to July 1; (e) persons for whom the Japanese American Joint Board established in the Provost Marshal General's office did not affirmatively recommend leave clearance; (f) persons about whom there was other information indicating loyalty to Japan.[3]

As thus formulated, the segregation program was far more comprehensive than the registration program. Included as potential segregants was not only the No-No group,[4] as defined by registration (Class II), but also a very large number of persons who had,

---

[2] WRA, *Administrative Instruction No. 100,* July 15, 1943.

[3] *Ibid.,* paraphrased.

[4] Official instructions called for classification on the basis of question 28 (allegiance) only. Negative answers to this question were, however, universally accompanied by negative answers on question 27 (willingness to serve in the armed forces). The group is therefore called "No-Noes."

since evacuation, indicated a desire to return to Japan by applying for repatriation or expatriation (Class I). In this class were both No-Noes and Yes-Yeses, among the latter many aliens who, even though desiring to return to Japan, had found no difficulty in answering registration questions affirmatively. Class III included No-Noes who had asked to have their negative answers changed to affirmative after registration, repatriates who had asked to have their applications withdrawn, and a miscellaneous group of persons, technically "loyal" by registration criteria but against whom various intelligence agencies or WRA project officials had filed "adverse" reports.

Persons in Class I were to be segregated without hearing. Those in Class II were to be given a "comparatively brief" hearing by a Board of Review, set up in each relocation project, to determine whether or not they still "held to their pro-Japanese views." If, in the opinion of the Board of Review, they did continue to hold such views, they were to be segregated. If, however, they indicated willingness or desire to answer the loyalty question affirmatively, they were transferred to Class III. Persons in Class III were considered on probation. They were not to be released to resettle on indefinite leave except by affirmative recommendation after hearings of "sufficient thoroughness to enable the Leave Section to determine the true loyalty of each individual."[5]

A fourth class comprised the Yes-Yeses, and the nonrepatriates against whom no adverse report had been filed and persons in this class were stated to be "eligible for leaving." These were not to be segregated, but it was provided that if they wanted to remain with or join members of their immediate families subject to segregation they could do so.

In summary, the composition of the group to be segregated was determined partly by a policy[6] of arbitrarily segregating applicants for repatriation or expatriation; partly by negative answers or refusal to answer the "loyalty" question at the time of registration and by persistence in holding to these answers after further examination; partly on the basis of ill-defined "other information . . .

---

[5] WRA, *Segregation of Persons of Japanese Ancestry in Tule Lake Relocation Center* (pamphlet), August, 1943.

[6] This policy was formulated by WRA as early as August, 1942, but never put into effect.

See footnote 10, Chapter III, for history of procedures regarding repatriation.

indicating loyalty to Japan," and partly on the basis of the desire of persons who fell in none of these categories to stay with "disloyal" members of their immediate families.

It is apparent from instructions issued, and documents prepared by WRA prior to segregation, that the official interpretation of "disloyalty" bore more heavily upon sentiment than upon behavioral attitudes. Thus "disloyals" were described as persons having interests "not in harmony with those of the United States"[7] and "people who have indicated their desire to follow the Japanese way of life";[8] while "loyals" were those who "wish to be American"[9] and those "whose interests are bound with the welfare of the United States."[10]

"Disloyalty" was not to be considered culpable; nor was segregation to be considered a punitive matter. "The program of segregation is not being undertaken in any sense as a measure of punishment or penalty."[11] The privilege of leave clearance for resettlement purposes would be denied to those assigned to the Tule Lake Center. Otherwise, the main differences between Tule Lake and other centers would be (1) that self-government on the same basis as in relocation projects would not be possible at Tule Lake, but an advisory council of evacuees would be recognized; (2) that while American elementary and high schools were to be provided, attendance would not be compulsory. Japanese language schools could be established at the will of the residents but without financial aid from WRA. In all other respects, WRA procedures for community management would continue, including adult education, vocational training classes, hospital services, a community newspaper, and coöperative enterprises. Freedom of religion, except for Shintoism,[12] would be maintained. Employment would continue to be voluntary and compensated at the same rates as in relocation projects.

The broad principles of the segregation program were announced

---

[7] WRA, *op. cit.*

[8] Colorado River War Relocation Project, Release on Segregation, 3A, August 7, 1943.

[9] WRA, *op. cit.*

[10] *Ibid.*

[11] *Ibid.*

[12] "Since State Shinto is not regarded by the Japanese government as a religion, it will not be permitted." *Ibid.*

in each of the ten relocation projects early in July; and the fact that
Tule Lake had been chosen as the segregation center became generally known before the end of the month. By the first of August
the administrative personnel on each project was geared to the job
of resifting the residents preliminary to the transfer, which began
with the departure of "loyal" Tuleans on September 13 and the
arrival of "disloyals" from other projects on September 18.

Unlike registration, segregation aroused no organized resistance
from the evacuees and the program was carried through smoothly.
But like registration, the decisions to be made by individuals and
families were the source of serious mental disturbance. Under the
registration program, all adult evacuees had faced the necessity
of declaring themselves "loyal" or "disloyal," in accordance with
administrative definitions of these terms. Under the segregation
program, the "disloyal," as defined at registration, had to decide
whether they would stand by their declaration or retract. In both
cases, decisions were often made for reasons highly irrelevant to the
matter of political allegiance. The most seemingly irrelevant of
these reasons, and the one having the greatest influence on the
evacuees was their belief that a declaration of "loyalty" would
imply eventual forced resettlement. Residents of the segregation
center would be denied leave clearance and could not resettle for
the duration of the war whereas residents of relocation projects
were being given leave clearance and subjected to intensive WRA
pressure to resettle. Many evacuees therefore believed that WRA
was planning to force them out of camps to face the hostile American public responsible for their evacuation and detention. To these
people, the choice offered was not between Japan and America, in
a political sense, but between Tule Lake and the rest of America,
in a security sense.

To some, the attraction of Tule Lake over that of America was
enhanced by an estimate of the rewards that would ultimately be
reaped by the technically "disloyal" if Japan won the war, and by
the belief that Japan actually was winning the war.

To others, bitterness and disillusionment over the abrogation
of rights, and the severe economic losses which evacuation had
brought, resulted in a declaration of "disloyalty" to America without any element of sympathy for or interest in Japan.

Contrasted with these irrelevant "disloyals" there was, even at this time, a minority of politically conscious adherents of Japan, who were willing to take a positive stand in favor of the "mother country," and a number of aliens who were unwilling to accept the stateless existence that any taint of "disloyalty" to Japan, or "loyalty" to America, would imply.

The manner in which decisions to remain "disloyal" and thus be eligible for segregation were reached is best illustrated by the documentation of individual cases recorded during "processing" for segregation.

The following four cases of Issei who had refused to register and were called for hearings before the Tule Lake Segregation Board, a fifth case of a Nisei woman married to an Issei, and a sixth of a Nisei man, illustrate the fear of forced resettlement and the tendency to use "disloyalty" as a means of maintaining residence in Tule Lake.

An Issei man, aged 59 (through an interpreter):

Q. Does he hope to return to Japan?
A. Yes, as soon as the war ends.
Q. Does he have any property in Japan?
A. He doesn't know for sure.
Q. How does he feel about going to another center and waiting for the war to end?
A. He dosen't want to move anywhere until after the war. That is the main reason why he didn't register. (The latter point was stressed.)
Q. Does he feel more loyalty to Japan?
A. He hasn't been back, but he can't get it out of his mind.
Q. He doesn't feel disloyal to the United States?
A. Before the war he felt sympathetic to the United States. Since being put here, he feels more sympathy to Japan.[13]

An Issei man, aged 54 (through an interpreter):

Q. Why didn't he register?
A. His intention was to return to Japan after the war. He didn't want to leave for the outside.
Q. Does he feel he is more loyal to Japan than to the United States?
A. Since he intends to go back to Japan his sympathies are with that country.[14]

An Issei man, aged 41 (through an interpreter):

Q. Was there any reason for his not registering?

---

[13] Robert Billigmeier, verbatim record of Hearings, August 20–21, 1943 (manuscript).
[14] *Ibid.*

A. He didn't register because of the rumor that those who registered would be forced to leave [Tule Lake] and he had no place to go.

Q. Does he understand now that that isn't so?

A. I guess he does.

Q. He can't understand or speak English?

A. Very little.

Q. Does he plan to return to Japan after the war?

A. Yes.

Q. Does he feel more sympathy to Japan than to the United States?

A. His sympathy lies with Japan.

Q. Why?

A. He was a law abiding citizen, worked hard, respected law, and yet he was placed here. He can't stand it any longer.[15]

An Issei woman, aged 39 (through an interpreter):

Q. She didn't register, why?

A. At that time she was sick, but she had no intention of signing the registration forms.

Q. Will she abide by the laws of the United States and not harm the war effort?

A. She says that if she answers yes, she might have to leave. Should I tell her that her fears are not valid?

Q. It's not a question of leaving, it's a matter of loyalty. We're merely asking questions—it's not for us to decide whether or not she stays. She can sign all the papers and still can go to Japan. That is for Japan to decide if it wants her.

A. She can't answer the question.

Q. She can't answer whether she'll harm the war effort and abide by the laws of the United States?

A. She says she can't do any harm anyway because she doesn't want to leave. She has that fear she can't squelch.[16]

A Nisei woman, wife of an Issei:

Q. Are you disloyal?

A. Yes.

Q. Why?

A. Well—no reason. If I say "loyal" will they take me or leave me here?

Q. We don't split families. If one member is on the segregation list the others in the family are given their choice of leaving or remaining. We don't want you to answer a certain way just because your husband does. This hearing is just to determine your loyalty.

A. Then it doesn't have anything to do with staying?

Q. No, you'll just be given the choice of following your husband or not.

A. Then I'm loyal.[17]

---

[15] Ibid.

[16] Ibid.

[17] Ibid. Billigmeier recorded all hearings (34 cases) at one Board meeting on

Jerry Kawamoto, 30 years old, married and the father of several children, said that he had too much at stake to risk leaving Tule Lake. He had lived with his parents and brothers and sisters prior to evacuation on a farm near Sacramento. It was a family enterprise which had assured all members of the family economic security. Jerry's father, now aged, and suffering from heart disease, despaired of rebuilding what they had lost at the time of evacuation, and was thinking of retiring to Japan with his meagre savings. Jerry himself had pleurisy, could not work full time, and believed that he would be unable to support his wife and two children on the outside.

At the hearing, Jerry told the interviewer that he desired to remain in Tule Lake with his family and later return to Japan with them. He claimed that the Board had assured him that he could stay in Tule Lake. He received a notice, however, stating that he was "loyal" and was to report for an interview to discuss his preference among relocation centers. He said:

"Hell, you can't consider me disloyal. I've been loyal too long. But if I can't stay by being loyal, I'm going to be disloyal. I told the interviewer that I wanted to stay here, and he said that I could."

When he protested against being removed from Tule Lake, he was given another hearing. In the rehearing, Jerry declared that he was no longer loyal to the United States. The interviewer's comments were: "You can be sure of staying here for the duration if you put it down like this, but I sure hate to see you do it."[18]

That fear of the insecurity of the "outside world" for these displaced people was enough to tip the balance in favor of a declaration of "disloyalty" is evident. That the decisions were made not only for self-protection but also to assure family unity and security for the duration of the war is also evident.

Similar fears and concern for the security of the family impelled numbers of residents of other relocation centers to undergo the inconvenience of moving and accept the stigma of disloyalty in order to achieve war-duration security in Tule Lake. The following excerpts are taken from an analysis by Morris Opler,[19] based on the records of the hearing boards in Manzanar and represent attitudes of a number of Nisei who had never been in Japan.

August 20 and 21. This is the only case in which "disloyal" status was changed to "loyal," and it should be noted that the woman's continued residence in Tule Lake was, in this instance, assured by her husband's eligibility for segregation.

[18] Field Notes, August 17 and 29, 1943.

[19] WRA, Community Analysis Section, "Studies of Segregants at Manzanar" (manuscript prepared by Morris Opler). Note that the word "relocation," as used in these hearings, means "resettlement."

The subject in this case is a young man, 22 years of age, unmarried, the oldest of seven children in a family of nine. On the strength of his answer the whole family will go to Tule Lake. At one time the subject was preparing himself for work in America's defense program. In December, 1941, he completed a course at the Welding Engineering School at Wilmington, California. . . .

Q. At the time of the registration you answered "no" to question 28. Do you want to change your answer now?

A. I don't want to change. In my position I have a big responsibility. I can't go out on relocation. That's the big fact.

Q. Do you know of anyone who has been forced out of a center yet?

A. No one has been forced to leave yet. But gee, if the war goes on for two or three years we figure that the place will be closed down. We don't know, something may be in the office now about closing. We never know about these things until they are sprung on us.[20]

A 20-year-old unmarried girl comes before the Board. She is accompanied by her mother. The family is from the Florin district. The girl is speaking, not only for herself, but for a 22-year-old sister who has a speech defect and who does not appear at all. The girl is advised by her mother, who whispers in her ear before she speaks. There are four other children, 15 to 5 years of age, who are affected by this girl's answer. In response to the questioning the girl explains:

A. My older sister can't talk. My mother changed it to yes, but I want to leave it "no."

Q. What is the reason for your answer?

A. Father is dead. Sister can't talk and mother is all alone. We can't go out. So we have all planned to go to Tule Lake. We have close relatives we can depend on in Tule Lake, that's why. We want to go to Tule Lake as soon as possible.[21]

The subject is a 23-year-old woman, the mother of a small son. She operated a beauty parlor of her own in Santa Monica until the outbreak of the war and claims to have earned a yearly income of $15,000. She is the graduate of the Santa Monica High School and a west coast "Beauty College." Her husband is a kibei who maintained his "no" answer in Spring before a hearing board. The subject objects to relocating during the war and gives this as one reason for the retention of the "no." . . . This may be the primary reason why her husband earlier insisted on a "no" answer. Kibei, who feel that they have a linguistic handicap and habits which may be resented in a time of war, are extremely fearful of relocation. . . . My notes on this occasion were as follows:

A. I feel loyal to the United States but I have no intention of relocating, now or ever during the war. I've heard that segregation and relocation are connected.

[20] Ibid.
[21] Ibid.

Q. We are not talking about relocation at this time. We are interested in finding out about your loyalty to this country. Do you feel loyal to this country?

A. Why yes, I feel loyal to the United States, for I was born here, but I want to do what my husband does. What I want to know is whether relocation and this answer mean the same thing?

Q. No, relocation is a separate subject.

A. Also there is my husband. He is not disloyal, but he is the first child and has to go to Japan after the war to see and take care of his parents. He is kibei.

Q. Your husband could have said "yes" and yet could have gone to Japan after the war to see his parents. Lots of people will travel all over the world after the war. And, for that matter, you can say "yes" if you really feel loyal and still go to Tule Lake with your husband.

A. I'm going to do whatever my husband does. I won't do anything that will separate me from my husband. Maybe I'd better say "no."

Q. This is a loyalty question and you have already told us that you are loyal. Isn't it a contradiction now to say "no" to a loyalty question?

A. As I told you from the beginning I'm not disloyal, but I'm going to do what my husband does. I'll feel better about it.[22]

Two young men from the Venice district are involved. One is 20 and the other is 23 years old. Both are graduates of Venice High School. The older leased land and operated the family farm, the younger worked on the farm. This is the substance of the exchange between [one of them] and the Board: . . .

Q. Have you thought over what you want to do about this question?

A. We want to keep it as it is.

Q. Do you realize that means we will have to send you to Tule Lake?

A. Our parents wish to go; to be segregated.

Q. We are more interested in how you feel on this citizenship status than how you feel on the family status.

A. We'd like to sit in Tule Lake for a while. We don't want to relocate. The discrimination is too bad. I see letters from the people on the outside. There are fellows in Chicago who want to come back [to camp] but who are not allowed to.[23]

A reinforcing influence upon the decision to stay in or go to Tule Lake was fear, on the part of the parents, that their sons would be drafted unless they were "disloyal" and reluctance on the part of many of the young men to be inducted. An Issei in Tule Lake described the situation as follows:

I'd be willing to go out now if it weren't for the draft. I have one son in the Army now, and I don't want my other sons to be drafted one by one.

---

[22] *Ibid.*

[23] *Ibid.*

You can't blame them for not wanting to serve in the Army when they've been treated the way they have. In Walnut Grove they had to attend a different [segregated] school. If we hadn't been evacuated, I wouldn't mind their serving in the Army. I'd be glad to see them go, but it makes you mad when you've been discriminated against so much. Ever since I came to America there wasn't a day when I wasn't made to feel small because I was a Japanese.

I've lost all hope of a future in America. I can't make money here any more. I've lost everything. My wife feels worse than I do about the whole thing. She wants to send the younger children back so that they can get a Japanese education over there.

I wouldn't mind going to another center, but I just can't stand the chance of my sons being drafted one by one. After all I haven't more than ten or fifteen years to live. I don't forget for a minute the son who is away from home. Unless you are a parent you can't tell how we Issei feel.[24]

Further questions and answers from the first case cited above from Opler's Manzanar analysis show how closely fear of forced resettlement and reluctance to be drafted were interrelated. The young man continued as follows:

A. What about the draft? If I and my brother get killed what happens to my family? My brother and I are the only ones old enough to help support the family.

Q. Lots of mothers are losing sons.

A. Yes, but they put us in here and then they expect us to fight for this country. It's one thing for a son to go off to war when the father still has his job and the family still has its possessions; its another thing to expect it after people have been through what we have and have lost everything.[25]

A young unmarried man who, before evacuation, had helped his father in farming operations and suffered severe economic losses explained his No-No answer, in part, as follows:

A. If I would say "yes" I'd be expected to say that I'd give up my life for this country. I don't think I could say that because this country has not treated me as a citizen. I could go three-quarters of the way but not all the way after what has happened.

Q. Would you be willing to be drafted?

A. No, I couldn't do that.

He later elaborated upon this situation in a talk with Opler:

My dad is 58 years old now. He has been here 30 years at least. He came to this country with nothing but a bed roll. He worked on the railroads and he worked in the sugar-beet fields. If I told you the hardships he had

---

[24] Field Notes, August 16, 1943.
[25] WRA, Community Analysis Section, op. cit.

you wouldn't believe me. I owe a lot to my father. Everything I am I owe to him. All through his life he was working for me. During these last years he was happy because he thought he was coming to the place where his son would have a good life. I am the only son. I have to carry on the family name. You white people have some feeling like this but with us it is greatly exaggerated.

I tell you this because it has something to do with my answer about the draft question. We are taught that if you go out to war you should go out with the idea that you are never coming back. That's the Japanese way of looking at it. Of course many in the Japanese armies come back after the war, just like in all armies, but the men go out prepared to die. If they live through it, that's their good luck. I listen to white American boys talk. They look at it differently. They all take the stand that they are coming back, no matter who [else] dies. It's a different mental attitude.

In order to go out prepared and willing to die, expecting to die, you have to believe in what you are fighting for. If I am going to end the family line, if my father is going to lose his only son, it should be for some cause we respect. . . . I would have been willing to go out forever before evacuation. It's not that I'm a coward or afraid to die. My father would have been willing to see me go out at one time. But my father can't feel the same after this evacuation and I can't either. . . .

My mind is made up. I know my father is planning to return to Japan. I know he expects me to say "no" so there will be no possibility that the family will be separated. There isn't much I can do for my father any more; I can't work for him the way I used to. But I can at least quiet his mind on this.[29]

Among many of the Nisei, the primary reasons for declarations of "disloyalty" were anger and disillusionment because of the abrogation of their citizenship rights. In Tule Lake, for example, a Nisei woman of 32, who had never been in Japan, replied to the question regarding her failure to register as follows:

A. I have American citizenship. It's no good, so what's the use?
Q. Has the evacuation caused you to lose faith?
A. I feel that we're not wanted in this country any longer. Before the evacuation I had thought that we were Americans, but our features are against us.

When asked whether she wanted her child brought up as Japanese, she said:

A. Yes, I found out about being an American. It's too late for me, but at least I can bring up my children so that they won't have to face the same kind of trouble I've experienced.
Q. You realize that you will have difficulty in adjusting to life in Japan?

[29] Ibid.

A. I know that, but I'm willing to try it anyway. It's too late for me. The important thing is that my children will not have to go through the same experiences as I have.[27]

A 21-year-old Nisei boy from Sacramento, immediately turned the question back to the examiner by saying, "Put yourself in my place" when asked if he was loyal. The interview proceeded as follows:

Q. Do you feel that you'd fit in well in Japan? Where do you think you'd best fit in—here or in Japan?
A. I can't say because of racial prejudices in this country.
Q. We're fighting against racial prejudices and persecution.
A. I don't know, the colored people have faced it ever since they came here.
Q. You mean the Negroes?
A. Yes.

After a debate with the interviewer on the matter of race prejudice, the young man held to his negative answer and remarked, "I want to stay in Tule Lake and see how the American people react."[28]

Opler's Manzanar cases are replete with statements of disillusionment and of angry protest, three examples of which are cited below:

Q. Are you a dual citizen?
A. No, we are not dual citizens. But in the first place if we are citizens, how come we are in these camps? The FBI had a record of all the bad ones. How come they took the rest? How come they took the citizens? How come they didn't intern Willkie, LaGuardia and Mayor Rossi?
Q. This is wartime and things were done because of military necessity that would not be done in normal times.
A. I'd rather leave the answer the same as it is.
Q. We know you are angry at what has happened in the past but there is no use in arguing about that here. What we want to know now is about your loyalty, your feeling toward this country.
A. I answered "no" because of resentment and because of how they treated us. When they asked us to come here, they told us that they would pay us union wages. They even used the Catholic church for such lies. How can I have faith in this country? I lost all my ideals about this country. In school I was even an Ephebian [member of a California high school honor society]. Do you know what that means? What will it be when the soldiers come back? I don't speak much Japanese, but at least

---

[27] Billigmeier, *op. cit.*   [28] *Ibid.*

I'll be among Japanese. (The young man's lips are trembling. He is almost crying.) [29]

A. Here is the thing. I'm supposed to be a citizen of the United States. At the time of registration, I asked them how far my citizenship went. I don't know if there is such a thing as restricted citizenship in this country. I refused to answer because if there is such a thing as restricted citizenship, I have the right to refuse to answer. What security have we? If this can happen now, why can't the same thing happen in five years?

Q. What has happened is unfortunate. But other minorities have had to face discrimination too. In my part of the country the Germans are probably treated worse than Japanese.

A. It's all right to be of a minority as long as you're of the same race.

Q. I can't see that. If you're discriminated against because you belong to a minority group, it's as bad whatever race you happen to belong to.

A. This is the reason you look at it differently; you are a white man. At the end of the war, animosities will be high. There will be high feelings against us. There will be a boycott of us if we start in business. At the end of the last war, the bad feeling didn't continue against the Germans. But you can't tell a German from an Englishman when he walks down the street. But when I go down the street they say, "There goes a Jap." Perhaps it will be 15 years before this feeling will die down. I disagree with you when you say that 100,000 Japanese can be assimilated now. I know the WRA personnel are doing what they can. But the one hundred thirty millions in this country are hostile. (After additional discussion of this same topic) Well, you'd better write me a ticket to Tule Lake. . . .

Q. Your record doesn't show any interest in Japan and you haven't said anything that would indicate that you want to go to Japan. Why is it then that you object so strongly to question 28?

A. I have not been given citizenship rights so I don't have to answer questions like that.[30]

Q. Don't you feel that whatever has happened you should express your loyalty to the only country in which you now hold citizenship?

A. At the time of the draft I was deferred because of my dependents. At that time I said I'd die for this country in the event of war. That's the way I felt. But since I lost my business when I was young and just starting up I've changed my mind. You Caucasian Americans should realize that I got a raw deal.

Q. But things like these happen in a time of war. Evacuation was a war measure, an emergency measure.

A. They shouldn't happen to citizens. What did a war with Japan have to do with evacuating me? You've got to realize that I am an American citizen just as much as you. Maybe my dad is not, because of Congress. He couldn't naturalize. But my associates in school and college were Caucasians. It's been a hard road to take. It's been hard for my dad. He lived

---

[29] WRA, *op. cit.*   [30] *Ibid.*

in this country for 30 years. He was never in jail; never in any trouble. Yet he was pulled in [interned by FBI on suspicion]. Even though they let him out for lack of evidence it hurt him.

Q. We really want to know whether you are disloyal. It isn't how angry you are, we know about that.

A. I leave my answer "no" definitely.[31]

Opler also cites the case of a girl aged 22, who said: "I'm going to say 'no' to anything as long as they treat me like an alien. When they treat me like a citizen, they can ask me questions that a citizen should answer"; and of a 19-year-old boy who remarked, bitterly: "You people are just not loyal to us; so that's the way we feel."[32]

Among many Issei and Kibei, and some Nisei, the hope and expectation that Japan would win the war and that rewards would accrue to them through this victory, were often underlying motives for negative replies on the loyalty question. Some Issei thought that Japanese victory would mean indemnification for the losses they had suffered through evacuation and either restoration of the place they had made for themselves in the economic life of America or a brighter future in Japan. To numbers of Nisei, and particularly to Kibei, it would mean the possibility of a postwar career in the Orient. These hopes were postulated on a Japanese victory, or, at worst, a negotiated peace. The belief in a Japanese victory was a very prevalent one, reinforced by broadcasts from Radio Tokyo, which were listened to avidly by the few who had access to short-wave radio sets, or read in the widely circulated vernacular newspapers, and passed on, in exaggerated form. A few examples from Tule Lake will illustrate these beliefs and hopes.

A young Tulean Issei, married to a Kibei girl, had, although strongly antiadministration, and initially opposed to the registration procedure, finally answered question 28 in the affirmative. His wife had given a No-No answer, and residence for both of them in Tule Lake was thus assured. To a neighbor, he gave the following explanation of his reluctance to leave the project:

If I were sure that I was going to live here in the U. S. and not return to Japan, then I'd go out and start working right now. Under those circumstances that's the best thing to do. But after the war I expect that something's going to come out of the negotiations beween Japan and America. That's why I'm not going out right now.[33]

---

[31] *Ibid.*
[32] *Ibid.*
[33] Field Notes, June 26, 1943.

An older Issei who had fled to the Free Zone at the time of evacuation and from there had been sent to Tule Lake, had joined in a mass refusal of his block to register. He gave his reasons as follows:

The main thing is that the war's got to end soon. Japan will probably attack the mainland, but still I suppose it might take some time for Japan to win the war. America was sure dumb in thinking that she could beat Japan in a couple of months. . . . Japan used China as a sort of practice ground for her Army. But America was not smart enough to see that. She's losing all over the place. You can't believe the news you read in the American newspapers because all they do is to tell lies. One reason Americans are weak is that they don't have any guts. . . . Japan won't weaken now, because look at all the resources she has at her command.

The people in my block haven't registered yet, and they aren't going to do it either. It's better not to change the answer and leave because they might draft the boys, and it's dangerous going out. Well, yes, it might be all right for single men to go out, but I wouldn't advise it. People with families can't go out, anyway. I'm staying for the duration. When the war's over I can go back to Japan. Of course, it depends on the kind of peace that is made, but America's losing the war.[34]

Another Issei, who had been a successful farmer before evacuation, and worked on the hog farm in Tule Lake, remonstrated with his foreman, a Kibei who was leaving Tule Lake with the "loyals," as follows:

Are you going to leave? Why don't you stay. If you leave you'll miss the *takara-bune* (treasure ship) from Japan.[35]

What's wrong with you Nisei is that you've got your hand on both objectives, Japan and America. If Japan wins you'd like to go to Japan, and if Japan loses you'd like to stay in America and make some money. Why don't you place implicit faith in Japan winning this war, for she will . . . After this war Japan will be a powerful nation, a nation of tremendous opportunities.[36]

A young Kibei advised a friend against resettlement on similar grounds:

I think it's best not to go out. There's been broadcasts from Japan saying that the Japanese people should stay inside the center. If you go out, then Japan will assume that you are loyal to the U. S. and they won't do anything for you. That's why I think it's better not to go out. It was dumb of the administration to ask the Kibei to register. Even if we are put in jail, it'll only be for the duration. The war can't last very long now.

[34] Field Notes, April 27, 1943.
[35] Field Notes, July 22, 1943.
[36] Field Notes, July 31, 1943.

America is going to be invaded soon. And when Japan wins they won't be able to keep us in jail. The trouble with the administration is that they think America is going to win.[37]

The idealization of the Orient, as a place of unlimited possibilities for their sons, had begun long before the war, when many of the Issei found that the children they had sent to high school and college were unable to find jobs for which they were qualified. Within the confines of the barbed-wire fence, the feeling that there was no longer a chance for success in America was intensified. The hope of a future without discrimination in Japan-controlled Java or Manchuria became, in many cases, the basis of plans for the future. One Kibei explained that there would be a good future in Manchuria for Nisei who spoke both English and Japanese. He himself planned a career there where he could "enjoy his Japanese face."[38]

A Nisei, brought up in a rural community near Los Angeles, in the midst of a sizable Japanese settlement, had attended the University of California. At the time of registration he was caught by the pressure of both his parents and his block. His block wavered between not registering and doing so, and after much discussion, decided to permit registration of its residents. For several weeks the young man vacillated between affirmative and negative answers. He had hoped to leave the center and complete his college education or to take a job as judo instructor. An uncle told him not to register in the affirmative because he would be drafted if he did. His parents expounded the idea of a bright future in the Orient. His uncle proposed that they pool resources, and start a cleaning business in the Orient. The young man finally accepted the idea that America offered no future for Nisei, and registered No–No. When the segregation hearings were held, he did not change his stand even though most of his close friends were leaving Tule Lake.[39]

Administrative insistence on the terms "loyalty" and "disloyalty" as applied to Issei posed a dilemma for many honest Issei who could not accept status as "loyal" to America if it carried the implication of being "disloyal" to Japan, for "disloyalty" to the country of birth and citizenship implied lack of integrity. In Tule Lake this matter came to the front when the Project Director (Best) stated in the *Tulean Dispatch* that a rumor was prevalent that Issei who went "to a so-called loyal center . . . will lose their citizenship rights in

---

[37] Field Notes, April 18, 1943.
[38] Field Notes, April 23, 1943.
[39] Field Notes, March 8 and 14, 1943.

Japan." Best denied the rumor and assured the evacuees that "segregation hearings are entirely confidential and are not seen by any other government."[40]

This attempt at reassurance merely confirmed the Issei's suspicion that status as "loyal" to America would detract from the moral character of Japanese citizens. An Issei block manager said:

Whatever did Best mean when he said that the documents would be kept secret? Many people had made up their minds that they would go if they had to. None of them are going willingly. But if they have to go and then try to keep the fact a secret from the Japanese government, many of them don't want to leave. I'm not sure what Best meant, but he shouldn't have said what he did. Do we have to keep the fact that we are leaving Tule Lake a secret?[41]

Another Issei expressed the same fear even more forcefully:

I can't leave this place. If you do you're going to be considered disloyal to Japan. Best said that they would keep it secret whether you've been in one center or another, but how can you keep a matter like that secret? You just can't do it. I tell people: "Don't get fooled! What do they think we are, fools?" They should make it clear that people will be able to go back to Japan even though they go to another center without having to keep it secret.[42]

While a third Issei remarked:

No Issei would disobey the laws of the United States. They've always been law-abiding. In that sense they can be called loyal to the United States. On the other hand, none of them are disloyal to Japan. You can't use the word "loyalty" or "disloyalty" for Issei because it just doesn't apply to them.[43]

It was not unusual to find Kibei also who found it impossible to make an honest declaration of loyalty to America if this meant forswearing allegiance to Japan. The following case was recorded at Poston:

A Kibei, 23 years of age, answered negatively to the loyalty question at the time of registration because he could not see how he could forswear allegiance to the Emperor of Japan. The day before his registration his friends had informed him of the nature of the question but he could not decide how to answer it at that time. However, the moment the question

---

[40] *Tulean Dispatch,* Supplement, August 20, 1943.
[41] Field Notes, August 17, 1943.
[42] Field Notes, August 22, 1943.
[43] Field Notes, August 17, 1943.

was read to him by the Nisei sergeant he said he knew there could be only one answer—a negative one. He calls himself "the tragedy of the Kibei." He was taken to Japan at a very early age and called back five years ago. He feels that if parents had not sent their children to Japan this sort of tragedy would not have occurred.

He despises those people who changed from No to Yes because a thing like loyalty should not be played around with for personal convenience. He brands these individuals as cowards and of no value to either country. He said, "How can a Kibei be comfortable in a U. S. uniform when his convictions lie elsewhere? I know what I'm doing. I'm satisfied in the knowledge that I'm sticking it out according to my convictions even if they take my life away."[44]

In the same center, another Kibei remarked:

If I change to Yes, I won't be able to walk on the streets of Tokyo with a clear conscience after the war. I can't forswear allegiance to the Emperor of Japan.[45]

In summary, the documents cited show the complexity of the motivations leading to an assumption of "disloyal" status. On the part of aging and dispossessed Issei, fear of forced resettlement and the economic and social uncertainties of the "outside world" were often of primary importance. Among their citizen children, the potential supporters of the family, the fear was felt that "loyal" status would result in their induction into the armed forces and further destruction of family security.

Among Nisei schooled only in America, the abrogation of the "rights" which their indoctrination had led them to believe were implicit in American citizenship, often resulted in a negativistic protest reaction to the registration questions, and among many of these, negativism toward America was accompanied by no positive identification with or hope of a future in Japan. Others had built up prospects of a future in the Orient, free from race discrimination. This last group was especially receptive of the propaganda, expounded by some Issei and Kibei, of Japanese nationalism and imperialism directed toward the Greater East Asia Co-Prosperity Sphere.

In two important respects the residents of Tule Lake were in a unique position at the time of segregation. In the first place, the unfortunate bungling of the registration program in Tule Lake

---

[44] Field Notes, August, 1943.
[45] *Ibid.*

had resulted in over four times as many potential "disloyals" in proportion to population as the average in the other relocation projects. This meant a much greater spread of "disloyalty" among the various classes of the population, a much lesser degree of selectivity, than was true elsewhere. In the second place, the fact that the home project had been selected as the segregation center gave an incentive, lacking elsewhere, to hold to the status of "disloyalty" to avoid what was, in a very real sense, an eviction process. Tuleans who remained in Tule Lake would not have to undergo the inconveniences and hardships of a move similar to those previously enforced and vividly remembered, from home to assembly center, and from assembly center to relocation project. These two factors promoted a tendency among large numbers of Tuleans toward narrowly opportunistic decisions to hold to the status of "disloyalty"—a tendency reinforced by the belief that "disloyal" status could be changed, at a more convenient time, to that of "loyal."

Among both Tuleans and residents of other relocation projects, administrative policies operated further to stimulate declarations of "disloyalty" on practical rather than ideological grounds. The most important of these were (1) WRA's propaganda for resettlement which was being intensified during the period of segregation hearings in the hope of persuading as many as possible of the "loyal" to reinstate themselves immediately in the "normal stream of American life." This propaganda for resettlement implied closure of some, if not all, other relocation projects, once the segregation movement had been completed. At the same time, resettlement from the segregation center was strictly prohibited by administrative regulations. The only sure war-duration refuge for evacuees would thus be the Tule Lake Segregation Center, residence in which could be attained only by the assumption of the status of a "disloyal" by at least one member of a family. (2) Statements from authoritative Army sources[46] that "disloyals" were not wanted in the armed forces. "Disloyalty" was thus to be rewarded administratively by the assurance of freedom from forced resettlement and freedom from induction into the armed forces.

Nor were these the only rewards awaiting the "disloyal" in Tule Lake. The promise was made of plentiful postsegregation jobs, particularly on the widely publicized Tule Lake farm, and at the same

---

[46] E.g., by Major S. A. L. Marshall, see pp. 79–80.

time a drastic reduction of employment quotas was announced in all other projects. Tule Lake residents were assured administrative sanction for leading a completely Japanese way of life after segregation, including the possibility of establishing their own language schools, and WRA had stressed the point that the segregants were not being and were not to be punished for their "disloyalty." Under these conditions a large number of "loyals" desired to avoid transfer altogether and to remain in Tule Lake with the "disloyals."

When the time for departure arrived, an appreciable number of the "loyals" followed the well-established pattern of passive resistance and, although all members of the family were Yes-Yeses and ineligible for segregation, they refused to leave Tule Lake. This came about as follows: All those who had been put on "removal lists" were scheduled for interviews with members of the Social Welfare Department in order to indicate their choice of a center of residence.[47] An appreciable number failed to appear for the scheduled interviews and of those who appeared many refused to state any choice of center. Administrative policy in these cases tended to be lax in general and the project personnel had been instructed to use persuasion rather than force, from fear of creating organized resistance.

Thus by the end of the segregation movement, several hundred families, all members of which were technically "loyal," still remained in the Tule Lake Segregation Center for the "disloyal." The number of persons involved was approximately 1,100.[48]

Altogether, some 6,250 "loyal" Tuleans left the center for other relocation projects between September 13 and 30. A small number of keyworkers, who had been asked by the administration to help with the segregation movement, and a few of the resistance cases left some weeks later. Remaining in the segregation center were more than 6,000 old Tuleans.

[47] Choice of centers was allowed as a reward to "loyal" Tuleans, and as a means of counteracting anticipated resistance to moving. Individuals and families could designate the center in which they wished to reside. If, however, a larger group than a family wanted to be sure of going to the same center, it had to accede to an administrative selection.

[48] This estimate was made by the Relocation Planning Division of WRA. All but 34 of these 1,100 eventually "legitimized" their status by applying for repatriation or taking other similar officially sanctioned steps to become "disloyal," or, in a few cases, transferring to a "loyal" project.

It has been possible to analyze, in some detail, the nature of the selective process that held these 6,000 old Tuleans in the Tule Lake Segregation Center. One factor of importance was location in the project, for there are clearly defined areas of "loyalty" and "disloyalty" on a blockwise basis. Blocks near and adjacent to Block 42, where the registration incident occurred (see pp. 75–77) represent the most clearly 'marked "zone of disloyalty," as shown by Chart IV.

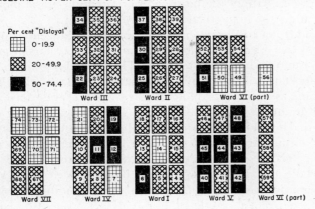

Chart IV

Within a given location in the project, the "loyalty" issue was also subject to varying interpretations by different classes of the evacuees, and was closely dependent upon preëvacuation background, economic status, and social distance from the majority group. Statistical analysis of variations in proportions "disloyal" indicates significant and systematic "net" relationships (when all possible factors are held constant) with a number of exogenous factors. The most striking relationships are in factors manifesting variations in acculturation or assimilation; religious preference for the Occidental patterns of Christianity or agnosticism versus the Oriental pattern of Buddhism; biculturalism in training and education, the extremes being the "pure" Nisei, educated only in America, and the Kibei returning recently after years of education in Japan; origin in certain areas of California, where economic and social segregation from the majority group was pronounced, as against origin in the more tolerant Pacific Northwest; occupation in nonagricultural pursuits, where, on the whole, contact with and accommodation to the majority group occurred to a greater degree than was true with the farming element. In brief, Buddhists were proportionately more "disloyal" than Christians or agnostics; the order of "disloyalty" proportions descended from Kibei to Issei to Nisei; Californians were more "disloyal" than Northwesterners. Less consistent on a "net" basis, but suggestive, were the differentials in occupation, the farming groups tending to be more "disloyal" than the nonagriculturists.[49]

In addition to the systematic operation of exogenous or background variables, and endogenous variables or factors originating in the camp environment, the train of individual experience played an important role in motivating negative answers to the "loyalty" question, as documents quoted earlier in this chapter have shown.

While the sifting of "loyals" and "disloyals" was going on, the Tule Lake Relocation Project was being transformed physically and administratively into the Tule Lake Segregation Center. A double "manproof" fence, eight feet high, was constructed around the whole area, and a new gate was built between Ward VII and the administrative area. The external guard of military police was increased from a couple of hundred soldiers to full battalion strength, and new barracks were built to accommodate them. In the military area, half a dozen tanks, obsolete but impressive, were lined up in full view of the residents. At this point there followed numerous resignations among the Caucasian personnel in protest against the transformation of Tule Lake into what had the aspect of a concentration camp. Notable among these were some socially minded persons who had been in close and coöperative relations with the evacuees and had promoted their efforts to develop a democratic organization within the center.

Beginning on September 18, trainloads of "disloyals" from other relocation projects began to arrive in Tule Lake. During a 25-day period, some 8,600 transferees were added to the population of

---

[49] Statistical analysis of "The Ecology of Disloyalty" will be presented, in full, in a forthcoming monograph in this series by George M. Kuznets. This brief analysis is based on his manuscript.

the center. First to arrive were those from the Arkansas projects (Rohwer and Jerome), the last were those from the Arizona projects (Gila and Poston). At the end of this movement, old Tuleans com-

Composition of Adult Population of Tule Lake Segregation Center by Project of Origin

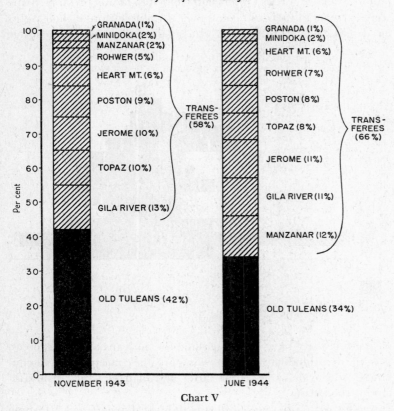

Chart V

prised 42 per cent of the population of the segregation center; transferees 58 per cent. Later, in February and May, 1944, 3,600 other transferees, in the main from Manzanar, Rohwer, and Jerome, were added to the population, and for these new barracks had to be built in the overcrowded project. When this movement was completed, old Tuleans comprised 34 per cent of the population, transferees 66 per cent (Chart V).

Among the transferees there was the same range of motivation as among the remaining old Tuleans. Many had accepted the stigma of "disloyalty" to achieve security for themselves or their families. Numbers of the technically "loyal" had come to Tule Lake to avoid family separation. Many had come because of unwillingness to enter the armed forces. Others had yielded to family pressure. Some were extreme in their bitterness over the abrogation of their rights as citizens. Some were ardently pro-Japanese. But though the range

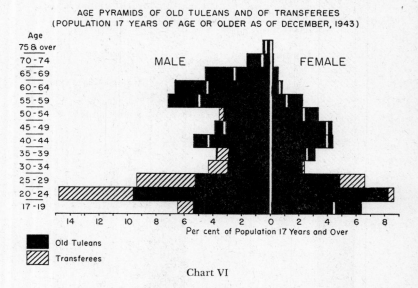

AGE PYRAMIDS OF OLD TULEANS AND OF TRANSFEREES
(POPULATION 17 YEARS OF AGE OR OLDER AS OF DECEMBER, 1943)

Chart VI

of attitudes may have been the same for Tuleans and transferees, it is highly probable that there was a greater concentration of convinced "disloyals" among the latter and of irrelevant "disloyals" among the former.

Age-sex pyramids of old Tuleans and transferees (Chart VI) show a striking difference that throws some light on the problem of motivation. The concentration of transferees among young males of ages subject to selective service induction suggests the strength of the protest faction within this group. Correspondingly, concentrations of old Tuleans in the older age groups tends to confirm the hypothesis that the desire for security, and general inertia, motivated the declaration of "disloyalty" for a large proportion of this group. The strength of this selective process can be inferred from comparison of this chart with Chart I,[50] where it is seen that the basic populations from which these two groups were drawn differed but slightly in age-sex composition.

Transferees contrasted with the old Tuleans in another important respect. Whatever their motives in declaring themselves "disloyal," the transferees found themselves, upon arrival in the segregation center, in the position of disadvantaged migrants, whereas the Tuleans were well-established "old settlers." The Tuleans represented the "haves," the transferees the "have nots," and with the arrival of the first trainload of transferees, antagonism flared up between the two groups.

The first disadvantage the transferees felt was that they were often widely scattered throughout the project, separated from friends, and crowded into inferior apartments. Because of an expected housing shortage, transferees were put into apartments in accordance with maximum WRA quotas of persons per apartment.[51] When apartments of the proper size were not immediately available, they were forced to take quarters in excess of the maximum quota, or were placed in hastily arranged dormitories in recreation halls. Old Tuleans, who had had their apartments assigned at a time when housing was relatively plentiful, had not been required to maintain maximum quotas. As described in Chapter II, when the evacuees originally entered Tule Lake in 1942 they found the apartments extremely meagerly furnished. In the meantime they had made a number of "improvements," including shelves, closets and partitions. When now these apartments were assigned to the incoming transferees, they had been stripped by their former occupants of all these improvements, and in addition plaster board and wood had been ripped from the walls for crating purposes, leaving gaping holes and unsightly walls. Where furniture and shelves had been left, they had often been appropriated by other residents during the short period of vacancy before transferees took possession.

Upon applying for job placement, transferees found that the old Tuleans had secured or retained the most desirable jobs. Vacan-

---

[50] See p. 31.

[51] Apartments of 20 by 25 feet were assigned to a group of 6 members; 20 by 20 to groups of 3–5 members; and 12 by 20 to groups of 2–4 members, often without reference to sex, age, or closeness of relationship.

cies created by departing "loyals" had been immediately filled by promotions of old Tuleans from lower to higher grades. For example, the 31-year-old "loyal" Kibei foreman of the hog farm, and a graduate of the University of California, College of Agriculture, was replaced by a "disloyal" Tulean Nisei only 20 years old. The head of the Adult Education English Department was succeeded by a young, inexperienced Tulean girl. Replacement was especially rapid and complete in the Coöperative Enterprises. Takeo Noma, who had held a minor position in the Coöp before segregation, became General Manager upon the departure of the "loyal" incumbent. Similarly, Milton Sasaki, who had been little known before segregation became Executive Secretary.[52] By the time the transferees arrived, there were no major positions left unfilled in this important organization.

In addition to their resentment of the fact that the "old settlers" had secured a monopoly of housing and jobs the transferees manifested an immediate contempt for the Tulean situation as a whole and made loud and disparaging comparisons between this center and their "home" project regarding the "spineless," proadministration behavior of the settled residents, the overstocked canteens on the one hand, and the poor food provided by WRA on the other, the defects of the physical facilities (e.g., latrines), and they disparaged the climate and natural surroundings. Taken altogether there was thus a wide cleavage between the new transferees and the old Tuleans.

Typical of the attitude of the transferees was a remark made by a Rohwerite after his first meal in the segregation center: "This won't do. We'll have to get organized and lodge a complaint."[53]

A young Kibei was overheard saying: "The people here are no good. In Rohwer we had a *Seinen-Kai* (Young Men's Organization) and never did anything the WRA told us to do."[54]

Old Tuleans, on their part, were quick to characterize the transferees as troublemakers, agitators, "a sad bunch," and people who would be "hard to handle."[55]

---

[52] The roles later played by Sasaki and Noma are described in chapters VII and X.

[53] Field Notes, September 21, 1943.

[54] Field Notes, September 19, 1943.

[55] Field Notes, September 20, 1943.

An old Tulean Issei characterized the two opposing groups as follows:

> Tuleans who are staying are often doing so because they didn't want to move. Those who are coming in are among the worst because they wouldn't bother to pack and come here unless they were fairly bad.[56]

The dissatisfactions of the transferees soon manifested themselves in a series of minor outbursts of violence. A group of recently "processed" transferees refused to pass through the gate between the administrative and residential area until the American flag, raised by old Tulean Boy Scouts, had been lowered.[57] On several occasions, evacuee police were unable to control crowds pushing against the fences to welcome incoming groups. The windows of the Housing office and of the Coöp magazine stand in the administrative areas were broken. In the latter, copies of the JACL weekly, the *Pacific Citizen,* were destroyed. Rumors of violence toward women spread, and a voluntary curfew was imposed on young girls. A group, said to be Kibei, broke up a dance, and after this incident no public dances were held. A man in charge of the public address system at a basketball game was forced to stop playing American jazz and instructed to play Japanese national music.[58]

The transferees also quickly assumed leadership in the promised "pursuit of the Japanese way of life." Japanese language schools sprang up in different parts of the project (first in blocks 32 and 26), and a board was formed to supervise the organization of such schools in every ward. Buddhist religious ceremonies flouished, with ten active priests, and Christian activities were relegated to a minor place, with only one minister officiating. Etiquette classes for girls involving, for example, practice in sitting on the floor, were initiated.

A Nisei high school boy, worried about the lack of recreation and of American schooling asked: "What are we going to do if we stay in here?"[59] And a young Kibei wrote to his former English teacher:

> It isn't very good for a nice boy like myself when things turn out like this, is it? And what is more the people who came from other camps are

---

[56] *Ibid.*
[57] Field Notes, October 16, 1943.
[58] *Ibid.*
[59] Field Notes, September 25, 1943.

all rough. They shout loudly "Banzai to the Emperor!" and even the police, it seems, are afraid to cross them. If you are caught at anything like [American] dancing, you are likely to be practically killed. . . . Japanese schools have sprung up everywhere. They say that the American school will not start until next February.[60]

Most important to the transferees in their vigorous campaign for control was the fact that by the removal of many of the Tulean leaders to other projects, and the restrictions imposed by WRA on self-government after segregation, the political field was left in a chaotic state. The Community Council, which had resigned during the registration crisis had never been reconstituted. The Issei Planning Board, which had not been officially dissolved, had nevertheless lost many of its members through segregation and had not proceeded with reorganization. A number of "loyal" block managers had left, and their positions were in most cases not filled until after the arrival of the transferees.

This political disorganization opened the way for the consolidation of the transferees as a protest bloc, opposed to both the old Tuleans and the administration. How quickly and effectively they utilized this opportunity will be described in subsequent chapters.

---

[60] Field Notes (undated letter) October, 1943.

Chapter V

REVOLT
Strikes, Threats, and Violence

———————————————————————

IN THE DISORGANIZED and chaotic Tule Lake Segregation Center, where hurried exchanges of hundreds of unwilling evacuees were being made daily, the transferees, as described in the preceding chapter, began immediately to give violent expression to their feelings of discomfort and dissatisfaction with respect to living conditions in general, housing and food in particular, the availability of employment, and working conditions. Block managers, both old Tuleans and newly chosen transferees, had constantly to take the brunt of pugnacious criticism from block residents. Evacuee supervisors and foremen received incessant complaints.

The first overt manifestation of dissatisfaction over working conditions occurred when a labor dispute arose within a crew assigned to handling coal. On October 7 while segregation movements were still taking place, the administration abruptly terminated the employment of forty-three members of this crew who had vigorously protested the discharge of three coworkers for alleged insubordination. The following day these vacant positions were thrown open to anyone who would take them, but no evacuee came forward. Meanwhile, in order to help settle the controversy, the workers called upon several transferees who had been well known in their respective relocation centers for aggressive antiadministration attitudes. Among them were Watanabe and Kato from Topaz, Abe from Jerome, Sano from Rohwer, and Doi from Heart Mountain,[1]

———————

[1] Soon after his arrival, Doi and some of his Heart Mountain associates had formed a *Kenkyu Kai* (study group) to investigate conditions in camp. Watanabe, Kato and Sano formed a clique which met frequently for similar purposes. Abe was regarded as leader of the Jerome faction, which, while not formally organized, represented a compact interest group.

who were to take leading roles in events that followed. The matter was taken to the administration and was successfully arbitrated by Harry Mayeda, former chairman of the Community Council, and Bill Mayeda, chairman of Civic Organizations, the central organization of block managers. In spite of disapproval of outsiders' intruding in a labor dispute, the administration gave way on October 12, rehired the forty-three terminated workers, and made certain concessions, promising the crew members coveralls, gloves, and a midmorning snack. Although this dispute was on a minor scale, the residents regarded the settlement as strengthening their position. The advisors gained prestige from the incident, in spite of the fact that the administration had discouraged their intrusion.

Shortly after this labor dispute two serious accidents occurred, involving a number of evacuees and precipitating a series of outbreaks. The administration was held to have been culpably negligent in connection with these accidents, and when adequate compensation was not forthcoming, fear of loss of life and limb was added to the many smoldering grievances of the residents. When a partial strike of the evacuees was called, pending settlement of these multiple grievances, it was broken by the administration under conditions which pyramided on the existing bases for the grievances.

The accidents occurred on October 13 and 15, 1943. On October 13 a fire truck, speeding to answer an alarm, overturned, and three firemen were seriously injured; on October 15 at about 1:30 P.M., a farm truck, carrying twenty-nine workers, attempted to pass another truck, hit a soft shoulder, and overturned. All of the workers were cut and bruised, five were pinned under the truck and seriously injured, and one of them, Kashima, died soon afterward.

Hundreds of the workers on the farm turned back to the center immediately after the accident. Just a few hours earlier a number of them had refused to report for work, having been angered by an Army sentry, who had held them up at the main gate leading to the farm, because of some procedural technicalities. Scarcely an hour had passed since they had acceded to an appeal made at the noon meal and reported for the afternoon work. The dispute in the morning had left them resentful and suspicious; the accident in the afternoon added to their state of confusion. These were, however, only the most recent of a long series of difficulties.

The farm situation had always been a source of grievance to the old Tuleans, and, from the inception of their employment, to the newly arrived farm workers also. Together they had made some effort to organize in order to bring their complaints about working conditions, equipment, and food to the attention of the administration, and a representative had been elected from each crew. The morning after the accident these representatives, together with various foremen, held a meeting in a mess hall, outside which the workers milled about in an angry mood. A rumor that the driver of the farm truck was a boy only 16 years of age,[2] quickly spread among them and from them to the residents in general. WRA, in its capacity as employer, was blamed for negligence in placing the lives of the evacuees in the hands of an inexperienced minor. Shocked, frightened, and angry, the residents then strove primarily to devise means of self-protection. They agreed to refuse to leave the center for work at the farm unless safeguards against further accidents were set up and adequate compensation for the injured persons provided. At the same time the farmers realized that the circumstances of the accident and the resulting work stoppage provided an unparalleled opportunity for applying pressure on the administration to alleviate other grievances and to improve living conditions. The work stoppage of approximately eight hundred farm workers jeopardized many thousands of dollars worth of crops which were then just ready to harvest.[3] Appreciating the power of the weapon in their hands, the representatives of the workers passed a resolution "to request and demand legitimate action from the administration and also to prevent any such happenings in the future." The resolution reads in part:

We wish to make justifiable demands on behalf of the victims for the settlement of this regrettable incident. In addition, we ought to try to solve all problems [in camp] so that such an incident will not occur in the future. This problem is of vital interest to all the residents. Therefore, we resolve to make the problem center-wide. We farm workers pledge ourselves to stay away from our places of employment until our demands are met.

[2] The driver was actually 19 years of age. The reason for the residents' belief that he was younger was the fact that minors were known to be employed on the farm at this time and that, among the injured workers, were two boys of eleven and twelve years of age, respectively.

[3] About 2,900 acres were under cultivation, the crops consisting of alfalfa, potatoes, cabbage, cauliflower, lettuce, turnips, beets, spinach, etc.

At this meeting, various prominent evacuees were called in for consultation and advice on how to get camp-wide support for a camp-wide issue. Among the participants were Watanabe and Kato from Topaz, Abe from Jerome, Sano from Rohwer, and Doi from Heart Mountain, i.e., the same advisors who had been called in to help settle the coal crew dispute. As in the dispute of the coal crew, the farmers decided to approach the Civic Organizations to report their specific grievances and to obtain center-wide support for their cause. When approached, the Civic Organizations, however, referred them to the Planning Board, the Issei advisors of the administration. The Board was reluctant to handle the dispute and returned it to the Civic Organizations. There is reason to believe that neither the Board nor the Civic Organizations, both of which were dominated by old Tuleans at this time, was willing to handle the grievances of the farm group, particularly since the request was engineered by known recalcitrant and belligerent transferee leaders. As a result the Civic Organizations, at the request of the farm representatives, referred the question to a general meeting of block managers. The block managers, among whom were now many transferees, were much more intimately acquainted with the mood of the community since they had had to deal constantly and directly with complaining residents in their blocks. They speedily and unanimously decided on a plan for holding block meetings to elect representatives from each block and passed the following resolution:

With respect to the October 15 incident we block managers resolve to support unconditionally the resolution of the farm workers. Furthermore, for solution of this problem we request visits by the WRA Director and the Spanish Consul. Because of this favorable opportunity, we resolve to solve, in coöperation with all the residents, all important general problems pertaining to living conditions.

It is to be noted that emphasis was placed on the fundamental problem of improving living conditions in the center.

On the same night block-wide elections were quickly organized, and sixty-four representatives, one from each block, were chosen. The resulting choices reflected the existence of diversified interest groups in the community. In the process of segregation, the old Tuleans had lost, through relocation and transfer, many of their formal leaders (councilmen, block managers, Planning Board members, etc.). And following segregation, groups of newcomers were introduced into almost every block, for apartments made available by the departure of "loyals" had to be occupied soon after they were vacated in order to assure smooth functioning in exchanges. Since the newcomers arrived from the several relocation centers on different trains, there was an unavoidable concentration of Topazians in certain blocks, Jeromites in others, and so on. The remaining vacancies were then filled indiscriminately, according to the size of the families. The result was a very considerable heterogeneity of blockwise population, each block containing "cores" of people from one or more relocation centers. Such cores within the various blocks exercised a strong influence in the selection of representatives and in the formation of policies by the evacuees.

The recently transplanted cores tended to remain solidary, acquaintance and intimacy tended to be limited to former neighbors, to the exclusion of present neighbors, and in the selection of representatives newcomers from within a transferred core had in the main a greater chance of support than members of the old Tulean population. If, for example, a bloc of transferees from Topaz immediately nominated an antiadministration, aggressive Topazian, this nomination was likely to overshadow any choices of the remaining residents, who might comprise a heterogeneous mixture of old Tuleans and blocs of transferees from half a dozen other projects. There was evidence of an inclination to elect belligerent, vociferous individuals who had gained the reputation of being aggressive opponents of the administration in the centers from which they had come. Under the circumstances the selection in many blocks favored transferees.

Quantitative analysis of the results of the election shows that old Tuleans outnumbered the combined population of all transferees in 21 of the 64 blocks, but managed to elect Tulean representatives in only 10 of these 21 blocks.[4] In 28 other blocks they outnumbered any other transferee bloc; but Tulean representatives were elected from only 12 of them. Two other Tuleans were, however, elected where Tuleans were outnumbered by one or more transferee groups. Thus, while mere numerical preponderance per block

---

[4] Most blocks elected alternates as well as representatives. Associate representatives were also frequently elected. This analysis is based on representatives attending the first meeting of *Daihyo Sha Kai.*

might have been expected to result in the election of some 49 Tulean representatives, only 22, or less than half the "expected" number were elected, although 2 others were elected from blocks where Tuleans lacked numerical preponderance.

The effectiveness of relatively small blocs of transferees in electing representatives is shown by the following facts: In no block in the project were there more than 50 Jeromites[5] of voting ages, yet 13 Jerome representatives were elected. In 29 blocks, the representative elected came from a relocation project which had contributed less than 30 potential voters to the population; and in 6 of these, the representative came from a relocation project contributing fewer than 10 potential voters. Gila and Poston segregants, arriving later on the project than those from Jerome, Rohwer, Heart Mountain, and Topaz, were less successful than the latter in electing representatives, in spite of the fact that they were less dispersed on a blockwise basis.

In other words, although dispersal throughout the project had produced a situation favorable to old Tulean control of any blockwise election, the leaderless old Tuleans were unable to take advantage of this situation and lost, by default, to the more aggressive but much smaller cores of transferees. If proportional representation of old Tuleans and transferees, respectively, is considered from the standpoint of total rather than blockwise distribution, the results of the election seem far less biased. Old Tuleans comprised 42 per cent of the total population and elected 24 out of 64, or 37 per cent of the possible representatives. Correspondingly, transferees, with 58 per cent of the total population, elected 63 per cent of the representatives. Among the transferees, however, there is evidence of greater strength of some blocs than of others, e.g., Jerome and Rohwer elected representatives in twice the frequency of their proportions in the total population; Topaz, Poston, and Heart Mountain in about the same frequency as their proportions in the total population would predict; but Gila River transferees, who arrived only a few days before the election, were markedly underrepresented; and the scattered and numerically unimportant transferees from Manzanar, Minidoka, and Granada did not succeed in electing any representatives at all.

---

[5] The average potential voting population per block was 159, with only one block having fewer than 100.

To summarize: In so far as "representativeness" was concerned, the election had produced a body composed of old Tuleans and transferees in about the proper proportions, but some blocs of transferees were markedly overrepresented and were soon able to obtain and hold positions of control in the organization.

By common consent the elected body became known as the *Daihyo Sha Kai,* which is the Japanese equivalent of "Representative Body." On October 17, the day after the elections, the *Daihyo Sha Kai* held its first meeting, and the injured farmers formally placed all claims against and all proposed negotiations with WRA in its hands. The meeting was attended not only by the elected representatives, but also by representatives of groups with special interests in the farm incident, e.g., the Motor Pool, the Hog Farm, and the Agricultural Division. Officers were elected, with George Kuratomi of Jerome and H. Doi of Heart Mountain defeating Watanabe of Topaz by a wide margin for positions of chairman and vice-chairman, respectively. Watanabe's defeat should be remarked upon here, for later it was widely believed that he, a prominent Topaz transferee, coveted and expected to obtain the position of chairman, or some other position of prominence. A number of informants have hinted that he carried his jealousy of the elected leaders to the point of betraying the *Daihyo Sha Kai* to the administration and obstructing its progress.

As chairman, Kuratomi called on a leader of the Farm Group for its recommendations, and the latter presented a five-point proposal:

(1) Prosecution of the persons responsible for the accident.
(2) Termination of the employment of all minors as drivers.
(3) Consultation with WRA officials.
(4) Report of results of consultation to the Spanish Consul.
(5) Adequate compensation for the injured.[6]

After considerable attention to the circumstances surrounding the farm accident, discussion became focused on some of the basic grievances regarding living conditions: shortage of ambulances, defective fire apparatus, broken-down plumbing in the latrines, overcrowding, scarcity of jobs, lack of unemployment compensation, and, above all, deficiencies in the food supplied to the mess halls. To make possible more detailed attention to these numerous

---

[6] Paraphrased from minutes of the meeting, October 17, 1943.

grievances, a plan for the formation of a series of subcommittees, to be selected by the representatives on a ward basis, was drawn up. These were to cover sanitation and betterment of living conditions, farm-incident settlement, the hospital, education, and mess halls and food supply. Finally, there was to be a central committee to coördinate the activities of the other committees and to negotiate with the administration. This became known as the Negotiating Committee.

On the morning of October 18 the *Daihyo Sha Kai* representatives met on a ward basis to select one ward representative for each committee. These meetings were in general poorly attended and extremely informal. The important Negotiating Committee of seven men was selected in this informal way, on the ward basis. The original committee of seven ward representatives and the ex officio chairman and vice-chairman of *Daihyo Sha Kai* comprised seven transferees (four from Jerome and one each from Heart Mountain, Topaz, and Poston) and only two old Tuleans. Thus power of the organization was vested largely in the transferee protest bloc. Later, the committee appointed other members, and consolidated its own position. As described by a member, "The Negotiating Committee was more or less given the power to appoint any person as a member of the Negotiating Committee."[7]

For days the *Daihyo Sha Kai* made no attempt to negotiate with the administration, largely because of time-consuming preparations for a public funeral for Kashima, the deceased farmer, and because of the necessity of getting the various subcommittees on a working basis, of carrying on investigations, of reporting to and receiving reports from the residents, and of deciding upon the proper approach to make to the Caucasian officials.

Meantime, the administration, not knowing the extent to which the residents were organizing their protest movement, and faced with the loss of a valuable crop, issued[8] the following ultimatum to the farm workers:

In the immediate situation the entire farm crop needs to be harvested. These are the vegetables that the residents of Tule Lake will be eating this winter. The crop will not be lost. If evacuees do not harvest it, the Army will be asked to. This means that the WRA will have to ask the Army

---

[7] Statement by Bill Kato, Field Notes, November 10, 1944.

[8] The statement was read by the block managers in the mess halls on October 20; it was published in the *Tulean Dispatch* on the following day.

Quartermaster for vegetables for the evacuees' tables this winter. These requisitions must be prepared for 50 days in advance of the period to be used. We would not be in a very good position to expect our demands to be filled if we fail to harvest the splendid farm crop now available.

The situation is the responsibility, pure and simple, of the residents of Tule Lake Center. The administration is ready and willing to discuss and work out on a fair basis any and all difficulties that may arise. If the farm workers are not interested enough in the settlement of this problem to send official spokesmen to the administration by 8:30 A.M., October 21st, it will be necessary for the WRA to request harvesting by the Army and consequent loss of the crops to the evacuees.[9]

In response to this ultimatum, the farm foremen met on October 20 with the Caucasian Chief of the Agricultural Division. They informed him, first, that they could not return to work until their planned negotiations with WRA officials had been completed, and, second, that they had delegated responsibility for contact with the administration to the Negotiating Committee. They pointed out further that "we are not striking, but for our own protective precautionary measure we will not go to work until the issue involved has been settled." This fine distinction between "work stoppage" and "strike" was emphasized because of the justified fear that a "strike" would provide valid grounds for termination of their employment.

Failing in his attempt to negotiate directly with the farmers, Project Director Best on the following day (October 21) invited, through the block managers, "any representative committee to discuss any problem," with him. But before this invitation could be acted upon by the *Daihyo Sha Kai,* tension reached a new height.

Kashima's death had moved the people deeply. "They felt that the people who got hurt represented the whole center. They wanted to give Kashima an honorable funeral because he represented all of us."[10] The desire for an honorable funeral soon became crystallized into an intention to have a public ceremony. "Since Kashima was riding on the truck which was checked out of the Motor Pool, the Motor Pool people would want to come. Since he was from Topaz, his Topaz friends would want to come. Since he was a farmer, the farmers would want to come."[11]

[9] By "loss" was meant only the loss of food; the evacuees did not share in profits or losses resulting from the sale of the crops.

[10] Statement of a Nisei informant, Field Notes, March 23, 1944.

[11] Statement by Bill Kato, Field Notes, September 11, 1944.

The decision to have a public ceremony was apparently made by two groups independently, one composed of the deceased's fellow workers from the farm, the other organized on a camp-wide basis through the *Daihyo Sha Kai,* which delegated the responsibility to Mr. Watanabe, a friend of the Kashima family.[12]

The first of these groups to contact the Project Director was the farm workers, evidently without the knowledge of the *Daihyo Sha Kai* group. The farmers wanted permission to hold a public funeral on the outdoor stage, and assurances that the Project Director would attend the funeral and send a letter of condolence to the widow. Best refused, and confirmed his refusal in a letter to the committee on October 21, in which he said:

> In reply to your statement that a public funeral will be held at 2:00 P.M. on Saturday, October 23, at the outdoor stage in the firebreak, you are hereby notified that permission is not granted to hold such a public funeral.
>
> For your information, funerals will be held in the customary locations as they have since the opening of this center.

He later justified this refusal on the grounds that

> they didn't ask me, they demanded that I appear at the funeral and speak. They demanded that I transmit a letter of condolence to the widow. I do not recognize demands.[13]

Shortly thereafter Watanabe and his colleagues, acting for the *Daihyo Sha Kai,* approached Mr. Best in a conciliatory manner on the same errand, but evidently without knowledge of the Farm Group's earlier attempt. Best is said to have given them a half-promise that the high school auditorium could be used. This was withdrawn the day before the funeral in the following curt note:

> In reply to your request to use the outdoor stage or the high school auditorium for funeral purposes Saturday, October 23, my final answer is that no public funeral will be allowed at this particular time. Permission to use the outdoor stage or the high school auditorium is not granted.

---

[12] The attitude of Kashima's widow complicated the plans. According to Kato, she approved the plans of the *Daihyo Sha Kai* group and stated that she felt deeply honored. When approached by the administration, however, she is reported to have said that she did not want a public ceremony. This was later interpreted by the administration as evidence of pressure tactics by *Daihyo Sha Kai.* Evacuee informants (Kato and Kuratomi), however, interpret the refusal as "Japanese psychology," i.e., Mrs. Kashima, although pleased with the honor, felt impelled by modesty to refuse.

[13] Minutes of meeting with the Negotiating Committee, October 26, 1943.

Angered by this refusal, Watanabe proceeded with his plans to use the outdoor stage. The notice that a public funeral was to be held had appeared in the *Tulean Dispatch*. Donations of money were made by each block and by various individuals and groups.[14] It is said that groups of young men from Jerome and Topaz cleaned up the firebreak in preparation for the funeral.[15]

In defiance of Best's instructions, the funeral was held on October 23 as scheduled by the *Daihyo Sha Kai* group. Since it was not authorized by the administration, the *Daihyo Sha Kai* decided "that no Army or Internal Security representative nor any Caucasian whatever should come to disturb it."[16] There is evidence that a group of young men, said to have been transferees from Jerome and Topaz, had banded together to enforce this ruling. Best, nevertheless, instructed the Reports Officer to attend the funeral and to take photographs[17] of the proceedings. When the Reports Officer appeared and stepped out of his car, the young men moved in formation on him, took his camera away, and tossed him into the air. The episode was brief and the ceremony proceeded as scheduled.

The administration contributed a further source of irritation by turning off the electric power on the project during the funeral, with the result that the public address system could not function. WRA officials claimed that the public address apparatus had been taken by force from the Community Activities Section following the intimidation of Nisei workers in charge of it.

Best's refusal to sanction a public funeral was generally regarded as a discourteous and heartless act. It increased existing tension and added to the developing sense of persecution and of hostility toward the administration. Concomitantly, Watanabe's successful defiance resulted both in further loss of public respect for the administration and a corresponding increase in the prestige of the *Daihyo Sha Kai*. The unrestrained public attack on the Reports Officer further deteriorated respect for law and order among the residents and encouraged irresponsible boys, who had for some time been destroying government property and obstructing dances and social functions, in more frequent outbursts of lawless behavior.

[14] Field Notes, September 11, 1944.
[15] Field Notes, October 12, 1944.
[16] Field Notes, December 12, 1944.
[17] Or, according to some reports, to act *as if* he were taking photographs, and not to leave his car.

On the same day (October 23) a further blow was dealt the evacuees when an official report from the United States Employment
Compensation Commission was made public. This report stated
that the amount of allowable compensation for Kashima's widow
and children would be two thirds of his monthly wage as of the
date of the accident. This brought to the fore the smoldering resentment regarding WRA wage levels and wage policy. As one informant expressed it, "The widow and son of the deceased are entitled
to the grand sum of 60 per cent[18] of whatever he is making in a
month, namely, 60 per cent of the kingly wage of sixteen big
dollars."[19]

That evening *Daihyo Sha Kai* met to receive reports from its
several grievance subcommittees. Attention was centered on deficiencies in living conditions and on proposals for bettering them.
Overcrowding should be eliminated; private enterprises should be
restricted; the coöperative enterprises should not be permitted to
sell luxuries and food items; the latter should be provided by
WRA; wages should be increased to the new level of pay received
by men in the Army; lumber should be provided free for making
furniture, etc. It was alleged that the food provided in the mess
halls cost only eighteen to twenty cents per day per person, whereas
WRA regulations called for forty-five cents.[20] From this discrep-
ancy, and the fact that products of the chicken and hog farms were
not reaching the evacuees' tables, it was inferred that the Caucasian
personnel were disposing of food illegally for private profit. In this
connection, also, the question of status as "disloyals" was intruded.
It was said that the best of the Tule Lake farm products were being
shipped to the "loyals" in relocation projects and to the U.S. Army
and Navy. "Disloyal" Tuleans, who planted, cultivated and harvested the crops were receiving only second-grade products, and
in insufficient quantities at that.[21]

By October 26, the Negotiating Committee was ready to accept
Mr. Best's invitation to discuss project problems with him. Some
ten members of the committee and three Caucasians, including Mr.
Best, were present. Kuratomi acted as spokesman for the Negotiating Committee.

---

[18] Actually, 66⅔ per cent.
[19] Field Notes, December, 1943.
[20] WRA, *Administrative Instruction No. 33,* August 24, 1942.
[21] Paraphrased from minutes of the meeting, October 23, 1943.

Although Best was unwilling to recognize the Negotiating Committee as "representatives" of the evacuees, and although antagonism between Kuratomi and Best[22] was evident, some of the more important grievances were met by an evident attempt on the part of the administration either to devise means of alleviation, or to open the way for further consideration, and Best even stated at one point:

> There is no reason why we can't come to an understanding. We can lay our problems right here on the table. I am here to help you. I am not here for any other purpose. I want to spend 90 per cent of my time with you and your committee. That is what I am here for. . . . I don't think there is a problem that we can't solve if we get together. . . . We can get right down to the bottom of these things.

The agenda prepared by the Negotiating Committee covered four main points, namely (1) clarification of the status of Tule residents; (2) settlement of the farm incident; (3) request for community government; (4) request for betterment of living conditions.

Concerning *status,* the question was raised of the desirability of resegregation, involving the separation of "loyals" or "fence-sitters" from the genuinely "disloyal" and sincere repatriates for whom Tule Lake had been designed as a segregation center. Best agreed that "that is a good idea and is something that will have to be worked out."

With respect to the *farm incident,* very little was settled. Discussion degenerated into recriminations, Kuratomi reproving Best for his "inhuman attitude" and demanding that WRA accept "full responsibility" for the accidents and issue a statement expressing regret; Best claiming that the residents had been pressured into attending the funeral. The only concrete concession made by the administration was an assurance that minors would not be permitted to drive automobiles or trucks. On another point concerning the farm, however, Best agreed with the Negotiating Committee

---

[22] The administration is said to have believed that Abe and Kuratomi had organized a pressure group while still at Jerome and had come to Tule Lake prepared to enforce their program on the residents. When Kuratomi and other Jeromites were introduced to Mr. Best shortly after their arrival, Best is alleged to have prefaced his greeting with the remark: "I don't recognize any group activity. I don't care what you have done in the past, but as far as this center is concerned, you shall represent no group or groups of people." (George Kuratomi, Personal Notes, October, 1943.)

in principle, namely, that farm acreage be cultivated only to the extent dictated by the needs of the Tule Lake residents.

Concerning *community government*, both parties agreed to its desirability. Best, however, emphasized the fact that self-government, as such, would, under WRA regulations, be impossible in a segregation center, but that an advisory committee would be desirable provided it included "complete representation."

About *living conditions*, many questions were raised, in accordance with the reports of the *Daihyo Sha Kai* subcommittees. The most pressing points related to food: insufficient milk for children, lack of eggs, poultry, pork, etc. As Kuratomi said, "Food is the major problem of every individual." Best sidetracked these important points by suggesting that the question of mess-hall distribution of food should be investigated by the Mess Management Division. He agreed, however, to initiate improvements in latrine facilities, to request permission from Washington to build uniform porches on the barracks, and, in general, "to make this as decent a place as we can make it." Interestingly enough, he blamed Congress for the existing state of community disorganization and discomfort. He stated:

> The Congress of the United States . . . demanded and ordered segregation. The Tule Lake Center was selected as the place. We had all of these trains coming in and going out and I don't believe that you or I or anybody else could have done better with what we had. We didn't have time. I didn't get here until the first of August. Other centers knew all about it before the first of August, but Tule Lake had no preparations made and had no plans. Other centers moved out one to three trains. We moved 14 trains out and received trains from every center. I believe there were 18 or 19 trains in. . . . I guess we will just have to blame Congress. I don't want to blame you and I don't want to take the blame. I guess the blame rests on Congress.[23]

On the basis of evacuee statements concerning this period, the points brought up by the Negotiating Committee seem to have been a fairly accurate presentation of public sentiment. Only on the matter of the creation of a "permanent governing body" can the committee be said to have anticipated the wishes of the people. This does not mean that the people were against the formation of such a body, but there is no evidence that they considered it an immediate need or desired to make it one of the salient items re-

---

[23] Minutes of the meeting, October 26, 1943.

quested of Mr. Best. With this one exception, it can be said that every issue put before Mr. Best at this October 26 meeting had an appreciable amount of public support. According to informants' statements, the institution of proper precautions to prevent recurrence of accidents, improvement of general living conditions, and the dismissal of the Caucasian Chief of the Hospital (Dr. Pedicord), were the most emphatic desires of the people. This last issue was not mentioned at the meeting, although it later assumed great importance. Kuratomi explained that the committee members believed their chief efforts at this time should be directed toward the attempt to straighten out the farm accident and, furthermore, that the report of the hospital subcommittee was not yet complete.[24] They intended to bring up this issue at a later meeting. The policy of the Negotiating Committee at this meeting has never been criticized by evacuee informants. The general attitude at this time was that these men had been selected as representatives: whatever they chose to do "for the benefit of the people" was approved.

The important question of the work stoppage of the farm crew was not mentioned specifically during the conference of October 26. Best touched twice, however, during the meeting on the subject of the disposal of the farm crop. Once in discussing the distribution of hogs and poultry he said:

If you have a tie up and have no one out to the farm to work of course I am going to have to dispose of the produce. If you don't have a work crew out there we will just have to find a buyer and sell it.

Kuratomi took this warning to have reference to the hog farm crew and the poultry crew, and replied, "As far as I know they are working out there." Best then said, "I mean if you should stop working I couldn't give you any of the crop."

At another point Best said:

We are going to be short on some vegetables until they can be picked up, as long as we have our own crop out here and won't use it. I am going to sell this crop. There is a food shortage. There is a war on. We are going to salvage this food. I am going to sell it to the government. We will never see any of the money. I am going to sell the crop to save it. The crop is going to be harvested. We will work out this winter what to farm and what size you want, if any.[25]

---

[24] Field Notes, April 9, 1945.
[25] Minutes of the meeting, October 26, 1943.

Believing that the administration was receptive to their pleas and hopeful of an early settlement of disputes and grievances, the Negotiating Committee gave an optimistic résumé of the meeting to the *Daihyo Sha Kai* and the Farm Group.

The optimism of the Negotiating Committee turned out to be unjustified, however, for the administration had, two days before the meeting, made plans for recruiting evacuees from other relocation centers to harvest the farm crop[26] and had telegraphed the Project Directors at Topaz and Poston for their aid.[27] This information was withheld from the evacuees at Tule Lake.[28] With successful recruiting of harvesters in prospect, Best announced on October 28 that "due to failure of farm workers to report for work, they have been terminated as of October 19." Having taken this action, he left the project for San Francisco.

The termination of employment of the farm workers, entirely without warning, was a serious set-back for the Negotiating Committee and for the farmers who had insisted that they were not engaged in a strike but in a "work stoppage." A further blow was dealt them on the next day when they learned through newspapers that "loyal" harvesters, at prevailing wages, were to be brought in to break the "work stoppage." The "prevailing wage rate" was set at one dollar per *hour,* which contrasted sharply with the sixteen dollars per *month* wages of the striking—or "work stopping"—farmers at Tule Lake.

The evacuees had now completely lost their main bargaining point. Their anger and humiliation because of this situation were increased by the fact that it was "loyals" who were being brought

[26] WRA, Tule Lake Incident, Sequence of Events (manuscript).

[27] The Project Director of Topaz was definitely assured, and in turn reassured the residents, that no strike was in progress at Tule Lake. He stated: "In discussing the job I have been asked to find out if there is any trouble like a 'strike' at Tule Lake. Last night I phoned to Tule Lake and received this information: 'There is no "strike" or labor trouble in Tule Lake.' The residents of Tule Lake have had meetings with their project director and have said they did not feel they should harvest crops that were going to the other centers." (*Topaz Times,* October 28, 1943.)

[28] WRA, *Semi-Annual Report,* July 1 to December 31, 1943, states: "The administration . . . recruited evacuee volunteers from the regular centers to save the crops. The recruitment was so successful that by October 26, the day set for a meeting with an evacuee committee . . . many recruits from other centers had already been recruited. . . . In view of the attitude of this committee, the project director did not announce the fact that the harvest was being completed by volunteers from the relocation centers" (p. 12).

in under these favorable conditions to break a strike of "disloyals," in spite of the fact that "disloyalty" had been defined, administratively, as neither disparaging nor culpable. Seeking to forestall or delay their termination, the farmers, without waiting for the Negotiating Committee to intervene, immediately sent their own committee to discuss the matter with the administration. They reiterated the interpretation of their action as a "work stoppage" rather than "strike," and thus challenged the right of WRA to terminate their employment. They emphasized the contrast between conciliatory statements made during the Negotiating Committee's conference with Mr. Best and this abrupt retaliatory action. They asked the administration to retract the termination by noon of the following day, and threatened that "if this problem cannot be settled . . . we will again have to turn the matter into the people's hands." At the same time they pleaded, "It's possible that all of us should return to work. We don't believe any of us would have any objection to returning to work."[29] The administration, however, paid no attention to their threats or pleas and issued the following statement on October 30:

The Farm Committee met with the Assistant Project Director . . . and discussed various subjects relating to the farm. These subjects will be discussed further with Mr. Best and Mr. Myer on either Monday or Tuesday, November 1 or 2:

Due to Administrative Instruction 27, Revised, dated August 4, 1943, it is impossible for me [as Assistant Project Director] to reverse the decision regarding the turning in of badges which was received by the former farm workers on October 28, 1943.

On the same day the first contingent of "loyal" strike breakers arrived and was housed in tents some distance from the project proper. Meanwhile, evacuees discovered that Caucasian employees had, during the previous night, transported food from the warehouses to the farm for the use of the harvesters. A morning check-up by evacuee employees revealed that, not only were appreciable quantities of staple foods missing, but that certain luxury items which the evacuees rarely or never enjoyed in their own mess halls had also been removed.[30] Since discontent about food was one of

---

[29] Field Notes, December 26, 1944.

[30] According to an evacuee informant, the warehouse employees found deficiencies of 120 sacks of rice, 50 cases of milk, many cases of canned corn and pineapple and much flour and catsup.

the most persistent of camp grievances, and since food supplies that had been bought for Tule Lake residents were to be diverted for the use of "loyal" harvesters from other centers, this situation led to further feelings and expressions of bitterness against the administration. Resentment against the "double-crossing WRA"—Mr. Best in particular—and the "double-crossing loyal Japanese" rose to a high pitch. A group of young *Daihyo Sha Kai* members and adherents immediately organized night watches on the warehouses and Motor Pool. When on October 31 evacuee employees of the Motor Pool were ordered to service trucks to be used for transporting a second contingent of harvesters from the railway station to the farm, they refused, and Caucasian employees had to take over the job. By this time, unrest and tension were general.

Learning of Dillon Myer's imminent visit to the project, *Daihyo Sha Kai* leaders approached Zimmer, Assistant Project Director, early on the morning of November 1 and requested an appointment with Myer on behalf of the Negotiating Committee. Zimmer refused to make this appointment, insisting that the proper procedure would be for Myer to meet with the Farm Group on the following day. This administrative decision was consistent with the policy applied at the time of the coal strike, i.e., to deal with an aggrieved labor group as an entity and to impede evacuee efforts to make a labor issue a matter of camp-wide concern. Since the Farm Group had already delegated responsibility to the Negotiating Committee, the latter was unwilling to comply with this policy. When informed by an evacuee janitor in the administration building that Dillon Myer had arrived at about 11 A.M., and fearing that they would miss the chance of seeing him, members of the committee decided to force a meeting, and *Daihyo Sha Kai* representatives announced at the noon mess that Myer would meet with the Negotiating Committee that afternoon and would speak to the people. All residents were exhorted to attend.

After lunch a veritable multitude streamed to the administration area. As the crowd was gathering, Myer and Best, being alarmed, "got in a car and made a reconnaissance of the [evacuee] area, with a view to determining whether the situation warranted calling in the military. They saw people walking from every block toward the administration area. Old and young, women with babies in arms or in baby carriages, and children of all sizes were moving in a steady stream toward the administration building. The presence of these women and children and the aged in the crowd convinced the Directors that violence was not part of the plan."[31] They returned to the administration building and waited in the Project Director's office for developments.

A Kibei woman informant describes the proceedings and the temper of the people vividly in the following words:

> It was announced in the mess that Mr. Myer was here and that the representatives of the *Daihyo Sha Kai* would see him on matters that the residents of the colony wanted determined. . . .
> They said they didn't care whether we were young or old. They wanted us to go and they told us that we would not be permitted to come home when we wanted to.
> About ten minutes after we came home from lunch, every one of us got ready and formed a line in front of the mess hall and we walked to the administration building. When we reached there, the place was packed with people from other blocks.
> Everyone of us went from my block.[32]

By 1:30 P.M. the crowd, variously estimated from 5,000 to 10,000, completely surrounded the administration building. Most of these people knew that the demonstration was intended as a gesture of support to the Negotiating Committee and they participated for this reason. Curiosity and fear of criticism if they absented themselves were important motives for others. Tension and resentment against the administration were at a high point, and the people in general were deeply aroused. The *Daihyo Sha Kai* leaders, however, were unwilling to risk a slackening of interest, and groups of young men were assigned "to keep order" and to block any efforts made by the masses to return to their barracks.

The demonstration had been entirely without warning. Before lunch none of the Caucasian personnel had the least inkling that it was contemplated. Completely surrounded by thousands of evacuees and virtually imprisoned in the administration building, Dillon Myer consented to see the Negotiating Committee. According to Caucasian witnesses, the members of the committee approached the building "as if they knew exactly what they were doing and had everything well planned," and saw to it that a public address system was set up. Meanwhile, evacuees were stationed at

---

[31] WRA, *Semi-Annual Report*, July 1 to December 31, 1943, p. 14.
[32] Field Notes, October 12, 1944.

the doors of the administration building to see that no Caucasian left. According to a statement made by Reverend Abe, these young men took this task upon themselves, and the Negotiating Committee not only had no voice in the matter, but disapproved it too.

In the meantime a WRA employee "kept in close touch by telephone with the commanding officer of the Military Police, who stood by, ready to rush in soldiers at a moment's notice. Early in the afternoon the tanks in the military area were warmed up to be in readiness for an emergency."[33]

While the crowd was still gathering, and just as the conference between Myer and the Negotiating Committee was getting under way, a serious incident occurred between Dr. Pedicord and unidentified evacuees. The incident is described in the official WRA report thus:

The Chief Medical Officer [Dr. Pedicord] soon observed that groups of three to five evacuees who were not hospital employees kept coming in at intervals and circulating among the hospital employees presumably to get them to leave work and join in the demonstration. He told the intruders to leave, and they did so, but he noticed that fifteen or twenty were congregated on the steps outside. He commissioned another Caucasian doctor to guard the door and let no one in, and then went into his office, which is at the right of the entrance and entered by way of an outer office.

The young men on the steps pushed past the doctor at the door and began to crowd into the outer office used by the Chief Medical Officer's secretary. The secretary screamed; the Chief Medical Officer thrust his head out from his own office to see what was happening and had his glasses removed and laid on a shelf by one of the intruders. The Chief Medical Officer struck this man, whereupon the others moved up, pressing the doctor back into his office. Five of the group took an active part in the attack; the others stood on the sidelines. The assailants got the doctor down, kicked him twice, once in the side of the face and once in the body, and dragged him outside of the building. The doctor's nurse rushed out to the rescue, the leader of the gang gave the order to stop the beating, and the gang took itself off. Other hospital attendants came out, carried the doctor inside and administered treatment for his injuries, which were painful rather than serious.

The fight was over, the injured doctor was receiving medical attention, and the assailants had vanished when the doctor who had been commissioned to guard the front door put his call through to the Project Director's office. Naturally there was nervous tension in the hospital. Few of the hospital attendants had witnessed the violent incident, but word of such an event spreads rapidly.[34]

[33] WRA, *Semi-Annual Report,* July 1 to December 31, 1943, p. 14.
[34] *Ibid.,* p. 17.

The doctor's telephone message to the Project Director interrupted the conference that had just begun. Best asked Kuratomi what was going on at the hospital. Kuratomi answered, "I don't know."

The Project Director informed the group that the Chief Medical Officer had been beaten and property was being destroyed. At this point every WRA staff member in the room was aware of the surprise and consternation which the news produced in the committeemen: it was obvious that this episode in the hospital was no part of the committee's plan. Recovering himself [Kuratomi] said: "We will stop it," and sent some of his men to the hospital. Discussion stopped until the men returned and reported that the Chief Medical Officer was being cared for and that all was quiet in the hospital.[35]

The meeting between the Negotiating Committee and Director Myer was then resumed. The Committee had been augmented informally to include seventeen persons, and Kuratomi acted as spokesman. In addition to Myer and Best, some half-dozen Caucasian representatives of WRA participated. Kuratomi emphasized repeatedly that his function was to present the people's grievances, and over and over again he called attention to the great mass of demonstrators outside, who had come "to express their dissatisfaction and anger about center administration." He stated that, should the administration continue its mistreatment of the evacuees, the affair could be reported to the Japanese government. He added that he believed American democratic principles were at stake and that if the conditions prevailing were allowed to continue, "the democratic quality of the United States will be greatly injured." He accused Mr. Best of failing to keep faith with the Negotiating Committee and of inhumanity in regard to the funeral of Mr. Kashima.

The administration refused either to explain its actions or to negotiate with the committee on two of the three important current issues of (1) termination of the farmers' employment, (2) importation of "loyal" harvesters as strike breakers, and (3) use of food from evacuee warehouses for the "loyal strikebreakers."

In regard to the farmers' employment, Kuratomi accused Best of bad faith in terminating them retroactively, after inviting representatives to meet with him to discuss and settle the difficulties.

---

[35] *Ibid.*, p. 16.

Myer agreed that the termination notice issued by Best should be retracted with the understanding that the farmers would be notified of their termination *before* rather than *after* the action itself was taken, and it represented little in the way of a concrete concession to the evacuees directly concerned.

Myer refused to discuss the presence of the "loyal" harvesters, saying merely:

We are going to take care of the harvesting of the crop outside and I have no comment to make now. You folks did not want to do it so we arranged to have it done outside and I cannot make any comment.

Regarding the use of food for these harvesters, the following discussion took place:

BEST: It is our property and we are accountable for that property. We can do what we want to with it.

KURATOMI: Because of the fact that some merchandise was taken out of this center some mess halls suffered a shortage.

BEST: I would want to get into that thoroughly. I would want to find out exactly what was supposed to be delivered and was not and what mess halls were short. I want to know that.

KURATOMI: When you do find out what happened, will you take proper action?

BEST: What would be proper action? Maybe I don't know what the proper action is. I certainly will see that all staple commodities as far as the Quartermaster can supply will be kept here. I will see that the mess department keeps those things in here and supplies them to the mess halls.

KURATOMI: I am not satisfied with your answer as yet. We have to make a definite statement as to why this food was taken out and why the mess halls suffered.

MYER: Mr. Best gave you his answer. I am sorry but there will be no report why the food was taken out. I don't feel that it is necessary to report every movement made. If you request an investigation regarding such a case, and if it is proven that they were short, proper action will be taken. . . . I am sorry to say we cannot be in a position to report to the community on every movement of trucks.[36]

On the vital issue of disposal of the farm crop, Cozzens, the Field Director in charge of the San Francisco office, who was present at the meeting, is reported by the *Pacific Citizen*[37] to have said that "a committee of the assemblage . . . asked what was to be done about the crops which the Tule Lake residents had refused to harvest . . . Cozzens said that the Japanese Committee was told 'it was none of their business' what would be done about the crops."

---

[36] Minutes of the meeting, November 1, 1943.   [37] November 6, 1942.

Much against his will, Kuratomi had to accept these negative responses. His statement of the importance of the issues was by no means an exaggeration. For months afterward Mr. Best was denounced by the residents for bringing in the "loyal" farm workers and for feeding them "food belonging to us."

The matter of hospital difficulties was brought up after the conference had been again interrupted by a Caucasian nurse, who, already shocked and frightened by the Pedicord incident, telephoned the Project Director that a large number of evacuees were milling around in the corridor of the hospital building and going into a wing of the ward section.[38]

When the discussion was resumed, Kuratomi informed Myer that the *Daihyo Sha Kai* had decided, on the previous evening, to ask for the resignation of "each and every Caucasian doctor and each and every Caucasian nurse who feels so superior that some of them believe they know more about medicine than the Japanese doctors who have had big practices and lots of responsibility." Myer was then informed of specific cases of alleged neglect and malpractice, and he promised to have the complaints investigated thoroughly. Kuratomi refused to accept this reply, pointing out that the evacuees, having failed to get anywhere with "complaints" were now making "demands" for immediate removal of all Caucasian doctors and nurses and "a definite answer today."

MYER: That is impossible because I have been on the project only six or seven hours and haven't even had a chance to look around.

KURATOMI: Let me say this much. This has been a request from the evacuee doctors and nurses. . . . I don't want to see any violence . . . unless you . . . remove those people . . . from the hospital . . . I cannot guarantee the actions of the people. This is not a threat. I cannot stop these people from swarming over to the hospital and getting after the doctors. I don't want to see any violence take place, but I cannot guarantee what the people will do if we have to give them this answer.

MYER: I have never taken any action under threat or duress.

KURATOMI: It is not a threat; it is a fact. I am just explaining the actual tension.

---

[38] "There was a fairly steady stream of evacuees from the crowd passing in and out of one door which led across the long corridor to a wing of the ward section which was not used for patients but which contained class rooms, and what is highly significant in this instance, rest rooms. The residents, herded from lunch to the administration area and not allowed to leave the area for more than three hours, were understandably making use of the rest rooms available within the area." WRA, *Semi-Annual Report*, July 1 to December 31, 1943, p. 18.

MYER: I realize what exists. Someone is responsible for that. The people are pretty well whipped up. I am sure the tension would be much greater if I made concessions without going into the facts. . . . I am very sorry that is the situation. In view of what has happened at the hospital today, I cannot take action until we investigate the matter. That is final.[39]

Failing to gain any concession on this point, Kuratomi proceeded to review, for Myer's benefit, the many complaints of the residents about living conditions: qualitative and quantitative deficiencies of food, lack of porches, defective plumbing, insufficient supplies of items needed for cleaning, etc.

With reference to the deficiencies of food, the Negotiating Committee made specific accusations. Seki, who was called on by Kuratomi to report the findings of the food investigating committee of the *Daihyo Sha Kai,* charged that for the month of September an average of only 27 cents per person per day was spent for food instead of 45 cents per person per day, which was allowable according to WRA regulations.[40] That is, only 60 per cent of the money allocated for food had been expended during September. He also alleged that a spot check made for October 3 indicated that the food expenditure for the day was 27 cents per person, identical with the average for the previous month. He claimed that ration points for meat and processed food were being misappropriated, the Caucasian personnel receiving thousands of points in excess of their allotment at the expense of the residents. Seki concluded:

Between the time of September 17 and September 30, there is a record of 1880 pounds of beef being dumped for reason of being unfit for human consumption, and we thought this beef was to [have been] government inspected. Investigation reveals that the Caucasian mess hall not only gets some of the project meat but takes the choicest part of it. They get the cuts such as T-bone, rib steaks and tenderloin steaks. That part goes to [Caucasian] personnel mess hall and the evacuee mess halls get what is left. All of these items are contributing factors about which these evacuees in this camp are complaining, because they are not getting their proper share of food that comes into the project.[41]

[39] Minutes of the meeting, November 1, 1943.

[40] That Seki's charges were correct is suggested by a summary of improvements between November, 1943 and November, 1944, prepared by the Community Analyst (Special Report on Center Trends, November 16, 1944, manuscript), where it is stated that "the residents can taste the difference between three meals at twenty-odd cents, and three [meals] at forty-odd."

[41] Minutes of the meeting, November 1, 1943.

In regard to these grievances, Best stated merely that the complaints were "under consideration." Kuratomi thereupon presented a statement from "the residents" demanding the removal of Mr. Best and various others of the Caucasian personnel. Myer answered by reaffirming his confidence in Best and stressing the fact that "we can't operate on the basis of demands . . . [but] are willing to investigate charges and are willing to take action if we find they are based on facts."

During the course of the meeting two other important issues were raised, the first by Kuratomi, the second by Myer. (1) Kuratomi tried once more to get some definite statement on the status of Tule Lake residents. He pointed out the friction that existed in camp "between the people who have expressed their desire to go back to Japan and those who are still loyal to this country" and reiterated that "the residents would have this center designated for all those who have intention of going back to Japan sooner or later."

He received no assurance that the desired process of resegregation could be carried through. (2) Myer indicated, at several points, his lack of faith in the "representativeness" of the Negotiating Committee, pointing out that "you folks are serving in a temporary capacity until a truly representative committee has been chosen" and, again, "I don't know how many people you represent. I doubt that you represent all of them. . . . It is difficult to represent everybody's point of view when there are 15,000 here."[42]

The conference lasted for two and a half hours. During this whole period the great crowd of evacuees stood quietly around the administration building. A young man, Sadao Endo, spoke to them from time to time through a loud speaker and urged them to be patient.

When the meeting ended, Dillon Myer, at the request of Kuratomi, made a very short address to the people. This address was preceded by a report from Kuratomi on the progress of the negotiations and was followed by a speech by Reverend Abe. Kuratomi assumed a much more conciliatory attitude in his speech to the people than he had in his meeting with the administrators. He made no threats and expressed the hope that something concrete could be accomplished through negotiation.

---

[42] *Ibid.*

The résumé of Myer's speech as reported in the *Tulean Dispatch* of November 2 follows:

At the end of the negotiations Myer addressed the local residents over the public address system and stated that he has met with the people's delegates to discuss their representations. Expressing utmost confidence in Director Best, Myer concluded by asking residents to coöperate with the administration in settling all problems.

Abe said in part:

We have been here a long time. A great many things have been discussed and no conclusions have been reached. We will have to enter into further negotiations in the future. You people must remember that you are Japanese and must act as Japanese to hold together for the sake of the Empire and the Emperor.

At the conclusion of Abe's speech, Endo called on the people to bow. This they did in unison, according to Kuratomi, "not only in gratitude to Reverend Abe but also as a gesture of gratitude to Mr. Myer."[43] After Abe's speech the crowd dispersed quietly.

Immediately after the meeting, fully aware that the atmosphere was tense, the WRA officials took two steps which had far-reaching consequences. First, they conferred "with the commanding officer of the military police and [made] detailed arrangements for guaranteeing protection of life and property within the center in any emergency that might arise. The military stood in readiness to take immediate occupation of the center at need, and it was agreed that authority to summon military assistance should be given any Internal Security Officer, whereas previously only [Best]—or [Myer] himself—was authorized to call in the Army."[44]

Second, the officials instituted nightly patrols of the administrative areas and assigned Chief of Internal Security Schmidt to general surveillance. The plan was to have patrol officers check in hourly to the sergeant of the military guard and the WRA employee in charge for the night with the understanding that the military should investigate any check-in more than five minutes overdue.[45]

The state of mind of most of the Caucasian employees immediately following the meeting was one of indecision, tension and

[43] Field Notes, December 26, 1944.
[44] WRA, *Semi-Annual Report,* July 1 to December 31, 1943, p. 19.
[45] *Ibid.*

fear often bordering on hysteria. "At the suggestion of the Chief Medical Officer, the Caucasian hospital staff was relieved from duty that night and sent home to get some rest." One Caucasian employee remained on duty through the night. "A few members of the appointed staff spent the night in Klamath Falls or Tulelake (the nearest town)."[46] Newspapers printed lurid accounts of "Jap riots" and obtained highly colored statements from many of these Caucasians. For example, this "eyewitness" account of a WRA employee, who resigned after the incident, appeared in the *San Francisco Examiner:*

From a newly resigned official of the Tule Lake Relocation Center—a man who frankly says, "I quit because I like my sleep, and you can't sleep when you don't know when you're going to have your throat cut"—the *Examiner* has obtained a detailed report . . .

Japs began coming across the compound, between the hospital and the administration building. They came in droves, and they simply wiped away the low barbed wire fence which formed a deadline they were not supposed to cross.

One group of about a thousand, led by the Judo boys—the strong arm boys who rule the camp by intimidation—stopped at the hospital to have it out with Doctor Pedicord . . . And one nurse had had her hair pulled and her face slapped.

Meanwhile, several thousand Japs—my guess is about 6,000 or 7,000— were outside the administration building. . . .

I saw Japs walk up to the building with sacks full of straw, and poke the sacks under the building. Later, we learned that the straw was soaked in oil. And I saw the Judo boys ostentatiously take up positions guarding every door of the building. . . .

The Japs outside stood stolidly by . . . I know enough about the Jap to know that he's most dangerous when he's quiet. My knowledge wasn't any more comforting when added to the fact that most of the Japs outside carried knives—long, curved bladed beet knives or butcher knives . . .

That's why I quit. I couldn't sleep. I kept waking up with the expectation of feeling a knife against my throat.[47]

On November 2 the Caucasian employees held a series of meetings, culminating in one which Myer attended. They demanded that a fence be erected between the administrative and the evacuee areas. Several of the appointed personnel made speeches expressing their fears of violence. Some staff members resigned.[48]

46 *Ibid.,* p. 19.
47 *San Francisco Examiner,* November 4, 1943.
48 WRA, Tule Lake Incident, Sequence of Events (manuscript).

On the same day Best issued an order prohibiting public gatherings of evacuees in the administration, Caucasian personnel, hospital, and warehouse areas. This order was printed in a special supplement to the *Tulean Dispatch*, distributed to the evacuees on November 4, 1943.

Later in the day, members of the appointed personnel, prominent among whom were staunch supporters of Dr. Pedicord, held a meeting at the town of Tulelake. Dillon Myer again was asked to attend and is said to have done so unwillingly. The irate members of the WRA personnel demanded military protection, machine guns and tanks. Myer stated that he was against a show of violence, for violence bred violence. He voiced the opinion that the members of the personnel were justifiably scared but insisted that adequate military protection was quietly in operation. Soon after this meeting, Myer left the project in accordance with his original schedule.

Two days later the construction of a high barbed-wire fence, separating the evacuee section of camp from the Caucasian section (the Administration Building, living quarters, warehouses, and the hospital) was begun. Sentries were stationed at the gates and no evacuee was allowed to enter without a special pass.

Entirely unaware of these administrative attitudes and actions, the Negotiating Committee lost no time in publicizing and exaggerating the actual concessions and the alleged promises made by Myer and Best. Their claims achieved a certain credibility when Mr. Best informed Kato that "there are no facts to the rumor that Dr. Pedicord will return to the Tule Lake hospital."[49] Best also stated that he planned to have uniform porches erected, if Washington gave permission. When later events made it impossible to carry out these plans, the actual and imaginary broken promises were greatly magnified and were referred to repeatedly by the residents as evidence of the "double-crossing" character of Mr. Best.

On November 2 the *Daihyo Sha Kai* met to work out a procedure for the election of a permanent representative body (i.e., a permanent Negotiating Committee) and of permanent subcommittees. It was agreed that each block should prepare lists of suggested personnel, that *Daihyo Sha Kai* was to elect a "selection committee," that the selection committee should choose from the block lists a

---

[49] Letter addressed "To whom it may concern," given by Mr. Best to Bill Kato on November 4. Dr. Pedicord, however, later returned to the hospital for a short period.

slate of nominees, and that their selection should be subject to popular review. At the same time, a plan was also worked out to celebrate the *Meiji Setsu,* commemorating the birthday of the late Emperor Meiji, grandfather of the reigning Emperor, Hirohito.

The *Meiji Setsu* ceremony took place on the morning of November 3, without the permission of project officials. Some 10,000 residents participated in the elaborate and solemn ceremony, with most of the workers taking unauthorized leave from their jobs.[50]

In the afternoon the Spanish Consul came to the project, on invitation of the Farm Group, to investigate the disturbances, and met with a group of twenty-one evacuee representatives, including the members of the Negotiating Committee. The same ground was covered as in the meeting with Dillon Myer: the status of "disloyals," maladministration by WRA, hospital difficulties and malpractices, alleged graft by Caucasian personnel, deficiencies in food supplies, Best's "inhuman" behavior with respect to the Kashima funeral, etc.

At one stage of the conference De Amat, the Consul, asked if the main cause of the disturbance of November 1 was dissatisfaction with the hospital. Kuratomi, the spokesman for the meeting, replied that that was one cause and food deficiencies was another. The discussion that followed reflects difficulties confronting the *Daihyo Sha Kai* leaders:

DE AMAT: You know that I am here to help you. Why haven't you come to me before instead of going on strike?

KURATOMI: The reason is we have come here very lately; we have been here only a month. It was very fortunate for us to have Mr. Myer visit us and we thought he could take our grievances first to see if [he] would take proper action to rectify some of the wrong doings.

DE AMAT: But up to that moment you resorted to violence. . . .

KURATOMI: That wasn't done by the residents. There were two or three—some of the hotheads. That was not the [procedure] or part of [our] program at all.

In closing the conference, Consul De Amat made the following encouraging remark:

I enjoyed talking with you. Everything was very reasonable, which is an exception. Frequently I have complaints that have no foundation but

---

[50] According to the WRA *Semi-Annual Report,* July 1 to December 31, 1943, "Young evacuee men rounded up evacuee workers and herded them [to the ceremony]" (p. 20). Evacuee informants deny this statement.

everything we have talked about today makes quite a lot of sense, and I am very hopeful that part of it will be arranged, not all of it, but part of it.[51]

The major difference between the two meetings was the greater frankness and lack of restraint exhibited by the committee in the presence of the Spanish Consul, and the latter's sympathetic attitude in regard to the difficulties the evacuees were facing, in sharp contrast with the defensive attitude of the WRA officials. This difference was psychologically important in reinforcing the evacuees' dependence upon Japanese rather than American protection in time of need. Having relied for aid on the Spanish Consul, and through him on the protection of the Japanese government, the evacuee representatives were confidently hopeful of an early settlement of difficulties. In the light of events that soon occurred, an informal conversation between the Consul and Kuratomi is particularly significant. Kuratomi reported afterward:

He (De Amat) asked us, "Is it all right for me to leave [Tule Lake]?" I told him frankly that everything was under control.[52]

Contrary to Kuratomi's optimism, as will be seen, everything was far from being "under control."

On November 4 *Daihyo Sha Kai* met to complete arrangements for selecting the permanent representative body. Prior to this meeting, the residents of each block had handed in their lists of suggested persons for each committee, and it was the task of the "Selection Committee" of the *Daihyo Sha Kai* to choose the permanent committeemen from these lists. "The only thing left to do," said Kuratomi, "was to bring this up to the administration for their approval. We also intended to have the mass meeting and explain this to the people."[53]

The meeting was interrupted dramatically by the entrance of Yukio Baba, a twenty-two-year-old policeman, formerly of Heart Mountain, who reported that Caucasians were transporting food supplies to the outside by truck—presumably to the strikebreakers. Mr. Tada, the chief of the evacuee police force, instructed him to return, take the license numbers of the trucks, keep note of the

---

[51] Minutes of the meeting, November 3, 1943.
[52] Field Notes, September 18, 1944.
[53] *Ibid.*

foodstuff being taken out, and report to the supervisor at once. According to the minutes:

He further advised Baba not to go alone but stop at the Internal Security and pick up three or four night patrols to go along with him and he further warned him to refrain from taking rash actions by all means. Baba bowed and went out. Upon hearing this conversation, several youths followed Baba.

On his way back Baba picked up a number of young men, some of whom were shortly engaged in violent clashes with Caucasian employees. The circumstances leading up to Baba's participation in the affair and the subsequent riotous behavior are described in the WRA official report, where it is stated that at 8:15 that evening, a staff member had gone to the Motor Pool to requisition three trucks to meet evacuee harvest workers arriving at Klamath Falls from other relocation projects. Refused service by the evacuees in the Motor Pool, he corralled Schmidt, the Chief of Internal Security, and several other staff members and returned to the pool. After servicing the trucks, he and two other Caucasian drivers set off for Klamath Falls.

No sooner had the other staff members turned away from the motor pool than an evacuee [Yukio Baba] jumped in a truck and headed at full speed for the evacuee colony. [Schmidt] anticipating a reaction to the removal of the cargo trucks, stopped at the room of [his assistant] and assigned him to watch the broad, open space between evacuee colony and administration area for signs of action. He detailed another officer to stay with the switch-board operator at the telephone office to forestall any attempt to cut communications, and then went to the military compound to report the situation to the sergeant of the military guard and make sure that everything was in readiness for quick action. . . .

When word reached the colony that the trucks were taken, about 150 to 200 of the strong-arm squad rallied with the intent of preventing the trucks (already well away from the center) from being loaded with food and taken from the center. The messenger's [Baba's] truck and others similarly appropriated were used to carry men to the motor pool and warehouses to mount guard; auxiliaries set off for these areas on foot. Trucks darted about the center in pursuit of the missing trucks. Failure to find any trace of the three trucks baffled and enraged the young men. A number of them were armed with base ball bats, pick handles or short lengths of two-by-four lumber. Internal Security men on patrol or guard duty began to be aware of groups congregating in the shadows of the warehouses and around the motor pool. The guard at the high school called his chief to report that gangs of men were robbing the lumber pile. Two officers in a patrol car had their way blocked by a black pick-up whose evacuee driver announced that no produce trucks were going to get out of the center that night but who shortly drove away leaving the way clear. The officers headed back to the administration area to report. . . .

In the Military Compound . . . [Schmidt] stopping only to tell the sergeant of the guard that a request for the Army to move in would probably be made very soon, drove into the center, stopping about 75 yards from the gates when a car approached him, shining a spot light in his face. Thinking it an Army radio patrol car, he got out and walked over to it, discovering it to be the black pick-up previously mentioned. There were evacuee men riding in the rear. One of these and the driver jumped down and tried judo on the chief. After a brief interchange, the Chief got back into his car and headed for the Project Director's house. He parked his car across the road from the house and walked toward the house, suddenly perceiving 30 or 40 men with clubs in the shadows. Six of these attacked him, but he used the judo hold on two of these, wrenching an arm of each from its socket. In the lull following this feat, he got back to his car, hearing the men yell in English: "Get Best! Take Best!" He started in his car for the military area and out-maneuvered the driver of the pickup who tried to cut him off, reaching the military area to call in the Army.[54]

Schmidt's summons, however, was the second of the two emergency appeals to the Army in the short span of a few minutes. Previously, Project Director Best had called for the entrance of the Army when he had seen a number of men gathering near his residence.

In the meantime,

the two men on patrol and the officer assigned to the area between colony and administration area reached the telephone office in the administration building intending to report by telephone to [Schmidt]. The switch was open and they overheard the Project Director's call to bring in the Army. They started on foot for the Project Director's house, hearing the cries of "Get Best! Take Best!" Just outside the Administration Building, the driver of the same black pick-up attempted to run them down, but they jumped out of the way and the driver had to stop to avoid hitting some posts. He and his men jumped out and a fight began, in which one of the officers was injured. The other two, reinforced by several staff members from the administration building, fought off the others and took three prisoners in the few moments that remained before the Army arrived and took over.[55]

There were conflicting versions of this fight. According to the injured Caucasian officer, the evacuees attacked him. According to

[54] WRA, *Semi-Annual Report,* July 1 to December 31, 1943, pp. 21–22.
[55] *Ibid.,* p. 23.

another Caucasian in the fight, he himself "lit into the Japanese" after they had called him "dirty names." Whoever may have started the fight, a score or more of evacuees were very badly beaten.

Thus, at about ten o'clock on the evening of November 4 the Army entered the Tule Lake Center with guns and tanks to take over the administration. With the assistance of the Internal Security force, the Army arrested eighteen young men in the warehouse and closely adjoining personnel residence area and in the part of the camp adjoining that area. All but nine[56] of these young men were released the same night. Several had been severely injured, were hospitalized under guard after questioning, and later removed to a stockade. In all, "possibly six shots were fired (none by evacuees as no firearms have been in their possession in centers at any time) but no one was found to have been wounded by gunfire."[57]

There is great confusion and disagreement in the records and reports about what actually occurred, beyond the bare facts mentioned above. Among the important controversial points are the use for which the trucks were intended: whether food was actually being transported or not; the contention of some of the members of the Caucasian personnel that the evacuees intended to kidnap Mr. Best and the denial by evacuee informants of any such intention; the question whether or not certain arrested evacuees were brutally beaten in the statistics office by members of Internal Security before being turned over to the Army.

Even though the entrance of the Army was accompanied by the noise of light tanks and jeeps and the glare of floodlights, most of the residents did not know until the next morning that the Army had taken over the camp. The members of the *Daihyo Sha Kai,* however, who were discussing the selection of permanent committees, learned of the grave situation at about 11:30 that night. A Kibei youth ran into the meeting and reported that the Army had entered the center. "Noise of guns and machine guns, which broke the tranquility of a cold dark night, increased."[58] Abe instructed certain young men present in the room to order the boys to disperse before anyone was injured, and the discussion was resumed, the representatives evidently unaware of the melee that had taken place.

---

[56] Some evacuee informants reported that only five men were detained.

[57] WRA, Report, *op. cit.,* p. 23.

[58] Minutes of the meeting, November 4, 1943.

The selection of the committees was not completed until 2:00 A.M., after a meeting of more than six hours. Out of this meeting came a new permanent Executive Board, composed of Tetsuo Kodama, M. Tada and three others. These men were later to take on the important task of negotiating with the Army.

The reason for rushing the selection of the various committees was explained by Kuratomi: "The Negotiating Committee wanted to be relieved of the responsibility as fast as possible. I myself wanted to get the Buddhist center church organized. That was my primary thought at this time. If I continued in politics I wouldn't be able to do other things I wanted to."[59]

At the same time it may be safely concluded that the representatives were aware of difficulties in store for them, for the minutes have further dramatic references to the activities of the Army.

It was now 1:30 a.m. and the thundering roar of the tanks, armored trucks, and jeeps rumbled near the block 15 Mess Hall [where the meeting was held].

The minutes end:

Sound of the guns were no longer audible; however, the rumbling of the Army trucks and tanks were heard.

As stated in the WRA official report, "the acts which culminated in military intervention were committed in high temper and on the spur of the moment by young men acting on their own initiative. There is no reason to believe that the political leaders were in any way involved in the action taken by the young men."[60] Concerning Baba's report earlier in the meeting, Kuratomi lamented later:

When Baba came in to report the trouble at the motor pool, I did not think it would develop into a fight of major proportion. If I had known then that the fight would be as significant as later events proved it to be, I certainly would have taken more precautions and had Mr. Tada go out to investigate. The *Daihyo Sha Kai,* especially the Negotiating Committee, did not want to see such a thing happen. We had everything to lose and nothing to gain by having such a fight take place at this crucial time.[61]

---

[59] Field Notes, January 2, 1945.

[60] WRA, *Semi-Annual Report,* July 1 to December 31, 1943. This statement is significant in view of the fact that the political leaders were later arrested by the Army and confined on WRA orders in the stockade for periods up to eight months.

[61] George Kuratomi, Statement, November 14, 1945.

Chapter VI

SUPPRESSION
Martial Law

THE ARMY TOOK OVER Tule Lake on November 4, 1943, and declared martial law on November 13. Not until January 15, 1944, was martial law lifted and the administration returned to WRA. The intervening period was one of turmoil, idleness, impoverishment and uncertainty for the general population, who continued their partial strike and passive resistance. For the leaders of the *Daihyo Sha Kai,* for various other alleged instigators of the "riot," and for numbers of other individuals who had opposed the administration in one way or another, it was a period of increasingly severe repression: midnight pickups, isolation and incarceration in a stockade and "bull pen." It resulted in the disintegration of the *Daihyo Sha Kai* as a political organization, the emergence of an organization with collaborative aims (Coördinating Committee) and of an underground antiadministration pressure group (Resegregationists). Coincident with the development of these divergent policies came a sharpening of the distinction between the "disloyal" and the "loyal," an intensification of race-consciousness, and a wave of hate, fear, and suspicion toward dissenters, "fence-sitters," collaborationists and informers.

The Army had been brought into the center on the evening of November 4 to inhibit, by a show of force, an outburst of violence which WRA officials feared was in the offing. It was not expected that it would remain longer than was necessary to achieve these immediate ends. Events taking place between November 5 and November 13, however, led to the declaration of martial law and a two-month period of Army control.

The tanks rolled into the administrative and warehouse areas on the night of November 4 "making a big noise, shooting, and what not,"[1] but because of the distance of the evacuee living quarters from these areas, and because it was late at night, most evacuees did not hear the commotion and had no idea that anything untoward had occurred until the next morning when workers, attempting to enter the administrative area, were stopped at the gates by a cordon of soldiers and told to return to their barracks. About a thousand workers involved in this unannounced lockout pressed toward the gates, and the crowd was augmented by parents and relatives of workers in the hospital area who had not been allowed to return to their homes the previous night and by curious residents from the nearer barracks. Faced with a milling, rapidly increasing crowd and unable to disperse it by oral commands, the soldiers released tear gas into its midst. The scene is described by a Nisei informant:

> The next morning everybody, as usual, went to report to work and all the Japanese truck drivers were stopped by the guards, searched and told to go back. They said they had to go to work. The soldiers told them to go back, not to come near the place. Some of the fellows still argued and the soldiers kicked some of them. Everybody was gathering. So the Army started throwing tear gas at them and told them to go home.[2]

The evacuees were completely cut off from the administration. Even telephone calls between the evacuee and the administrative area were not accepted. Finally, M. Tada, head of the evacuee police,[3] was able, by virtue of his position, to establish contact with one of his Caucasian superiors and to request his mediation in arranging an interview with the Project Director. He was referred, instead, to Lieutenant Colonel Austin, the Commanding Officer of the Army unit, who, he was told, had now taken over the administration of Tule Lake. Escorted into Austin's presence, Tada immediately asked for a delineation of the conditions under which the Army would withdraw. Describing this interview, Tada reported:

> Colonel Austin told me that if the center goes back to normal conditions, there is no need of the army remaining. So naturally I asked what he would call "normal conditions." He didn't reply. I asked, "Does it mean if the residents resume the same activities as yesterday?" Colonel Austin said, "Yes."[4]

---

[1] Statement by M. Tada, Field Notes, January 11, 1945.

[2] Field Notes, December, 1943.

[3] Tada was also a member of the Executive Board which was formed the night before (November 4).

[4] Field Notes, January 11, 1945.

Since the Army was responsible for the evacuees not being able to go to work "as yesterday," Tada felt that the difficulties could be quickly ironed out if evacuee leaders and Army officers could get together. With Austin's approval he therefore approached key members of *Daihyo Sha Kai* and George Kuratomi, the chairman. These men together worked out a plan for getting essential workers back on their jobs, first the hospital workers on change of shift, then the coal and garbage crews. The Army acceded immediately in the case of the hospital workers, and ninety of them were permitted to pass through the Army cordon and take up their duties. In regard to the other crews, however, difficulties arose, for the authorities decided to limit the number who could return to work. This plan of limitation seems to have been evolved by the Army in consultation with WRA and to have been directed toward two objectives: (1) to purge from the work crews all those who were under suspicion of antiadministrative aims or acts; and (2) to introduce a more efficient plan for organizing the work, i.e., more intensive work per man employed rather than the existing system of spreading available employment over a rather large labor force. The plan met with immediate opposition from the evacuees. The Army, for example, wanted the coal crew cut from about 300 workers to seventy who had been "cleared." A similar cut was proposed for the garbage crew. A stalemate resulted, with neither crew reporting for work. Other troubles developed in regard to distribution of food supplies, with serious repercussions on the evacuees in general. An evacuee described the situation as follows:

Then on about the fifth and sixth of November, people began hollering about there not being enough coal. There was no milk. Only children under seven months old were getting milk. Children over seven months old were going hungry and crying.[5]

The Negotiating Committee, according to Tada, appealed to the workers, on the one hand, stressing the coal shortage, which "was being pretty much felt by the colonists and it isn't our idea to let the colonists suffer" and the necessity of garbage collection; to the Army, on the other, stressing the low wage scale, the fact that work was "voluntary," and that "the Army could not expect any of the Japanese to work as hard as Colonel Austin expected his soldiers to work." The Negotiating Committee asked, further, that "every

---

[5] Field Notes, December, 1943.

person in the center who had been working be permitted by the authorities to resume his job."[6]

The Army relented so far as the coal and garbage crews were concerned, and work by the complete crews was resumed on November 11; however, difficulties were now developing with other crews.

On a certain day, the butcher shop workers were cleared by the Army to go back to work. Of course, the number of workers was very much decreased compared to the number working before the incident. So a dozen or fifteen men went to work in the butcher shop. They were told that under Army supervision they would have to put in their hours stringently. Mr. Matsui, a Nisei from block 48, spoke up and said, "With the small number of workers, we cannot complete as much of the work as we used to do. You should get more men and also rehire the foreman." That afternoon Mr. Matsui was pulled in by the Army for making this speech and agitating or being insolent.[7]

Only twenty-five of the ninety-eight warehouse workers were cleared for reëmployment. But, Tada claims, he explained to the Army representatives:

It would be impossible for us to go back and tell the group that only 25 of the 98 could be approved by the FBI, WRA and the Army. That would have left a queer impression on those selected. The remaining people would be thinking they were *inu* or informers [i.e., collaborators with the administration].[8]

Those warehouse workers who had been cleared refused to report for work. The authorities refused to reinstate the remainder of this and of other crews. In some crews, essential "cleared" workers agreed and returned to work "for the sake of the Japanese," but as they reported to work and found that many of their fellow workers were not included in the recall orders, ill-feeling increased.

The rapport established between the Army and the Negotiating Committee in their joint attempt to bring order into the colony was strained by failure to come to terms on the matter of reëmployment. The breach in the relations between evacuees and Army was further widened by the inception on November 4 of a policy of removing persons suspected of antiadministrative acts or designs from the residential area and detaining them, without formal charges or trial, in an isolated, closely guarded area later designated as "The Stockade." The first persons confined in the stockade were

---

[6] Field Notes, January 11, 1945.   [8] Field Notes, October 26, 1944.
[7] Statement by M. Tada, *ibid.*

young men, variously reported in number from five to nine, who had been picked up during disturbances in the administrative and warehouse areas. On the night of November 4 the Army selected a site near the hospital, set up tents for temporary quarters and placed the arrested men there under heavy guard. Within a few days Matsui, who was involved in the butchers' dispute, was added to the group. After further arrests were made, the stockade was moved to another area, and five complete barracks, a mess hall, and a bathhouse were erected.

Until November 9 the reëmployment issue far overshadowed the stockade issue as a matter of concern, both for the Negotiating Committee and for the residents in general, and at an emergency meeting of *Daihyo Sha Kai* on November 6, the people's representatives passively accepted the statement of the chairman that "those detained by the Army will not be permitted to return to the center until they have had their hearings" and his admonition that "because of several youths' rash actions, an incident . . . occurred, which is very lamentable. You *Daihyo Sha Kai* representatives are requested to see to it that people refrain from such actions in the future."[9]

On November 9, however, when the Spanish Consul arrived (for the second time within a week) to investigate the incident at the request of the Japanese government, his attention was called to the stockade, and he was asked to ascertain the reasons for the Army's action and the physical condition of the detainees and to assure the Japanese government "that the colonists will remain loyal as Japanese subjects until the day we are allowed to return home . . . [and the Japanese government is] not to worry about us." The Consul, in turn, asked the Negotiating Committee to "expend its utmost effort to bring about an amicable settlement." He continued:

If negotiations for the settlement fail, the body should report to the Consul at once. Upon such notice, the latter will immediately call, inasmuch as he is assigned by the Japanese Government to insure the happiness of the Japanese colonists. The Consul asked for the promise of the body to see to it that such incident will not re-occur. Thus the block representatives [*Daihyo Sha Kai*] assured him that they will not resort to any rash or inconsiderate action, upon their honor. The Consul was very grateful.[10]

[9] Minutes of the meeting, November 6, 1943.
[10] Minutes of the meeting, November 9, 1943.

After promising that he would visit the center regularly, twice a month, and would make special trips whenever necessary, the Consul left Tule Lake

By this time *Daihyo Sha Kai* leaders were leaning heavily upon the Japanese government for aid in solving the difficult impasse. Their views of the situation were carried to the residents by the camp paper, the *Tulean Dispatch*. Censorship, which had previously been exercised by WRA, had ceased when John D. Cook, Reports Officer, left the project following the disturbances of November 4. Since the newspaper was published in the evacuee area, *Daihyo Sha Kai* opinions were freely expressed. The *Tulean Dispatch*, for instance, carried articles which gave the residents the impression that Japan would soon intercede and protect the Japanese in Tule Lake. For example, an article headed "Tule Lake Japanese Intimidated by Tanks" read:

The fact that the Army had entered this center was reported to Japan. Radio Tokyo on November 8 stated:

The American Army has entered the Tule Lake Center with machine guns and tanks, and is intimidating the residents. Nevertheless, the Japanese in the center are holding out by displaying their *Yamato damashii* [Japanese spirit].[11]

Again the Japanese Section carried an editorial, "Mother Country That Has Not Forsaken Us":

Being worried about us who are loyal to our mother country to the bitter end and about the entrance of the Army into the center, the Japanese Government has instructed the Spanish Ambassador, the representative of the Imperial Government, to investigate the conditions of the center. . . .

Remembering that our mother country will not forsake us to the end, we should be patient, avoid rash acts, and endeavor to promote peace and public welfare. We should show greatness worthy of Japanese.[12]

The committee issued a public statement through the *Tulean Dispatch* of November 11, in which the members threatened to resign unless the residents coöperated:

In asking the residents for their full support, the seven members of the Negotiating Committee stated that in case the residents do not obey their request for coöperation, they will be forced to resign. Also in case the Army does not recognize the truth of the incident, they will have to relin-

---

[11] *Tulean Dispatch*, Japanese Section, November 9, 1943.
[12] *Tulean Dispatch*, Japanese Section, November 11, 1943.

quish their position. The Committee asked residents that whenever a request for workers is made by them, to report immediately after the call is issued.

On the morning of November 12, however, Colonel Austin told the Negotiating Committee that, on the basis of information received from evacuees, he doubted its claims of representing the people and that he would no longer recognize it as medium for negotiations. In spite of this, the authorities and the committee proceeded with plans for a mass meeting on November 13 at which reports would be made by Army, WRA, and Negotiating Committee representatives. The Army and WRA were of the opinion that the Negotiating Committee was not giving the residents the true facts about the conferences between the committee and the authorities, and they hoped to use the meeting to make clarifying statements,[13] while the Negotiating Committee and the *Daihyo Sha Kai* planned to make a public justification of their actions. The pending meeting was announced in the *Tulean Dispatch*.

On the same afternoon, the day before the scheduled mass meeting, the *Daihyo Sha Kai* assembled, and, in a stormy session, reached a unanimous decision to cancel the meeting. The reasons behind this decision were many: internal dissention in *Daihyo Sha Kai*, apparent in the meeting and attributable to the refusal of the Army to "recognize" the Negotiating Committee, and suspicion among representatives that *inu* were making "false reports . . . to the authorities" to the effect that the committee did not have the backing of the residents; dissatisfaction with the arbitrary actions of the Army in terminating the employment of workers on crews while negotiations were still proceeding; and annoyance because the Army had decided to limit the meeting to forty-five minutes.

Suspicion of informers (*inu*) had crystallized when Army representatives told the Negotiating Committee that they were receiving reports from evacuees discrediting the *Daihyo Sha Kai*,[14] and its Negotiating Committee. They are said to have pointed out among

---

[13] WRA, "Tule Lake Incident, Report of Talks by Col. Verne Austin and R. B. Cozzens at Outdoor Stage in Japanese Colony" (manuscript), November 13, 1943.

[14] Under the title, "Army's Attitude Toward the Representatives Abruptly Changes; Our Demands Completely Refused; Informers Disrupt Unity in Our Midst," the Japanese Section of the *Tulean Dispatch* (November 13) states: "The Army believes that . . . these representatives do not represent residents as a

other things, that in spite of more than half of the population being old Tuleans, only two men from among them were on the Negotiating Committee, suggesting that "old Tuleans are not supporting you."[15] They are said, further, to have expressed skepticism as to the proportion of the residents who would support the committee by attending the meetings. The committee had estimated attendance at 3,000 on the assumption that one member per residential unit would participate and report back to other members of his apartment. The Army chose to interpret this estimate as proportional to the total population rather than to the number of residential units. According to Seki, "the Army pointed out that mere 3,000 attendance was only a small part of the colony," and disregarded Kuratomi's assurance that "we have the backing of 15,000 colonists."[16] Piqued by this skepticism, irritated by the frictions among the members, and fearful of the further acts of *inu,* the Negotiating Committee members offered to resign. They were, however, persuaded to carry on until evidence of general support could be presented to the Army, through a popular "vote of confidence" on a petition which would be submitted forthwith through the block managers.

The "arbitrary and oppressive" actions of the Army were described by Seki as follows:

Reinstatement of all evacuee workers have been agreed yesterday and they [the Army] promised to answer by 10 a.m. today, but they haven't kept the promise. Authorities [the Army] know how many workers are required in certain departments, yet they evaded responsibility by bringing in WRA to handle employment matters.[17]

By Tada:

Yesterday they [the Army] showed sincerity of recognizing the Negotiating Committee. Yet, they abruptly terminated hospital employees

---

whole. This belief, it is presumed, is a result of the work of some unknown Japanese informers who have reported to the Army that it is of no value to listen to the statements of these representatives."

An editorial in the same issue mentions scathingly that "the presence of traitors" in camp had been "exposed."

[15] Minutes of the meeting, November 12, 1943. See pp. 117–120 for analysis of the composition of *Daihyo Sha Kai* and the Negotiating Committee. It is evident that old Tuleans were elected as block representatives in approximately their proportion to the total population, which was not "more than half of the population" but about 42 per cent. The Negotiating Committee, however, was markedly overweighted with transferees.

[16] *Ibid.*   [17] *Ibid.*

without notice [while negotiations were still going on]. Virtually, negotiation has totally ruptured.[18]

By Kuratomi:

Seven hospital employees have been terminated and Matsui has been arrested and his whereabouts is unknown.[19]

Watanabe was the chief proponent of the cancellation of the meeting on the ground of the time limit. He said:

I object to tomorrow's meeting. . . . Forty-five minutes for the mass meeting is absolutely not sufficient. I suggest that we give full support to the Negotiating Committee and the *Daihyo Sha Kai*. I request the Chairman to remain in his present capacity until the end for the sake of the colonists. . . . If the Army doesn't allow more than 45 minutes for the meeting we should notify the Army that the mass meeting will be postponed indefinitely.[20]

In spite of Watanabe's suggestion that the Army be informed of the decision to cancel the mass meeting, no hint of the decision reached either Army or WRA representatives. Residents had, however, been notified in their mess halls at breakfast time that there would be no mass meeting in the afternoon.

A few minutes before 2 P.M. Colonel Austin and Mr. Cozzens drove into the Japanese section, down the main firebreak to the outdoor stage. Army units had moved into position earlier. As they reached the stage about 30 foot soldiers formed in a circle around the stage at a distance of about 50 feet from it. Soldiers at the front of the stage fixed bayonets. Scout cars and soldiers took up positions in and along the firebreak at a distance of about two blocks from the stage. Armored scout cars and jeeps patrolled the streets of the entire colony.[21]

Austin and Cozzens mounted the outdoor stage and prepared to deliver their addresses. In spite of the lack of evacuee audience, they proceeded doggedly to give their speeches to an empty firebreak. A prominent WRA official from Washington, who was present, reported the event as follows:

Colonel Austin . . . arrived at the scene a little before the set time with a detachment of M.P.'s. Armed guards were stationed around the stage and armored cars made a cordon around the ground where an audience

---

[18] *Ibid.*
[19] *Ibid.*
[20] *Ibid.*
[21] WRA, "Tule Lake Incident, Report of Talks by Colonel Verne Austin and R. B. Cozzens at Outdoor Stage in Japanese Colony, November 13, 1943" (manuscript).

was supposed to gather. In preparing this space the M.P.'s had to clear out some kids playing football in part of the field, but the kids moved on willingly. At two o'clock, no one came and there was no sign of anyone coming to hear his speech. Like an Army man, true to his tradition, Austin began his speech. No one was there. Not a single soul! Colonel Austin spoke to the air. There were some young girls coming along. They stopped, looked on, and a few moments later moved on to resume their walk toward their destinations. There were other men who passed by while the Army officer spoke to the air, but they did not pay any attention and passed on. It was a pitiful sight which I cannot forget. I was there.[22]

In his speech Colonel Austin stated that the Army had assumed control of the Tule Lake Center

to provide for the safety and welfare of every resident. . . . The providing of . . . essentials [food, shelter and warmth] shall be directed so that it shall benefit the greatest number, *but in the manner as prescribed by the military*. . . . I shall continue to welcome visits and suggestions from *representative* groups. . . . The sooner normal center operations . . . can be resumed, the better. . . . We will make the determination of the number who are to be employed. . .

I know that the majority of you want peace and the opportunity to live unmolested by hoodlums and goon squads, as well as others who apparently lack respect for order. I expect to see to it that you have it. Those who instigated and participated in the disorders leading up to the Army's occupation shall be dealt with.[23]

He then read the following proclamation, which was later posted:

1. That between the hours of 7 P.M. and 6 A.M. all persons of Japanese ancestry, except as directed by the military, shall be within their place of residence. This shall not be interpreted to prevent access, however, to laundry and lavatory facilities.

2. No outdoor meetings or gatherings shall be permitted without express military approval.

3. Normal Center operations shall be maintained, insofar as is practicable, under direct military control and in the manner prescribed by the military authorities.

4. Persons of Japanese ancestry desiring to engage in useful work at the Center shall be accommodated as promptly as the situation permits.

5. No incoming or outgoing telephone or telegraph messages will be permitted without prior military approval.

6. Failure to observe strict adherence to all military regulations will result in disciplinary action forthwith.

7. All persons of Japanese ancestry shall reside in the apartments assigned to them by the WRA.[24]

[22] Field Notes, March 13, 1943.   [24] *Ibid.*
[23] WRA, *op. cit.*, Italics his.

Colonel Austin closed with the statement that "the military is prepared to meet any and all situations."[25]

Mr. Cozzens' prepared speech described Mr. Best as an able administrator and deplored the fact that, since segregation, "a few people from the colony attempted to cause as much trouble and discord as possible." He complimented the people for their orderly behavior on November 1, "when you did not really know the purpose behind your presence at the meeting," and expressed his belief that "the majority of the people in this colony do want to live in peace and harmony."[26]

At 2:13 P.M., Austin and Cozzens left the stage with their military escort. It was noted that some evacuees along their route "smiled, laughed, pointed and stared at the departing Army and WRA people."[27]

The *Daihyo Sha Kai* explained its cancellation of the mass meeting in the November 13 *Tulean Dispatch:*

> Feeling that there wasn't any necessity for a mass meeting, the sixty-odd block delegates present at the representatives meeting held yesterday afternoon at mess 18 voted unanimously to cancel the meeting scheduled for this afternoon at the community stage.
>
> The Negotiating Committee had planned to make a detailed report to the entire residents as to the proceedings of the conferences. However with the temporary termination of the negotiations with the Army officials, the committee members felt that there wasn't any report to be made to the center at such a meeting.
>
> The committee reported to the elected delegates present that the negotiations with the Army had been cancelled because the Army did not recognize the committee as true representatives of the people.
>
> According to the committee, the Army felt that they knew how many workers were needed in each division and the WRA, having worked with the Japanese, should know who should work in each division.
>
> The entire congregation expressed unanimous accord that there wasn't any necessity for negotiations if the Army had taken such an attitude.

In retaliation for this humiliating act of passive resistance by the residents, which it attributed to pressure from *Daihyo Sha Kai,* the Army moved quickly in an attempt to root out the antiadministration leadership and ordered the arrest of members of the Negotiating Committee, other leaders of *Daihyo Sha Kai* and prominent members of the Farm Group, coincident with a declaration that martial law was in effect. Two members of the Negotiating Com-

---

[25] *Ibid.*   [26] *Ibid.*   [27] *Ibid.*

mittee were forthwith arrested and placed in the stockade; four others were, for various reasons,[28] not listed as subject to arrest; Abe, Kuratomi and one other member of the Negotiating Committee, and Kodama and Seki, prominent assistants to the committee, escaped arrest by going into hiding.

Kato, who was arrested, wrote in his diary:

I was picked up on November 13. It was at 8:30 P.M. Four armed soldiers came. They searched me and brought me to the army compound. There they searched me again and took off all my clothes so that I was naked.[29]

With the forced dissolution of the Negotiating Committee, the *Daihyo Sha Kai* block representatives engaged in a desperate campaign to retain the backing of the residents. Their petition for a "vote of confidence" in the Negotiating Committee, which had been agreed upon the night before, was presented to the residents on the day of the arrest of the committee members. It was worded as follows:

VOTE OF CONFIDENCE—We, the undersigned, residents of Block —— have this day hereby resolved to vest full power and authority to the above-mentioned Negotiating Committee to study, discuss, negotiate, and exercise, incidental or conducive to the carrying out the objects and purposes, for which the Committee was formed; wherein to bring about amicable settlement of our general welfare in the Tule Lake Project. Signed and dated this 13th day of November, 1943.

The petition was presented at block meetings in such a way that anyone who did not sign would be plainly observed. Somewhat over half of the residents 18 years of age or older affixed their signatures, many out of support of their oppressed representatives, without apparent regard to the context or meaning of the resolution; others out of fear of censure from the more aggressive supporters. The feeling of pressure that must have borne on many of the signers is exemplified by the statement of a young Nisei woman, who signed against her will:

They had everything written down and would put it in front of your face and say, "You sign it!" If you didn't sign it the next thing you'd know, you'd be beaten to a pulp. It nearly broke my heart when I had to sign

---

[28] Pro *Daihyo Sha Kai* informants claim that one of them escaped arrest because he was a close friend of Watanabe; and that two others were exempted because of their favored status as old Tuleans.

[29] Field Notes, September 15, 1944.

it. They said, "Don't anyone walk out that door." I wanted to walk out but my husband wouldn't let me.[30]

Another young girl added:

I fooled them. I said I was under age and walked out.[31]

Once signed, the obligation to stand by the declaration was an important factor in the stubborn support given the *Daihyo Sha Kai* as the hardship of Army rule continued.

Simultaneously, however, the *Daihyo Sha Kai* campaign for popular support was embarrassed by a radical move made by an anonymous group, which, under the name of the "Second Negotiating Committee," issued a manifesto calling for a hunger strike and general resistance to the Army:

The only way to oppose and protest the Army's oppressive barbarous action is to internationalize[32] the problem from the angle of humanity.
1. Demand immediate releasement of all those detained.
2. Demand resignation en masse of WRA appointed personnel.
3. Demand immediate withdrawal of the Army from the center.
4. Close all mess halls from this afternoon and enter mass hunger strike. All mess chiefs are hereby instructed to distribute whatever available food supplies among block residents.
5. Even at the risk of a torn-down door, everyone should prevent the entrance of the Army into the living quarters when search is conducted.
6. Close all canteens.

Some members of the rapidly disintegrating *Daihyo Sha Kai* met in Ward VII[33] and countered with a resolution of their own, discrediting the manifesto and asking for continued confidence in the *Daihyo Sha Kai:*

1. Second Negotiating Committee's urgent instruction is premature.
2. All colonists are requested to remain cool and calm until the arrival of the Spanish Consul, at which time negotiations will be properly conducted in compliance with the International Agreement.
3. Do not close mess hall, despite many circulating rumors.

[30] Field Notes, September 14, 1944.
[31] *Ibid.*
[32] The reference to "internationalization" exemplifies the growing tendency of the protest factions to rely on the Japanese rather than on the American government for solution of problems, especially in connection with such radical measures as a hunger strike and general resistance to the Army. Retaliation by the Japanese government on American prisoners of war and internees was hoped for.
[33] Watanabe was said to be the chief instigator of this meeting.

4. Colonists should keep calm until the formulation of a definite future policy by the *Daihyo Sha Kai.*

5. Signatures of the colonists obtained yesterday should be withheld by *Daihyo Sha Kai* for the time being.

6. Colonists are requested to entrust full confidence to the block representatives [the *Daihyo Sha Kai* members] and refrain from believing rumors.

Meantime, Abe and Kuratomi attempted to direct policies from their hiding places, but met with increasing difficulties. The *Daihyo Sha Kai* tried to give them support by electing a temporary substitute committee to carry out the policies of the hidden leaders. This body was called the *Renraku-iin* (Communications Committee). It was selected by the *Daihyo Sha Kai,* not to replace the original committeemen, but rather to transmit the wishes of these leaders to the administration. As Kuratomi described the situation:

After the Negotiating Committee was put on the spot and was hunted down by the Army, the remaining block representatives (*Daihyo Sha Kai*) didn't feel they should elect any other body until the incident was satisfactorily closed. So they felt they shouldn't elect any committee to negotiate with the WRA and the Army and that was the greatest difficulty. As a substitute they had the so-called *Renraku-iin.* On it were Kami [and five others]. They made it clear that they would not negotiate except through the Negotiating Committee.[34]

This body met almost daily from November 14 to December 1 in a futile attempt to carry on *Daihyo Sha Kai* policies, but was split by internal dissention, uncertainty, fear, and by the difficulty of contacting Abe and Kuratomi. The members looked to the Spanish Consul as final court of appeal, and on November 15 sent him a telegram signed by Kami. On November 19 the Spanish Consul replied, "No instruction received from the Spanish Embassy, Washington. State the reason for my coming to Tule Lake Center." The *Renraku-iin,* after consultation, sent the following reply:

Colonists are no longer able to endure the inconveniences caused by the martial law and desire nothing but normalcy; we request for your immediate visit.[35]

The words "martial law" were deleted by the censor—a deletion that must have left the Spanish Consul temporarily in ignorance of what the colonists were "no longer able to endure."

---

[34] Field Notes, September 18, 1944.
[35] Minutes of the meeting, November 19, 1943.

Dissension between the *Renraku-iin* and the hiding Negotiating Committee members came into the open at the meeting of the *Daihyo Sha Kai* on November 16. Composed largely of Issei of the Watanabe clique, the new committee immediately ran into difficulties with the residents who "bring all their complaints and grievances to the [*Renraku-iin* for immediate correction, but] . . . don't realize that we have no authority to negotiate with the administration or the Army."[36] The ill-feeling between the *Renraku-iin* and the Negotiating Committee is clearly apparent in the statement made by Mr. Kami, a member of the former committee, in the minutes:

We, the [*Renraku-iin*], are trying our best not to override the authority of the Negotiating Committee. The decision of the matter rests upon the Negotiating Committee's jurisdiction. Yesterday, as I was waiting for the co-op truck to be transported to the warehouse where I work, Kato [Secretary of the *Daihyo Sha Kai*] approached me and made threatening remarks[37] to the effect that if I didn't support the Negotiating Committee, he will see to it that I be duly penalized. I have been doing my best to contact the Spanish Consul to visit this center. Yet, my integrity has been doubted by some Negotiating Committee [members] which I just can't stand for.[38]

Instructions from the hiding Negotiating Committee members were regarded as "undeniably dictatorial," and Tsukai, who was operating as messenger between the hidden leaders and their substitute committee, was instructed by an irate member to

go back and tell those spineless Negotiating Committee [members] to come out and work together with the [*Renraku-iin*]. In spite of the bad reputations [that we are getting] we are doing our utmost for the Daihyo Sha [Kai's] mission.[39]

The policy which the hidden leaders had decided upon for the residents was that of passive noncoöperation with the Army and WRA, continuance of the partial strike, refusal to betray the hidden leaders, and refusal to elect a new representative body. This policy was termed the *genjo-iji* or "status quo." These conditions were thoroughly debated, but finally accepted by the *Daihyo Sha Kai*.

---

[36] Minutes of the meeting, November 16, 1943.
[37] Kato presumably shouted from the stockade.
[38] Minutes of the meeting, November 16, 1943.
[39] *Ibid.*

On November 18 the Army made its last attempt to deal with the *Daihyo Sha Kai* on a partly negotiatory basis. A meeting was called which was attended by Colonels Austin and Meek, Mr. Cozzens, nine block managers and the *Daihyo Sha Kai*'s *Renraku-iin*. The Colonels attempted to place the maintenance of colony order on the shoulders of the block managers and to convince them that it was their duty to give up the hiding negotiators. This and all other responsibilities the block managers refused to accept. Colonel Austin stated unequivocally that the Army would never recognize the Negotiating Committee. The *Renraku-iin* reiterated its position that the Negotiating Committee had been duly elected by the Block Representatives for negotiating purposes and had the confidence of the residents.

Having failed to obtain coöperation from the block managers in apprehending the hiding men, the Army, on November 26, took another forceful step, a camp-wide search. This search was held ostensibly to look for contraband, hidden weapons, intoxicating liquor and rice from which sake could be made. WRA personnel was enlisted in this search. The Army formed

two principal teams which worked from each side of the camp towards the center firebreak . . . [using] a large number of soldiers to insure that no colony resident could slip back into an area that had been searched. Small squads of soldiers searched every barrack, top to bottom. Boxes were examined. Space between the ceiling and roof was looked into. Floors were tapped. . . . The Army confiscated all rice found in barracks.[40]

Among other items confiscated were wooden canes, axes, hatchets, binoculars, cameras, and radios with dials which had short-wave bands.[41] Locked boxes and suitcases were taken along if the owners were not present to open them at the time of the search.

In spite of the thoroughness of the search, four of the five leaders were not found. Seki, the investigator of the mess situation, was found hiding in a corner of a friend's room. Approximately ninety other persons were picked up, some of whom were people without Army identification cards but the majority were Hawaiian Kibei wanted by Internal Security.

---

[40] WRA, "Tule Lake Incident, Report of the Army Search of the Colony, November 26, 1943" (manuscript).

[41] No attempt was made to determine if the radios still had short-wave receiving equipment. A set from which the short-wave receiving mechanism had been removed was not contraband.

By the end of November the leaders-in-hiding found their position untenable. Instead of coöperation and assistance, they were receiving constantly hostile criticism from the *Renraku-iin*. Their hope that the Spanish Consul would appear, with assurance of the support of the Japanese government, had proven fruitless. They feared further loss of prestige if they continued in hiding while the apprehended leaders of *Daihyo Sha Kai* were suffering in the stockade. They determined, therefore, to give themselves up "in the interest of the people," after one final gesture to obtain popular support: a new petition which, they believed, stated their position clearly and would reinforce the vague "vote of confidence" received on November 13.[42] They, therefore, submitted the following resolution and petition, through the block managers, on November 29:

Whereas, the negotiation committee, which was duly elected by the block representatives who were in turn elected by the block residents is our sole mean of conducting negotiations necessary for the well-being of the residents of this center and especially in view of the fact that we, the residents of this center, give our undivided support to the above-mentioned committee, and,

Whereas, we, as the residents of this center know that the present situation was caused by the failure of the WRA administrators to heed our request not to take commodities out of the center warehouses in the middle of the night, and

Whereas, Mr. Raymond R. Best, the Project Director, gave as his excuse for calling in the military that a group of center residents threatened to kidnap the Caucasian personnel, which statement is a plain *false*. As a result many unnecessary arrests have conducted.

Therefore, in order to bring this unfortunate incident to a satisfactory and complete solution we, the center residents, feel that we must put forward the following resolutions to express our unqualified support of our representative committee.

RESOLUTION

1. Not to enter any negotiation with camp administrators other than through our negotiation committee.

2. To demand the wholesale resignations of the WRA appointed personnels, who were here prior to November 4, 1943.

3. To ask the withdrawal of the U.S. Army from the camp site.

4. To put into practice the promises made by Mr. Raymond Best, the Project Director, during the conference held on November 1, 1943, in Mr. Dillon S. Myer's presence.

5. To request for the immediate and unconditional release of all of the persons who are held without evidence.

[42] Field Notes, September 18, 1944.

6. Not to conduct further arrests in connection with this incident in the future.

7. To ask for the reëmployment of all the workers who were terminated without reason.

Be it further resolved that without the satisfactory conclusion of the above resolutions we will not consider this incident closed. We, the residents of the Tule Lake Center, 18 years of age or over, hereby signify our determined stand by our signatures on the 29th day of November, 1943.[43]

This petition, like the earlier one, was signed by about half the adult residents, although some of the conditions were held to be too radical even by those who signed. On December 1, however, the committee members decided to give themselves up, but they surrendered to the FBI rather than to the Army.[44] Their surrender was accompanied by considerable formality and was preceded by a meeting of Abe with the FBI, and an extremely dramatic meeting of the *Daihyo Sha Kai,* for which the Army had granted permission. This meeting was held at 9:30 on the morning of December 1 with no absentees. Watanabe was elected chairman to succeed Kuratomi. When the leaders entered they were greeted with thunderous applause.

At this meeting Abe said:

We, the Committee, have been fortunate to obtain signatures of majority of the colonists that our next problem is how to use this for the solution of the problem. We, four Negotiating Committee, have, in order to evade injustice of the Army, hidden. But realizing that the solution of the problem could not be initiated without us, we have decided to come out, by meeting with the FBI. We will submit to them a complete record of our activities up to date to Washington. Second, the responsible party or the key to the solution of the problem is Colonel Austin, who will be met immediately and we will do our best to make him expedite the solution. We shall force him to accept the resolution of the colonists for the mentioned two reasons. We are going to give up. Before we leave, there's one thing I'd like to plead to you and that is, since you have promised to give absolute support to the Negotiating Committee and recognize no other Committee than this one, I assume that I have authority to appoint an Acting Negotiating Committee during our absence to carry on the demands of the colonists. There will be four Acting Committee [members], which you must support as you have supported us in the past: Hachi, Block 49; Yokota, Block 32; Samejima, Block 36; and Koike, Block 18.[45]

[43] Community Analyst to Head of Community Analysis Section, December 10, 1943.

[44] It is said that they hoped thereby to impress the FBI with the necessity of investigating WRA.

[45] Minutes of the meeting, December 1, 1943.

Kuratomi reiterated the necessity of full support by the residents and recapitulated his analysis of the causes of the existing tensions:

Injustice done since the incident was the responsibility of the Army. On that day we met Myer and asked him to stop such practice as transporting food to the outside by night because colonists feel uneasy lest they be subjected to hunger. Their resentment may result to violence. Myer agreed. In spite of the November incident, Project Director broke this promise and called in the Army with silly excuse that some of the Caucasians were kidnapped. Colonel Austin also made similar statement, which is more than injustice. They have made unnecessary arrests. In order to solve problems of this nature, such would require eight demands or articles,[46] we have instructed all the block representatives to call meetings to get signatures of the colonists. With that resolution, we have consulted the WRA. As a result, WRA recognized the institution of all departmental committees with WRA pay to assist the management of the Center. Negotiating Committee also expressed desire of controlling the block managers, since they are directly connected with the colonists. WRA rejected this on the grounds that they are the coördinating body of the WRA and the colonists. We demanded mass termination of Caucasian personnel, including the Project Director, Peck, Pedicord, Kirkman, and Caucasian nurses and doctors. We also demanded an unconditional release of all those arrested and at the same time the stoppage of all future pick-ups. Since we have with us the resolution signed by most colonists of 18 years or over signifying that they were supporting us, we have sound grounds to proceed with our demands. Once again I shall meet with Colonel Austin to remind him that the incident has created international problem and that the Japanese Government itself is aware of this. With that in mind, I shall expend my effort to bring about amicable solution on the matter. I feel I must do this because after the war when negotiation between U.S. and Japan starts, Japanese government should not be placed in an embarrassing position. FBI is waiting for us and time is so valuable, we must leave now.[47]

The four men who surrendered were placed in a separate stockade in two tents which were very cold quarters for this time of year. Later they were removed to the larger stockade where, by this time, about 190 other detainees were housed.

After the four leaders were removed to the stockade, and the dissolution of the *Renraku-iin* was announced, the *Daihyo Sha Kai* continued with its meeting and ratified Abe's proposal for an "Acting Negotiating Committee," delegating complete authority to this committee to act for *Daihyo Sha Kai* and, through it, for the resi-

[46] Kuratomi meant the seven demands listed in the resolution of November 29.
[47] Minutes of the meeting, December 1, 1943.

dents. The new committee immediately attempted to resume negotiations with the Army, but the latter refused to recognize it. *Daihyo
Sha Kai,* therefore, met again on December 4 to consider the situation. This meeting, which was very well attended, gives an unusually clear picture of the *Daihyo Sha Kai* state of mind. Rebuffed by
the Army, their leaders held incommunicado, the depleted *Daihyo
Sha Kai* was now faced with extraordinarily difficult and important
decisions of policy. If it disbanded, leaving its leaders in the stockade, this would be a betrayal and an admission of guilt. Moreover,
it had no assurance that the leaders would be released if the body
disbanded. This, the most important point in the discussion, remained a major camp issue for more than six months.

Eventually three policies were suggested, and each had adherents:

(1) to continue the status quo
(2) to call a general strike
(3) to dissolve the *Daihyo Sha Kai*

Yokota, who was one of Abe's nominees, took the chair and
reported that the Army had announced (1) that the original "Negotiating Committee, held in the stockade . . . will not be permitted
to return to the center *under any condition,*"[48] and (2) that neither
the original nor the new Negotiating Committee would be recognized as representing the center.

One *Daihyo Sha Kai* member urged maintenance of status quo:

My suggestion is that if we maintain the status quo at this time and
Washington officials having been informed by the WRA, the Japanese
Government will not neglect making protests for the colonists, that U.S.
Government will be forced to settle this matter, which means the instruc-
tions will be issued from the higher ups. That may be one way to solve.[49]

Several other members favored a general strike, but there was
division of opinion as to whether the evacuees should be consulted
before or after the strike was declared. The more radical members
proposed approaching the evacuees with a *fait accompli,* justifying
themselves by the claim that the evacuees had, in any case, delegated
power to them, but indicating their underlying fear that "slackers
among the colonists" and the *inu* would, if given a chance, fail to
support the strike. Watanabe opposed this policy on the grounds
that a general strike might well destroy all possibility of negotia-

---

[48] Minutes of the meeting, December 4, 1943. Italics ours.   [49] *Ibid.*

tions; the detainees would then presumably be "transferred to another concentration camp" and would have no chance of being released to the center. He proposed instead that *Daihyo Sha Kai* be dissolved:

> Then those who are not connected with the *Daihyo Sha Kai* can continue negotiation for the releasement, center betterment and other problems. General strike will bring us misery and grievance, whereby we gain nothing. If there's no alternative, strike should be our last card until we have no other way out.[50]

Watanabe's proposal met with considerable opposition. Among others, the following objections were raised by various delegates: (1) "The Army claimed that they will recognize the representatives[51] but not the Negotiating Committee. . . . [This makes] it apparent that the Army's intention is to confuse the colonists. . . . To select a new body means to discredit the Negotiating Committee"; (2) "Just because the Army revoked the original Negotiating Committee, that doesn't mean that we have to select a new body"; (3) "If we select a new body, not only the [original] Negotiating Committee but those 200 [detainees] will be a sacrifice."[52] Agreement was finally reached that the only fair procedure was to consult the residents in advance of so weighty a decision.

Unanimous agreement was then reached to present three possible procedures (as formulated by Yokota) to the residents in each block for a vote:

1. To declare a general strike and at the same time enter a hunger strike.
2. By dissolution of the *Daihyo Sha Kai,* select a new body, then request the Army for the releasement of 200 persons.
3. Maintain status quo and maintain the present condition no matter how long, until the authorities give in. In other words let time solve the problem.[53]

That night the residents of each block met, and votes were cast behind locked doors. The results, as announced at the *Daihyo Sha Kai* meeting the next day, were

2 blocks undecided	4 blocks for dissolution
3 blocks for general strike	56 blocks for status quo[54]

---

[50] *Ibid.*

[51] The evacuees, of course, considered the *Daihyo Sha Kai* and the Negotiating Committee as their true representatives.

[52] Minutes of the meeting, December 4, 1943.

[53] *Ibid.*   [54] Minutes of the meeting, December 5, 1943.

Having obtained an overwhelming vote favoring the maintenance of status quo and desiring to strengthen the partial strike, the *Daihyo Sha Kai,* in its meeting of December 5, unearthed the smoldering issue of resentment against the Coöperative Enterprises, which, dominated by old Tuleans and favored by the administration, had become increasingly an object of suspicion both by *Daihyo Sha Kai* and by many of the residents. *Daihyo Sha Kai* feared that *inu* were operating against them through the Coöp. Residents had noted that fruits which appeared on purchase orders by WRA were conspicuously absent from the mess halls, but were on sale at the canteens. It was strongly suspected that Coöp officials, collaborating with WRA personnel, were diverting government-purchased goods for private profit. In addition, residents resented the Coöp policy of selling candy and other "luxury" items which most of the unpaid, striking evacuees found it difficult to provide, and equally difficult to deny their children. This policy accentuated the differences between the rich and the poor, who could not afford such items, some of which, such as fruits and vegetables, the evacuees felt should have been provided in the mess halls by WRA. It was considered desirable either to limit sales or to close the canteens completely during the period in which status quo must be maintained. A not uncommon attitude was expressed by a delegate, who said:

Canteen is the cause of all the misery. Since it's colonists' canteen, we have no reason to hesitate from closing it altogether. This will be only for a short while, since status quo will win [a victory over the administration].[55]

The more radical plan of closure was discarded, and it was agreed to approach the Coöperative Enterprises immediately and demand that they cease selling unessential "luxuries": chicken, fish, fruits (except oranges which were to be allowed because of their medicinal value), vegetables, candies, hardware, gifts, silk and woolen yardage, cakes and pastries, and ice cream and soft drinks during the winter months.[56]

When the *Daihyo Sha Kai* representatives met with the Coöp Board of Directors on December 6, they admitted that their demands had not been approved by popular vote. Their chief argument for restriction of the canteen was that all food should be

---

[55] *Ibid.*   [56] Minutes of the meeting, December 6, 1943.

furnished by WRA. The Board replied that it, as "an elected body which is governed by the By-Laws and the members," could not decide this matter. It must be referred to the ward assemblies of members of the Coöperative.[57]

The Coöperative Enterprises, in fact, faced ruin if the demands of *Daihyo Sha Kai* were met. Their total sales in November were more than $110,000. If the items listed by *Daihyo Sha Kai* had been withdrawn, it is estimated that their gross sales would have been not much more than $40,000.[58] When, on December 10, a second conference was held between the Coöp Board and *Daihyo Sha Kai* representatives, the vice-president of the Coöp, who presided at the meeting, pointed out that if this proposed step were taken it would mean that the Coöp would be forced to sever connections with purchasing firms, that these connections could not be renewed, that the redemption of certificates of indebtedness would be postponed and that nearly 100 employees would have to be terminated.

A spokesman for the *Daihyo Sha Kai* said:

Let me tell you our side of the story. Up to November 3, negotiations with the WRA officials were progressing very satisfactory, but after the departure of Mr. Myer, Director of WRA, negotiations was abruptly terminated by them. To date the WRA has notified the *Daihyo Sha Kai* that they no longer recognize the *Daihyo Sha Kai* as representatives of the colonists. In the meantime, a great number of evacuees lost jobs and on top of that, up to date nearly 250 persons were picked up and detained in the Army quarters. It is evident that the WRA is about to give in to our demands . . . in spite of the fact that we are not recognized. Co-op does not cooperate with us. Too indifferent. Work daily without considering the difficulty encountered by the people who are without jobs. That's not fair. I presume you Co-op officials are evacuees, and of course, think of your native land. We are at war with this country, I want you to remember that, that is why we are asking you to cooperate. If you want to make money you should have gone out where there is opportunity.[59]

Replying for the Coöp, after consideration of the practical issues, Milton Sasaki, the executive secretary, said:

Referring to . . . statements that the Co-op's representatives, as a whole, are busy with the effort to make money only, and ignore the time and condition of this center, we want to make it clear to you that as far as

---

[57] *Ibid.*

[58] Board of Directors, Tule Lake Coöperative Enterprises, mimeographed statement, December 12, 1943.

[59] Minutes of the meeting, December 10, 1943.

loyalty and the seriousness and integrity are concerned, we allow no one to question us. We, the Board members and the Executives, on behalf of the 7500 Co-op members and colonists as a whole, must prevent the Co-op from disaster. I want you gentlemen to understand just that.[60]

It was decided to put the issue to a popular vote. The Coöp engaged in a hurried propaganda campaign, and distributed a mimeographed justification of its action to its members, in which the following points were emphasized: (1) If the purchases of many of the "so-called luxury items" were "cancelled, the difficulty of renewing the quota at a later date will be insurmountable"; (2) the evacuees would then have to buy these items from mail order stores at higher prices; (3) the financial status of the Coöp would become so precarious that 100 employees would have to be discharged; (4) under these circumstances it would be highly questionable if the Coöp would be able to redeem its outstanding certificates of indebtedness; (5) if the present camp difficulties could be solved in the near future, "the time will eventually arrive when the people will be more able to afford some of the things used in comforting our lives in this center, which is otherwise very much dull and sullen."[61]

The returns on the vote do not lend themselves to a simple interpretation. In the first place, voting was limited to Coöp members, who were by no means a representative sample of the general population. As of September 30, the Coöp membership was only 3,417. By this time the outward movement of "loyal" Tuleans, except for a few hundred essential workers, had been completed. Since the newly arrived transferees had not yet had time to join the organization, it is safe to assume that these were, almost without exception, old Tuleans. By November 30 total membership was reported as 6,393, and by December 31 as 6,508. As of the date of the referendum, therefore, membership could not have exceeded 6,500. Assuming that *all* of the increase in membership consisted of transferees, old Tuleans comprised at least 52 per cent of the potential voters, and it is probable that their proportion was considerably higher than this. Since at this time the proportion of old Tuleans in the total population was around 42 per cent, it is clear that the population eligible to vote on the Coöp issue was overweighted with old Tuleans, underweighted with transferees.

---

[60] *Ibid.*

[61] Board of Directors, Tule Lake Coöperative Enterprises, mimeographed statement, December 12, 1943.

In the second place, the popular vote was recorded for only 29 blocks, while 22 reported the result merely as "unanimous vote," "with condition" or "recommendation" (unspecified) on the issue, and 13 refused to hold a meeting. Of the 29 blocks reporting the number voting, the average number of votes recorded per block was 60. If the other 22 voting blocks had the same average number voting, the total popular vote must have been around 3,000. It seems obvious, therefore, that somewhat less than half of the Coöp members acceded to the request to vote on the issue.

In the third place, interpretation of the stand of the 13 blocks which refused to hold the election is open to some question. It seems reasonable to infer that, since the Coöp had initiated the procedure, refusal to vote indicated an antagonistic attitude toward the Coöp.

The blockwise status of votes can be broken down as follows:

I	II	III	IV
Clearly favoring Coöp (popular vote or unanimous decision)	Favoring Coöp but setting up "conditions"	Clearly opposed to Coöp (popular vote)	Refusing to vote
38	8	5	13

The administration apparently added classes I and II and set them in a ratio to class III, completely neglecting class IV. On this basis, the result was interpreted by WRA and by the Coöp officials as a "9 to 1" victory for the Coöp and "the best job . . . to date . . . of discrediting" the *Daihyo Sha Kai*.[62] If, however, we assume that only Class I represented an attitude favorable to the Coöp proposal and that all other classes were more or less antagonistic,[63] the ratio becomes a "1½ to 1" victory, a result far more consistent with later cleavages than the official interpretation of an overwhelming victory for the Coöp and an overwhelming defeat of *Daihyo Sha Kai*,

[62] Community Analyst to Head of Community Analysis Section, December 20, 1943 (appended to his December 10 report).

[63] A procedure that the Community Analyst later followed, by implication, when the more important community-wide issue of maintaining status quo was voted upon. Thus in his report of January 15, 1944 (appended to his January 14 report), to the Head of the Community Analysis Section, he refers to these classes as indicating "more or less negative results."

and as proof of WRA's constant contention that the *Daihyo Sha Kai* had never had a strong following in camp.

On the day of the vote on the Coöp issue the Spanish Consul, accompanied by a State Department representative, made his long-awaited visit. In a series of meetings[64] initiated largely by the pro-*Daihyo Sha Kai* element, these men made lengthy speeches in which they emphasized the international aspects of the problems developing out of the Tule Lake disturbances, and proposed as a solution the abolishing of the old Negotiating Committee and the election, by popular vote, of a new committee "composed of members in proportion to the various classes in the community; that is, Issei members should elect Issei, and Nisei should elect Nisei representatives."[65] The proposed committee was to be selected under the supervision of the Army. The residents paid little attention to the speeches, but pressed their various demands and complaints and vociferously expressed the deep resentment they felt because the Consul had delayed so long his coming to Tule Lake, in spite of the many urgent requests of the evacuees. Underlying all their demands was the urgency of recognition of the Negotiating Committee and release of the stockade detainees. Spokesmen for the residents insisted that the Army's treatment of the Negotiating Committee be reported without delay to Japan, e.g.:

They want you to report to Japan the fact that our Negotiating Committee has been detained by the Army from November 4.[66] That is our demand. They don't want shall or will business, they want you to make sure.[67]

The Spanish Consul gave no assurance of compliance with the residents' demands, other than a halfhearted promise that the matter would be referred to the Spanish Embassy and "if it is necessary, they will report it to the Japanese government. If they think it is not important, they will not do so." Spokesmen also insisted that the Consul meet with the detained Negotiating Committee members, and they raised the issue of status as Japanese citizens for Nisei who, "even if they are American citizens should be equal as

[64] The meeting described here is the only one of seven held during the two-day period for which minutes were available.

[65] Minutes of the meeting, December 13, 1943.

[66] As a matter of fact, the first arrests of members of the Negotiating Committee occurred on November 13.

[67] Minutes of the meeting, December 13, 1943.

Japanese nationals." When the Consul insisted that his protection extended to Japanese subjects only, and the State Department representative insisted that "no American subject can throw off his citizenship," the pertinent question was raised: "why did the United States government put American citizen Nisei in camp?" The reply was recorded as:

That was done for the security of the United States in time of war. If they think I am a dangerous person they would put me in the camp also.[68]

The temper of the meeting was reported by a young Nisei girl (George Kuratomi's fiancee):

The people didn't listen to their speeches. As soon as the speech was over, they'd yell, "That's not what we want. We want the Negotiating Committee!" All through the meeting the Consul would get up and say something and the people would say, "Oh to hell with you, we want the Negotiating Committee!"[69]

The conference between the detained Negotiating Committee members and the Spanish Consul, in the presence of Army representatives, was equally unsuccessful, according to Kuratomi's account:

We spoke with the Spanish Consul on December 13th or 14th in the Administration building because the people in the colony requested that he see us. Colonel Austin and Lieutenant Forbes were present at this meeting. I believe there were nine of us [Negotiating Committee and Executive Board] present.

The conversation was very interesting in that we asked Colonel Austin for the reason of our detention. His contention was that he thought we were trouble makers and that was the reason he was keeping us locked up. We asked, "Can the Army, just because the commandant thinks a portion of the people are trouble makers, can they detain us?" He didn't make a very clear reply and had to think a long time.

We also asked what was the evidence for our apprehension and detention. He thought a long moment and said, "We'll get the evidence while we keep you boys in the stockade."[70]

At this meeting, Kato reports, Colonel Austin remarked, "I think you are troublemakers and therefore you are troublemakers."[71]

When it became apparent that there was no disposition to accede

---

[68] *Ibid.*
[69] Field Notes, January 10, 1945.
[70] Field Notes, January 10, 1945.
[71] Field Notes, September 15, 1944.

to the Spanish Consul's appeal for the resignation of the Negotiating Committee, the Army, at the suggestion of WRA, began to arrest and detain the Block Representatives, the main body of the *Daihyo Sha Kai*. Some of these men attempted to go into hiding but on December 17 seven were picked up and on December 18, fifteen more.[72] There were well over 200 persons confined in the stockade by this time.

The Spanish Consul, representing Japan, had been the last resort. Failing to obtain either sympathy or encouragement from this source, chagrined by increasing signs of lack of support from the general population, and faced with concrete evidence of the Army's intention to apply even more drastic measures than in the past, the stockade detainees took matters into their own hands, and, on December 31, began a protest hunger strike. The precipitating cause was a minor conflict between several detainees and the Army officer in charge of the stockade concerning responsibility for the lack of cleanliness in the living quarters. When the detainees involved in this episode were isolated in a "bull pen," some 200 others signed the following document and began a hunger strike which lasted "six days and two meals."

As of supper, December 31, 1943.

We the undersigned have solemnly vowed to undergo hunger strike until such time as everyone here in the stockade is released back to the colony simultaneously and unconditionally!

Kuratomi later reconstructed the events of the day as follows:

On the morning of December 31, the Army made a sanitary inspection of the stockade and as a result of this inspection Lieutenant Shaner and a corporal came into the stockade and complained to Kato about the unsanitary condition of the latrine, shower and the barracks. Kato countered by saying that he did not have the necessary implements of sanitation, therefore he demanded that if he were to be given buckets, brooms and mops and the tubs for laundry he could have the place cleaner. Somehow Kato's attitude appeared insulting to the Army, and he was confined in the bull pen. The same complaint was directed against Tada, who was in charge of mess hall in the stockade at that time. When questioned about the unsanitary condition in the mess hall, Tada made similar demands as Kato. He, too, was sent to the bull pen. The detainees became angry at this act on the part of the Army, and asked the reason for having these two men sent to the bull pen and in the course of the argument detainees and the

[72] Community Analyst to Head of Community Analysis Section, December 20, 1943. (Appended to his December 10 report.)

soldiers became very heated and it was decided on the part of the detainees that they would not answer the roll call which was conducted at about 1 o'clock afternoon each day. The corporal's answer was that the Army was prepared to meet any such situation and that if the detainees did not report for roll call, proper action would be taken to have them out for roll call. At this point, Yamada said: "You just try and do it," which evidently irritated the corporal. When the time came for the roll call, none of the detainees went out. Soldiers numbering about 75 were called in at the request of Lieutenant Shaner, and Colonel Austin appeared in person. Yamada was immediately taken to the bull pen for his run-in with the corporal in the morning. Lieutenant Shaner reprimanded the detainees for the incidents in the morning and said to the effect that "anybody else who feels that he wants to join those men in the bull pen, step out." To the embarrassment of Lieutenant Shaner, everybody stepped forward. This was the last straw, and Lieutenant Shaner immediately ordered all the foodstuffs to be removed and said that the detainees would be put on a bread and water diet. Two trucks were brought in and the foodstuffs in the mess hall, as well as the presents that the colonists had sent in to the detainees over the holiday season, were picked up. Among these gifts were apples, oranges, nuts, cakes and pies, also about 300 cartons of cigarettes. Valuables such as money, fountain pens, wrist watch, etc., were also taken. The detainees in the front row were asked by the soldiers to remove the foodstuffs from the barracks to the truck. Some detainees hesitated and, being slow in their actions, were kicked and prodded with bayonets. This was the direct reason which started the detainees on the hunger strike, starting on December 31.[73]

Kato reported his own behavior as follows:

I really talked to the Army and gave them a piece of my mind. I said I didn't know the United States Army was like this. Lieutenant Shaner got burned up. He brought in soldiers and told me to pack up. He put me in the bull pen.[74]

On January 4 some of the strikers weakened in their determination to continue, and two days later the leaders decided to abandon the hunger strike.

The matter of confiscated gifts and valuables was taken up with the Army at a meeting of the Divisional Responsible Men[75] on January 17, 1944. According to the minutes

Colonel [Austin] was questioned whether the story concerning thefts of many articles, such as tobaccos, money, watches, fountain pens, etc. by the

[73] George Kuratomi, Statement, November 16, 1945.
[74] Field Notes, September 15, 1944.
[75] Evacuee representatives of work units. See Chapter VI for the role they played in community affairs.

soldiers during the Army's search of the stockade barracks recently was factual. The Colonel admitted that "lots of things were taken, but many were returned. Theft of money? I question money. I doubt whether people ever leave money in their barracks. I don't question watches or tobaccos."

By the end of December the residents had been on a partial strike for six weeks, most of this time under the rigid conditions of martial law. The strike had been entered into as a protest against the suppressive tactics initiated by the Army after the November 4 incident, involving the separation of evacuees from the administrative area, enforced by soldiers with bayonets, tanks, and tear-gas bombs, "man-proof" barbed-wire fences, watchtowers, and searchlights; the arbitrary curtailment of essential work crews; and the arrests and incarceration of leaders.

The mechanism through which the protest was organized was the *Daihyo Sha Kai,* whose leaders attempted to direct procedures first from hiding, later from the stockade where they had been detained. As time went on, however, they began to lose their precarious hold on the general population. In late November, in spite of great pressure, only half the adult residents signed a petition pledging unqualified support to the Negotiating Committee, although a few days later the block residents in a secret vote gave a clear majority favoring the continuance of status quo. When, shortly after this, the *Daihyo Sha Kai* adherents tried to gain further support for the strike by forcing the canteens to restrict sales, the people voted them down. When, as a last resort, they turned toward the Spanish Consul for support from the Japanese government, their demands met a cold reception and a stern warning that their tactics might have international repercussions and slow down or negate the possibility of exchange of repatriates to Japan. And a hunger strike initiated by the stockade detainees failed to win popular support.

The burden of maintaining status quo, involving, as it did, unemployment, idleness, impoverishment for so many, was bearing heavily on the people. As Niiyama, a member of Civic Organizations, expressed it:

During those dark moments of camp life many people with children had no shoes, no money, no clothing. Some of the children were beginning to go barefooted. The camp condition was critical.[76]

[76] Field Notes, January 8, 1945.

Similarly, Tsuruda said:

Their finances were petering out. Here—they're still paying off on October checks [statement made February 1]. Now these fellows who were not working got no clothing allowance, no welfare, no income.[77]

And Higashi describes similar hardship:

Criticism grew as status quo dragged on. People had no clothes. They tried to get their shoes fixed. . . . With the canteens and things, the people were going broke.[78]

In addition many people lived in constant fear of being picked up and confined in the stockade, as exemplified by the following statements:

I'll say this: I think the Army went too far in sticking those people in the stockade. My husband almost got pulled in. He was as much against *Daihyo Sha Kai* as I was. A neighbor came and told us that the Internal Security had come and that he should hide.
I said, "He can't hide." I even got his suitcase packed with pajamas, tooth-brush and a deck of cards. But they didn't come. However, they pulled in many innocent people.[79]

A bachelor Kibei, transferee from Poston, wrote to a friend:

Everything seems and looks cold and still and melancoline. . . . Everything seems unchangeable like yesterday. The confine has not cleared out yet. No parcel and no money order can send out and every letters has examined. Three Niseis who came from Hawaii to live in this block were arrested this morning at 3 A.M. If you will not hear from me for the quite few days in the near future, you must understand that I am arrested. Don't forget that it will be possible.[80]

Finally, the prisonlike atmosphere of camp and the cessation of all recreational activities resulted in feelings of extreme uneasiness and deep depression.

A young Nisei girl said:

I just thought, "What's this camp coming to?" After the Army came in I really felt like a prisoner . . . All during the time when the Army was controlling the camp, naturally, we were sad. There were no activities. Everything stopped. We had a curfew. Oh, it was a miserable life. . . . We got baloney for Thanksgiving.[81]

---

[77] Field Notes, February, 1944.
[78] Field Notes, April, 1944.
[79] Field Notes, September 14, 1944.
[80] Field Notes, November 26, 1943.
[81] Field Notes, August 30, 1944.

A married Kibei woman wrote:

Right now curfew is in effect and martial law at the same time. No one can go out from 7 P.M. to 6 A.M. Anyway, there's no place to go, it's too cold. . . . Right now there's no movies or *Engei Kai* [Japanese entertainment] or anything. . . . The army is still in: they're delivering all the vegetables and food stuff to the mess halls accompanied by armored cars, jeeps . . . Perhaps this letter will be censored, if so tell me.[82]

Under these conditions many longed for "normalcy," even if it meant yielding in matters of principle, and WRA was equally anxious to get rid of the Army and to reëstablish a working relationship with the evacuees. Mr. Best had established an Advisory Council, composed of project officials, before the November disturbances, and to this body he delegated responsibility for reinstituting rapport with the evacuees. They, in turn, looked to the leaders of the crystallizing *Daihyo Sha Kai* opposition, and first approached a group from the Civic Organizations (the central organization of block managers) on December 11. Two old Tuleans, Mayeda and Niiyama, along with Kitagawa of Rohwer and Minami of Heart Mountain, met with the Advisory Council. Their attitude toward *Daihyo Sha Kai* was extremely antagonistic and rapport was quickly established between them and the Advisory Council. They reported to the council that the Negotiating Committee represented the interests of a minority only; that the recent trouble had arisen because the "Jerome faction," which, they said, was organized prior to arrival at Tule Lake,[83] dominated the Negotiating Committee; and that the basic reason for popular acquiescence in the strike, was fear of terroristic actions by the *Daihyo Sha Kai* supporters. Niiyama said:

A lot of people would [like to] speak up . . . but they have to sleep in the colony at night; it would be different if we didn't have to live there.[84]

After the successful meeting of December 11, the Advisory Council drew in other prominent evacuees known to be critical of *Daihyo Sha Kai* policies. Most prominent among the newcomers were

---

[82] Field Notes, November 26, 1943.

[83] Kuratomi and others deny that the Jeromites were formally organized before coming to Tule Lake. There were informal cliques, existing prior to segregation, which tended to persist after arrival in Tule Lake.

[84] Community Analyst to Head of Community Analysis Section, December 20, 1943 (appended to his December 10 report).

Oyama of the Civic Organizations; Sasaki,[85] Kami,[86] Matsushita, and Noma of the Coöperative Enterprises; Kunisaki of Housing, and Watanabe, who, although formerly prominent members in *Daihyo Sha Kai,* had become increasingly critical of its policies and tactics. Meetings between these men and the Advisory Council took place almost daily during late December and early January, with discussions centering on ways and means of breaking status quo. Meanwhile, the Army continued to arrest alleged *Daihyo Sha Kai* supporters, "much to the satisfaction of the opposition groups.[87]

Some of the evacuees included in these meetings volunteered names of people whom they considered troublemakers. The administration and the Army regarded this as a sign of willingness on the part of the evacuees to collaborate with the officials. The evacuee leaders who were drawn in by the Advisory Council were preponderantly old Tuleans, and they represented vested interests. A number of them had remained in Tule Lake for purely opportunistic reasons. Niiyama, for example, was the father of five young children and the sole support of aged parents who wanted to return to Japan. Several of these men decided that Tule Lake was no place for them and were discussing the possibilities of resettlement. With some of them, too, the pattern of close coöperation with the administration had been established before segregation. They seemed to share the belief that improvement of the miserable conditions under which the people were living could best be achieved by working, in a conciliatory manner, with the WRA personnel.

By January 7 the coöperation of a group of some forty "responsible men" of the various sections and divisions, had been secured (including evacuee foremen of the Packing Shed, the Coal Crew, Garbage Crew, Maintenance, Time Keeping, Payroll and Account-

---

[85] Sasaki's militant stand on the luxury issue antagonized *Daihyo Sha Kai* supporters. The Community Analyst wrote that several days after the vote on the luxury issue, "Mr. [Sasaki] was threatened with personal attack and bodily harm. On learning this, he went directly to the headquarters of [the *Daihyo Sha Kai*] and informed the gentry assembled there that if any bodily harm befell his person, the organization and the gentlemen in particular would be sorry for it." (Community Analyst to Head of Community Analysis Section, December 29, 1943.)

[86] Kami was a member of the *Daihyo Sha Kai* and of the *Renraku-iin* but later resigned.

[87] Community Analyst to Head of the Community Analysis Section, December 29, 1943.

ing, Placement, Coöperatives, Civic Organizations, Housing, Clothing Unit, Construction, Furniture Industry, Mess Management,
Warehouse, and the Garage) and a joint meeting with Army and
WRA representatives took place. It was decided that a resolution
for the abandonment of *Daihyo Sha Kai*'s policy of status quo and
in favor of a general return to work be prepared and that members
of the various divisions should meet separately and decide whether
to accept or reject the resolution. The result would then be announced to the evacuees and a resolution be put to a secret vote in
each block. Since the divisional vote was markedly in favor of the
proposal, a committee of seven, including Kitagawa, Sasaki,
Oyama, Takayama, Sugano, Kami, and Minami, was chosen by the
Divisional Responsible Men to make plans for the taking of the
referendum.

Faced with the necessity of working so fast that the remnants of
the *Daihyo Sha Kai* would not have time to organize an effective
opposition, the committee members scheduled the referendum for
the evening of January 11. On the morning of the election they
distributed a mimeographed justification of the proposed action
throughout the project. The evacuees were asked to support the
following resolution, prepared by the Divisional Responsible Men:

BE IT RESOLVED THAT, as a vital preliminary measure in liquidating this so-called status quo as maintained by the *Daihyo Sha* [*Kai*] and in
order to bring forth normal condition to this colony in the very immediate future, every colonists, respectful and peace-loving residents, should
return to work immediately.

It was pointed out that the *Daihyo Sha Kai* representatives had
"utterly failed in their negotiation"; that the Army would not recognize them; that they had been unable to secure the successful
intervention of the Spanish Consul; that far from achieving the
release of the original detainees, they "were wholly unable to check
the increasing number of persons being detained each day"; and
that above all,

they have conclusively failed in their principal and initial purpose of bettering the condition of the center.

At present increasing number of families are suffering economically
and they are requesting for relief through the Social Welfare Department
and the Spanish Consulate. C'est domage! Every colonist in this Center
has no other desire than to exist as a true Japanese.

Every colonist in this Center should keep in one's mind that such a self-imposed suffering in itself does not reflect upon one's loyalty to his country.[88]

The men responsible for the resolution pledged themselves to two aims:

1. Equitable distribution of employment
"It is our duty to materialize an equitable distribution of employment because it is the principal source of income for most of the colonists residing in this center. After restoring this center back to normal condition, a plan can be worked out in which there will be employment possibility for the greatest number of residents."

2. Aid in obtaining the release of persons detained in the stockade
"The return of the colony to normal condition will create a favorable atmosphere where the justifiable release of detained colonists will become a greater possibility.

It is unwise contention that if the status quo is liquidated, the persons detained will be deemed as guilty. If the status quo is maintained, there will be no possibility whatsoever for negotiation for the release with either the WRA or the Army. Not only that, but also it has become evident that the longer the status quo is maintained, the more colonists would be looking out of the stockade."[89]

Voting was by secret ballot, with soldiers present at every polling place. Of 8,713 valid ballots cast, 4,593 were against, 4,120 in favor of status quo. Thus the decision to return to "normalcy" was won by a plurality of only 473. Blockwise tabulation also showed a relatively slight margin, some 35 blocks against, 28 favoring the maintenance of status quo, and 1 block refusing to vote.[90]

Daihyo Sha Kai remnants who opposed return to work, distributed a report challenging these results. Calling themselves the "Nippon Patriotic Society," they claimed that the vote was taken by force and that unopened ballots were carried away by the Army. By their estimate 31 blocks favored status quo, 29 opposed it, 4 were not clear, and the residents of 1 block refused to vote.

Whereas there is no evidence to support the claim that force was used during the voting, it is a fact that the Army had picked up a

---

[88] "What Is This So-Called 'Status Quo'?" Mimeographed statement distributed by Divisional Responsible Men, January 7, 1944.

[89] "The Motive and Course of Events of the Meeting of Division and Section Heads." Mimeographed statement distributed by Divisional Responsible Men, January 7, 1944.

[90] Community Analyst to Head of the Community Analysis Section, January 15, 1944 (appended to his January 14 report).

number of *Daihyo Sha Kai* members and sympathizers early that morning. Thus the impression that a vote in favor of status quo might lead to arrest undoubtedly impeded freedom of action in some sections of the camp.

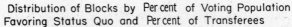

Distribution of Blocks by Per cent of Voting Population
Favoring Status Quo and Per cent of Transferees

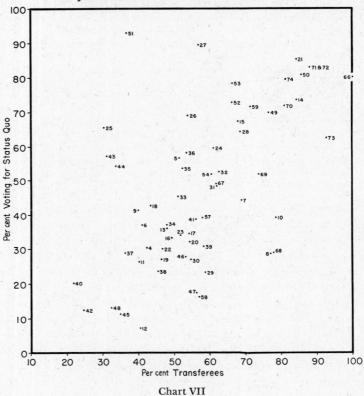

Chart VII

Statistics of the vote cast for and against status quo are available for all blocks except Block 56 which refused to hold a meeting. Chart VII shows that a positive relationship existed between proportions favoring status quo and proportions of transferees per block; or, conversely, between the proportion favoring "return to normalcy" and the proportion of old Tuleans. This relationship, based on 62 block units, is expressed as $r = .54$, a statistically significant result. It strengthens the assumption that the active protest faction was overweighted with the newer arrivals who, as has been shown, had a controlling interest in *Daihyo Sha Kai* and who were still willing to endure the hardships of a partial strike, while old Tuleans, more firmly established in the community, were predisposed to assume an attitude of accommodation to the administration-sponsored proposal of resumption of work. Nevertheless, the wide scatter in the observations reflects also the fact that many Tulean blocks voted strongly for status quo, while a number of transferee-concentrated blocks favored its abolition.

As soon as the vote had been counted, plans were drawn up to effectuate the return of the workers to their jobs. The Committee of Seven,[91] which had prepared the referendum, was officially recognized on January 15 by the administration and by the Army to coöperate with the Advisory Council in these plans, and it became known as the "Coördinating Committee." Simultaneously, the Army announced the lifting of martial law, withdrew most of the soldiers from the center, and returned the management of Tule Lake, except for the stockade, to the WRA personnel.

---

[91] The "Committee of Seven" requested official recognition by the administration at a meeting of the Divisional Responsible Men on January 12, 1944. Of 31 "responsible men" present at this meeting, 24 were old Tuleans and 7 were transferees. Of the 7 transferees, 4 were appointed to the Coördinating Committee, while only 3 were old Tuleans. The executive secretary, Sasaki, was an old Tulean, however, and it is clear that the committee received its backing from the Tulean rather than from the transferee bloc.

Chapter VII

ACCOMMODATION

Rise and Fall of the Coördinating
Committee

Fʀᴏᴍ ɪᴛꜱ ɪɴᴄᴇᴘᴛɪᴏɴ as a Relocation Project, Tule
Lake was split by dissensions reflecting the sharp contrasts in the
experiences and attitudes of its population. The split was, in general, between those who had progressed farthest along the path of
assimilation to American behavior patterns and those who were
oriented more to Japanese culture. The extent of segregation, discrimination and competition, or of tolerance, acceptance and coöperation by the Caucasian majority group prior to evacuation had
had much to do with the early camp dichotomization into accommodators and protestors. The earliest dichotomy was, broadly
speaking, Northwesterners as accommodators, versus Californians
as protestors. This territorial dichotomy, however, was blurred by
clusterings of certain interest and circumstantial groups. Of the
Japanese Americans educated primarily in American schools and
oriented to American culture, the majority clustered around the
"accommodation pole." They were predominantly Nisei; but
among them were minorities consisting of the older immigrants
(Issei), particularly those with American-born children and with
property interests in America, and other minorities composed of
the American-born, Japanese-educated second generation (Kibei),
particularly those who before evacuation had secured a foothold
in the American economy.

At the protest pole were clusters of those whose assimilation had
been weakest: immigrant bachelors who had "followed the crops"
as seasonal laborers for decades, and Japanese-educated, second-

generation Buddhists who had been hampered in economic and social adjustments by linguistic and cultural barriers between them and the Caucasian Americans. At this pole, too, were smaller clusters of the American-born, American-educated—some of them highly intellectual, some of them emotionally unstable—who had become embittered and disillusioned by the abridgment of their rights as American citizens.

The Registration crisis spurred resettlement of many of those who clustered at the early accommodation pole: first the active JACL members, then others of the more highly assimilated Nisei, Northwesterners and urbanites, far out of proportion to their numerical importance in the population. Segregation speeded up the process of withdrawal of the original accommodators, with the movement of vast numbers of the residuum of Northwesterners and urbanites, leaving behind a disproportion of Californians, ruralites, Kibei Buddhists, immigrant bachelors, the dispossessed in general, as well as a very large number of families, usually with many children, who, with no appreciation of the stigma of "disloyalty," simply resisted change and held tight to their "homes" in Tule Lake. While segregation was in process, this residual group consolidated its position, took over key positions, appropriated the more desirable housing units, built up rapport with the administration, and eventually established vested interests in the project.

The first dichotomy after segregation, then, found the previously protesting "old Tuleans" clustered around the "accommodation pole," while the incoming transferees from other projects, unable to find the jobs they wanted, overcrowded into what was often the less desirable housing, suffering from the psychic shock of another "evacuation," beset by the uncertainties and fears which their more positive decision to be "disloyal" had engendered, were found in the main at or near the "protest pole."

With the automobile accidents, the death of Kashima, the unsatisfactory compensation decision, the farm work stoppage, the arrival of "loyal" harvesters, who as strikebreakers were paid as much in two days as the strikers had received in a month and were fed with food taken from the project warehouses, unity of the whole population was achieved. Newcomers and old Tuleans merged in a general protest against what they conceived to be overwhelming injustice. This unity was short-lived, for the newcomers, achieving dominance in the selection of the Negotiating Committee of *Daihyo Sha Kai,* once more split the interest-groups in the community. When the violence of November 4 occurred, and the Army moved in to administer the project, the *Daihyo Sha Kai* was able to obtain an appreciable majority in favor of passive resistance and a partial strike, which became known as the maintenance of status quo. When their leaders were arrested and detained in a stockade under military guard, however, the *Daihyo Sha Kai* began a losing fight to hold the population at its pole. Successive "votes of confidence" in the Negotiating Committee were signed by scarcely more than half the adults. Status quo was maintained against increasing popular opposition. A radical proposal to extend the effect of passive resistance by restricting the sale of articles in the canteen was defeated by the voting members of the Coöperative Enterprises. Appeal to the Spanish Consul to strengthen its position by assuring the backing of the Japanese government met with a cold denial. Efforts to negotiate with the Army or WRA for release of those detained in the stockade were fruitless. Burdened by the inconveniences and hardships of status quo and the oppression of Army rule, most of the old Tuleans and many of the transferees veered away from the protest pole. When a group dominated by old Tuleans proposed a conciliatory solution and achieved recognition by the administration, status quo was defeated in a popular vote. The Army withdrew, and WRA, with the accommodation-polarized leaders, now known as the Coördinating Committee, set about the task of reëstablishing "normalcy." That this task would be a difficult one was obvious from the beginning, for the defeat of status quo had been achieved by a plurality of less than 500 out of nearly 9,000 votes cast. The Coördinating Committee faced the same problem the *Daihyo Sha Kai* had been unsuccessful in solving: how to unify a community split by a major cleavage.

Statements of informants are unanimous in indicating that it was weariness, impoverishment, and fear, more than rallying around a new set of leaders, that led to the conclusion of the strike, e.g., according to J. Y. Kurihara:

> The main reason status quo broke was not because they didn't want to stick with the Negotiating Committee but—lack of finance. Another reason is they didn't want to loaf along doing nothing. Time lags so monotonous.[1]

---

[1] Field Notes, March, 1944.

And Mr. Tsuruda stated:

It was my opinion that status quo wouldn't accomplish a darn thing but would only increase the peoples' sufferings. While we have status quo, we can't expect things to improve.[2]

While Kurusu, a conservative block manager, remarked:

I thought, deep in my heart, that it was very silly to keep on in a situation like this. We might as well change the system and have a better way to run the camp. If we kept going on strike forever, we're just sunk.[3]

The narrowness of the margin in favor of abandoning status quo, however, reflected the strength of antiadministration feeling: "If they had been in favor of the administration, the vote for liquidating status quo would have been overwhelming";[4] that fear of being picked up and distaste of Army rule had played an important role in the results, e.g., "People got wise that the longer they maintained the status quo, the more they were going to yank them and stick them in the stockade";[5] that there was little popular enthusiasm for new leaders, regarding whom, as Sasaki's secretary (Miss Yamaguchi) admitted, "The people say we're *inu*."[6]

The Coördinating Committee began its difficult task in the middle of January with the cordial backing of the administration. "The members . . . were put on the WRA payroll, given an office, and provided with the use of an official car."[7] It had committed itself to the people to carry out two policies, (1) full employment and (2) "justifiable" release of stockade detainees. It had every reason to believe that the administration would support it in these two programs as a reward for coöperation in the difficult task WRA faced in achieving "normalcy," a task which is described by WRA as follows:

Under the military authorities the center had almost ceased to operate as an organized community. . . . All employment under the War Relocation Authority had stopped when the Army took control, and no wages were paid.[8] The Army had imposed a curfew on the whole population,

---

[2] Field Notes, April, 1944.

[3] Field Notes, April, 1944. It should be noted that the informant, in spite of this attitude, had voted in favor of maintaining status quo.

[4] Field Notes, May 21, 1944.

[5] Field Notes, February, 1944.

[6] *Ibid.*

[7] WRA, *Semi-Annual Report,* January 1 to June 30, 1944, p. 29.

[8] A definite contradiction to the statement in WRA, *Semi-Annual Report,* July 1 to December 31, 1943 (p. 55) that as of December 31, 1943, 3,047 evacuees were

first from 7:00 P.M., later 9:00 P.M. All troublemakers, particularly those considered to be fomenters of the strike, were confined in what the Army termed the "stockade." When the War Relocation Authority took over in January there were 352 men[9] confined there. No assembly of any kind had been permitted in the center; if any group was found meeting it was immediately broken up. Nor had there been any schools in session; evacuee teachers were unemployed and the Caucasian teachers spent much of their time in staffing the administrative mess and performing other necessary tasks. All mimeograph machines had been removed from the evacuee area and no publications were permitted. That was the status of the center when WRA administration replaced the Army.

After January 14, it was the job of WRA to restore the camp to a functioning community insofar as the conditions permitted.[10]

The Coördinating Committee was, at first, hopeful of fulfilling the promise of "full employment." Its Executive Secretary, M. Sasaki, for instance, presumably relying on information from the administration, announced on January 9 that since "this center is considered a special project . . . plan had been laid out whereby placement of as many people as possible on various jobs will be instituted."[11] And Huycke (Head of Community Activities Section), representing the administration, assured the Divisional Responsible Men, a few days later, that

I'm quite sure we'll get more workers than November 4. . . . We believe that we can devise work for everyone who wants work here. Don't worry. I believe we can develop work for everybody.[12]

In spite of these assurances, the difficulties that the Coördinating Committee was to experience in the transitional period were immediately brought into sharp focus. It met obstacles to its "full employment" program from both sides—the Caucasion personnel and

"employed and paid by WRA." An official notice, signed by Colonel Austin and dated December 8, 1943, confirms the version that there were appreciable numbers working and paid during the status quo period. Thus, Colonel Austin stated that there were 2,837 employed and requested 267 "additional essential workers" to report for employment at that time. He added that "those now working on the payroll and those needed for the additional essential work will be processed and placed on the payroll."

[9] According to George Kuratomi, the peak population of the stockade was 253. According to the minutes of the joint meeting of the Divisional Responsible Men and stockade detainees on January 13, 1944 (two days before WRA took over), there were 247 men in the stockade.

[10] WRA, *Semi-Annual Report,* January 1 to June 30, 1944, p. 25.

[11] Minutes of the meeting of the Divisional Responsible Men, January 9, 1944.

[12] Minutes of the meeting of the Divisional Responsible Men, January 13, 1944.

the evacuees. In the January 13 meeting of the Divisional Responsible Men, the aim of WRA became apparent. In the first place,
WRA had every intention of continuing the policy of purging the
labor force of antiadministration elements by insisting that the
names of workers be cleared by both the Army and Internal Security. In the second place, dislodging of Caucasian personnel who
had certain jobs formerly open to evacuees was meeting with resistance from the divisions concerned. There was an especial reluctance
to reinstating evacuee employees in the Mail and Files Section and
in the Statistics Section "inasmuch as vital information may be
forwarded to the Spanish Consul and WRA will be put in a bad
light and they do not want to be fools again, and that the WRA
cannot take the risk." Resistance to the reinstatement of the evacuees was also met from the Operations Division, where the Caucasian personnel, according to Huycke, formed "a solid block" that
felt "somewhat uneasy" and feared "insubordinate sassiness" and
"lack of respect for their authority." The touchy issue of what comprised a day's work was raised also, as it had often been raised in
the past and without any greater concurrence of opinion. Huycke
urged that "the foremen . . . control their crew to see that they do
an honest day's labor, not for sixteen dollars [monthly] salary. . . .
You are working for yourselves not for the WRA." To this a member of the Coördinating Committee replied that because of the
meager wages it was impossible to compel such labor gangs as the
coal crew, engaged in disagreeable work, to work steadily for eight
hours a day and that, when pressed too hard "some bunch of radicals all get on trucks and just go home."[13] Finally, the evacuees
wanted some assurance that certain articles of work clothes would
be furnished them, and that food provided in the mess halls would
be immediately improved. As in the past, solutions of these problems were slow and incomplete.

On the following day (January 14), at a joint meeting of the
Advisory Council, comprised of several members of the administration, and the Divisional Responsible Men, the refusal of Caucasian
supervisors to accept employees who had been "cleared" and recommended for immediate recall to their former jobs was brought up.
It was reported that the Project Director had recommended "that
such a situation should be discussed and thrashed out by the em-

---

[13] *Ibid.*

ployer who refused the employee and the employee who was not wanted," both meeting with the Project Director.[14] This plan of arbitration, however, did not work out to the satisfaction either of the workers or the Coördinating Committee. The administration's failure to reinstate workers remained one of the major problems for the committee during its entire tenure, as it became increasingly evident that key WRA personnel were reluctant to enforce the committee's recommendations for employment recall upon their Caucasian subordinates. This administrative bottleneck, which had been described by Huycke on the previous day, was again emphasized by the Community Analyst in this meeting:

Inasmuch as the appointed personnel must be 'nursed' into this new plan, each division head will decide the problems according to his own discretion in that particular case.[15]

In the course of the next week the committee's efforts to place evacuees in their former jobs were repeatedly rebuffed by uncoöperative Caucasian supervisors; for example, the supervisor of the Motor Pool is said to have stated to the representatives of the committee:

Damn, what the hell is this Committee always butting into other people's business? What does it stand for? I don't care to know. I can get along fine without your (Committee) advice, in fact, I can get along better. I don't take any orders from anyone.[16]

Obstruction of the committee's efforts was also met from the evacuee side. In the first place, many evacuees who actually wanted to return to work hesitated to do so because of rumors of violence perpetrated on workers by nonworking *Daihyo Sha Kai* supporters, who had voted for status quo and who were continuing to oppose the back-to-work movement. That these rumors had some basis in fact is suggested by reports received by the committee of the intimidation of a number of reinstated workers. In the second place, would-be workers, who had been refused "clearance" by the administration or whose employment had been terminated,[17] accused the

---

[14] Minutes of the meeting, January 14, 1944.

[15] *Ibid.*

[16] Memorandum from the Coördinating Committee to Supervisor of Motor Pool, February 24, 1944.

[17] During this period, numbers of workers are said to have been dismissed because close relatives were officers or strong supporters of *Daihyo Sha Kai.*

committee and the Divisional Responsible Men of exerting influence on the Army and on Internal Security to keep their political opponents out of certain jobs. The committee also took the brunt of the blame from workers whom the Caucasian supervisors refused to reinstate. In one instance a group of workers who had been denied "clearance" threatened the life of one of the Divisional Responsible Men.[18] Many of these workers and their friends claimed that the fault lay with the committee because of its failure to press its program upon the administration.

In spite of these difficulties the Coördinating Committee, supported by the Divisional Responsible Men and consulting almost daily with the Advisory Council, achieved a considerable measure of success in getting jobs for the job-hungry population. While reëmployment proceeded slowly at first, it gradually gained momentum,[19] and, within a month the center was, on the surface, operating normally. But it soon became apparent that there were not enough jobs for those willing and able to work. The need for the sixteen dollars a month wage became more and more acute for the involuntarily unemployed. They pressed the Coördinating Committee, the Coördinating Committee pressed the project administration, and the project administration pressed Washington, with few or no concrete results. The committee proposed that farm operations be resumed in order to enable former workers to return to jobs. The administrative attitude, as expressed by Mr. Best, was that "the time is not appropriate to talk about a farm program of any scale."[20] The committee proposed that the portion of the farm land in the surrounding district that had been lost due to the policy of the Negotiating Committee, be regained in order to create more jobs.[21] This was declared to be impossible at the time. Not until late in the spring were farm activities resumed, and the farm program was then greatly curtailed.

Creation of additional work opportunities was stressed repeatedly. As early as January 24, for example, Sasaki, on behalf of the

[18] Minutes of the joint meeting of the Advisory Council and the Coördinating Committee, January 24, 1944.

[19] Between January 15 and January 22, 784 workers had been reinstated. (Minutes of the meeting of the Divisional Responsible Men, January 22, 1944.)

[20] Minutes of the joint meeting of the Coördinating Committee, the Project Director and the Commanding Officer, January 20, 1944.

[21] Memorandum from the Coördinating Committee to the Project Director, February 2, 1944.

committee, asked for a clean-up crew of thirty men. To this request Best replied: "New projects such as the above-mentioned are not yet in order; until such time that the center reëstablishes itself to its former sound normal stage and all old activities function as usual, such plans should be withheld. . . . However, all such plans will be duly considered."[22]

On February 2 the committee sent an urgent memorandum to Mr. Best, pointing out the political dangers that might ensue from the presence of a disgruntled body of unemployed persons on the project.

Approximately 750 persons [who were not employed when the Army took control] have applied for jobs up to date. In view of this fact that many are still on the waiting list, new applicants are aware that their chances of employment are remote, hence a growing impatience is noted among them. We, the Committee, fear the result, lest they be instigated by the pro-status quo group who may aver that this back-to-work movement is beneficial only to those who had worked previously.

In order to relieve this situation, may this Committee again request for your special consideration on this matter of creating new employment opportunities such as general camp cleaning or sawing of kindling wood.[23]

When this suggestion was brought up in the meeting of the Coördinating Committee and the Advisory Council on February 3, Mr. Best and Mr. Black[23a] countered with the employment statistics which apparently showed that there were only 165 fewer persons employed than there had been before the strike. Black said, "We don't have to step very far before we have more people working than before."[24]

Repeated attempts to prevail upon the Project Director to increase work opportunities continued throughout the Coördinating Committee's tenure. At almost every meeting with the Advisory Council, the unemployment problem was described in detail, and alleviation was earnestly requested. On February 25 Sasaki stressed the fact that "because of lacking of opportunities, people are losing faith."[25]

---

[22] Minutes of the joint meeting of the Advisory Council and the Coördinating Committee, January 24, 1944.

[23] Memorandum from the Coördinating Committee to the Project Director, February 2, 1944.

[23a] Assistant Project Director in charge of Community Management Division.

[24] Field Notes, February, 1944.

[25] Minutes of the meeting of the Advisory Council and the Coördinating Committee, February 25, 1944.

The committee was constantly pressed by the Divisional Responsible Men to reinstate workers and to alleviate the labor shortages in various crews. At a meeting of the Coördinating Committee with the Divisional Responsible Men on February 26,

> slaughter house employees ... took the floor and requested for the body's aid in investigating the reason why they were not recalled to work despite their long wait for assignments.[26]

The head of the construction crew complained:

> We have requested for 40 more carpenters, however, the request seems to have been bottlenecked at the Placement [office]. Would like to request the Committee to investigate the bottleneck.[27]

Few of these complaints, which the committee channeled to the administration, resulted in amelioration. As a result the Coördinating Committee, during February and March, lost much of its already tenuous hold on the people because it could not obtain effective collaboration from the administration in fulfilling the first of its promises to the residents to work out "a plan . . . in which there will be employment possibility for the greatest number of residents."[28] The precarious employment situation which was jeopardizing the committee's status was described by Sasaki, "People are desperately trying to get jobs and there are about 1,000 on the waiting list already."[29] The problem was further complicated by the arrival of nearly 2,000 new segregants from Manzanar toward the end of February. Although some of this group had been given service assignments (e.g. mess hall jobs) before arriving in Tule Lake, the bulk of them found it impossible to obtain employment. During the period from February 22 to March 25, there were among them some 924 job seekers who represented 40 per cent of all job seekers on the project.[30] To the extent that they obtained employment, they decreased the openings for the still unemployed earlier transferees and old Tuleans. To the extent that they were unable to obtain jobs, their own group solidarity was strengthened by the impression that they were at a disadvantage in comparison with

[26] Minutes of the meeting, February 26, 1944.
[27] *Ibid.*
[28] See p. 181.
[29] Minutes of the joint meeting of the Coördinating Committee and Stockade detainees, February 28, 1944.
[30] *Newell Star*, April 20, 1944.

earlier transferees and original residents. In any case, their arrival had an immediate influence in depressing the percentage employed on the project as a whole and led to administrative restrictions on the number employed per family.

In late March it became evident that employment would have to be spread among families, and it was determined that no family should have more than two employed when there were other families with only one or none.[31]

Even by June, 1944, Tule Lake Segregation Center had not been able to absorb its employables to the extent that was possible in other relocation projects. At this date, two months after the Co-ordinating Committee had given up the struggle to achieve its program, less than 31 per cent of its population was employed, compared with an average of about 40 per cent for all other relocation projects.

The committee was even more seriously balked in attempts to fulfill its second promise of "justifiable release of detained colonists."[32] On January 13, two days after the status quo referendum and two days before the committee was officially recognized by the Army and WRA, it took the initiative in establishing rapport with the detainees. With the permission of the Army, but without the knowledge of WRA, six detainees were interviewed. None of these was a key member of the Negotiating Committee, the Army having refused Sasaki's request to include one or more of them in the conference. A member of the Coördinating Committee explained the results of the referendum to the detainees and stated that "efforts in trying to get you people released from the stockade should be the preliminary step, prior to our ultimate objective (return of normal conditions)." Of the six detainees interviewed, only one, Yokota, was inclined at that time to be coöperative with the Coördinating Committee, and he promised to compile opinions of the detainees on the plan for establishing "normalcy."[33]

On the following day the Coördinating Committee met again with the same six detainees. The latter criticized the former severely for not consulting them before the referendum was taken; pointed to the small plurality as evidence that most people still favored

[31] WRA, *Semi-Annual Report,* January 1 to June 30, 1944, p. 29.
[32] See p. 181.
[33] Minutes of the meeting, January 13, 1944.

status quo; deplored the split among the residents and the fact that a program was being foisted upon them," after all the hardship and misery [they] had gone through," without united support. They insisted that release of detainees should be assured before the return-to-work program was embarked upon. As Yokota pointed out:

> The reason why status quo came into existence was chiefly for the purpose of getting our release. . . . You cannot remedy and settle this situation . . . by merely liquidating status quo. Normalcy will automatically come back if you solve the root of it.[34]

Kitagawa and Sasaki explained the Coördinating Committee's helplessness in view of the administration's determination that normal conditions, i.e., abandonment of the partial strike, must precede releases. The detainees were at first adamant in demanding unconditional release of all 247 as the price of their coöperation in supporting the return-to-work program, but later modified this to a proposal to release the detained members of the Negotiating Committee for a few hours in order that they might convince the residents of their support of the Coördinating Committee's program. Yokota also promised, on behalf of the Negotiating Committee, that the members, if released, would abstain from political activities.

The administration's attitude toward this meeting was one of disapproval that "their"[35] group should initiate a contact with the "opposition."

> On January 15th we learned, too late to prevent it, that meetings were being arranged between "our" majority spokesmen . . . and the stockade group. . . . Our group apparently wished to hold a trump card, by being the only faction in the village in contact with the stockade. They further sought information on the hunger strike. . . . As feared, the meetings were a misstep, the stockade bargaining ever so diplomatically for our group to work for unconditional release of all inmates; the committee asking for stockade backing to promote a program which would bring their best representatives closer to freedom.[36]

---

[34] Minutes of the meeting, January 14, 1944.

[35] Administrative personnel, at this time, consistently referred to Coördinating Committee members as "our" group, in contrast to antiadministration factions such as *Daihyo Sha Kai* supporters.

[36] Community Analyst to Head of Community Analysis Section, January 15, 1944. (Appended to his January 14 report.)

At a meeting on January 17, the Coördinating Committee members were sharply rebuked by WRA officials for having approached the detainees without prior approval of the Advisory Council. Kami apologized "for the committee's negligence in not consulting the Advisory Council previous to the interviews"[37] and mentioned that one of the detainees had stated that "the detainees really desired liquidation of status quo; nevertheless, due to some great pressure from the 'big bosses' of the 'headquarters,'[38] such feeling could not be expressed outwardly."[39] Mr. Oyama added that, according to a recently released detainee, some 170 detainees opposed status quo and about 30 favored it.

The committee and the administration were unable to reach any agreement at this meeting; the former insisting that "justifiable" stockade releases, which would be credited to its efforts, be initiated immediately; the latter being equally insistent upon delay until normal conditions prevailed. It became apparent that the administration was not willing to give the support on this issue that the committee considered essential if its promises to the people were to be fulfilled. At the same time, the project officials were reluctant to weaken the community position of the committee, which was performing important functions in channeling information to the people and in getting people back to work. In an attempt to absolve the committee from blame because of failure to obtain releases, Best sent the chairman the following letter on January 18:

It is noted that the first accomplishment has been the back to work program. This we learn is a direct reward of your labor in the Colony as the result of the ballot in which the entire people over 18 years of age participated.

While you have not been successful in securing the release of all the men detained in the Army Stockade you can be assured that the cases of these men . . . and those persons who meet the requirements for return to the Colony will be returned to the Colony at the earliest possible time. Be assured that your interest or requests in this connection are being given due consideration.[40]

---

[37] Minutes of the joint meeting of Divisional Responsible Men, the Project Director and the Commanding Officer, January 17, 1944.

[38] By "headquarters," was meant Barrack F, where Abe, Kuratomi and other prominent *Daihyo Sha Kai* men were confined.

[39] Minutes of the joint meeting, *op. cit.*

[40] Community Analyst to Head of Community Analysis Section, January 20, 1944. (Appended to his January 14 report.)

Meantime, a group of *Daihyo Sha Kai* supporters made an independent and unsuccessful attempt to obtain the release of the detainees through an approach to one of the project officials. The negotiations carried on by this group will be described in the following chapter.

The Coördinating Committee continued to press the administration for release of the detainees simultaneously with a campaign for increased work opportunities. Some releases were made on an individual basis, and on January 29 Sasaki was able to report to the Divisional Responsible Men that

up to yesterday, 55 persons were released from the stockade and more will be released in the very near future. The Army has definitely stated that release en masse is impossible unless the Center has returned to its normal condition.[41]

In its attempt to get favorable publicity for its efforts in releasing men from the stockade, the Coördinating Committee was frustrated by the desire of the administration that no publicity be given these releases, lest undue pressure be put upon the Coördinating Committee by the "opposition." On January 20, at a meeting with the Project Director and Army representatives, the committee was promised preferential consideration for four detainees whom it recommended for immediate release and was also authorized to publicize the release of various other detainees from the stockade.[42] However, on January 26, at a meeting with the Advisory Council, Mr. Best "cautioned the Coördinating Committee to proceed very slowly in its undertakings and he thought it advisable to refrain from publicizing matters pertaining to the releases of the detainees, especially their names, too strongly."[43]

The committee had earlier been informed of a split within the stockade. It was alleged that the overwhelming majority of the detainees had turned against the Negotiating Committee at the time of the hunger strike, claiming that Abe, Kuratomi and others of the leaders who were confined in "Headquarters" were fortifying themselves with vitamin pills and food obtained surreptitiously. For example, a crudely printed anonymous letter from the stockade reached the military authorities on January 16.

[41] Minutes of the meeting, January 29, 1944.
[42] Minutes of the meeting, January 20, 1944.
[43] Minutes of the meeting, January 26, 1944.

Lt. Shaner: "Rats" plenty here and getting fat. Only place "rats" can get something eat is kitchen. You send soup few days ago. We not eat soup because "rats" catch soup first. "Rats" have plenty smoke every day. They have package we get only two cigaret. One day apple on menu breakfast we no eat apple. This morning apple half box no more. All us know where "rats" live. In Barrack F big rats no good. They like go out first that not right. . . . We no do nothing but here long time. That not right here too. Like go home quick go work. "Rats" getting coffee every night. Lots sugar. Why you no do something. Pretty soon trouble. Somebody getting mad. Hit "rats" head with shovel. No like trouble me. More better you do something.[44]

In its meetings at about that time with the detainees, the Coördinating Committee had sought help from part of the group which seemed to be willing to coöperate in return for freedom. Its efforts paid dividends on February 4, when two of the remaining detainees (Yokota and Koike) asked the military officer in charge of the stockade to arrange a meeting with the Coördinating Committee. The meeting took place the following day and was opened by Yokota with an expression of confidence in the committee:

The reason why we asked for this meeting was because we heard many true stories and actual reports of the Center's existing condition at the present time, by many men who recently came into the stockade. We heard about you people who were working so hard for the benefit of the colony and how straightforwardly the Committee had been working in attempting to get the stockade people released.

Yokota stated forcefully that among those still detained there were now many who were ready to abandon their stubborn support of the Negotiating Committee and to give a solemn agreement not to engage in political activities in the colony.

Mr. Kodama, Mr. Koike and many others believed that it was just of no use being so stubborn—there's no limit to it. Army's attitude toward the Negotiating Committee hasn't changed a bit since their December 4 statement.[45] We felt that there's no hope in relying on those Negotiating Committee. At that time we had strong convictions, but since we failed once, we have no intentions of being block representatives again. Many of those men have this same opinion.

The older detainees, furthermore, were said to be distressed by the fact that so many young men, who had engaged in no political

---

[44] Community Analyst to Head of Community Analysis Section, January 20, 1944. (Appended to his January 14 report.) The pidgin English used in this letter suggests that the writer was a Hawaiian Kibei.

[45] See p. 166.

activities, were confined in the stockade, and that, in spite of the releases that were made, new arrests and new detainments were not uncommon. Some of the allegedly unjust imprisonments were described in detail, e.g.:

There are cases which are really pitiful—boys who are merely 20 or so have been detained in there for three months just because their past records weren't too good or something.

Since I became captain of the barrack, I met boys who come in to fill coal and do other works. They have told me that they were detained simply because they didn't carry or because they lost their temporary passes. Some of them are really handicapped because of their inability to speak English. Recently I have noticed many fellows like that. There are three boys in particular, who have been in Tule Lake since the inception of this center. I think something should be done for them, even before us. Once when I heard that a young boy dreamt about his mother, I felt so sorry for him. I think it's urgent that such boys be released as soon as possible.

Referring to a young man, the speaker continued:

His younger brother went out but he's still in there and he doesn't even know why he came in. He told me that he wasn't at the Motor Pool at the time of the incident as the Army thinks so. He told me that he was willing to testify strongly and even provide evidence, a time punch, to establish proof that he was in a mess hall.[46]

Yokota gave the Coördinating Committee a list of sixteen persons whose immediate release he recommended. The Coördinating Committee thereupon agreed to draw up a pledge for these men to sign before the Project Director, and presented the list to the Advisory Council on February 8. At the meeting on February 8 it was agreed to give consideration to these persons provided there were no charges against them other than allegiance to the Negotiating Committee. The committee's tactics to win over the detainees, however, were again frustrated by the slowness of the administration in acting upon its recommendations. Negotiations for the release of the sixteen men progressed slowly, and, on February 11, a formal request for the release of two of the sixteen, Yokota and Otsuka, was presented by the Coördinating Committee as a means of expediting the matter:

The releasement of such persons will have great influence upon the welfare of the colonists; thus, we have arrived at a conclusion that without

---

[46] Minutes of the meeting, February 5, 1944.

any risk on our part, the Committee will profit immensely by their release-ment. . . . We feel that such . . . would bring the finishing touches to the work which the Committee could not otherwise undertake.

These two men were released the following day.

Extra-committee pressures for release proceeded concurrently with these activities. In several instances block meetings were held and block petitions drawn up for the release of detained block members; e.g., on February 14, the residents of Block 9 petitioned for the release of four detainees on the grounds that

the releasement of the above-mentioned persons will bring about the solution to the problem of the block. Therefore, please consider this matter for the future maintenance of peace among residents. . . . We will assume responsibility to see to it that these parties will not be involved in politics of any kind after their release.

Similar petitions were presented by the families of detainees, e.g., an Issei woman petitioned, on February 16, for the release of her husband who, she said, "has done nothing whatsoever in the past that may be detrimental to the peace of the block residents, as well as the residents of the center."

However, Best stated at a meeting of Advisory Council and Coör-dinating Committee on February 18 that petitions of this sort would receive no consideration and that appeals would have to be made through regular channels, viz:

Release shall be based on individual merits and block petitions will not be acted upon.[47]

By this time the committee was weary of the difficulties that it faced and discouraged by lack of support from residents. It was anxious to organize a new central committee, with campwide sup-port, to succeed itself. It recommended the appointment of Taro Watanabe (the *Daihyo Sha Kai* renegade) as an advisor and as head of an Arrangements Committee to make plans for the election of this proposed Central Committee. The recommendation was ac-cepted by the administration, and at the regular meeting of Febru-ary 25 with the Advisory Council, Watanabe made a strong plea for "releasement of those considered leaders,[48] also innocent youths" as the first step in winning support of the status quo adherents and

---

[47] Minutes of the meeting, February 18, 1944.
[48] By "leaders," Watanabe did not mean the Abe–Kuratomi clique.

thus unifying the community prior to the establishment of a sound central governing body.

While continuing its efforts on behalf of the stockade detainees, the committee acceded to administrative pressure to place primary emphasis on extension of work possibilities. The administration's standpoint was emphasized by Assistant Project Director Black as follows:

The Committee's work should not be measured by the number of releases from the stockade. It should be on the basis of employment, living conditions, decent community atmosphere, etc. Moreover, process of releasing is slow because of Army and FBI clearances. Furthermore extracts from the FBI Washington office is being forwarded, clearing some of the detainees.[49]

Watanabe, however, presented a memorandum to the Advisory Council on February 27, in which, admitting frankly the lack of popular support of the Coördinating Committee, he recommended various steps that must be taken in establishing "ground work" prior to the "formation of Colonists' central body," and again, insisted upon release of stockade detainee leaders in order to obtain their coöperation:

Let the leaders of those more than half of the colonists who support pro status quo take the initiative to pacify their followers, in other words, the conversion of the leaders of status quo and make them see our point in the future. For this reason I have conferred with Mr. R. Best, Project Director some three weeks ago with regard to the releasement of those detained internees on condition that I, myself, will be responsible for their future activities and again I repeat my unchanged opinion, at this time.

Among those released in the past are men who are considered influential leaders. Mr. Kazuo Yokota has been expending his utmost effort for the conversion of the pro status quo group; however, there is a limit to a single person's effort on such a great undertaking. Therefore, my desire is the releasement of some of the detained internees with whom Mr. Yokota could work together. Then I believe accomplishment would be expedited in reference to the formation of a central body, to which Mr. Yokota has requested me to convey this message to you. If the administration should accept our suggestion, I would like to have the Coördinating Committee, including myself, interview those detained internees prior to their releasement to assure that upon their releasement they would willingly coöperate with Mr. Yokota's effort for the educational campaign among the colonists.

My suggestion for the condition of their releasement will be aided with utmost importance. Leaders of those released up-to-date will issue a co-

[49] Minutes of the meeting, February 25, 1944.

signed statement, to be distributed throughout the Center, that they are supporting Mr. Yokota's movement which ultimately supports the work of the Committee. As to the above laid suggestion it is definitely arranged and agreed between Mr. Yokota and several others who have already been released. By this statement which may be experimental factor as to its effective result, this will be our step toward the formation of such central body.

Now we enter the second step. I wish to see that with the exception of the same Negotiating Committee and those who had profound relations with them, the majority of the block representatives and others released. I appeal to the Administration since success or failure of the formation of this new central body depend on them. If this is materialized the second step will be made public by those released and I believe, as a result, not only the status quo but also all the colonists, as a whole, will be impressed and recognize our righteous standpoint and thereby profit by their utmost support. Then the friction in this center and the unsavory atmosphere will gradually be obliterated.

The next day (February 28) the committee, along with Watanabe, and the recently released Yokota, met with fourteen "selected"[50] stockade detainees. One after the other of these pledged "unreserved coöperation" and "whole-hearted support" for the "restoration of peace and order," and gave unstinted praise to the Coördinating Committee for its efforts in this direction. At the conclusion of the meeting Sasaki apologized for the stand of his committee and the Divisional Responsible Men in limiting their requests to "justifiable releases":

When the divisional responsible men's body was born, we emphatically resolved to obtain justifiable releases. You people may construe this insertion of the word "justifiable" as a word of cowardice. However we have always based our all undertakings on "within reasons" principle when dealing with the Administration or otherwise. Even upon your releasement I want you people to understand and realize thoroughly this point of view. That is the only way we can restore perpetual peace.

To this apology, two of the detainees replied:

Your work up till today has evidenced that it is truly not cowardice.[51]

The Coördinating Committee, on March 1, sent a memorandum to Schmidt, Head of Internal Security, again urging release of the fourteen who had been present at the meeting on February 28,

---

[50] The remainder of the sixteen detainees whom Yokota on February 5 recommended for release.

[51] Minutes of the meeting, February 28, 1944.

giving as its reason the excellent results obtained through the earlier release of Yokota and Otsuka who "have proven to us by their utmost efforts for the conversion of the opposition," but pointing out that "there is a limit to their efforts on such a great undertaking," and that

as to the above-listed persons, this Committee recommends that they are trustworthy as to their sincerity to help as assured by Mr. Yokota and then by the interview with them the other day.

On March 3 the Advisory Council assured the Coördinating Committee that the Army and WRA were attempting to accelerate clearance and subsequent release of the men recommended, but, when, by March 9, no action had been taken, the Coördinating Committee sent a further urgent memorandum to the Chief of Internal Security, the Advisory Council, and the Army, pointing out that there were signs of popular unrest and that

in view of the sign of possible re-flare-up, the Committee earnestly feels that it could be prevented if detainees whom we have interviewed and recommended were released as soon as possible to work together with those already released. . . . They have agreed to put out a statement stating their clear position.

We request for your special consideration to expedite the releasement of the 14 detainees.

In the meantime, a larger list of sixty-one detainees considered worthy of release had been prepared and submitted to the administration. In spite of these efforts, releases were made very slowly. On March 11 it was reported that Kodama had been released; and on March 14 two others from the list of fourteen, four from the longer list of sixty-one, and one whom the committee had not recommended obtained their freedom. There is little reliable evidence of the use which those who were released made of their freedom. Sasaki has said that some did their best to help the Coördinating Committee and others double-crossed it.

By the middle of March, in spite of the committee's efforts, about 120 persons were still confined in the stockade, partly because the continuing pick-ups tended to offset releases. At a meeting with Dillon Myer on March 18, the question was raised once more, and, according to the minutes:

Mr. Myer went on to say that doubtless there are many who earnestly desire to get friends out of the stockade, but one should be reluctant in making demands, until WRA has a chance to get the inventory taken and get all papers in order to check the stockade list. He advised that one should withhold making too many recommendations which are inclined to embarrass the administration.

In the course of its relations with both the administration and the residents, from the middle of January to the end of March, the Coördinating Committee found itself in an increasingly difficult and unpleasant predicament. The policy of collaboration with the administration which the members and their supporters had adopted was probably dually motivated by (1) a genuine desire to have more settled conditions in the project, and to improve the situation of the residents, and (2) a desire to maintain a position of political control over the residents partly because the tactics of the *Daihyo Sha Kai* had become a threat to their vested property and employment interests in Tule Lake and their stake in a future in America, which they were by no means willing to abandon. The administration had in the beginning shown itself willing enough to give the committee nominal support and backing if it brought the people in line with predetermined administrative policies in regard to employment and developed an effective opposition to the *Daihyo Sha Kai*. When, however, the committee attempted to initiate policies in regard to extensions of employment and release of detainees, the administration disregarded or pushed aside its proposals. Yet these proposals had to be met if the committee could hope to strengthen its tenuous hold on the people.

The committee was fully cognizant of the seriousness of its situation within a few days of its recognition by the administration. In desperation, the members adopted the tactics of "playing both ends against the middle." As described above, they interviewed stockade detainees without administrative sanction, and they pressed for better living conditions and for increased employment opportunities against administrative indifference. At the same time, they tried to crush all "radical" (i.e. *Daihyo Sha Kai*) opposition,[52] and at a meeting of the Divisional Responsible Men on January 22, formu-

---

[52] A plan for protective espionage was probably developed very soon after the status quo referendum. The Community Analyst stated, "The important thing for the Coördinating Committee is results. To aid them in what [Sasaki] calls his 'researches,' they are getting a staff." (Community Analyst to Head of Community Analysis Section, January 20, 1944, appended to his January 14 report.)

lated a plan for "a liaison body acting between the Coördinating Committee and the Divisional Heads and workers to receive all reports, complaints, suggestions, plans, etc."[53] Two days later, when the matter was put before the Advisory Council, the liaison body was described as a

sub-committee . . . [which] will refer such matters as it may deem necessary to the attention of the Project Director. Mr. Kami reiterated that inasmuch as the Committee is still encountering much difficulties with the antagonistic minority of pressure groups, it is definitely imperative that this sub-committee be established immediately to accelerate the progress of this great task.[54]

By January 28, when the committee again met with the Advisory Council, the proposal for the subcommittee was stated, frankly, as a request for the appointment of "30 men with WRA remuneration for the purpose of *performing intelligence work* which is to be used only for the advantage and benefit of the colony." At the same time the necessity of restricting meetings within the center was brought up, and on Mr. Black's suggestion the restriction was deemed unnecessary "since the creation of an intelligence unit should alleviate the task to a certain degree by insinuating within these [meetings] investigators and spotting and identifying the nature of the meeting and possibly the leaders."[55]

The organization of this intelligence unit was approved by the administration, and the agents, known as "fielders," were placed on the WRA payroll. They kept a constant watch for "agitation," and "general unrest," as well as for complaints about mess halls, housing, and employment. On February 1, two fielders were assigned to work in Ward VII since problems had been reported in blocks 66, 69, and 70. Trouble was reported on February 3 from Ward VI, to which three fielders were dispatched the next day. They reported "general unrest" in blocks 49 and 52. On February 5, B-9, a fielder (the fielders were known by numbers) reported that troublemakers in blocks 27, 53, 54, and 67 were "busily plotting to overthrow the committee." The next day three fielders were instructed to work in wards II and VII. On February 7, fielder K-3

---

[53] Minutes of the meeting, January 22, 1944.

[54] Minutes of the joint meeting of the Advisory Council and the Coördinating Committee, January 24, 1944.

[55] Minutes of the joint meeting of the Advisory Council and the Coördinating Committee, January 28, 1944. Italics ours.

reported that Block 67 was the headquarters of the pressure group and named Tsukai[56] as an agitator. On February 10 it was reported that Sawamura, Shiba, Tsukai, Tsuchikawa, and others were involved in an organized plot, were obtaining signatures of the residents under the pretense of giving them priority on the exchange boat, were attempting to get the release of everyone in the stockade, and were discrediting the Coördinating Committee by propaganda.[57] The committee passed on the information received in this way to the administration in a further attempt to consolidate its collaborative position.

When, in late February, a contingent of 1,876 segregants arrived from Manzanar, the Coördinating Committee made a vigorous attempt to win the new arrivals to its side. In this it was aided by WRA personnel, who arranged elaborate welcoming ceremonies, giving the Coördinating Committee a prominent part, and had built new and superior living quarters for the newcomers, who thus escaped many of the inconveniences and hardships that had been the lot of the other segregants. Fires were lit in their barracks prior to their arrival, and they were presented with a mimeographed expression of welcome, signed by Sasaki on behalf of the committee, ending with an appeal for coöperation:

> None of us know how long will our stay in Tule Lake be. All Tuleans have been trying to make it a better place to live under the circumstance. Yet they have no other desire than to live in peace and happiness for the duration. Our ideal is Utopia. Ideal of Utopia may not be attained, however, we must strive to attain that goal as much as we can for ideal is like a North Star. Sailor never reaches North Star, yet without North Star he cannot come to the port.
>
> We appeal to you, MANZANITES!! Now you are in the same boat with us. Let's make the best of it and lay up for the future happiness.

The success of this gesture was marred by two circumstances, (1) the resentment by the other residents of the considerate treatment given the Manzanar people, and (2) a blast of propaganda from former status quo supporters, now operating as an underground pressure group, "unmasking" the Coördinating Committee.

Resentment over the comparative luxury of the Manzanar quarters was not limited to any political segment of the population. An Issei who was noted for his proadministration attitude complained:

---

[56] See p. 161.
[57] Diary of the Coördinating Committee, February 1 to 29, 1944.

They tried to do everything for the Manzanar people. When we came in here we were treated like criminals. We were treated dirty. When Manzanar people came in they were treated like princes. Even their stoves were started already. They had showers and everything.[58]

Mrs. Kurusu, a Kibei transferee from Gila, noted for her disapproval of radicals, stated:

It seems that the administration is afraid of them. They had a riot in the Manzanar Relocation Project you know. They've gotten very good consideration if you ask me. I think Gila people had the raw deal. We were the last in here and when it came to work, Gila people didn't have any. Manzanar people already got work before they came in.[59]

These statements differed little from the outburst of Higashi, a strong status quo supporter:

We are all glad they're here, but we don't like the things the administration does for them. We've been here six months. We haven't yet received broom, mops, or soap. The people from Manzanar all received a new mop, broom and a cake of soap for each person. What's the difference between those fellows and us?[60]

Similarly, two ex-Gila housewives:

Mrs. A: They got everything!
Mrs. B: My sisters tell me, "Gosh, they got treated so good they thought something was fishy!"[61]

The propaganda from the underground pressure group was distributed early in March in the form of a pamphlet, presenting the "true picture of this center." It analyzed the "root of the [November] incident" in terms of the policy of WRA of "converting reluctant evacuees to so-called loyal ones."

For the love of their native land and recognizing the conflict as a racial war, the evacuees have resorted to repatriation and willingly segregated from the other centers. Among the evacuees, there were many young people in indefinite status because of American citizenship and there was no action taken as to the legislative action of denouncing citizenship. The greatest inconsistency to which the colonists were subjected was forced to keep silence. Nonclarification of the status was the root of all center troubles up to date. The present incident precipitated by the accident occurred in the agricultural department. The fundamental root was the accumulation of resentments on the part of the evacuees for the above-mentioned hypocritical and inconsistent policy on the part of the Administration.

---

[58] Field Notes, March, 1944. [60] Ibid.
[59] Ibid. [61] Ibid.

The pamphlet minimized the violence connected with the incident itself:

Because of the incident, the resulting suppressive policy made colonists' life more unbearable. On the other hand, it seems as if it were planned as in a drama. At any rate for a little incident of that nature, they the Army, used even motor trucks and tanks and fired great number of ammunitions. Since then, forced suppression prolonged, until today. During the incident over 200 innocent ones were picked up and every apartment was searched, for which even a mere child of three years of age was indignant.

It pointed to the "dark stream of a sinister plot" by the executives of the Coöperative Enterprises, who were supporters of the Coördinating Committee, and who

resolved to pacify the colonists' feeling by vile absurd statement that they were expending utmost effort, as if to risk life even, and attempted to dissolve the *Daihyo Sha Kai* by the use of contemptible publication and speech, inveigling the colonists. On the other hand, those who rallied [support for] this campaign with the executives of the Co-op were gamblers, bootleggers, and shameless egoists, or the so-called money makers of the center. To . . . [aid them] the WRA employed, in order to carry out their damnable policy, the "dogs" [informers; i.e., *inu*] hired with excellent salary.

It claimed the status quo referendum "was taken by banditlike methods . . . with the coöperation of armed soldiers" and that the "true result is more than questionable."

Furthermore, it branded the Divisional Responsible Men as *inu* and "betrayers of the Fatherland," because they had disregarded "Fatherland's stiff protest for the sake of the colonists" and nullified "the accomplishment and altruistic spirit created by the former *Daihyo Sha Kai.*

It claimed that the Army withdrew from the center as a result of a "stiff protest" delivered by "the Imperial Government repeatedly." The protest was

considered stronger than an ultimatum. Stipulation was made that unless the Army withdrew from the center by January 15, reciprocal retaliation will be made to the American prisoners.

It ended with the following warning:

Don't be fooled, Manzanites! Special consideration and hospitality upon your arrival to this center was a plan . . . camouflaged by hypocrisy . . . to enslave you. We can definitely tell you so brothers and sisters from Manzanar.

Disillusioned by the failure of the Coördinating Committee to live up to its promises regarding employment and release of detainees, irritated by and suspicious of the activities of the "fielders," fearful because of the continued pick-ups, and resentful of the committee's attempts to win over the Manzanar group, the residents, in general, veered more and more from support of the program of the Coördinating Committee. By the middle of March the attitude of many had changed from indifference to hostility. Kurihara expressed a prevalent attitude of suspicion that the Coördinating Committee was impeding releases of detainees and was instrumental in the recent pick-ups when he said: "The Japanese are held in the stockade by the Japanese."[62]

Wakida indicated the general state of pessimism regarding releases: "I don't think the people in the stockade will ever be released,"[63] while Higashi said, "The majority of the people are against status quo but in their hearts they don't like to see people in the stockade,"[64] and later added: "The people haven't gained much confidence in Sasaki. They don't thank the Coördinating Committee for anything. I'd still like to know how they got in there."[65]

Some informants, however, continued to express approval of the Coördinating Committee members, e.g., Wakida, who stated:

I know the Coördinating Committee works hard. I respect them. But I think status quo against anti-status quo will be a big trouble in the future too.[66]

And a Nisei ex-*Daihyo Sha Kai* member said:

The Coördinating Committee did get people out of the stockade and tried to do their share.[67]

A few even approved the administration's policy in regard to detainees, e.g., the proadministration Issei, cited above (p. 207, note 58), who said:

I suppose some of the fellows in the stockade should be let out. A good many didn't mean anything—not knowing what the consequence was to be. The real agitators—the leaders were nothing but agitators—should be kept there their whole life as far as I'm concerned. They want to start trouble.[68]

---

[62] Field Notes, March, 1944.
[63] *Ibid.*
[64] *Ibid.*
[65] *Ibid.*
[66] *Ibid.*
[67] *Ibid.*
[68] *Ibid.*

A Caucasian informant (WRA employee) described the difficulties, as follows:

> On the subject of releases the Army is telling the Coördinating Committee that WRA is holding out, and the WRA is telling them the Army is holding out. It's a vicious circle. There are too many cooks with a hand in the broth, the Army, WRA and the Coördinating Committee.[69]

Kurihara is one of the few residents who recognized the difficult position of the Coördinating Committee, and the inevitability of blame, deserved or undeserved, being heaped upon it. Of the committee he said:

> The Coördinating Committee, I think, is the unconscious tool of either the Army or WRA.[70]

And concerning Sasaki:

> There are a couple of men under him. They express themselves better in English than he does and they go over his head in doing things. If he could wriggle out of the committee, all right. But if he waits longer, some day it's going to be too late. He will be blamed regardless of the consequences that follow. If he keeps on and sticks at it, even if he's really for the Japanese, he's going to be branded as an *inu* and blamed for working for WRA.[71]

Throughout all the maneuvers described in the preceding pages, the position of the Coördinating Committee as a political party was an anomalous one. It had not been elected by the people, but appointed by a group of "responsible men." The narrow popular margin by which status quo was liquidated could not reasonably be taken as a vote of confidence in this committee, about whose very existence a large part of the population was ignorant. Yet the Army and WRA officially "recognized" this committee, as a mechanism of collaboration, although both agencies had earlier refused to "recognize" *Daihyo Sha Kai* and its Negotiating Committee on the grounds of lack of evidence of "true representativeness" of the former and of appointment, rather than election, by a "minority faction" of the latter. As suggested earlier in this chapter, the Coördinating Committee was by no means unaware of its anomalous political position. When the Divisional Responsible Men requested "official recognition" of the committee on January 12, it had been unanimously voted that the committee be dissolved as soon as nor-

---

[69] *Ibid.* [70] *Ibid.* [71] *Ibid.*

malcy was achieved. At the meeting with the detainees on January 14, Sasaki stated:

> We have no political ambitions whatsoever. We have strongly resolved to dissolve this group as soon as the center returns to its normal conditions, as soon as people go back to work, as soon as we succeed in getting the release of those justifiable colonists detained, and finally when the responsible political group is established.[72]

By February 3 the committee felt so insecure that it made a serious proposal, at its meeting with the Advisory Council,[73] to initiate a popular election of representatives. Sasaki said:

> If we made preparations to replace the committee, the colonists would feel better. That way, everybody is responsible for recommendations in the center.

The Army and WRA representatives, however, hesitated to act on this proposal, for fear "radicals" (i.e. *Daihyo Sha Kai* supporters) might be elected as representatives. They were completely frank in the reasons for their reluctance, as indicated by the following exchange of views:

> LT. FORBES: To put it in words of one syllable, do you think you can win it the same way you won the last election [status quo referendum]?
> SASAKI: I don't think so. But we want the people to realize that we are not like the Negotiating Committee but are interested in the welfare of every colonist in the center.
> HUYCKE: If you have an election, I'd say the chances are you'd have a committee selected with about 40 per cent negative point of view.

The only Caucasian supporting the committee's point of view was the Community Analyst, who suggested that an election might be advisable because of the difficult position of the committee. He urged some delay, however, at the same time proposing an immediate public announcement.

Black supported Huycke's negative stand:

> BLACK: If we have a referendum now, we're not going to get the quality of men on the committee we want.
> COMMUNITY ANALYST: The main point is, this group is begging to be released. I thing that this responsibility lies on us, since we want them to continue.

---

[72] Minutes of the meeting, January 14, 1944.

[73] Official minutes of this meeting are not available. Quotations are from our own field notes.

The discussion continued, with pros and cons as follows:

ROBERTSON:[74] What does the committee feel would be the reaction of the colonists to the fact that the committee wants to leave. Do you think they'd clamor for a referendum?

COMMUNITY ANALYST: (answers for the committee) Yes.

ROBERTSON: The committee does not entirely approve of this statement from the administration?

SASAKI: Not exactly.

LT. FORBES: I think the opposition would seize on it and demand a vote.

SASAKI: It's not quite democratic. We should leave before our welcome is worn out.

At this point, Kami fell in with the suggestion of the administration and stated:

It's too early yet. I feel personally there is more to be accomplished before we submit a referendum. We don't want people to think we're doing this because we like it. We want to accomplish something before we retire. When this is all fixed up, let Mr. Best give a big steak dinner for the incoming and outgoing committee.

The members of the committee, asked if they were willing to accept Kami's standpoint, agreed, somewhat hesitatingly, while Sasaki insisted "At least let the people know." The meeting ended with no concessions made by the administration, and the Coördinating Committee remained in its insecure and uncomfortable position of prominence, appointed by a small group, the Divisional Responsible Men, but standing as representatives of the people and supported by the Army and the administration.

The struggles of the committee with both administration and residents, which continued throughout January and early February, finally made a plan for self-liquidation imperative. The committee called in Watanabe on February 7 and obtained his agreement to act as head of an "Arrangements Committee" to plan an election. On February 16 it sent an urgent memorandum to Mr. Best, recommending that this Arrangements Committee, headed by Watanabe, be approved; and that, when the personnel of the Arrangements Committee had been finally agreed upon, "the Coördinating Committee, as previously understood as a temporary one, will duly dissolve." It justified its decision, as follows:

Viewing great improvement of the Center to normalcy, this body should not, by any means, lose this ripe opportunity of dissolution, which was

[74] Assistant Project Director in charge of Operations Division.

made public in our previous statement; otherwise, colonists' misunderstanding and misconception toward this Committee will accrue. It is imperative that this organization's standpoint be clarified, as announced previously, whereby the Committee may be replaced by election by means of secret votes.

The members expected, they said, that their elected successors "will thereon continue to settle the problems among colonists and simultaneously coöperate fully with the administration for the betterment, peace, and order of the community," and that the Coördinating Committee itself would, even after dissolution, continue to "assist and coöperate for the betterment of the Center." Two days afterward, this proposal was approved by the administration.

At about this time it was made clear that the Coördinating Committee members expected full administrative backing in the planned reorganization and election, and were not willing to share their prerogatives and prestige with any other group before the election, which they obviously hoped to influence through their favored status. A self-styled minority group championing a "peace-movement" had been given a hearing by the Advisory Council. It had proposed the dissolution of the Coördinating Committee to permit its group to form "a temporary acting committee." This "temporary acting committee" was to "be at liberty to coöperate fully with the administration's 'back-to-work program.'" When "normalcy" was achieved by this committee "another shall be elected by the colonists in compliance with the authorities' announcement."[75]

The end, a general election, was the same for which the Coördinating Committee had been pressing, but the means—manipulation of the election by a rival group—was not to be tolerated. On hearing of the meeting, the Coördinating Committee sent an indignant memorandum to the Advisory Council on February 18. The committee, so the memorandum stated, had made "extensive study and investigation through fielders . . . almost daily" for any such "plot" or "movement" on the part of status quo supporters. It deplored the Advisory Council's consultation with this group, which should "have come to us first." The fact that the Advisory Council had conferred with this minority, without the Coördinating Commit-

---

[75] Hisao Shiba, Negotiator of Minority, to Chief of Internal Security, February 8, 1944.

tee's knowledge, would, the latter said, lead to rumors of lack of administrative support of the committee and would strengthen the hands of the opposition:

> We are fatigued mentally and physically and could no longer invite and increase our burden. The reason why we resent is that we feel that such frivolous action on the part of the Advisory Council will give an impression that the Committee has been discredited and also noncommitment statement are often interpreted in a wrong sense and in favor of those who are against us. We have been up-to-date obliged to exhaust our efforts to rectify such rumors spread by misunderstandings. . . .
>
> This Committee has no intention to ask you to stop altogether such interviews or consultations, however, hereafter, please bear in mind that such opportunity given to such delegations will give an impression that anyone can consult the administration directly on this matter, thereby ignoring the Committee's position and curtailing its work.
>
> Perchance that should you find these delegation more fitted for the work than the Committee, we are always ready to wash our hands on the matter any time.

The committee apparently gained nothing from its protest, except an intensification of the feeling of its insecure position in its relations with the community and administration. It nevertheless went ahead with its plan for establishing "ground work prior to the formation of colonists' central body," and Watanabe presented his plan, toward this end, in a memorandum to the Advisory Council on February 27. He conceived the release of friendly leaders from the stockade as an essential part of this groundwork. He admitted frankly that "about 50 per cent of the colonists are still for status quo despite [its] liquidation . . . by the effort of the responsible men of all divisions," and pointed out that the other 50 per cent of the colonists "are less organized comparatively, their standing is very unstable, and their belief is not concrete as to the solution of the existing problem; they are reluctant to take active part to the opposition." If, he added, "we disregard such a condition and if we should proceed with the formation of a new central body, those prospective representatives from each block will refuse to assume office; thus, the formation of a central body will become a failure." Therefore, he concluded, the gap between the opposition and the followers of the committee could be bridged only by utilizing the leaders, including the detainees, to educate the general population in "willingness to . . . coöperate."

The efforts of the committee in preparing the groundwork for an election were met with a general indifference by the residents. Even persons who felt that the election of a representative body might do much to bring order into the camp were pessimistic, for they believed that responsible persons, realizing the difficulty of getting caught between the administration and the people, and the possibility of incurring criticisms for dissatisfactions for which they could not be responsible would, if elected, refuse to accept positions on the central body.

Tsuruda said:

I don't think an election would do any good anyhow. What do we want representatives for? They don't do us any good. Let us roam around here and feed us three times a day. We'll wait until the war ends. Nobody likes trouble. If they treat us like human beings and not like dogs, nobody starts kicking.[76]

Wakida said:

If a general election were held in this camp, who's going to be a candidate? I won't. We wouldn't have any power to do anything here anyway.[77]

Less typical is the statement of a young Nisei, employed in the Community Analysis Section, who was hopeful of the results:

In order to have the camp back to a normal basis, the only way to do is to dispose of the Coördinating Committee and let the blocks elect at least two representatives from each block and then let them be the peoples' representatives.[78]

The majority of the people in camp were relieved that the status quo period of discomfort and tension was over; people had gone back to work and were making some money, although more than 1,000 were unemployed, awaiting job openings. Living conditions, in general, had improved, although there were still dissatisfactions, with food in particular. These people, however, had learned the futility of fighting the administration and had resigned themselves to the ineffectual outcome of protest activities. It was better to let well enough alone, and give passive support to the Coördinating Committee, rather than initiate any step which might bring on another period of tension and discomfort. A minority, however, while disapproving of the Coördinating Committee, found this attitude unacceptable. Some sort of rapport between the residents

---

[76] Field Notes, March, 1944.   [77] *Ibid.*   [78] *Ibid.*

and the administration should be established, they believed, but fear of being thought proadministration or *inu* rendered them helpless. At the opposite extreme was another minority, or a cluster of minorities, determined that some organization should be formed on their terms. Persons of this way of thought were biding their time, agitating continuously against the administration, and particularly against Mr. Best, and campaigning vigorously to discredit the already very insecure Coördinating Committee. Some of the younger extremists among them were reported to have threatened to beat committee members.

At this time the administrative attitude was marked by optimism, as exemplified by Dillon Myer's speech to the Caucasian employees on March 17, when he is reported to have said:

I think WRA has passed its worst crisis, assuming we don't have another blow up. I feel more confident about Tule Lake than ever before. Things are on the beam now. Everything's going to be all right. Once I decide I have the right people in the right place, I'll support them.[79]

At Myer's meeting with the Coördinating Committee the following day, the question of replacing the committee (in which Best expressed "full confidence and faith") was raised. Myer pointed out that the matter had to be cleared with the Secretary of the Interior, and that

if the Secretary agrees (it is hoped that he will), some plan could be worked out where Tule Lake may have a representative type of election, actually selected in the same capacity as this Committee. It will not be a community government in the same sense as those functioning in the other relocation centers, but as a group representing the colony to serve as a channel of information and understanding between the colony and the administration and a body representing the point of view of the colony to present to the administration, and vice versa.[80]

Before these plans could be developed, however, the Coördinating Committee found itself in a position so strained that its resignation could no longer be put off. A group of *Daihyo Sha Kai* sympathizers, which, as will be described in the following chapter, was involved in an underground movement in opposition to the committee, obtained administrative sanction to circulate a petition for signatures of those who had applied for repatriation or expatriation and who wanted to be separated from "loyal" residents until

---

[79] *Ibid.*   [80] Minutes of the meeting, March 18, 1944.

they were afforded an opportunity for exchange to Japan. Although sanction was withdrawn on April 10, the petition had meantime been circulated and obtained some 6,500 signatures.[81]

To the Coördinating Committee members, the recognition of these people whom they termed *Daihyo Sha Kai* sympathizers was the last straw. As a final resort they went over the head of the WRA and appealed to the Army for support. They received no encouragement from the Army and incurred the disapproval of Mr. Best.

On April 7, the day on which the petition was circulated, the members of the committee resigned en masse, sending the following communication to Mr. Best:

> . . . We, the Committee, have expended our utmost in order to restore normalcy in this Center, in spite of threats, intimidations, bad names, such as "dogs" [informers]—literally we have exhausted ourselves physically and mentally for the good of the colonists by our utmost faith toward the Administrative personnel to attain our object. . . .
> At this time, we, the Committee, feel that it is most proper and opportune for us to keep our promise, which we made at the time of the formation of this body, to dissolve and make way for the future responsible body, which will be selected by the entire colonists' vote. Prolonged existence of this Committee will wear out the welcome of the colonists. . . . We, the Committee, hereby submit our resignation to be effective immediately upon due consideration.

The following day the committee was reprimanded by the Divisional Responsible Men for resigning without consulting "the body which elected them." The committee members, while apologizing for their "rash action," presented a lengthy justification, including the following points:

(1) The fact that WRA had granted permission for the circulation of the resegregation petition without consulting the Coördinating Committee.

(2) The fact that the committee had been rebuffed by the Army when asking for intervention in respect to conditions "endangering the peace and normality of the Center. . . . Colonel advised that the Committee should not 'tell' on such a trifling occurrence."

(3) The fact that consultation with the Army had led to strained relations with WRA. "Project Director felt indignant toward the committee because the committee had over-ridden the Administration."

[81] See p. 233.

(4) In view of all of the above-mentioned difficulties, and the fact that "the center condition had returned to normalcy and the object upon which the committee was formed has been accomplished, and in order to expedite the formation of a new colonists' representative body," the committee had seen fit to resign without consulting its sponsors, the Divisional Responsible Men.

Because of this action of the committee, the Divisional Responsible Men took under consideration plans for their own dissolution. It was finally agreed to postpone this step until

April 29, 1944, which does not mean that the body will irresponsibly sever relations with the colonists or the Administration. Until that time (April 29), the body will expend its utmost to prepare for the replacement of this body. Furthermore, there are many unfinished business yet to be completed prior to dissolution. In other words, for the maintenance of peace and harmony among colonists, the resigned Coördinating Committee, as part of the Divisional Responsible Men's body, will give its undivided attention as heretofore.[82]

Sasaki, in an interview, later expressed his own opinion of the need for resigning, in view of WRA's evident lack of confidence in the committee:

Mr. Black told the committee that the Coördinating Committee was not the only body representing the colonists. At that time we sort of felt it might be WRA policy to keep confusion among the colonists.

Up to the 19th of February the Advisory Council would coöperate with us, but lately I was told, "You people are making too many requests and getting in my hair." It may be WRA's policy to stir up confusion.

We worried a good deal when this resegregation petition was presented. It showed us that there have been some members of the administration working hand in hand with the *Daihyo Sha Kai*.[83]

Sasaki's secretary, Miss Yamaguchi, summed up the dissatisfactions as follows:

Every time when something good was suggested, the administration would over-ride us. The committee members feel the longer they stay in, the longer they'll be called *inu*.[84]

Niiyama, of Civic Organizations, who had been instrumental in bringing the Divisional Responsible Men together, said:

---

[82] Minutes of the joint meeting of the Divisional Responsible Men and the Coördinating Committee, April 8, 1944.
[83] Field Notes, April, 1944.
[84] *Ibid.*

The administration used the Coördinating Committee like a crook uses a crowbar to get into a house. After robbing the house, they threw the crowbar away.[85]

That it was not only "betrayal" by the administration, but also awareness of the increasing hostility of the colonists that motivated the resignation of the committee is also suggested by the following expressions of opinion recorded just before its resignation:

A few days before the news of the committee's resignation, Kurihara said:

I heard that the members of the Coördinating Committee were going to resign and have the people elect persons in whom they can have confidence. If they do that it might help. The Coördinating Committee and the Civic Organizations group are suspected. From our point of view, they are "loyals."

The administration knows that the people consider the Coördinating Committee and the Civic Organizations group *inu,* yet they continue to employ these people. They should know better.

The general trend of opinion of the people is: they've got to get rid of, sever the heads of, the men on the Coördinating Committee. Unless they get rid of these men there's going to be trouble![86]

The conservative Mrs. Kurusu, stating that the Coördinating Committee was more unpopular than ever before said, "This would be a fine time for the Coördinating Committee to resign."[87]

Mr. Kurusu added:

I think the people are so against the anti-status quo group, because they don't like the Coördinating Committee. They don't trust the members. If the members of the Coördinating Committee had been chosen by election, that would be another story. But they're self-appointed. We don't trust them. We don't know them.[88]

The news of the committee's resignation, announced in the *Newell Star* of April 13, was received with general approval. The removal from power of the group of "self-appointed loyals" and "Coöp *inu*" would, many people hoped, decrease unrest among the residents.

On April 29 the Divisional Responsible Men held their last formal meeting, and Milton Sasaki listed, for their benefit, the chronology and the accomplishments of the Coördinating Committee.

[85] Field Notes, January 8, 1945.
[86] Field Notes, April, 1944.
[87] *Ibid.*
[88] *Ibid.*

1. On January 8, return-to-work voting was held at various places and by majority of affirmative votes, ex-employees of various sections and divisions resumed work.

2. On January 11, referendum vote was taken and by a margin of 473 votes or 35 blocks against status quo and 28 blocks for, policy of status quo was liquidated. . . .

3. On January 12, seven members were selected from the Divisional Responsible Men as Coördinating Committee, which was officially recognized by the administration and the Army forthwith. The Committee, since it felt that its purpose for which it was organized had been accomplished, tendered its resignation on the 10th of April.

4. On the 15th of January, the Army withdrew from the center and the WRA resumed administration.

5. On January 19 and 20, first releasement of 26 internees was made.

6. By February 4, total of 3,848 was at work. This figure was only 165 less than the full employment mark of October, 1943.

7. Curfew was lifted on February 21.[89]

8. 5,145 employees were on the payroll on April 17.

9. 257 stockade internees were released and 19 recently released.

10. Since the center returned to normalcy, the Divisional Responsible Men resolved to dissolve on April 30 at its meeting held on the 8th.[90]

It will be noted that almost equal emphasis was placed on the two planks in the platform on which status quo was defeated, (1) full employment, and (2) release of detainees. That the Administration held a much more limited view of the functions, accomplishments and reasons for liquidation of the committee is suggested from the following appraisal in the WRA Report:

> . . . The Coördinating Committee . . . resigned . . . ostensibly . . . because it was under considerable pressure from certain of the residents to force the release by WRA of all of those detained in the stockade. Actually, however, it had about outlived its usefulness in getting the people back to work. To this Committee should go considerable credit for bringing about a more coöperative attitude among the residents.[91]

[89] Although the Army had turned the center back to WRA on January 15, some features of martial law were continued for many weeks. Among these were the curfew and the maintenance of military patrols within the center. The Coördinating Committee made repeated efforts to have these restrictions relaxed. At its meeting with the Advisory Council on February 18, it had again petitioned for removal of the curfew, and Best had agreed that "such a recommendation is permissible if such is the desire of the colonists." The revocation was made effective by Colonel Austin on February 21. The patrol was, however, maintained until June 1, 1944.

[90] Minutes of the joint meeting of the Divisional Responsible Men and the Coördinating Committee, April 29, 1944.

[91] WRA, *Semi-Annual Report,* January 1 to June 30, 1944, p. 29.

Chapter VIII

UNDERGROUND

Inception of Resegregationist Pressure

As DESCRIBED in the preceding chapter, collaboration became a policy for evacuee-administrative relations in the middle of January, 1944. It was mediated, on the evacuee side, by the Coördinating Committee, which had been appointed by a relatively small group of "Responsible Men." Its popular backing was dubious. Its platform of "back to normalcy" versus "status quo" had won by a margin of only a few hundred votes. It soon met administrative indifference in effectuating the two main planks of its platform: "full employment" and "justifiable release of stockade detainees," and its popular margin of support narrowed to such an extent that its control of the community was imperiled. It sought in vain both to enlist opposition leaders and to crush opposing factions. It proposed self-liquidation repeatedly, but reacted negatively against attempts made by other groups to obtain administrative recognition. When, in spite of all its efforts, popular confidence ebbed still further, the opposition gained strength and organization, and the administration vacillated in its encouragement of first one group and then the other, the committee resigned.

The activities of the opposition were touched on briefly in the preceding chapter. In its early development, it consisted of several small groups operating independently and informally around nuclei of supporters of the detained *Daihyo Sha Kai* leaders. From time to time these nebulous groups merged to bring pressure upon the administration. This merging of small groups eventually resulted in an underground movement of considerable strength.

Because they were subject to the constant danger of arrest and confinement in the stockade, its leaders carefully concealed their identity from the administration. When it was necessary to come out into the open, they chose, as spokesmen, persons whose arrest would not seriously weaken their organization.

Throughout January, February, and March, their activities were directed toward two ends: (1) the attempt to bring about the release of the stockade detainees, and (2) the reopening of the status quo issue. In contrast to the Coördinating Committee, which fought for only "justifiable" releases and acceded, however unwillingly, to the administrative policy of giving priority to other factors in achieving "normalcy," the opposition leaders emphasized release of *all* detainees and usually made these releases a prerequisite for abandonment of the status quo. They strove to maintain the partial strike as a bargaining weapon in dealing with the administration for correction of many actual and imagined grievances. Concomitantly, they relied on the intervention of the Japanese government for the alleviation of their humiliation and sufferings. They were convinced that Japan was winning the war and would be the only effective source for their protection. Many of them firmly believed that the Army had relinquished control over the center and had later lifted the curfew because of protests by the Japanese government. In furthering their aims, they publicized their dependence on Japan as the "savior" for those "disloyals" now segregated at Tule Lake and at the same time they did everything possible to discredit and embarrass the Coördinating Committee. Before the people they accused the committee of conniving with the administration in "oppressing" and impeding the release of detainees; to the administration they complained that the committee did not consist of true representatives of the people; and toward the committee itself, they used various tactics to intimidate its leaders.

Many of the stockade detainees were close relatives or friends of members of this group, which regarded them as martyred leaders. The group made many efforts to obtain the release of the Negotiating Committee and other detainees from the stockade. They sent appeals to the Secretary of the Interior, the Attorney General of the United States, and the Spanish Consul at San Francisco. They also made at least two direct appeals to the project officials. The first of these was on January 16 when Robertson, an Assistant Project

Director, was asked by five or six *Daihyo Sha Kai* members, in an interview shrouded in secrecy,[1] to intercede on behalf of the detainees. The meeting was held at the home of Mrs. Tsuchikawa, sister of the Sadao Endo who had been arrested on November 4 and confined in the stockade. She assumed a position of leadership in the underground movement and also agitated constantly and openly for the release of her brother. In the course of time she came to be regarded by the administration as the instigator of most of the trouble that later developed.

The meeting with Robertson led to no concrete results. Robertson urged that the *Daihyo Sha Kai* back the Coördinating Committee in the latter's efforts to bring the center back to normal. The group appeared willing to take this advice provided Robertson could gain the approval of some of the more prominent detainees. Accordingly, Robertson called seven men, among whom was George Kuratomi, to his office. After an hour-and-a-half session, Kuratomi said, "If you'll promise us that we'll eventually get out of the stockade, we'll go for that plan." Robertson pointed out that he was in no position to make a promise of that sort, but that *Daihyo Sha Kai*'s support of the Coördinating Committee would probably be a necessary preliminary to their eventual release. Kuratomi is said to have replied, "If I ask the boys in the stockade to adopt this plan, I'll have to give them my word. If anything goes wrong, I'll have to commit hara-kiri." Robertson refused to allow Kuratomi to take the risk, since he could give no guarantee of release. Kuratomi then suggested that two detainees be granted temporary freedom "to convince the people that this is the thing to do,"[2] since the group Robertson had talked to was not strong enough to lead the people. Kuratomi promised, "If you release two, we'll resign and tell the people to hold an election." Robertson agreed to approach the administration with this plan, but pointed out that he had little hope of success. His pessimism was justified, for, upon approaching Mr. Best, he obtained no concessions.[3]

[1] Robertson reports that he received "a frantic telephone call" from Block 11 (one of the strong *Daihyo Sha Kai* blocks) asking him to come to an address in Block 11. He went there and was told that someone in Block 6 wished to see him. The next day he was invited to a meeting in Block 6, where he met six members of the *Daihyo Sha Kai*, none of whom he had ever seen before.

[2] On January 14, two days previously, Yokota proposed a similar plan to the Coördinating Committee. See p. 195.

[3] Field Notes, March, 1944.

Early in February the group made another attempt to negotiate with the administration—this time using one Hisao Shiba as its spokesman. As described in the preceding chapter (see p. 213), Shiba claimed to be a "negotiator for the minority" and was granted a conference with members of the Advisory Council. He proposed dissolution of the Coördinating Committee and assumption of responsibility for "peace and order" by the minority. After the promised "peaceful conduct of the colony" had been achieved, the stockade detainees were all to be immediately released. Again, nothing came of this effort, and the administration, as described, reaffirmed confidence in the Coördinating Committee.

The underground group was evidently responsible, also, for the preparation and distribution of the propagandic pamphlet circulated in early March among the newly arrived segregants from Manzanar (see pp. 207–208). Investigation by the Coördinating Committee's "fielders" revealed a possible common source of publication of Manzanar pamphlet and of the material distributed by the "Nippon Patriotic Society,"[4] challenging the validity of the status quo referendum.

There is no evidence that the underground group had any positive popular support throughout January, February, and March. Its position was, however, indirectly strengthened by the uncertain status of reinstated workers and by the growing popular attitude of suspicion and hostility toward the Coördinating Committee. Many of the workers who had quietly returned to their jobs, thus breaking status quo, giving indirect support to the policy of collaboration with the administration, and indirectly jeopardizing communal solidarity, were often most vociferous in their complaints about camp conditions and in their denunciations of collaborationists. The general residents, too, while not inclined to support an aggressive, radical, overt antiadministration movement, were disposed to make scapegoats of the proadministration Coördinating Committee and its supporters.

At the same time the tactics of the Coördinating Committee in utilizing fielders for "intelligence work," concomitant with the continuation of the Army's and WRA's policy of making new arrests and confinements in the stockade, brought about an almost

---

[4] The "Nippon Patriotic Society" was believed to be composed of *Daihyo Sha Kai* members.

pathological state of fear of being informed upon by *inu,* or of being classified as an *inu.*

The members of the Coördinating Committee, and many of their supporters among the Divisional Responsible Men had, by this time, achieved the unenviable reputation of being *inu* par excellence or, in camp parlance, "Public *Inu* Number One," while a larger slate of men, the composition of which might almost be said to vary in the mind of each individual resident, was suspected of *inu* activities. So great was the fear and suspicion of being informed upon that no one could be sure whom he could trust. Many residents believed that a casual, joking remark in the latrine or mess hall might be reported unfavorably to the administration by *inu* and might result in imprisonment in the stockade. And the fear of being branded as an *inu* was the more intense, because a person so suspected was not only subjected to the most severe social ostracism but was often in very real danger of physical violence.[5]

The underground leaders made effective use of this fear by branding as an *inu* anyone who made a statement which could be interpreted as proadministration, or critical of themselves or their group. Since few of the residents explored the basis of the rumors arousing these suspicions, a man's reputation could be ruined by a few whispered words or by an inspired "smear" campaign.

The underground group also sought to force a realignment of the population in respect to the attitudes that had been developed in regard to "loyalty" during segregation. To understand its maneuvers, it is necessary to review briefly attitudes prevailing at the time of registration and segregation, and the changing alignments that resulted from the increasing tension in the segregation center.

As has been explained in detail elsewhere, a negative answer to questions 27 and 28 at the time of registration had many different meanings. To some it reflected an intense bitterness toward and alienation from America, as a reaction against the rejection by America, and the humiliation which evacuation implied: the abrogation of citizenship rights, the uprooting from homes, the destruction of means of livelihood. To others it represented a protest against the intolerable oppression which was a necessary concomitant of even the most humanely operated concentration camps. To many others it was a highly opportunistic decision, offering a haven

---

[5] See Chapter X.

of security from which, they believed, neither relocation into a hostile world nor induction into the armed forces of a country which had placed them behind barbed wire would be required. Since segregation was based on the ex post facto definition of "disloyalty" which had resulted as a by-product of registration, it was necessary for those who had answered the crucial questions negatively at the time of registration to reiterate their "disloyalty" at presegregation hearings if they wished to remain in or be removed to Tule Lake. This act of reiteration branded the registrants as "disloyals" and made them eligible for segregation.

Also eligible for segregation were very appreciable numbers of persons who, though answering the registration questions in the affirmative, came under an administrative regulation designed to avoid the hardships of split families and permitted them to accompany a "disloyal" member of their immediate family to the segregation center. It often happened that a single member of a family, perhaps a young man of draft age, gave a No-No answer on the registration questionnaire and thus achieved the coveted status of segregants for his parents, sisters, and brothers, all of whom thereupon registered as "loyal." Similarly, "loyal" wives accompanied "disloyal" husbands to Tule Lake, and vice versa. All persons under eighteen years of age were ineligible for registration and were therefore technically "loyal," even though segregated. Finally there was a large group (estimated at more than 1,000 persons) of Tule residents who registered as "loyals" but simply refused to leave the project while the segregation movement was in process.

In respect to alienation from America on the one hand, and predisposition toward Japan on the other, the segregants, at the time of segregation, fell into three rather well-defined attitudinal and motivational groups:

I. Those who were extremely bitter toward America and aggressively vociferous in their expressions of loyalty to Japan. They stated that since they had been cast off by America, they had decided to become Japanese; that they had suffered financial loss, indignity, and great inconvenience by evacuation; that they placed all reliance for assistance and eventual justice and repayment for injuries on Japan. Japan, they hoped, would accept them without prejudice or discrimination. "Life in Japan could not be any worse than life in the United States." They repeated over and over again that they had become segregants because of "a sincere desire to return to Japan" and that they "saw no future for themselves in America." They were "true Japanese" who had "made up their minds once and for all."

II. Those who had made no hard and fast decision favoring either America or Japan as a future place of residence or symbol of allegiance. They believed that this decision could and should be postponed until the war was over. Many of them possessed a considerable attachment to the United States and to the American way of life. Others, of the immigrant generation, tended to be nostalgic for the Japan they had known thirty or forty years ago. Almost all of them were extremely ambivalent in their attitudes toward a future in Japan or a future in America.

III. Those to whom Japan as a symbol of allegiance or a future place of residence held no attraction. In spite of the discrimination they had met, they preferred the prospect of a future in America to a future in Japan.

Although we have no direct statistical measure of frequencies in each of these classes, documentary evidence suggests that, at the time of segregation, Group II contained the overwhelming majority both of those who had remained at Tule Lake and of those who had arrived from other relocation projects. Groups III and I were both a great deal smaller than Group II. Group III was overweighted with old Tuleans because of the inertia of the old Tulean population at the times of registration and segregation, but it also contained numbers of new "loyal" transferees accompanying their families. Group I, on the contrary, drawing as it did the radical dissenters from nine relocation projects, necessarily contained a greater number of transferees than of old Tuleans.

During the period immediately following the segregation movement, competition and rivalry between the in-migrating segregants, as a whole, and the settled old Tuleans, brought about a largely artificial cleavage that obscured the margins between the attitudinal groups described above. At this time almost all transferees acted *as if* they belonged to Group I and gave at least lip service to the extreme views expressed by this group. This is, in large part, to be attributed to the tensions connected with the segregation movement; the loss of the familiar atmosphere of their former "homes" in other relocation projects; the feeling that Tule Lake was, in all respects, inferior to these other projects; in particular, the shock connected with the "man-proof" fences, the numerous watchtowers, the searchlights playing over the camp at night, and the finger-printing at time of entrance; the need to assert themselves against the vested interests of old Tuleans, who seemed to have entrenched themselves in the best apartments and the best jobs. Opprobrium heaped on the old Tuleans by Group I took the form of claims that the former were not "true Japanese"; that they were all either loyal to America or, worse still, were "fence sitters" waiting to decide their allegiance, and that they, therefore, did not belong in the segregation center designated for "disloyals." Group II among the transferees took over the attitudes and expressions of Group I so far as to claim that *they* were "true Japanese" and that the old Tuleans were, by and large, persons "loyal" to America who should be removed from camp.

Although many transferees in Group III had no desire to become "true Japanese," their resentment toward the old Tuleans was so great that they found it convenient to adopt the disparaging term of "loyals" in referring to them. Others, realizing the incongruity of the accusations, were unwilling to risk social disapproval by expressing dissent from the prevailing attitude. So far as the old Tuleans themselves were concerned, the radical, "pro-Japanese" Group I expressions of the transferees gave some of them an effective weapon to use against their rivals in assuring the maintenance of their status with the administration. To many others, however, status with their fellow-residents was of more importance than status with the administration and they began vociferously to protest the injustice of the accusation made against them and to proclaim the depth and sincerity of their "disloyalty."

During the period we have termed "Revolt," the margins of the attitudinal trichotomy described above were further blurred. The strike was a collective movement; passive resistance to the administration was general; the necessity of maintaining status quo was an obligation felt deeply by all segments of the population. Unification was, however, of relatively short duration. With the suppression and inconveniences that were necessary concomitants of Army rule, the monotony and boredom of life without productive activity, the impoverishment of a wageless existence, cleavages again became manifest. Protest tactics had failed to bring about any noticeable improvement in conditions of living, and the cohesion of the protest movement had been destroyed by the arrest and confinement in the stockade of most of its leaders. New leaders appeared and, with them, the assumption of a policy of collaboration with the administration in breaking status quo and achieving "normalcy." This policy, however, failed to gain general support, even at its inception. Its backers and leaders were predominantly old Tuleans upon whom, in return for their collaboration, the administration bestowed many favors: positions of prestige, priority in job placement, offices, paid assistants, use of project automobiles. Dormant resentments against the old Tuleans flared up once more among the transferees. Suspicion that the leaders were *inu* grew into a confident belief that they were "loyal to America" and therefore predisposed to betray the "true Japanese." J. Y. Kurihara, for example, said:

We have a lot of loyal people here. Probably they are here for the administration to make use of them.[6]

while Tsuruda stated:

One hundred per cent of the *inu* are of the loyal bunch. I wouldn't be surprised if Sasaki and that bunch are all loyal.[7]

A tendency to attribute the difficulties facing the colony to the failure to separate the "loyal" from the "disloyal" by segregation became more and more apparent, along with expressions of loyalty to Japan and denunciation of "fence sitters." These denunciations were usually followed by some such statement as "The *inu*, the Yes-Yes and the loyal people should be forced out of camp." As these attitudes spread to the old Tuleans, they felt the same compulsion to find scapegoats who could be denounced as fence sitters or "loyals."

Most of the members of the underground movement belonged unequivocally in attitudinal Group I. They were predominantly transferees and had, from the time of their arrival, been ardent exponents of separation of themselves from their "loyal" opponents and rivals (by definition, old Tuleans). They had backed *Daihyo Sha Kai*, forced the adoption of radical policies on the more moderate leaders (most of whom were at this time detained in the stockade), and instigated gangs of younger men to acts of violence. They

---

[6] Field Notes, March, 1944.   [7] *Ibid.*

had opposed the collaborationist leadership of the Divisional Responsible Men. Their opposition had not diminished but had, on the contrary, become sharper when status quo was defeated by a narrow margin. They welcomed the arrival of new contingents of Manzanar, Jerome, and Rohwer transferees in the spring of 1944, who, they correctly concluded, would be predisposed to accept the protest definition of the solution of community problems. They made every effort to strengthen this predisposition through propaganda against the anti status quo elements, who, they claimed, were "loyals" and collaborators. They succeeded in enlisting the enthusiastic support of the new arrivals and, fortified by this support, sharpened the criteria for resegregating the "loyal" who were undetermined about repatriation, and the "disloyal" who wanted to go to Japan as soon as possible.

Pending the realization of the ultimate goal of return to Japan for themselves, resegregation in separate areas of the Tule Lake camp was sought. Since Ward VII had been fenced off by the Army after the November disturbances,[8] the protest leaders pressed to have this ward set aside for themselves and "like-minded" people, including those who were still detained in the stockade. Simultaneously, they made efforts to determine more accurately the composition of the "like-minded" group. Early in February, attempts to obtain signatures of persons who wanted to be sent to Japan on the "earliest exchange boat" were reported,[9] and rumors were prevalent that the Japanese government was negotiating for an exchange ship. The underground group thereupon made an open bid for resegregation and priority in repatriation. A letter signed by one Ishikawa, a comparatively unknown person, on behalf of a "committee" asked permission of Attorney General Biddle and the Spanish Embassy to circulate a petition for the signatures of those residents who desired early return to Japan and who, meanwhile, wished to be separated, in Tule Lake, from those who were not so inclined.

Ishikawa's letter was channeled from Biddle to Ickes to Myer and finally to Best, who, being about to leave the project on official business, passed it on to Black, who sanctioned a survey.[10]

---

[8] Presumably because of an abortive plan to segregate "troublemakers" and their families in this area.

[9] See p. 206.

[10] As described, pp. 216–217, this was the act which led to the resignation of the Coördinating Committee.

This is to confirm my statement to you and your committee during our conference yesterday to the effect that there is no objection on the part of the administration to the proposal that you and your committee make a survey to determine the wishes of residents with respect to further segregation within the center.

The information to be derived from the survey would be as follows:

1. Persons and families who have applied for repatriation or expatriation, who wish to return to Japan at the earliest opportunity, and who wish to live in a designated section of the center among others of like inclination.

2. Persons and families who have not applied for repatriation or expatriation, who have reached no conclusion with respect to an early return to Japan, and who wish to live in a section of the center not specifically designated for persons and families of the first group.

It is understood that the survey is to be made merely on a factual basis with the entire liberty of choice resting with the subject interviewed. The survey committee is to make no attempt to influence the decisions of the residents. It is pointed out that no sound speculation can be made as to any prospect of return to Japan because at present the Japanese government is entertaining no consideration of further exchange.

It is further understood that the survey will be made without commitment on the part of the administration, either stated or implied, that the results of the survey will be made the basis of administrative action beyond that which is already established for housing adjustments through the Housing Office.[11]

The last paragraph of Black's letter, which is ambiguous in English, was made even more ambiguous in the Japanese translation where it conveyed the impression that the results of the petition would be made the basis for future administrative action. This led to a general belief that WRA approved of and was contemplating the early development of a plan for resegregation.

The petition was circulated from April 7 to April 9. While it was being circulated the pressure group released a statement signed by Ishikawa, the wife of Reverend Abe, and twenty-eight other persons. In this statement, it was pointed out that, upon arrival in Tule Lake, "we discovered a large number of heterogeneous elements, with whose thoughts our ideas could never harmonize, mingled among us. Hereupon scores of like-minded people petitioned for resegregation to the high government officials in Washington."

Conduct and attitudes compatible with the "honor of Japanese subjects" and "discipline and education of our children adapted to

---

[11] Letter, Black to Ishikawa, March 29, 1944.

the system of the wartime Fatherland" could not be achieved "as long as the objectionable elements are present."

The proponents of this statement reaffirmed alleged WRA support by adding that "fortunately, the intelligent authority has given its consent to our earnest petition." They, therefore, urged all "who wish resegregation because they desire the opportunity to board an exchange ship . . . to sign this petition of your own free will and judgment."

The circulation of the petition threw the residents into a state of turmoil and confusion. Many suspected that it was not authorized by the administration and that signing it might result in arrest and confinement. But the rumor spread that failure to sign might mean that one would not be allowed to repatriate or expatriate. Arguments for and against the petition raged. Beatings and violence were reported. Sasaki stated:

> Due to the diversity of opinions, a brawl, which hospitalized one, has already been noted in Block 16. Many cited that various arguments pro and con were noted in various blocks.[12]

The fundamental cause of the confusion was the narrow and radical exposition of loyalty propounded by the underground group; that the only "true disloyals" were those willing (a) to repatriate as soon as possible, and (b) in the meantime to be resegregated, either in a separate section of Tule Lake[13] or possibly at some center other than Tule Lake. Anyone not willing to fulfill these conditions was, by definition, a fence sitter or "loyal to America." Loudly as they denounced the fence sitters, most of the residents did not want to go to Japan immediately and were, in fact, neither loyal to America nor to Japan in a political sense. They had segregated to Tule Lake with the idea that they could stay there and make up their minds, depending upon the outcome of the war. Moreover, they did not want to move again even if the moving entailed only a shift to another section of the camp.

It should also be kept in mind that a strict separation of ardent repatriates and expatriates from the other camp residents would necessarily have resulted in extensive separation of family members. Many families had come to Tule Lake because the parents had

---

[12] Minutes of the meeting of the Divisional Responsible Men and the Coördinating Committee, April 8, 1944.
[13] Ward VII.

requested repatriation, while the children remained Yes-Yes. In other cases parents had merely accompanied No-No children, particularly sons, without themselves requesting repatriation. To base resegregation solely on the desire for immediate repatriation or expatriation was objectionable to such families and also to the Nisei No-Noes who had not requested expatriation.

The petition therefore placed the residents in a difficult position. Some 6,500[14] resolved this by signing, some because they sincerely desired to repatriate immediately, others because they believed that their signatures were not binding. Among those who did not sign were many who complained that the underground group was going too far. Some of them pointed out that they had already taken all necessary steps in applying for repatriation or expatriation before segregation and that coming to Tule Lake as segregants was in itself sufficient proof of their intentions. In additions, they objected to setting off the petitioners as the only ones worthy of being called "true Japanese."

The excitement which this petition engendered in the colony caused the administration great alarm. Mr. Black, feeling that the petitioners had not kept faith with his stipulations and had gone "ahead on their own initiative and started this 'return to Japan rumpus,'"[15] issued the following memorandum on April 10,[16] stating that the administration had had no intention of carrying out resegregation and that no petition had been authorized.

It has come to the attention of the administration that two unauthorized reports have caused some uneasiness in the colony during the past week.

The first rumor was to the effect that there would be a further segregation within the center so that all individuals and families who had applied for repatriation or expatriation would be *required* to live in one area of the center and all other individuals and families in another area. It is officially announced that the administration has no intention to carry out a further segregation. Under present procedure individuals and families who wish to move from one part of the center to another, may do so voluntarily by making application . . . at any time to the Housing Office.

[14] Included in the 6,500 are dependents whose signatures were appended by parents. It should be noted that according to WRA records, at least 7,265 residents had been classified as repatriates and expatriates at the time they were segregated (WRA *Semi-Annual Report,* January 1 to June 30, 1944, p. 26). It seems reasonable to infer that signers of the Ishikawa petition were among these 7,265.

[15] Field Notes, April, 1944.

[16] By this date the petition had been circulated and signed by 6,500 persons.

The second rumor was to the effect that persons who wished prior consideration of applications to return to Japan at the first opportunity should sign a petition which was cirulated among the colonists. It is officially announced that no authorization or authenticity was given to the circulation of such a petition. At present the government of Japan is giving no consideration to further exchanges. It is our understanding that if and when further exchanges are considered, the Japanese government will make selection of persons to be exchanged on an individual basis, as has been the case in the past. Affiliation with any group within Tule Lake Center, or place of residence within the Center, will have no bearing upon the selection or rejection of the individual.

It is requested that this announcement be posted conspicuously for the information of all residents of the Center, and that announcements in all mess halls invite attention to its contents.

In view of the fact that Black had been said to have authorized the circulation of the petition just a few days previously, this retraction was regarded, even by opponents of the underground group, as another example of "double-crossing" by the administration.

The disturbing effect of the petition on the general camp residents wore off in about three or four weeks. Since the administration had denied its authenticity and nothing more was done about it, many of those who did not sign and those who signed under pressure, appeared to think it was a closed issue. Some informants, however, realized that resegregation, as such, was not a closed issue and that the cleavage in the colony would probably persist.

The underground group felt that its cause had been greatly strengthened by the petition. On April 24 five of its members sent a copy of the petition to the Spanish Embassy in Washington:

We, the residents of Tule Lake Segregation Center, Newell, California, whose names are listed below in total numbers of ——, do hereby earnestly and respectfully wish to request your excellency to contact the proper authority of the Japanese Imperial Government immediately for the purpose to convey our most desired wishes stated below.

1. All the petitioners desire an immediate repatriation.

2. Upon arrival at the destination if our wishes is granted, all the petitioners have decided to give up everything, materials and manpower, to the country we love so dearly, willingly and gladly as loyal service at this time of national emergency, for her disposal.

Respectfully submitted this 24th day of April, 1944, A.D.

Representatives: Torakichi Ishikawa   Tokuichi Matsubara
                       Tomoichi Kubo   Kenichi Wakasa
                       Hideki Tsuchikawa

They adopted a name, *Saikakuri Seigan*,[17] and soon became known as the Resegregation Group, or Resegregation Committee. Receiving no satisfaction from their appeal of April 24, they followed it up by a more elaborate petition to the Spanish Consul in San Francisco on May 30, appending the names of "6,500 residents …and a supplementary list thereto," and they requested the Consul

to expedite negotiation with proper authorities regarding the said matter through the Spanish Embassy as it is our sole intention to be included in the priority on the next exchange vessel to Japan. We are determined and fully convinced that it is intolerable for us to remain entirely indifferent while our mother country is at war. We, Japanese disloyals, have no egoistic ambition but we only hope for the exchange ship in order to fulfill our duties as Japanese subjects. . . . Furthermore, we wish to be resegregated whereby we Japanese with same thoughts and ideals of mutual understanding can prepare and wait for said order of repatriation.

They reiterated their dissatisfaction at having to live among

loyal citizens of the United States who should enter the Army or relocate outside to help the government; loyal citizens who came here merely by family ties who do not desire repatriation or expatriation; persons who are taking advantage of this center as more or less for safety—[united in] their beliefs to evade draft calls; persons who do not wish to return to Japan until the war is over, etc.

They emphasized their desire to avoid "disturbance and restlessness," and to "keep away from such shameful behaviors [as] that of fighting among brothers," and to receive education and discipline "in accordance to the organizations of our mother country." These ends could be achieved only by resegregation, and

the resegregees, if granted to live in a separately established area, will guarantee full coöperation with center officials in keeping peace and harmony within that area.
The resegregation will tend to lessen the burdens of center officials for the maintenance of peace and harmony within and also shall be easier to deal with in all daily problems.[18]

After submitting the petition of April 24, the several active proponents of resegregation organized frequent, informal meetings among themselves in order to develop plans for implementing their program. Not until August, however, did they come out into the open with plans for a formal, overtly nationalistic organization.

[17] The literal translation is "appeal for resegregation."
[18] Petition from Resegregation Committee to F. De Amat, Consul of Spain, San Francisco, California, May 30, 1944.

Chapter IX

INTERLUDE
Period of Apathy

THE PERIOD FROM THE end of April to the middle of June, 1944, was, politically and psychologically, characterized by indifference and apathy on the part of the residents. The protest movement had failed, and its leaders were still confined in the stockade. The Army had taken over and then relinquished control of the center. A partial strike had been succeeded, if not by "full employment," at least by a wider distribution of jobs, and wages were being paid. Some improvements had been achieved in food and living conditions generally, and the unpopular and disillusioned Coördinating Committee had resigned. Although agitation for resegregation was being carried on continuously by the *Saikakuri Seigan,* popular interest in its program had died down after the Ishikawa petition.

On May 7 June Yamaguchi, secretary to Milton Sasaki of the recently dissolved Coördinating Committee, wrote to a friend

Tule Lake Center continues to be subjected to many trifle discords, unrest, and disharmony, which probably will never end....

Divisional Responsible Men's group as well as the Coördinating Committee are practically out of existence. Sure hard to trace the members now ... The place is so quiet...

In spite of many things, Center's social activities continue to function as if there's no trouble whatsoever. Baseball, basketball, dances, shows, *engei kais* [Japanese entertainment], bazaars, and field day of various track games are some of the activities which enliven our almost "dead" spirit.

J. Y. Kurihara remarked early in May,

Things have changed a great deal.... Right now things are simmering down pretty fast.[1]

[1] Field Notes, May 14, 1944.

And Higashi said at about the same time:

. . . All quiet on the western front. Things are going pretty good except for the reduction of persons working in the family. . . .

I think the Japanese people as a whole made a big mistake at the warehouse [November 4 incident]. If the food had been as it is now, it couldn't have happened. Now we have all the Japanese food we want, and plenty of rice and vegetables.[2]

Tsuruda described the state of affairs as follows:

Things are quieting down. People are forgetting Sasaki. He stays in the background. As long as you don't keep floating something in front of peoples' faces, they forget about it.

The food has really improved. We have 48,000 pounds of cured ham sitting there in cold storage. In the coming months we are going to average eight eggs per person per week. That's an egg a day.[3]

Co-existent with this lessening of tension, and perhaps to some extent responsible for it, was a marked change in administration policy. Mr. Best, in the words of one of his staff, was "putting himself out to be agreeable."[4] He had proposed a half holiday to permit the people to celebrate the Emperor's birthday on April 29; he ordered the big meal of the week to be served on that day; he threw the first baseball at the game which celebrated the occasion. He had also had the fence which separated Ward VII from the rest of the colony removed, an act which had a pronounced effect on morale. As noted in Chapter VIII, the Resegregationists were pressing to move en masse to this ward pending their return to Japan. Many residents, particularly those living in Ward VII, were opposed to this plan since it would have subjected them to the inconvenience of moving. When WRA took down the fence they inferred that the plan for intracamp resegregation would not have administrative approval and that they would, therefore, not have to submit to forced change of residence. Every informant visited in Ward VII made some such remark as the following: "The fence has been taken down. It certainly makes us feel better."

The chronic causes of dissatisfaction were, of course, still present. The prisonlike conditions of camp had, after all, been modified only in relatively slight details. The underlying dissatisfactions were, however, rarely verbalized during this period. Most people

[2] Field Notes, May 15, 1944.   [4] *Ibid.*
[3] Field Notes, May 13, 1944.

seemed to have resigned themselves to the inevitability of the thwarting of their desires for a fundamentally better way of life. The more obvious, presumably remediable dissatisfactions continued to be commented upon: the stockade situation, physical conditions in camp, and employment deficiency.

The stockade situation was discussed, at this time, mainly by the relatives of those who were still detained, or by pressure group agitators. The lack of overt concern by other elements is probably to be attributed to the rapid rate at which detainees were being released. On May 18 the administration announced that 264 detainees had so far been released; that the number remaining in the stockade at that time was only 55; and that "releases of from 2 to 5 persons are being made almost daily."[5]

Preoccupation with deficiencies in the physical conditions of life had shifted from food, which, it was generally admitted, was much better, to sanitary conditions; and comparisons were still made between the superior facilities in the Manzanar section and the inferior equipment in the older section of the camp.

Complaints continued to be heard, also, about the lack of employment opportunities, since WRA had in late March embarked on a policy of limiting employment of two persons per family. From the middle of April the administration intensified its efforts to effect voluntary terminations of the excess employees. The director of the Placement Office was quoted in the project newspaper on April 27 as saying:

One or more members of 78 different families have signified their intention to voluntarily terminate so that there will be no more than two in the family employed. . . .
However, terminations initiated by the administration will be necessary if this voluntary action is not taken.[6]

On May 11 the director stated:

It is urgently requested that terminations be made voluntarily as it will be much more satisfactory for all concerned.
To date, a total of 188 persons from 145 families have volunteered to terminate immediately . . .
Of the 301 families requested to make voluntary terminations, 156 families with 225 excess people employed have not volunteered terminations.[7]

[5] *Newell Star,* May 18, 1944.
[6] *Newell Star,* April 27, 1944.
[7] *Newell Star,* May 11, 1944.

On May 25 the Placement Office reported that it was "now dismissing [excess] workers from the families where there are more than two working"; and on June 8, it announced that "voluntary terminations [of either husband or wife] will be appreciated wherever the family consists of only husband and wife and both are employed." It also stated at this time that those who were being terminated involuntarily were "accepting the decision . . . in a very satisfactory manner."[8] Reports from evacuees suggested, however, that the acceptance was often made with great unwillingness. For example, Higashi said:

Things are going pretty good except for the reduction of persons working in the family. In this block there were eight or nine families who had more than two persons working. In my opinion the administration is making a big mistake by saying that only two people in each family may work, because there are some families who have as many as ten members and they ought to be allowed to have more people working.[9]

In addition to the causes of dissatisfaction mentioned above, at least two happenings in early May might have been considered as sufficient cause for overt resistances.

On May 2 and 3 a number of young men received notices from Selective Service Headquarters to appear for physical examination. Of some 73 on the original list, only 35 were still in residence at Tule Lake and, of these, 24 refused to appear for examination.[10] Wakida, a Kibei, commented:

This is the way I think the Japanese feel. Anyway, it's the way I feel. If I get called for selective service and show up for my physical examination, the Japanese think that means we have some loyalty to the United States of America. If we are loyal to Japan and we are pure Japanese, we don't have to go. If we are going to refuse to go into the Army, we are going to refuse from the beginning. . . .

If I'm going to be a Japanese, I'm going to be pure Japanese and not

---

[8] *Newell Star,* June 8, 1944.

[9] Field Notes, May 15, 1944.

[10] WRA, *Semi-Annual Report,* January 1 to June 30, 1944, p. 31. The *Newell Star,* however, reported on July 20 that "27 Japanese failed to report for preinduction physical examinations for the Army." These twenty-seven were arrested, but when the cases were heard in the U.S. District Court at Eureka, California, the Judge dismissed the indictment. His decision was quoted in the *Newell Star* of July 27, 1944, in part as follows: "It is shocking to the conscience that an American citizen be confined on the ground of disloyalty and then, while so under duress and restraint, be compelled to serve in the armed forces or prosecuted for not yielding to such compulsion."

American at all. I didn't use to be like this. But now I just see this camp from the Japanese point of view only.[11]

These violators of the Selective Service Act were subjected to intensive questioning by FBI agents. Yet no expressions of resentment were heard about the questioning. The whole matter seems to have been taken very casually, as exemplified by Tsuruda's description:

All they did was come around and pull you in for a couple of hours of routine questioning. Some boys had their suitcases all packed. They asked, "Where do we go from here?" The FBI said, "You can go home now."[12]

The second happening was the arrival of a contingent (1653) of new segregants primarily from Rohwer and Jerome. This movement caused a great amount of inconvenience to the settled residents, who were required to take up smaller quarters in accordance with a new regulation alloting a minimum housing space of 80 square feet and a maximum of 100 square feet per individual. Many family groups had to be consolidated, and, while this process was going on, a large number of the new segregants were housed temporarily in recreation halls. The new segregants were thus exposed to the same conditions which had led to unrest among the earlier transferees. At this time, however, they made no organized protest, nor was there any overt attempt to propagandize them, such as occurred with the induction of the contingent from Manzanar. By late summer, however, their accumulated grievances made them receptive to the pressures of the Resegregationists.

During this outwardly quiet period the administration decided to take up anew the long-dormant idea of self-government. It will be remembered that a proposal of this nature had been made by *Daihyo Sha Kai* as early as October 26, 1943,[13] and that insistent and repeated proposals of the same sort had been made by the Coördinating Committee from the day it assumed office to the day of its resignation.[14] These proposals were consistently sidetracked by the project administration, in part because WRA steadfastly maintained that its policies for self-government of relocation projects could not apply to Tule Lake,[15] especially since antiadministration "radicals" might be chosen in such an election.

---

[11] Field Notes, May 18, 1944.
[12] Field Notes, May 15, 1944.
[13] See Chapter IV.
[14] See Chapter VI.
[15] See p. 216.

As described in Chapter VII, the Coördinating Committee had, on February 16, recommended the formation of an Arrangements Committee to plan the establishment of a permanent representative body to succeed itself. Although this plan was approved by the administration on February 18, it failed to materialize.

When it became apparent that the Coördinating Committee would have to resign, the administration found it imperative to sponsor some plan for organizing an evacuee committee with which it could deal in channeling communications to the evacuees. On April 15 the Project Director is said to have received official authorization from Washington to encourage the residents to select a representative committee.[16] On April 22 Myer's authorization was published in the *Newell Star,* along with an invitation to the residents from Acting Project Director Black, to participate in planning an election. Myer stated:

The residents of the segregation center will be invited to establish a Representative Committee. The membership of this Representative Committee shall be selected by orderly, representative, elective procedures. The members shall be selected on a geographical basis to represent residential areas within the center, shall be selected for fixed periods of time, and the total membership of the committee shall not be greater than 12 persons.

The function of the Representative Committee shall be that of acting as the official representative of the residents of the center in communicating to the project director the viewpoints, attitudes, and requests of the residents, in conveying to the residents information concerning WRA regulations and determinations affecting them, and in advising with the project director on matters as to which collaboration between the administration and the residents is needed.

Black requested that an Arrangements Committee be formed "to work out the final plans and supervise the election of the permanent committee." This Arrangements Committee was to be composed of one representative from each ward, selected by block representatives. Black added:

It is hoped that by May 1 a meeting may be held with this Arrangements Committee . . . and the administration can outline the requirements of regulations of the War Relocation Authority. . . .

The duty of the block delegates will be merely to select one representative from each ward to serve on the Committee of Arrangements.

This Committee on Arrangements will have two functions: (1) Make

[16] Field Notes, April, 1944.

plans for the election of a permanent Representative Committee. . . .
This duty will include the fixing of the tenure of office, provide for the
method of filling vacancies, prescribe the manner of conducting elections,
and make all necessary preparations so that an orderly election may be
held in the near future. (2) Supervise the election and certify the results
to the administration. . . .

There will be no community government within the Tule Lake center
similar to that which exists at the relocation centers. The Representative
Committee . . . will serve in an advisory capacity to the Administration.[17]

The administration waited in vain for the slightest sign of initiative on the part of the colony. On May 4 Mr. Best announced
that procedures for the organization of an Arrangements Committee to plan and supervise the establishment of a permanent
Representative Committee had been decided upon "in a spirit of
helpfulness and coöperation" . . . : and outlined plans for an election to be held on May 22, three weeks after the date originally set.

An election by secret ballot of block delegates to ward councils will be
held May 22 from 2 to 8 P.M. in each block manager's office, following preliminary block meetings on May 18, under the pro tem chairmanship of
the block manager, to nominate five candidates and to choose an election
board consisting of three to five members. . . .

The ward councils, composed of 18 block delegates from each ward (20
in Ward VI) will meet at 2 P.M., May 25. . . . A secretary will be appointed
and a representative and an alternate who must be able to speak and
understand both English and Japanese, will then be selected from among
themselves to serve on the Arrangements Committee; after which, results
of the meeting will be certified to the project director through Civic
Organization. The ward council will continue to exist for possible consultation by the Arrangements Committee.

The eight members of the Arrangements Committee so selected will
meet, with the project director or his designated representative as chairman pro tem, and select its own chairman as the first order of business.

The Arrangements Committee will then prescribe qualifications for
voters and for members of the Representative Committee; fix the term of
office of members of the Representative Committee; designate the date of
election; prescribe the manner of filling future vacancies in its own membership; supervise the election; confer with the project director or his
representative on matters related to the election and the inauguration of
the Representative Committee.

Members of the Arrangements Committee will be paid at the rate of
$19 per month and the secretary $16 per month. Other approved members
of any necessary sub-committees will be paid at appropriate WRA rates.[18]

---

[17] *Newell Star*, April 22, 1944.
[18] *Newell Star*, May 4, 1944.

On May 8 these items were repeated in the *Newell Star* and, under a section headed "Slow Response," the failure of the evacuees to take advantage of the invitation was pointed out:

> However, there has been no substantial response to the administration's invitation to proceed with the formation of the Representative Committee. This delay may be due to a number of factors, such as the size of the community, the diversity of interests, the more immediate importance of competent and sound leaders to assume the initiative which would put the program under way.
>
> Therefore, in a spirit of helpfulness and coöperation, the administration is prepared to assume the responsibility for proposing definite plans to bring about the organizations of the Representative Committee and the establishment of harmonious and practical working relationships with it as the recognized and official spokesman of the residents in accordance with the provisions of Mr. Myer's authorizations.

There followed an elaboration of the earlier instructions regarding the election planned for May 22 and the selection of the Arrangements Committee on May 25, with further, very detailed specifications of functions of the Arrangements Committee and procedures for election.

These elaborate plans never came to fruition. At the camp-wide block nomination meetings scheduled for May 18, only fifteen blocks[19] nominated delegates. Most blocks called meetings, but so few residents attended that valid nominations could not be made. A few blocks refused even to hold meetings.

Accounts are available from a number of informants indicating the procedural difficulties met in the separate blocks.

Wakida, from Block 58, reported:

> I didn't go to the meeting. Eighty-two people were needed for a quorum[20] and only seventy-five showed up. Then the anti-status quo people went around to get people to come. I went and I was nominated. I absolutely refused the nomination. I don't intend to engage in politics. Things dragged along and about ten people left. They refused to let me decline the nomination. Then I said that there was no quorum anyway, so the nomination was not valid. After a lot more talk the meeting ended. Nobody was nominated.

---

[19] New construction had added 10 blocks to the original project and there were 74 occupied blocks at this time.

[20] Each block could determine its own rules of procedure. Definitions of "quorum" varied greatly. In some blocks 75 per cent and in others 50 per cent of the eligible voters formed a quorum. In still other blocks, no specific quorum was required.

J. Y. Kurihara, who refused to attend the meeting in Block 7, said:

I was home and they came for me. But I refused to attend. I heard they had only twenty people attending. They seem to have appointed me and another gentleman next door. But I flatly refused to accept the nomination.[21]

Kurusu, block manager of the very pro status quo Block 59, tried to comply with the instructions given by the administration, but failed:

I had a meeting. Only twenty-five or twenty-six people attended. So there was no quorum and I just told them the meeting was adjourned. As you know, the block managers can't stick their noses in politics, so I must be neutral. I did my best, but the people feel that way.[22]

A young married woman living in the notoriously tough Block 21 reported that the people in her block had had a meeting but that they had shouted, "No, no, no, no!" No one was nominated.[23]

When Tomiyama, an Issei resident of Block 5 was asked how the nominations had gone, he replied with a smile, "Nobody was nominated," adding, "Of course, this is Reverend Abe's block."[24]

The Community Analyst reported the situation in other blocks as follows:

I heard that Block 73 had a long argument. The block manager arrived and was accused of being an *inu*, for helping in this. He said he had a fight (verbal, it seems) with the "worst radical" in the block. He added that there were others "too radical to listen." Anyway, the group couldn't be handled. There were no nominees.

In Block 9 there were no nominees.

In Block 69 they put up representatives; but they also had an argument. Apparently it was in the blocks which had no nominees that they had the worst arguments.

In Block 29 things went O.K. There was a nomination. But they had a one-hour wait before people came. I think that was usual. They had to go around in the block and get them to come in. In Block 16 an anti-status quo man said, "We had to drag them out of bed to get nominees." Block 16 is very pro-status quo.[25]

It is obvious that the old status quo issue was still very much alive; that the radicals, far from seeking election, were opposed

[21] Field Notes, May 21, 1944.   [24] Field Notes, May 20, 1944.
[22] Field Notes, May 23, 1944.   [25] Field Notes, May 20, 1944.
[23] Field Notes, May 22, 1944.

to the formation of any representative body; that the conservatives and moderates were unwilling to assume the responsibility of working with the administration in this way; and that fear of being called an *inu* if elected was a general deterrent. Statements of a variety of informants, both before and after the election, indicate clearly that the attitude of the general resident was one of skepticism about what could be gained by an election; of resentment that earlier "representative" bodies (*Daihyo Sha Kai* and Negotiating Committees) had not been recognized; of irritation that there were still detainees in the stockade; of fear that new representatives might be thrown into the stockade; and, above all, of unwillingness to accept any administration-sponsored proposal. Although an appreciable number of potential voters may have abstained from attending meetings because of overt pressure from the underground group or because of social pressure from their neighbors, it is apparent that a pattern of opposing the administration by merely ignoring administrative exhortations to attend meetings had become well established.

Kurihara had stated, several days before the nomination meetings, that, in his opinion, the election was doomed to failure because "people are not very enthusiastic about it." He regretted the lack of interest:

I think that a body ought to be formed to try to coöperate with the administration and get things rolling harmoniously. It would be best if the body stood up and spoke for the rights of the Japanese, even if they are thrown into the stockade.

He added, however, that "no respectable, well-educated Japanese" would be "willing to accept that position."[26]

Higashi, a former *Daihyo Sha Kai* supporter, foresaw that getting "new delegates will be pretty tough. People in general are saying 'What's the use? We put up representatives once and they wouldn't recognize them.' " He suspected also that the administration had a black list of residents of whom it disapproved and that if any of these were elected, "I know the administration will not OK him." He added:

As far as I'm concerned, I don't care if they elect representatives or not, as long as they take care of sanitation and family employment.[27]

[26] Field Notes, May 14, 1944.
[27] Field Notes, May 15, 1944.

June Yamaguchi, also before the election, emphasized the extent of *Daihyo Sha Kai* support as an impediment:

It doesn't seem as if this representative body will go through. I hear so many people say as long as they are obligated to the *Daihyo Sha Kai*, they will refuse to vote until they're released from the stockade.[28]

Wakida was extremely pessimistic:

I have no idea about it. They've asked me to be one of the representatives, but I won't. I'm not going to be in any political organization.

The people feel pretty bad. If you do good for the people you get put in the stockade. If you do good for WRA you get called *inu*. So I'm going to play baseball.[29]

Tsuruda, who had no strong allegiance to any of the camp's political factions, said:

Nobody cares a thing about having a representative government. So far as I can see, nobody is going to break their neck trying to work up a few representatives for the block. They just don't care. Things are going along pretty good, so leave well enough alone.[30]

Ex post facto explanations emphasized strongly the stockade issue. "Representatives" were still confined against the will of the community. How could the administration expect the people to elect new representatives? For example, J. Y. Kurihara said:

People are taking the attitude, why should they make a committee when the administration and Army refused to recognize them in the first place. If the administration had recognized the boys in November, they would have had success at this time.[31]

Wakida remarked:

It was unfair to put the representatives in the stockade. It was a dirty deal. That's really what the people feel. Eighty per cent of the camp feels this way, not because they support Abe and Kuratomi but because they think WRA treated them bad.[32]

Tomiyama made the same points:

When the people came into camp they were confused. They are still confused. The reason they are refusing to support this proposal is that the old matter of the men in the stockade is not settled. If they were all let out, the election would be proceeding in an entirely different manner. No intelligent able man would accept the nomination. I certainly wouldn't.[33]

[28] Field Notes, May 16, 1944.
[29] Field Notes, May 18, 1944.
[30] Field Notes, May 13, 1944.
[31] Field Notes, May 21, 1944.
[32] Field Notes, May 23, 1944.
[33] Field Notes, May 20, 1944.

And Itabashi, a transferee from Manzanar who entered camp in February, long after the *Daihyo Sha Kai* representatives had been incarcerated, and had expressed himself frequently as opposed to all "radicals" and "trouble makers," had also swung over to the prevalent attitude:

The first representatives we sent out were all put in the stockade. The administration was denouncing them that they were not representative of camp opinion. So we put in some new block representatives.

Then the administration said, "You don't represent camp opinion either." It sent them to the stockade. . . .

Then the administration formally requested the camp people to elect representatives. Everybody's opinion was, "What's the use? Every time we send representatives they are arrested. If we make more representatives, they will only put more people in the stockade." Everybody said, "What the heck! We don't want to send any more people to the stockade."[34]

Kurusu, conservative and anti-*Daihyo Sha Kai*, also felt that the stockade issue was still of paramount importance.

The people feel right now, I think, that it's better to release the men from the stockade. I feel pretty strong that way.

Another thing, the Coördinating Committee was organized for the purpose of releasing the men and bringing the center back to normalcy. As long as the men are in the stockade people will feel that it is not a normal condition.

Unless WRA releases the men in the stockade there is no necessity to organize another committee.

Besides people hesitate to be block delegates. They may go to the stockade if they are.[35]

A Nisei girl, an old Tulean, explained, later, that nominees refused because of fear of being beaten up.

They thought the best thing to do was to sit quiet and take what the administration dishes out. You're always in constant fear if you take that job.[36]

Yamashita, who was assuming leadership in the underground pressure group, summed up the situation as follows:

It shows that the majority of the residents have no confidence in the administration.

Much of it is due to the people still being held in the stockade. They are taking too much time for settling this little business in the stockade. Mr. Best every day is taking valuable time with the chief consideration of

---

[34] Field Notes, July 27, 1944. [36] Field Notes, August 17, 1944.
[35] Field Notes, May 23, 1944.

keeping the administration's face. They have to spend so much time on the stockade that they are disregarding other things such as watering the roads and improving the mess halls.[37]

And Mr. Tsuchikawa, husband of the active agitator for resegregation, remarked that "This is a great victory for the people."[38]

Project officials are said to have interpreted the nullification of their efforts as a mere postponement. A Caucasian informant describes the Project Director's reaction as follows:

Best said that if the center felt that this was premature, we will have it later. He isn't calling it off.

It's a curious inversion. Once, when they had the organization, Best was trying to slow it down. Now Best is saying "Go ahead," and the people are slowing down.[39]

In the course of time the matter was dropped, and no further official attempts were made to form a representative body. The project administration announced its stand, as follows, in the *Newell Star* of May 25:

Plans for the formation of the Representative Committee, a permanent intermediary body which was granted approval by the WRA, have been postponed for an indefinite period of time, announced Ray R. Best, project director. The block meetings, which were held Thursday evening to nominate candidates for the block delegates' election as the first step toward formation of the permanent body, did not show sufficient response from the residents.

"The failure of a large number of blocks to hold their meetings and select their nominees serves to defeat the purpose of the organization plan, and indicates that there is not enough popular sentiment in favor of the formation of the Representative Committee to warrant a continued effort to carry out the election at the present time," stated the project director.

He lauded the earnest effort made by the residents of many blocks to launch community representation in accordance with the outlined plan; and stated, "It is obvious that unless the residents are virtually unanimous in their participation in the selection of the Representative Committee, then the committee cannot be truly representative."

In conclusion he expressed the belief that the formation of the representative body should be postponed until a more favorable date "in fairness to the entire community."

In this same issue of the *Newell Star* it was also announced that WRA had taken over the stockade from the Army.

---

[37] Field Notes, May 21, 1944.   [39] Field Notes, May 20, 1944.
[38] *Ibid.*

The WRA is now in complete charge of the administration of the segregated area within the center, it was announced by Project Director Ray R. Best on Wednesday. This area which has been commonly termed the "stockade" had been established by the Army authorities and administered by the Army prior to this time. As stated in the *Newell Star* last week, releases have been made from the area to the residence section of the center by a WRA committee working with Army officials.

The administration of the segregated area by the WRA as announced by the Project Director means that complete supervision will be in the hands of the project officials.[40]

This act was to mean that the force of the irritation and anger of the evacuees about continued detention would shortly be directed entirely toward WRA, which could no longer pass along the blame for detention to the Army.

On May 24 an incident of extremely high explosive potentiality occurred. An evacuee worker in the construction crew, returning to the project from his assignment outside the area, had an altercation with an armed sentry and was shot at close range. He died on the following day. Here was a repetition, under even more distressing circumstances, of a situation which, late in October, had thrown the camp into turmoil: a worker had been killed, not accidentally as before, but apparently in cold blood. The incident was witnessed by some dozen evacuees.

Some time later an account of the incident was built up from these eyewitness accounts by a committee of eight Issei and formed the basis of a report submitted to the Japanese government via the Spanish Consul. This version follows:

Immediately after the incident of November 4, 1943, the Army with the aid of the WRA, constructed fence, segregating the Colony and the Administrative area. Four gates were constructed and Army sentries were assigned to examine the workers who passed through the gate from the Colony area into the restricted zone. Recently, evacuee workers were issued work buttons and blue cards. There have been complaints about the gate-pass procedure, which required different type of buttons, about two inches in diameter—white, green, and red. . . . Despite inconveniences of the gate-pass procedure, there was no evidence of generalized center hatred for the sentries.

On the morning of May 24, the Center was calm and undisturbed. Then, at approximately 2:20 P.M., May 24, 1944, the shooting occurred. The victim, Shoichi James Okamoto, was 30 years old, had been born in

---

[40] *Newell Star*, May 25, 1944.

Garden Grove, California, and had never been abroad. In the Center, he was a truck driver, properly licensed and assigned to the construction crew.

Okamoto was driving Truck #100-41 at the order of the construction supervisor . . . to get lumber piled across the highway from the old main gate, which is called Gate #4. He carried all necessary identification papers and badges and was qualified as a truck driver permitted to pass into the restricted area. In his truck, a swamper named Harry Takanashi . . . accompanied Okamoto on this assignment; he likewise was provided with all necessary identification to go outside the perimeter gate. The witnesses, besides Takanashi who rode next to Okamoto, included eleven boys from the heavy equipment crew who were waiting for an Army escort to go out to the cinder pit. This crew had three trucks parked in a semi-circular form, close to Gate #4. Okamoto and Takanashi were permitted to pass out the gate and the fatal shooting occurred when they were returning via the same gate.

According to Takanashi, the new sentry had just come on duty. Word has it that the new sentry was in a disagreeable mood and was known as one of the tougher sentries. The two on the truck went over the line a bit. The sentry, on Okamoto's side of the truck, could see Takanashi's badge, but could not at first see Okamoto's because of the high sidedoor of the truck, and because of the sentry's short stature. It is claimed that the badge was on Okamoto's jacket, as was necessary. The sentry asked to see the badge in a disagreeable fashion. Okamoto showed the pass, was allowed through, and returned with his truck and swamper in a few minutes. On the way back, his truck drove up close to the heavy equipment crew's trucks. There were 11 boys on the equipment crew, the trucks in a semi-circle form, standing near the gate with fellows on the running boards, fenders, and around the vehicles. It is said that the sentry made remarks to them. The most usual phrase which was repeated in the center was, "What the hell are you Japs doing—waiting to climb the hill?" At this juncture, Okamoto was driving in towards the gate and the sentry's attention was focused back upon him. While he had been waved through the gate a few minutes before, he was now ceremoniously halted. It is claimed Okamoto said words to the effect of, "Well, here's the pass." Perhaps this sounded cocky to the already irritated guard. The sentry ordered him off the truck and commanded Takanashi to drive. Without a driver's license, the latter explained, he could not drive a truck. The sentry, it is said, was infuriated at this delay. From then on, commands were well peppered with curses. This took time and raised tension all around. To Takanashi's answer the guard is said to have replied, "You Japs and your WRA friends are trying to run the whole camp." He then turned back to Okamoto. . . . Heavy equipment boys, not many feet away, were talking among themselves of the sentry's aggressive and insulting manner, and some despite the tension—were saying, "They're not all like that," "This one has it in for 'Japs,' etc." Okamoto was apparently apprehensive by this time. When ordered out of the truck he had done so reluctantly and had left the truck door opened. At this juncture a Ford V-8, driven by Roy S. Campbell, a

Caucasian WRA staff, arrived from the highway and stopped with engine running, about 7 feet from the end of Okamoto's truck.

According to Takanashi and other witnesses, the sentry at that time cocked his gun and went around via front to the other side of the truck where Okamoto was standing. The sentry then ordered Okamoto to the back of the truck. This would have been just outside the gate. Okamoto started but hesitated for an instant. At this point, speculate on the guards motives, with true concentration-camp psychology, the suspicion is that the guard wished to shoot him outside the gate. (Shot while trying to escape.) Okamoto's hesitation is explained by this point. In the moment of hesitation, in which most say no pipes were lit and no words said, the sentry struck Okamoto sideways on the right shoulder with a rifle-butt. Okamoto raised his right arm and moved his body slightly back to ward off any further blows. While in this defensive position, the guard stepped back one pace and from a distance of four or five feet fired without warning. In all accounts stemming from eyewitness testimony, the act was looked upon as an unprovoked attack, Okamoto fell with what seemed to have been a close-range stomach wound. Residents speculated on the possibility of the sentry having been overseas, having been shell-shocked, or being mentally below par. It is said, in the center, that Takanashi certainly must have been cool-headed about the affair since he summoned an ambulance in less than one minute. At any rate, the account which he and his co-workers gave as signed testimony to the Police Department in interviews with all eyewitnesses on the scene shortly thereafter is said to be factual and logical. The story of all eyewitnesses, despite already distorted newspaper versions, such as in the S. F. Examiner that the one Caucasian, Roy Campbell, eyewitness account,[41] probably fits the picture drawn for them.

The heavy equipment crew was thunderstruck. The sentry cursed, seemed nervous, and it is said, swung the rifle in their general direction. More cursing—"You people get the hell out of here"—and they fled, Takanashi trying to get the hospital on the phone. Another crew of five stumbling on the scene were ordered back by the sentry. The ambulance arrived. . . .

Okamoto was immediately hospitalized. How long a time elapsed before he was hospitalized is not known; some say 20 minutes. According to the attending physician and surgeon every possible means of treatment was

---

[41] The newspaper account, to which reference is made, stated: "The witness, a Caucasian employee of the WRA, said he did not know the cause of the argument.

" 'The guard said, "Don't get out of that truck," ' the witness related. 'Anyhow the Jap got out on the driver's side and I am sure the guard said, "Don't come any closer, you b———." '

" 'About that time he drew up his rifle, butt end. He was going to hit him on the head.

" 'The Jap moved, the guard backed up about three feet and shot.' " *San Francisco Examiner*, May 25, 1944.

administered. . . . In spite of the doctors' effort, Okamoto died at 12:10 A.M., May 25, 1944.[42]

As in the case of Kashima's death, the immediate reaction of the residents to this fatality was shock, intense fear, and anger. There was a reluctance to pass through the sentry-guarded gates. The construction crew, of which Okamoto had been a member, met and refused to resume work. Workers on many other crews failed to report for duty on the day after the shooting. Grievance meetings were held throughout the project on the evening of May 24 and the following day.

Due to quick and effective action by WRA officials, however, anger was turned against the Army rather than against the administration. As reported by WRA, "[the] event . . . somewhat reduced the opposition to WRA and made it stand, rather, in the light of protector."[43]

The strategy WRA used in handling the incident was in sharp contrast with its tactics at the time of Kashima's death. Mr. Best immediately circulated a statement of regret about the tragedy, and he and other project officials called on the bereaved family. Secretary of the Interior Ickes issued an indignant radio and press release, calling the shooting "completely unwarranted and without provocation on the part of the victim."[44] Two automobiles were placed at the disposal of the family, and another was sent to the Heart Mountain Relocation Project to bring other relatives to the funeral. Employment compensation papers were filed immediately. Plans for a public funeral were approved and facilitated. Caucasian and evacuee members of the WRA police force were stationed at the gates, near the sentries, to alleviate the workers' fears of passing the armed sentries.

Best's message of regret, which was circulated in both English and Japanese, was reported in the *Newell Star,* of May 25, as follows:

Mr. Best made a statement this morning which was read at all of the mess halls in the center. The statement follows:

"I regret very much that one of the center residents was shot yesterday afternoon by a military police sentry and that he died at the center hospital early this morning. Everything was done by the medical staff at the

[42] Report of the Investigation Committee on the Shoichi James Okamoto Incident, July 3, 1944.
[43] WRA, *Semi-Annual Report,* January 1 to June 30, 1944, p. 30.
[44] *Newell Star,* June 1, 1944.

hospital to save his life and a great many people stood ready to give their blood.

Investigation is being conducted by the military and proper disciplinary action will follow. The WRA was in no way responsible for the shooting, and I want you all to know that we regret that it happened. No further statement can be made at this time pending the investigation by the board, but as soon as facts are available they will be given to the residents in full detail."

At the same time Mr. Best expressed sympathy to the bereaved members of the family and offered to make available to them any facilities of the W.R.A.

In the same issue of the *Newell Star,* Okamoto's older brother was quoted as wanting

a complete and unbiased investigation of the circumstances surrounding the shooting and full justice meted, although he hoped that there would be no undue disturbance within the center over the affair.

The effectiveness of this policy is shown both by the fact that the construction crew and other workers immediately called off their strike and by the attitudes of many informants.

On May 25 J. Y. Kurihara reported:

I heard quite a lot of criticism about it, but one thing surprises me: the people are very calm. There is quite a lot of resentment, but they are not excited. The people are saying, "Let's be cool and find out more about it before we take any action. We must not make any rash judgment until we know the facts completely." The colony itself is taking it calmly.

You might find hot heads may start to agitate. But we must be fair. Mr. Best is not responsible.

We had an announcement here at noon in English and Japanese. As I say, they were very calm. The Japanese can take it. They'll take it more than any other race.

From the information that has been gathered, of course, I don't know. It looks as if the soldier used too rash judgment in using his gun.[45]

A young Nisei girl, at about this same time, said that the people were calm but that they were talking a great deal and had had a meeting that morning. "They do not as yet know who was right, but think the soldier was too quick with his gun."[46]

Tsuruda's wife, a Nisei, emphasized the quieting effect of Ickes' statement:

The people are angry about it. But we heard over the radio that Secretary Ickes said that it was the soldier's fault, that the soldier was going to hit Okamoto on the head. That made the people feel better.

[45] Field Notes, May 25, 1944.   [46] Field Notes, May 25, 1944.

They were all angry around here but nobody knew what it was all about. Some were saying, "Well, maybe Okamoto got fresh." But now even Secretary Ickes blames the M.P.[47]

Some informants, however, refused to exonerate WRA completely from blame. June Yamaguchi, for example, said that she felt the announcement made at the mess hall sounded as if WRA were trying to avoid responsibility.

It was Mr. Best's fault for bringing in the military in the first place.[48]

Immediately after the shooting, the sentry, a man named Goe, was placed under arrest and an investigation board was appointed by Colonel Austin. It was announced that a court-martial would be held after the completion of the Army investigation. Meantime an inquest by the Coroner of Modoc County was held, and on May 26 a verdict was released to the effect that Okamoto came to his death "by a soldier of the United States Army in the performance of his duty."[49] District Attorney Lederer of Modoc County reported on the inquest as follows:

Lederer said the [coroner's] jury received "eighteen different stories."

Sifting these stories, he continued, it appeared that Okamoto and the unnamed sentry first had words when Okamoto drove outbound through the gate to pick up a load of lumber.

When Okamoto returned to the gate, inbound with the lumber, he again exchanged angry words with the sentry over the latter's demand to see his pass, said the district attorney. Witnesses declared that Okamoto was "sarcastic."

"The sentry ordered him from the truck," Lederer said. "But Okamoto refused. Then the guard ordered him again and the driver left the vehicle.

"The guard then ordered him to the rear of the truck, where a WRA car was parked, and again Okamoto refused."

The soldier was holding his rifle at the port arms position across his chest when Okamoto made a sudden move as though to grab the rifle, said the district attorney. It was at that point that the sentry took two steps back and fired.[50]

From statements collected three or four days after the incident, it became apparent that many people believed that the court-martial proceedings would result in a "whitewash." Some feared an outbreak if the sentry was exonerated. Tsuruda, for example, showed the conflicting emotions that the strain had induced:

---

[47] *Ibid.*   [49] *San Francisco Examiner,* May 27, 1944.
[48] *Ibid.*   [50] *Ibid.*

A lot of how this goes is going to depend on how WRA handles it between now and the time the verdict of the court-martial is released. If WRA can prove to the people that they are sincere in their belief that the man who was shot was of no fault, and that they did their best to get justice, then things might quiet down. But if they justify the sentry completely, there's going to be a blow-off. They'll have to build a double fence around the administration section.

The smartest thing WRA could do is to start impressing the people now that the military is responsible and not WRA. After all, the man was a soldier. . . . It comes under the jurisdiction of the War Department. . . .

There are people who talk like this: "Well, we can't expect justice from the Army here inasmuch as we are disloyal Japs and their enemies. If that's the case and the soldier is exonerated, all we can do is learn his name and remember it until after the war and see which side wins." They want to bring it up at the peace conference.

Another faction says, "You won't hear anymore about this until after the war. By that time, they hope the people will have forgotten about it."

If the soldier is exonerated, that will give the M.P.'s the impression that the lives of the Japs in here are not worth a hell of a lot. That's just asking for more shooting. It all depends on what the verdict is.[51]

Wakida stated that he had a good deal of business to transact in the administrative areas but he was not going to risk going through the gates. His wife remarked that the sight of soldiers patrolling camp with machine guns was offensive. But neither Wakida nor his wife, however, believed that the people would make any demonstration. "What can we do?" asked Wakida, "We're only Japs. All we can do is take it."[52]

A young Kibei informant from Block 21 stated categorically that the soldiers should be kept out of camp.

Everytime the people see them they feel worse. If the soldier is acquitted, the best thing WRA can do to avoid trouble is to remove the soldiers completely and tear down the fence. Then trouble might not start. It would be all right to have the military at the main gate, but at the other gates—No.[53]

In this tense atmosphere the public funeral arrangements were made by a committee of block managers and representatives of the Construction Crew and Motor Pool. A wake, held in the high school auditorium on the evening of May 30, was said to have been attended by some 1,200 persons; and the funeral on May 31, held on

---

[51] Field Notes, May 27, 1944.
[52] Field Notes, May 28, 1944.
[53] *Ibid.*

the outdoor stage, had an attendance variously estimated at from 4,000 to 9,000. According to the *Newell Star* of June 1:

Thousands came from all parts of the center, in spite of the cold discomfort, to stand with bowed heads in tribute to the deceased. At the same time they were expressing a protest against the hate and intolerance engendered by this war. Men and women, young and old, mothers with babies in their arms, thus offered sympathy to the bereaved family. Every person present was moved by sorrow.

Mr. Best and other high-ranking project officials were present, and Best gave a memorial address:

I wish to express regret that this unhappy event has occurred. I have already assured the young man's family on behalf of the administration that all in our power will be done to assist them in their hour of grief.

The community is to be commended for the help that it has given the bereaved family and for the public expressions of sympathy. The spirit shown during the past few days gives me confidence that we have learned to live under the difficult and complex conditions that prevail in this center.[54]

After the funeral, reactions, in the main, were still favorable to the administration. Mr. Best's courteous gesture was evidently deeply appreciated by the residents in general, although some of the more cynical interpreted it as "a first-rate political gesture."

J. Y. Kurihara remarked with considerable emotion:

I felt happy that he came and made that talk. Not to do it would have made the people suspicious. I felt very good about it. Undoubtedly he created a better feeling by coming than by staying away.

The Japanese people thought sure he would send Mr. Black or Mr. Robertson and that Mr. Best wouldn't come. They were surprised. He has regained some confidence. Coming in and speaking showed courage.[55]

Wakida said:

He's good now, but think what happened last time [the farm accident]. He's learned. . . . Now he has confidence in our behaving peacefully.[56]

Yamashita gave the more cynical interpretation and expressed an attitude undoubtedly common among members of the underground pressure group:

As you know, the shooting took place in such a manner that it was liable to cause almost any kind of trouble with grave consequence. But

---

[54] *Newell Star*, June 1, 1944.   [56] *Ibid.*
[55] Field Notes, June 3, 1944.

with the experience of the past, residents of this center kept themselves very quiet, knowing themselves how serious a matter it was. The administration has done a marvelous job of taking the matter very cautiously, trying to calm the feelings of the residents.

The question of sincereness and sympathy to the family, on the part of the administration, is, in my opinion, doubtful. But they have worked in a very, very wise way to prevent some incident which might occur. Leaving the funeral to be a camp funeral was done very excellently and that I appreciate and admire. The administration was wise in persuading the residents to have a public funeral. That was one of the reasons which should be considered important in calming down the feelings of the people. Mr. Best was very wise in making the funeral so big. It made people feel very good, at the expense of the residents. [I.e., cash contributions were received from the residents.]

If this was a public funeral, which the administration sincerely recognized, it should have been paid for by the government or the administration.

The committee who arranged the funeral was more or less pulled in as tools of Mr. Best.[57]

Kurusu wrote an excellent summary of general camp attitudes about ten days after the shooting

Generally speaking, the attitude and sentiment of the colony toward shooting incident is very quiet and does not make sharp and strong criticism in comparison to the last year's incident. It seems to give me a hint that on account of the past experienced troublesome period, the colonists are acting much more sensibly and observing the present existing condition with the eyes of great interest.

As far as I can observe the present existing public sentiment, I hope that probably there will be no public disturbance or see the slightest tendency of trouble and pressure group. However, it appears to me that the colonists have received considerable shock and a tendency of great anger toward thoughtless cruel barbaric inhuman being attitude of the military police.

With the most prudent attitude and the greatest interest, the colony is observing the progress of the present affairs and those false communication and broadcasting over radio deeply degrade the public morale and extremely irritate the public sentiment and anger. As the most typical characteristic of the Orient races, especially, Japanese has a great tendency toward excitement, irritation and judge things sentimentally. In consideration of these facts I sincerely hope that the authority take thorough steps for the investigation and the justice will be done for a better solution. Also I have confidence that the colony is eagerly waiting with great expectation for the official announcement of the truth.[58]

---

[57] Field Notes, June 14, 1944.
[58] Isamu Kurusu, Letter, June 5, 1944.

Some evacuee leaders attempted to make political capital out of the tragic shooting. The Divisional Responsible Men, spurred on by former Coördinating Committee members, and the underground pressure group both attempted to intrude themselves into the picture.

The Divisional Responsible Men met on May 26, the day after Okamoto's death, ostensibly "for the purpose of discussing future preventive or precautionary measures to avoid the recurrence of an incident similar or diverse in nature to the one in which James Okamoto was a victim, as well as take steps in assisting in any way possible with the disposition of the case."[59] Pointing to the fact that no representative body had been formed to care for the residents' interests, they proposed that a "temporary group"

to deal with the immediately pending problems, such as insurance of safety when passing through the Gates, be formed. Then, future plans for a workers' group may be discussed and decided upon later, subsequent to the Administration's approval or rejection.[60]

A temporary committee was thereupon appointed, but, when it met with the Project Director on May 30, the members received a cold response on the grounds that they were intruding political considerations into a purely personal matter.

Mr. Best expressed great distress over the incident and stated that as our respect to the man who passed away, tribute must be paid purely on a religious and personal basis in which politics should be wholly uninvolved. He further mentioned that an establishment of a temporary body composed of responsible men of various divisions and sections may tend to divide the colony again. He felt that another trouble, presumably caused by this recent incident, will not recur; that is, he hoped it will not. If it should, it will be one in which people will be against the administration and in such an event, the people are the only ones who are going to suffer. If in the future, at any time, any incident of any nature occurs from which trouble starts, "we might just as well wash our hands and have the Army take over the camp," Mr. Best commented.

The program under way to establish a Representative Committee to disseminate information and to talk and counsel with brought no response from the Colony because there were some groups which disliked the administration and groups which disliked the Divisional Responsible Men, the Project Director informed. As a whole, Mr. Best felt that it was inadvisable to form such a body (committee) at the present time. Mr. Black pointed out that in view of the nonacceptance of the administration's invitation to proceed with the formation of the Representative

---

[59] Minutes of the meeting, May 26, 1944.   [60] *Ibid.*

Committee, setting up of a temporary committee, which will not be authorized by Washington, will stall off the time when we can bring about the required Representative Committee which Washington has already approved.[61]

Miss Yamaguchi (Sasaki's secretary) described the indignation and hurt feelings of the members of the former Coördinating Committee at this rebuff when she said:

Because of this shooting they wanted to make some sort of a labor organization to protect the workers. Mr. Best said he was really distressed over the incident but politics should not be involved in the funeral; it should be a purely religious matter, purely a matter of paying tribute to the deceased.

Mr. Kitagawa, Mr. Kami and Mr. Sasaki say, "No matter how hard we work and how much we try to do for the people we are always called *inu*. So we might as well leave the place alone and let it burn up."[62]

The underground pressure group used the incident to fan up resentment against the Army and the administration. Its leaders posed as protectors of the "oppressed," and one of them (Kira) is said to have threatened that if the sentry were exonerated in the court-martial, some Caucasian would pay for the verdict with his life.

The results of the court-martial were not announced until the end of the first week in July, about six weeks after the shooting. The sentry was acquitted. Nothing came of Kira's threats, and the predicted troubles did not materialize.

The institution of court-martial proceedings had been announced in the *Newell Star* of July 6, 1944:

Court-martial proceedings for the sentry ... commenced today at the military area here, announced the administration. Officers from other military posts have been detailed here to conduct the court martial.

Although it is contrary to military rules for any civilian to be present at a military court-martial, exceptions were made in this case. Arrangements were made by Dillon S. Myer, national director of WRA, with the War Department so that eight residents of the center may be present at the proceedings. Among those attending today will be a member of the Okamoto family and representatives of the committee of Japanese nationals which will make a report covering the case to the Spanish Embassy.

Representatives of the WRA project staff and Edgar Bernhard, WRA attorney from San Francisco Regional Office, will also be present.

[61] Minutes of the meeting, May 30, 1944.
[62] Field Notes, June 15, 1944.

The trial was described in the public press as follows:

Private Goe, charged with manslaughter in connection with the death of 30 year old [Shoichi Okamoto], a disloyal resident of the camp, testified in his own behalf before a board composed of five colonels, a lieutenant colonel, and two captains. . . .
The verdict was reached after an hour's deliberation.[63]

The verdict had relatively little impact on the residents generally. By this time the temper of the community had changed. A series of *inu* beatings had, just a few days before, culminated in a murder, and most of the residents were preoccupied and confused by this new crisis.

The acquittal of the soldier was, however, discussed resentfully by some individuals. Others regarded it cynically as an action that might have been expected from the American government. J. Y. Kurihara wrote:

The American laws are born out of Congressional incubator, turned out by the thousands to suit the occasions which benefit themselves. I would rather live among the barbarians than among the hypocritical, selfish, everything-for-myself Americans. Their laws are mockery to civilization. They can shoot and kill an innocent man for no reason whatever and be acquitted, as pronounced by the court-martial freeing Pvt. Bernard Goe, who shot Shoichi Okamoto on May 24. . . .
The resentment over this very unfavorable verdict is great. Why shouldn't it be? To kill a man just because he was afraid of him is no excuse, yet the officers have acquitted the sentry. A cowardly shooting and a shameless verdict. This is America, hypocritical America.[64]

A Nisei girl said:

There were harsh reactions to the acquittal. It was very shocking and disappointing news. It seemed so unfair and unjust.[65]

Another Nisei girl said:

The verdict was kind of expected. They knew the result before they even started. All those things are whitewashed.[66]

---

[63] "Sentry Exonerated in Tule Lake Jap Slaying," *San Francisco Examiner,* July 7, 1944.
[64] J. Y. Kurihara (manuscript).
[65] Field Notes, July 18, 1944.
[66] Field Notes, July 19, 1944.

Chapter X

INFORMERS
Suspicion, Beatings, and Murder

THE PERIOD DESCRIBED in the preceding chapter was characterized by extreme apathy and indifference to administrative proposals and actions. At the same time, however, the undercurrent of suspicion toward fellow-evacuee collaborators, fence sitters, and "loyals" was gaining strength. The dual fear of being informed upon by an *inu* and of oneself being classified as an *inu* has been discussed in Chapter VIII, where the tactics of the underground pressure group in labeling an ever-increasing number of its opponents with this derogatory tag have also been described. Most members of the Coördinating Committee, many of their backers among the Divisional Responsible Men, the old Tulean clique in general, and a number of the transferees who had taken a public stand in favor of coöperation with the administration, were being called *inu*. Most prominent among these alleged informers were Kitagawa, Minami, Niiyama, and Oyama of the Civic Organizations; Sasaki, Kami, and Noma of the Coöperative Enterprises; Watanabe, and other deserters of the *Daihyo Sha Kai* cause, all of whom were called "Public *Inu* Number One."

It will be remembered that Army representatives met with members of the Negotiating Committee daily after the November 4 disturbance until November 12, when they abruptly refused to have any further dealings with the committee members on the grounds that they were not truly representative of the community. The Commanding Officer admitted, at this time, that he was receiving information from evacuees discrediting the Negotiating Committee and *Daihyo Sha Kai*. The leaders of these evacuee organizations suspected that the hostile reports had come from Kami and Kitagawa. The suspicion soon became public information and these men were held responsible for the subsequent crackdown by the Army and the institution of martial law. When the leaders were arrested and thrown into the stockade, without specific charges filed against them, in November and December, *Daihyo Sha Kai* supporters firmly believed that informers, such as Minami, Niiyama, Oyama, Kami, and Noma were to blame. When the Army suddenly arrested other *Daihyo Sha Kai* supporters on the morning the status quo referendum was being taken, and when status quo was defeated by such a narrow margin in the subsequent vote, the two events were connected as further evidence of the use by the Army of informers hostile to *Daihyo Sha Kai*. Noma came under especial suspicion during the period of martial law because he was observed frequently entertaining Army officers at his apartment and was exempted from the Army-imposed curfew regulations.

When martial law was lifted the activities of the newly created Coördinating Committee, and the enthusiastic support it received from WRA, did nothing to diminish suspicions of its members, many of whom were the same ones who had been thought to be informing the Army. In particular, the administration-approved committee plan of using "fielders" for "intelligence work" confirmed these suspicions. The committee's policy of asking for only "justifiable" release of stockade detainees made it apparent that, with administrative sanction, it was determined to keep its most outspoken opponents incarcerated indefinitely. It was also blamed for the new arrests that were made sporadically. When Watanabe, who had been one of the original *Daihyo Sha Kai* members, joined forces with the Coördinating Committee and was given special status as advisor to the committee, his earlier obstructive tactics in regard to *Daihyo Sha Kai* were remembered. His frequent visits to project officials, and the fact that a few Negotiating Committee members and *Daihyo Sha Kai* block representatives, who were his close friends, escaped arrest while those known to be his enemies were apprehended, left no doubt in the minds of many residents that he was an *inu* par excellence. Without exception, members of the Coördinating Committee were considered informers, and Sasaki, its executive secretary, necessarily took the brunt of the blame for its activities. The tie-up between the committee and the Coöp was also viewed unfavorably by the residents.

On the imaginary list of Public *Inu* Number One were included also Police Chief Suzukawa and several members of the Evacuee Police Force. Ever since segregation the evacuee police had been under suspicion by the segregant transferees, who knew that after registration only Yes-Yes or "loyals" had been allowed to serve on police forces in relocation projects. They believed that the same policy held in the Tule Lake segregation center,[1] and that the administration was employing "loyals" in this capacity to spy on the "disloyal" residents. Furthermore, the police were in an inherently vulnerable position since they had to work closely with the administration and, in enforcing law and order, to carry out policies that often clashed with the residents' wishes. They were, for example, required to investigate alleged pro-Japanese activities which were disapproved by the administration but condoned by the community. In this connection they were frequently accused of informing on fellow evacuees, of obstructing "harmless" activities, of harrassing "innocent" people and, in general, of breaking the unwritten law which required every Japanese to keep damaging information about his fellow evacuees within his own racial group. The incompatibility of their duty to collaborate with the administration in enforcing law and order and their obligation as evacuees to observe the unwritten law tended to inactivate the police force. They avoided involvement in any action by which they might be considered *inu*. As a result social control by legal sanctions weakened progressively. Lawbreakers, who had been "legitimately" arrested, often took advantage of the prevailing state of pathological suspicion and called their arraigners *inu*, hoping thereby to establish their "innocence" in the eyes of the community. And, although the inaction of the police against gamblers, who were operating openly in the project, brought accusations that they were taking bribes from gambling and vice interests, the police chose in most cases not to arrest the offenders, for to do so might lead to the more dangerous accusation of being *inu*.

A man named Kurokawa was also included among Public *Inu* Number One. He had been confined in the stockade, but, after his release, was often seen in the administrative area and was said to be an unofficial advisor to the Project Director. After obtaining

---

[1] This was an erroneous impression. At Tule Lake there was no such requirement in force.

employment with the Reports Division he had, apparently on his own initiative, opened an office and set up a sign designating it as "Research Headquarters." Suspicious residents immediately dubbed the office "*Inu* Headquarters."

Residents did not hesitate to suggest that their private enemies, or persons whom they merely disliked, were *inu*. Usually no specific accusations were made. It was sufficiently damning to pass along the word that "so-and-so is an *inu*." By May it was difficult to find an informant who was not vociferously castigating the generally recognized Public *Inu* or giving vague hints about other suspicious characters. As a Nisei girl expressed it: "Every place you look you see an *inu*."[2]

Ever since status quo had been broken it was widely believed that the *inu* would be the objects of violence. It was even hinted, occasionally, that their lives were in danger. For many weeks, however, no overt punishment of *inu* took place. They were, instead, subjected to distressing forms of social ostracism. A suspected *inu* would be met with marked hostility in mess halls, block meetings, recreation halls, latrines. People would break off conversations at his approach, or would lower their voices to whispers. Children would bark at him suggestively.[3] Young men would shout "Hey, *inu!*" as he passed. Rumors that certain persons were planning to waylay and beat him up would reach his ears. His wife and children would be similarly shunned and insulted. The long-expected series of beatings did not actually get under way until the middle of June, when, within less than two weeks, at least four "*inu* beatings" occurred.

On or about June 12 Masato Noma, brother of Takeo Noma, the general manager of the Coöperative Enterprises, was so severely beaten in a night attack that he had concussion of the brain, and it was reported that he might lose his eyesight. The reasons for the beating were widely discussed. Many people believed that he had been mistaken for his brother, Takeo, who, it was agreed, was a Public *Inu* Number One. Others claimed that the beating was intended as an example and reproof for Takeo who had, upon Masato's recent arrival from the Santa Fe detention camp, favored him with the prized position of manager of the sewing factory in the Coöperative Enterprises. There seemed to be general agreement

---

[2] Field Notes, June 4, 1944.   [3] Cf. pp. 78–79.

that popular resentment against Takeo Noma was directly or indirectly responsible for Masato's beating.

On the night of June 13 Anzai, an Issei warden on the police force, was the victim of an assault so serious that he was said to have suffered a fractured skull. This incident was the culmination of friction between status quo and anti status quo factions in Anzai's block (Block 54). The block had been split almost in half on the status quo referendum.[4] Even after the referendum the status quo anti status quo cleavage dominated block meetings, and Anzai and another Issei became known as spokesmen for the anti status quo position. They were accused of threatening to report questionable activities of their opponents to the administration. A crisis had arisen several weeks before the beating when these two Issei had publicly criticized certain young men in the block for indulging in "morning exercises" in imitation of militaristic exercises customary in Japan. Resenting this criticism, several of the young men (said to be members of the underground pressure group) sought out the two Issei and, after a heated argument, locked one of them in the public ironing room. The second Issei escaped and called in the evacuee police, who released his friend but did not apprehend the culprits. The block residents, irrespective of their former stand on the status quo issue, now repudiated the two Issei completely. They petitioned the administration to remove them from the block, and they petitioned Suzukawa, the evacuee chief of police, to remove Anzai from the Police Force. Neither of the petitions was acted upon, and the two men continued as unwelcome, suspected residents of the block. When, less than a week later, eleven men from the block were arrested and placed in the stockade, suspicion that Anzai and his friend were culpable *inu* became a certainty in the minds of their fellow residents. Most residents, outside the block, knew little or nothing of the details of the friction that led to the violence. It was generally agreed, however, that Anzai was beaten because he was an *inu*. Few people questioned the validity of this accusation; the mere fact that other people were calling him an *inu* was accepted as justification for the act.

Reactions of the residents to the beatings varied from gratification and condonation to mild rebukes. J. Y. Kurihara reported that "the majority of the people are enjoying the beatings."

---

[4] Continued status quo was favored by 52 per cent, opposed by 48 per cent.

Kurihara added:

The beatings can be justified from various angles. The Japanese have grievances against the administration, but they know as a fact that they're helpless. Naturally, the only thing they can think of doing is how to get back at those who spy on them. I think these beatings will keep going on for quite a while. I think there will be at least a half a dozen more. The administration listens to the *inu* and not to the others. So such things happen.[5]

Yamashita said:

Knowing the Japanese as a race, knowing them for their courtesy and their good behavior, I say that if anyone is beaten there is a certain fundamental reason justifying it.

I hate to see any Japanese beaten by our countrymen. The fundamental reason for such beatings is the way this camp is governed.[6]

A few days after the Anzai beating, Harry Takanashi, the chief eyewitness of the Okamoto shooting, was threatened but escaped a beating. It was alleged that his testimony at the coroner's inquest, unfavorable to Okamoto, had resulted in exoneration of the sentry.

On June 21 a mentally deranged evacuee attacked his roommate and another elderly Issei with a hammer and almost killed one of them. Although it was widely known and acknowledged that the victims had never been called *inu,* the *inu* obsession was so universal that some people began to say that they must have been *inu.* A Nisei girl, for example, reported:

People are saying that even this beating was an *inu* beating. The old man found out that his friends were acting like *inu.*[7]

By the middle of June the project administration had become aware of the tensions and the disorganized condition in the camp. It was also cognizant of the unpopularity and inherent weakness of the evacuee police. In an attempt to improve the deteriorated relations of the police with the residents, the administration had planned to organize a Police Commission[8] composed of eight ward representatives. An announcement in the *Newell Star* of June 1

[5] Field Notes, June 17, 1944.
[6] Field Notes, June 14, 1944.
[7] Field Notes, July 2, 1944.
[8] There was an earlier Police Commission composed of three evacuee members selected by the Coördinating Committee. This body was very unpopular and ineffectual and soon went out of existence.

attracted little interest from the residents. But as the beatings continued, social disorganization in the community became more pronounced. Petty thefts and other crimes took place with increasing frequency; the WRA officials became alarmed and renewed their efforts to organize the commission by announcing on June 22 that "an election will be held Wednesday [June 28] in each block to select by ballot or by acclamation one man whom they consider qualified to act as a Police Commissioner."[9] Another election was to be held on July 5 to select three candidates from each ward from among the block choices; and from these three ward candidates the administration was to select one police commissioner.

By the formation of the commission the administration hoped to enlist evacuee leaders to cope with the situation and to bring "about an understanding and coöperation between the colonists and the police department in the enforcement of rules which have been set up for the good of the center."[10] This administrative action again met passive resistance from the residents in the form of non-coöperation. Before the election many evacuees predicted that it would be a failure. A man in Ward VIII remarked caustically, "Who wants to be a legalized *inu?*"[11] Kurihara predicted it would be a "resounding failure. Nobody with any self-respect would take the position because he would inevitably be labeled as *inu.*"[12]

And Tsuruda said:

I don't think it's going to be such a hot idea. The people aren't going to like it. It's giving them the impression that the administration is putting them under additional surveillance.[13]

Wakida was more optimistic:

It may have a fifty-fifty chance. You see the Internal Security is very bad. Somebody might think, "We're going to change this system." So the election might go better than the one to select a representative body in May.[14]

The Tsuchikawas, pressure-group leaders, stated that they hoped the election would be even a greater failure than the attempt to elect representatives in May.[15]

When the election was held on June 28, only three blocks elected candidates. Wakida's wife reported:

[9] *Newell Star,* June 22, 1944.
[10] *Ibid.*
[11] Field Notes, July 2, 1944.
[12] Field Notes, June 26, 1944.
[13] Field Notes, June 25, 1944.
[14] Field Notes, June 23, 1944.
[15] Field Notes, June 24, 1944.

The block manager announced it in the mess hall at lunch time. He said

The block manager announced it in the mess hall at lunch time. He said we'd have a meeting. But he said a certain number of people have to come to have the meeting and if you don't come we can't have it. I don't think many people went.[16]

According to a Nisei girl informant, Block 21, a very strong status quo block, did not have any meeting. The Tsuchikawas expressed disappointment that their block (Block 6) had actually selected a candidate, although only about ten persons attended the meeting. The block manager had stated that there was nothing in the announcement about a quorum and proceeded with the meeting. According to Kurihara his block (Block 7) failed to hold an election because only about four people attended.

The situation in the center was further complicated on June 28 by the transfer of nineteen Issei from Tule Lake to the Santa Fe camp operated by the Department of Justice. Fifteen Issei were removed directly from the stockade, and the others were taken from the evacuee area, presumably for having engaged in *Daihyo Sha Kai* activities. It was alleged that the administration had been contemplating their removal for some time. The residents considered this as unnecessary persecution, and many of them blamed a nebulous group of *inu* as being responsible for these arrests and the transfer. Some confidently expected reprisals, e.g., Mrs. Wakida said, "Both my husband and I think there's going to be a lot of trouble here since these nineteen men were sent to Santa Fe."[17] An Assistant Project Director, approached by some members of the pressure group, was told that the transfer was "the last straw." He was warned that the leaders had had difficulty in restraining young strong-arm boys and that they were no longer willing to keep them in check. As a result, the official was told, future attacks might not be restricted to beatings, but might result in murder.[18]

Meanwhile, incidents of violence continued. On June 29, a little over a week after the attempted hammer murder, a man named Sumitomo was waylaid and beaten at night. According to rumor he was a close friend of Mr. Kurokawa, a Public *Inu* Number One. Sumitomo was also said to have deserted the *Daihyo Sha Kai*, for which he was once a block representative. Although some informants claimed he was beaten because he was not liked in his block,

[16] Field Notes, June 30, 1944.   [18] Field Notes, July 2, 1944.
[17] Field Notes, June 30, 1944.

it was more widely reported that he had been beaten "because he was an *inu*."

A few nights later, Watanabe was beaten by unknown assailants, although he was not severely injured. His status in the Public *Inu* Number One group left no doubt in the minds of the residents about the cause of the assault.

During the latter half of June these beatings were discussed in almost every home and were the main topic of conversation in latrine, laundry, and boiler room. Gruesome details of injuries were repeated and elaborated. Imaginary black lists, on which *inu* were supposed to be ranked in order of their guilt, were described. There were frequent guesses about who would be the next *inu* to be beaten. Hints that the "worst" was yet to come were heard. Though the ordinary, peace-loving resident might secretly disapprove of violence, he rarely expressed this disapproval publicly for fear that he himself might come under suspicion. He tended, rather, to pass on every scrap of gossip he heard about the misdeeds of the victim and the activities of those who were "next on the list." Some people expressed disappointment that, so far, only the smaller fry were involved in the beatings. In discussing these happenings at a later period, Kurihara said, "Some of them deserved it and some didn't," and added, "Take Kami, he should have been buried."[19] Mrs. Tomiyama said at the time: "It's too bad about the Noma beating. They mistook the man for his brother."[20]

Regarding the tension in camp, Kurihara commented:

> Having *inu* around keeps everybody on edge. Everybody suspects everybody else and it has led to a great deal of hard feeling. It keeps the people in a constant state of tension.[21]

Mrs. Tsuruda, a younger Nisei who had often expressed violent hatred of *inu,* described the state of unrest when she said: "I think everybody is nervous in here. This place gives me the willies."[22]

Gossip about the misdeeds of the officials of the Coöperative Enterprises became intensified. Stories of the extent of their alleged graft reached fantastic proportions. It is almost certain that some of these stories originated with the underground pressure group which had bitterly attacked the Coöp for its stand on the luxury issue in December and for its role in breaking status quo in Jan-

[19] Field Notes, October 16, 1944.
[20] Field Notes, June 21, 1944.
[21] Field Notes, June 8, 1944.
[22] Field Notes, June 24, 1944.

uary. Whatever their source, the stories were accepted on their face value and spread from one family to another. Some informants accused General Manager Noma of attempting to buy off his opponents with Coöp money. Others accused Coöp officials and employees of outright theft.

An older Nisei woman stated:

People say that Coöp men are making big money for themselves. They say that in the old days whenever a Coöp man relocated he took a big pile of money away with him.[23]

An old Tulean Nisei later told of a woman who had reputedly found three hundred dollars in a box of cake purchased at the Coöp. When the honest finder returned the money to the store, the clerks made her a present of several more cakes in the hope that she would not betray the fact that they had secreted stolen money in a cake box. She added:

Employees in the canteens all graft. If you have a friend you can go to the canteen and buy things for half price.[24]

Kurihara remembered that:

Mr. Kami has said numerous times, "If I'm afraid of two by fours [the clubs used in beatings], I can't make money."[25]

Stories of graft by Coöp officials in connivance with WRA officials were also widely reported. An Issei stated:

The information I get from all over is that there are a few of the managers of the Coöp who have a close relationship with the WRA officials. Both appointed personnel and evacuees are getting graft out of the Coöp.[26]

A Nisei girl, an old Tulean, later stated: "They said the Coöp was buying WRA stuff and selling it in the canteens."[27]

These stories were brought into the *inu* context by claims that people who had criticized the Coöp and its officials were being arrested and confined in the stockade. According to Kurihara:

Any person who unflinchingly attacked the Coöperative was immediately reported to the administration . . . Without question, that person

[23] Field Notes, June 21, 1944.
[24] Field Notes, August 24, 1944.
[25] Field Notes, July 31, 1944.
[26] Field Notes, June 30, 1944.
[27] Field Notes, September 14, 1944.

was then apprehended and thrown into the stockade and confined there indefinitely without even a semblance of a trial.[28]

The interplay of intense hostility toward the Coöp, the breakdown of legal sanctions, and the tacit social approval of the beatings and attempted beatings finally culminated in murder. On the morning of July 3 the camp was electrified by the news that Takeo Noma, the general manager of the Coöperative Enterprises, who had long been known as a Public *Inu* Number One, had been slain the previous night while on his way home from a carnival. The *Tule Lake Coöperator,* the publication of the Coöp, reported in the July 3 edition:

Mr. [Takeo Noma], general manager of Tule Lake Coöperative Enterprises, Inc. was assassinated July 2nd, 10:40 P.M. in front of the entrance of his brother's unit in Block 35. He was attacked by several unknown assassins who stabbed him through his neck from right side of throat and cut a main artery with a sharp short sword. He fell on the porch and died instantly.

Mr. [Noma], on his way home from a visit to the Carnival that night, stopped at lavatory of block 35 where he resided. When he came near the entrance of his own unit, apparently he noticed the figures of several suspicious men, and so he tried to enter his brother's unit which was located next to his. But, it was too late. The assassins ran closely after and stabbed him before he could open the door. Hearing a sharp cry of anguish, his sister-in-law dashed out and saw to her surprise the tragedy. Despite the prompt search to north and south by Mr. [Noma's] brother and his neighbors, the men who committed the crime had fled.

Diverse rumors about the cause of the murder spread rapidly. Noma's *inu* status in the camp had been well established in the minds of the residents. He had been accused of graft and of nepotism. He had been prominent in resisting *Daihyo Sha Kai* in December. He had advised and helped the administration in its program of breaking status quo. He had backed the Coördinating Committee. Any one of these acts was considered sufficient cause for punishment. Some people, however, held that his prewar activities as an insurance agent, when he was alleged to have swindled fellow Japanese, had led to a "grudge murder."

The immediate reaction of many of the residents was that Noma had met the fate he deserved. Kurihara's sentiments, quoted below, were shared by many others.

---

[28] J. Y. Kurihara, manuscript, July 20, 1944.

The killing of T. Noma was a blessing to the residents. I have yet to see anyone who really feels sorry for him, other than those of his immediate family. Never have I seen such pleasant reactions to a murder in all my life.

Several others are said to be in line for the grave . . . and their deaths, violent as they may be, will be openly rejoiced by the residents.

The public sanction of T. Noma's murder will undoubtedly encourage the executioner to carry on his or their work. A good work. He doubtless is feeling like a hero receiving public approval and rejoicement. I hope he won't betray himself, feeling elated. . . .

Why do I approve it? Because there is no law here in this camp. . . . The administration has so far listened to the Rats [*inu*] and upon the strength of their flimsy charges, it arrested and threw many into the stockade.[29]

A Nisei girl stated:

This might sound awfully heartless, but nobody has any sympathy for Noma. The whole camp feels that way. It had a lot to do with the Coöp and people felt he was really behind all the things going on with the administration and sending people to the stockade—especially the more recent pickups.[30]

Two informants, discussing the murder much later,[31] described the attitudes prevalent shortly after the murder. A Nisei girl, an old Tulean, remarked:

The old Tuleans, I know, felt Noma got what he deserved. After all he did! They were all saying he was going to resign and leave camp. They said he had made his kill and was planning to go.[32]

An Issei said:

Of course, Mr. Noma was one of the most hated men in camp. I heard that he signed a petition to send the people in the stockade away to Santa Fe.[33]

Others, disapproving of this extreme act of violence, were hesitant to express sympathy. An older Nisei man said: "The funny thing is that the murder has split the camp into two parts. Half feel sorry for the guy and the other half are glad."[34] But, as Kurihara said, "Everybody shut up like a clam."[35]

---

[29] *Ibid.*

[30] Field Notes, July 18, 1944.

[31] It was necessary to collect an unusual number of ex post facto statements to cover this period, since our Caucasian field worker was asked by many of her informants not to visit them for fear they might be suspected of being *inu*.

[32] Field Notes, August 24, 1944.

[33] Field Notes, August 8, 1944.

[34] Field Notes, July 17, 1944.

[35] Field Notes, July 20, 1944.

Yamashita stated:

People were sorry for the victim. But they as a whole were afraid of consequences if they did not rejoice for such a happening. They thought that the murder was the last resort or last step to be taken to let the public on the outside and the administration know that wrong doings by WRA cannot continue here forever. Deep thinking people do not consider that this barbarous action was wise and they realized that it would be more or less criticized by the American public when it is known outside by the paper or radio. But the conditions of this camp were such that they were forced to use such a method.[36]

The residents speculated a great deal about the identity of the assailants, and many of them suspected that some members of the still nebulous Resegregation Group would be accused. The administration, too, attributed the murder to a deliberate conspiracy by members of the Resegregation Group and suspected that the stockade detainees had incited them. Several repressive measures were immediately instituted against the detainees. All mail to and from the stockade was stopped, and large pieces of plaster board were attached to that portion of the stockade which faced the evacuee residential area so that no signals could be exchanged between detainees and residents. Gate Number 2, near the stockade, was closed, and Gate Number 3, which was located several hundred yards away, was opened for the residents. These measures angered the detainees, irritated the camp residents and contributed toward keeping the stockade issue alive in the public mind. As described in the next chapter, the detainees, in protest, initiated a hunger strike in the middle of July. Later, the administration turned over several of the detainees to the Grand Jury of Modoc County for indictment on the charge of murder.[37]

Throughout the project a state verging on panic prevailed. The Board of Directors and the key officials of the Coöp immediately resigned. Anticipating closure of the canteens, people rushed to stock up on food supplies. Anonymous threats against other *inu* were reported to the administration and spread over the project. It was said that the assassination of all members of the Coöp Board of Directors had been threatened. Persons who feared that they were "next on the list" were taken into protective custody and housed in the administrative area. The entire evacuee police force resigned.

---

[36] Field Notes, July 28, 1944.   [37] See p. 301.

The *Newell Star* reported the resignations of the Coöp officials in its July 6 edition as follows:

As a result of [Noma's] slaying, an emergency Coöperative Board of Director's meeting was called Monday morning [July 3]; at which time all 17 members of the Board resolved to tender their resignations collectively.

Subsequently, the following officials of the Coöperative tendered their resignations which were approved and accepted by the Board of Directors: Masao Nishimi, assistant manager; Masamori Maruyama, business manager; Masao Iwawaki, personnel director; and Toshio Tomishige, information director.

For a time it seemed as if the Coöperative Enterprises would disintegrate completely. Under the shadow of increasing public opprobrium and suspicion, minor officials throughout the organization attempted to resign. Most of them agreed, however, to remain at their posts after an urgent appeal had been made by their former leaders who immediately took steps to insure the election of a new Board of Directors. In spite of the reluctance of many of the residents to assume the vacated positions and the turbulence and disorder of many of the meetings, a slate of ward representatives was elected by July 9. These, in turn, selected and installed a new Board of Directors on July 12.[38] The make-up of the new Board contrasted sharply with that of the old. Instead of being ultraconservative representatives of the old Tulean vested interests, two of the new directors were ex-stockade detainees who had been suspected of complicity in the November disturbances, and several others were considered "agitators" by the administration.[39] The administration was forced to approve these selections, for it recognized that the individuals were willing to step into positions which might cost them their lives.

On July 24 the new Board released, through the *Tule Lake Coöperator*, a statement requesting popular support of its officials:

The sudden death of the late General Manager [Takeo Noma] has made a great change of managing staffs. ... The Board is still facing fur-

[38] Ward II reëlected its former directors, who later refused to accept the positions and were replaced by new men. Ward VII failed to elect directors.

[39] The list of directors announced in the *Tule Lake Coöperator* of July 15 (no directors from Ward VII) indicates that two Tuleans were chosen. The breakdown of the list shows that besides these two Tuleans the new Board was composed of three transferees from Topaz, two each from Poston, Manzanar, and Rohwer, and one each from Heart Mountain, Gila, and Jerome. A transferee from Jerome was elected president of the Board.

ther difficulties in selecting the personnel for the key positions. If the actual condition of the Coöp has not been well presented to its members, then there will be a tendency to cause misunderstanding. . . .

Therefore, we appeal to you for the preparation to create a smooth and favorable operation of our Coöp in the future, you are urged and invited to assist in choosing the most capable men for this purpose. . . .

Your fine judgment and generous cooperation is needed to carry on this program. We may say there is a slight tendency of an atmosphere of "none of my businessism" can be found among us members. Doesn't it?

We must eliminate totally such unfavorable feeling because it might happen to be a cause of unwelcomed incident. We especially take this opportunity to appeal to you for your hearty assistance and cooperation which is essentially needed to adopt a successful plan for mutual benefit of all patrons.

The Board immediately adopted and adhered to a policy of referring important issues to the residents for criticism and approval. It proceeded to pay off long-deferred patronage dividends. It pledged itself to follow the "guiding principles . . . of courtesy and honesty"; to avoid high-pressure salesmanship and overexpansion; to give no discounts to anyone; to restrict radically the sale of "luxury items"; and, finally, to shun political activities.

We shall confine ourselves to the conduct of business and we shall not enter into any affairs having no bearing upon the proper discharge of responsibility.[40]

To remove any suspicion of graft, it employed as a special accountant for periodic checking of its books an evacuee of recognized integrity and prestige who had a considerable following in the community.

As these various changes went into effect, hostility toward the Coöperative Enterprises died down, and criticism of its policy practically ceased. Improved rapport was clearly manifested as early as July and August, 1944.

A Kibei girl stated, "People I know are very glad about the changes. It seems everything is in order now,"[41] and a Nisei girl said, "Well, as far as our block is concerned, the people were very satisfied with the new Board representatives."[42]

Although critical remarks were occasionally heard, the majority of the people seemed to agree that, at last, the Coöp had become a decent and properly run organization, working "for the good of the people."

Meantime, threats to other Public *Inu* Number One were considered such a serious menace that some fifteen men[43] were removed from the evacuee area and housed in the administrative area as a protective measure. It is said that some of these men fled from the evacuee area and sought refuge on their own initiative but that others left only under protest, after being informed by Internal Security representatives that, unless they acceded, the administration would not be responsible for their lives. They were all housed in the hospital where they immediately met opposition and scorn from other evacuee workers. Whenever any of them walked about in the administrative area, he was greeted by barking noises. The mess crew in the hospital refused to serve them food and when the refugees were then taken for meals to the Caucasian personnel mess hall, they met a similar reception from the evacuee crew employed there. Finally, facilities for cooking had to be set up for them in a warehouse.

Several of the refugees shortly returned to their barracks; but even after ten days others refused to leave their sanctuary, although the administration assured them that the danger of violence had passed and that the situation was under control. It is said that some of them claimed that return at this time was "equivalent to a death sentence." On August 15 three of them (Kami, Suzukawa, and Kurokawa) were, at their own request, transferred to other relocation projects. News of this transfer spread quickly among the evacuees, many of whom expressed satisfaction that *inu* had been removed from their midst. Some added hopefully that these people would undoubtedly meet their deserved fate in the centers where they had taken up residence. A rumor arose that Kurokawa had been forced to leave Heart Mountain, the center to which he had transferred, because of public feeling. Kurihara remarked:

Kami, Kurokawa, and Suzukawa—it was wonderful that they were transferred. That helped to relieve a great deal of tension. But I feel sorry for them; they're branded as *inu* for good. People from Tule Lake are writing to other projects telling their friends all about them.[44]

[43] Included were Sasaki, Kami, and Watanabe of the Coördinating Committee; Suzukawa, Chief of Evacuee Police; Kurokawa of the Reports Office; and several members of the Coöp Board of Directors.

[44] Field Notes, August 21, 1944.

Mrs. Tsuchikawa, the prominent Resegregationist, however, expressed disappointment at their removal and hinted that it would have been better for all concerned if they had remained in Tule Lake and met the same fate as Noma.

The remaining refugees returned to their barracks after several weeks. They were met with varying receptions. The hostility toward some of the old Coöp Board members seemed to have died down, and they had little difficulty in reëstablishing themselves in their blocks. Sasaki and Watanabe, however, were regarded as traitors and were completely ostracized by their coresidents. Sasaki found the reception in his own block so hostile that he left his family and took up residence with a group of devoted judo boys who acted as a constant bodyguard. Kurihara said:

> Those *inu* who fled the evacuee community and who returned—I don't think they could contrive to sleep without worries. The longer Sasaki maintains bodyguards, the longer he'll be hated. If he lived alone, the people might forget. Getting bodyguards was a very short sighted policy.[45]

The resignation of the evacuee police force was one of the most serious repercussions of the Noma murder. The administration experienced extreme difficulty in recruiting another force, and the change brought about in the attitude of those evacuees who finally consented to serve altered the character of the body a great deal. The explanation of their reputation as *inu* before the murder has already been indicated (p. 263), and their position in the community became extremely hazardous after the murder since, as an essential part of their duties, they would be required to investigate and act against Noma's assassins. The public in general tacitly condoned the murder, and the leaders of the underground pressure group had a special interest in preventing any investigation for fear their "strong arm boys" would come under suspicion. Immediately after the murder, threats (presumably by pressure-group adherents) were made against Police Chief Suzukawa and his assistant, and they resigned under duress. Other members, realizing their untenable positions, resigned one by one. The staff dwindled from 115 to 72 men within a little more than two weeks after the murder. Suspicion and pressure from the colony increased progressively. The remaining members of the staff, fearing that they would be forced to coöperate in the apprehensions of the murderers and

---

[45] Field Notes, August 7, 1944.

thereby incur the wrath of the powerful and violent underground group, resigned en masse. Itabashi aptly described the situation:

> The camp residents suspected that they were spies of the administration. That was the main reason the police couldn't get the coöperation of the residents.[46]

The resignation of the remaining seventy-two men on the police force was announced in an extra issue of the *Newell Star* on July 20. In this announcement Mr. Best asked the residents in each block to select two men to serve as policemen in their own blocks. "These persons selected by the blocks will be accepted by the administration without question and will be assigned to the colony police force."

The mass resignation left the administration in a difficult position since the project could not be policed without evacuee help. It was imperative that a new force be recruited immediately in accordance with the announced plan. Accordingly, Mr. Schmidt and Mr. Holding, of the Internal Security section, addressed the block managers and attempted to make the recruiting of this force the latter's responsibility. Mr. Holding is said to have stated:

> If there's a failure it's going to be your responsibility. You've got to see that people in the block coöperate with the policemen. For those blocks which supply no policemen, no protection will be given.[47]

Schmidt threatened to withdraw certain services, ordinarily provided by evacuee police, from blocks failing to elect representatives, e.g., passes to the administrative area, transmission of telegrams, etc. These coercive statements angered some of the block managers and impelled them to resist the administration-sponsored election.

Many informants expressed the opinion that the attempt to form a new evacuee police force would face many obstacles. Wakida said:

> People would like a police force but nobody wants to run for the job. They don't want to be *inu*. I think the attempt to get a new police force will fall to the ground.[48]

A Kibei block manager wrote:

> Up to date the reputation of police has been so grave that it seems to me that the colonists have no interest in police affairs.[49]

---

[46] Field Notes, July 24, 1944.   [48] Field Notes, July 24, 1944.
[47] Field Notes, August 8, 1944.   [49] Isamu Kurusu, Letter, July 20, 1944.

Itabashi, who lived in the Manzanar section, remarked:

I think they'll get a police force, but it will take time. So far, the police have been looked upon as administrative agents.[50]

Rumors that those chosen to serve on the police force would be required to sign a pledge of loyalty to the United States and that the record of their service on the force would be sent to Japan also had a deterrent effect on the progress of election. Kurihara reported:

There is quite a lot of argument about that. I heard this thing two months ago. I'm not sure whether it's true or whether it's rumor. Anyway, it is said that the records of all Japanese who ever acted as policemen and spied for the administration will be sent back to Japan when they are exchanged.

If that is true, then when they get back to Japan they'll be on the black list. That is the point many of them are worrying about. The previous police were made to swear some kind of statement that they will be loyal to America and even give up their lives if necessary. One who really is truly a Japanese will not sign that statement.[51]

Kurusu, quoted above, explained:

The Issei in our block are against it because they heard the rumor of sending records to Japan. Also the colonial police used to wear a badge of the regular United States police. It said United States Police on the badge. Most of the people are afraid to connect themselves so obviously with the United States government.[52]

Elections were, however, duly held and about two thirds of the blocks immediately selected policemen. As the *Newell Star* in the July 27 edition reported, "The breakdown revealed 33 blocks each chose two policemen, 13 blocks elected one each and three blocks elected three members." The article added:

It was also disclosed that 25 blocks failed to elect representatives. However, this report of 25 blocks failing to elect members is not to be judged as final. Some blocks have requested time for further study and information.

The Community Analyst wrote:

Blocks . . . wished additional information, indicating how much independence the wardens' organization would have from . . . [the Caucasian] Internal Security . . . People said generally that they "know complete inde-

---

[50] Field Notes, July 24, 1944.   [52] Field Notes, August 8, 1944.
[51] Field Notes, July 31, 1944.

pendence is impossible, yet we want to know how much is possible; the wardens will never succeed if they have to spy on the residents or be responsible for stockade pickups."[53]

Some of the blocks succeeded in the election of policemen, while others remained unpoliced for six months or more. It is perhaps significant that the blocks in Ward VIII, the Manzanar section, filled every position. There is reason to believe that the underground pressure group played an important role in the success of elections in these blocks where its leaders, who were soon to undertake numerous overt nationalistic activities, resided. There is some evidence that it desired to control the new force by having its own members selected in order that activities of the group might not be curbed.

Considering the deterrents against the election, it is significant that the police force was restaffed at all. The fairly rapid and successful recruitment in the face of the reluctance of residents to accept positions that might brand them as *inu* may be attributed in part to bizarre rumors of rape that spread through the camp for ten days after the resignation of the evacuee police. A Nisei girl reported that a young woman was covered with blankets and thrown into a ditch. She added, "In Ward VII another girl is supposed to have been attacked by some of the boys. Some of the boys in camp are bad."[54]

Mrs. Wakida said:

Some boy chased a girl in block 69. The boy had a blanket over his head. Also her girl friend who lives only with her mother and sister was annoyed by having boys knock on her door at night and shine flashlights in the window.[55]

These and even more specifically detailed rumors were taken very seriously by many people. For about a week girls and women imposed a voluntary curfew on themselves, and were seldom seen outside the barracks after dark. Wakida said:

The girls can't go to the Japanese night school. It's a fact that some people, especially girls, are scared. Even the movies are closed down.[56]

[53] WRA, Community Analysis Report, "Community Attitudes on Recurrent Crises in July," August 3, 1944 (manuscript).
[54] Field Notes, July 25, 1944.
[55] Field Notes, July 26, 1944.
[56] Field Notes, July 24, 1944.

Some residents were skeptical of the authenticity of these reports and saw the hand of the administration behind them. For example, Itabashi remarked:

> The bothering of girls is just rumor, I think. Of course, there is a possibility that such crimes could be committed when we are living this abnormal life, but I think it's a rumor started by the administration to make people form a police force.[57]

After the selection of police, stories—or events—of this sort abruptly ended.

The new police force, which had ninety-four men by the end of July, held a series of meetings among themselves and with the administration in order to formulate new policies to mitigate the "weaknesses and defects of the former police force." They deemed it "necessary first to dissolve the previous suspicions and opposition surrounding the old [evacuee] police force." They proposed to "create a police force operating for and by the people of the community," providing a rule that a policeman might be recalled by the wish of the people. They also requested that Director Best henceforth instruct Internal Security and the FBI to inform the evacuee police of the reasons for the arrest of any resident and specified that "problems arising between the administration and the residents did not come within the jurisdiction of the [police] force."[58]

The newly organized police force thus adopted a series of changes designed to insure that they would not be involved in any affair which might incur the displeasure of the residents. Soon the "wardens," as the police were now called, came to be looked upon as meek, ineffectual officers. Whenever any infringement of law occurred which might remotely be connected with politics or might conceivably offend the residents if action were taken, the wardens refused to act.

Concomitant with the reorganization of the Coöperative Enterprises, the liquidation of the old Tulean clique, the removal to places of safety of the Public *Inu* Number One, and the reorganization of the police force, public sentiment toward the wave of violence that had culminated in Noma's murder, underwent a marked change. People began openly to deplore the murder. Some

---

[57] Field Notes, July 24, 1944.
[58] *Newell Star*, August 10, 1944.

even questioned Noma's essential guilt as an informer. Itabashi said, "He wasn't bad enough to be assassinated."[59]

A Nisei girl remarked:

I never understood why Mr. Noma had to be killed. My parents knew him and feel sorry for him. I can't feel one bit of this hate that made someone stab him. Nobody seems to know why he was killed.

In camp there were so many rumors at that time. People believed what they heard was true. To prove its credibility they always said, "My friends say it." It made almost everybody believe the story.[60]

As an aftermath of the wave of *inu* hatred the pressure group gained strength by default. The administration was weakened with the thorough discrediting of many of the evacuees upon whom it had depended as a channel of communication and a means of collaboration. Failure to apprehend assailants and assassins weakened the official forces devoted to the maintenance of law and order. The more radical elements emerged from the underground and sponsored openly, and with impunity, programs that a short time before would have led to arrest and incarceration.

---

[59] Field Notes, August 8, 1944.
[60] Field Notes, August 30, 1944.

Chapter XI

INCARCERATION
The Stockade Issue

T HE STOCKADE WAS ORIGINALLY a circumstantial device adopted by the Army as a means of incarcerating a group of young men apprehended in the November 4 incident. It became institutionalized during the period of martial law and was firmly established as an essential element in WRA project administration by the time the Army withdrew from the center. It was in existence for more than nine months, from early November, 1943, to late August, 1944. During this period over 350 men were picked up and detained for varying periods, some of them for more than eight months. Its maximum population was reached during January when more than 250 were in confinement at one time. It was the source of grief and emotional disturbance to the families from which these men had been separated and of irritation, discontent and persecution reference among the general population. The surging suspicions against *inu,* described in the preceding chapter, were closely tied in with fear of arrest and incarceration in the stockade. The stockade was an important element in every political issue that arose between administration and residents, or within political factions among the residents. Status quo had its origin in the stockade issue; the Coördinating Committee's fate was largely determined by its actions in regard to the detainees; the administrative failure to realize its plan for representative government was directly connected with its stockade policy; and the underground pressure movement drew increasing popular support for its program of unconditional release of those who had been incarcerated. Eventually, the WRA policy of detaining people without accusation or trial led the American Civil Liberties Union to intervene.

In physical structure the stockade grew from a single tent, set up by the Army on November 4, to a barbed-wire enclosed area of 200 by 350 feet, comprising five barracks, a mess hall and a building with sanitary facilities. A detained evacuee described the stockade in the following terms:

There were four towers located on each corner of the stockade just outside of the fence and armed guards were stationed on each 24 hours a day. . . . There was only one gate and each time any of us were taken out to go for our food or to the office for various business, there was a guard standing at the gate and several Internal Security Officers attending.[1]

The barracks were of the same size as those in the center, 20 by 100 feet, and each accommodated on the average 43 or 44 persons. It was "one large dormitory"

without partitions . . . with two coal stoves for heating purposes and 12 windows to each side. These barracks were numbered A to F. One half of Barrack F was used for latrine and shower, the other half, for living quarters. Barbed wire fence was approximately 10 feet from the building on both ends. Barrack A had one row of lights in the center, which was poor. Barrack B, C, D, E had two rows of lights; hence, better than Barrack A.[2]

Living conditions were described as "poor" or "intolerable" with details as follows:

We were not given any convenience of sanitation to keep the barracks in order such as bucket, broom, and mop, etc., at first. They furnished cot beds with 3 or 4 blankets without any sheets or pillows which even refused to people with very poor health. . . . The stockade does not have any washing place and the people confined in the Area have to wash when taking a shower. Above that Tule Lake weather causes clothes to become dirty and have sweat odor making it impossible to wear long without washing. Soaps were furnished occasionally.[3]

The food condition that existed in the stockade were very poor and the ration for the number of people was not sufficient. We were only given 2 pounds of sugar per day when there were 155 odd persons. One box of orange or apples were sent consisting of rotten fruits so most of the people did not get any. We were on a carrot diet from January 16 for nearly one month and carrots day after day. Even these consisted of bad vegetable. There was no jam or butter (oleomargarine) for the bread. Black coffee for a long time without sugar. There were so many confined

[1] Letter from the files of the American Civil Liberties Union, Northern California Branch, August 20, 1944.

[2] Ibid.

[3] Letter from the files of the American Civil Liberties Union, Northern California Branch, August 11, 1944.

that people had to eat their meals in shifts for not having adequate dishes and silverware.[4]

When we were first in here we only had rice and carrots I don't know how many weeks.[5]

All mail, both incoming and outgoing, was censored by the Army while it was in charge and by WRA when it took over the stockade. No visitors were permitted.

First class mail has always been censored and has to be opened before it comes in. . . . They won't let it in unless it is open and a third party has to open it and I know it is against a Federal law. . . . And then you have heard about the fact that we haven't been given an opportunity to even see anyone.[6]

The first pickups on November 4 were on the initiative of the Army and were directed toward the quelling of what was believed to be a potential "riot." The next major move was made on November 13[7] when members of the Negotiating Committee, other leaders of *Daihyo Sha Kai* and prominent Farm Group representatives were ordered arrested. This move followed the successful act of passive resistance to the administration when the residents ignored the Army—WRA-sponsored mass meeting. Several of the Negotiating Committee leaders who escaped apprehension at this time by going into hiding gave themselves up on December 1 and were then put into the stockade. Meantime, a general search of the evacuee area had resulted in the apprehension of some ninety men, who were under suspicion on unspecified charges by the WRA Internal Security staff. And when by the middle of December it became apparent that incarceration of its leaders had not broken *Daihyo Sha Kai* resistance, a pickup of the block representatives of the organization was instituted and they were added to the stockade population. Arrests continued after martial law was lifted in January,[8] but not until late in April did the Washington office of

---

[4] *Ibid.*

[5] Stenographic record of interview between Ernest Besig and detainees, July 11, 1944; from the files of the American Civil Liberties Union, Northern California Branch.

[6] *Ibid.*

[7] WRA, "History of Area B at Tule Lake, 'The Stockade'" (manuscript), September 12, 1944, states, however, that on November 5 a number of evacuees were arrested "at the request of and upon information furnished by the Internal Security . . . on suspicion of being connected with the incidents of November 1 and 4." Detainee informants do not verify this statement.

[8] Officers of the Western Defense Command pointed out in an interview that,

WRA issue an ex post facto statement of its procedures for the "separation of residents within [the] center." An "isolation area" was then defined as necessary for the restriction of "the movement and activities of persons whose influence or actions may be disruptive to the operation of the center," for promoting "the orderly administration of the center," and for maintaining "peace and security for the residents."[9]

There is no evidence that any administrative plan for liquidating the stockade was contemplated at this time. On the contrary, it was stated that "residence of any individual in Area B [the stockade] . . . shall be for an indefinite period."

Correspondingly, no need for statement of charges against the arrested individuals, for intensive investigation of charges, or for regularized hearings was felt. "Since such . . . separation of individuals is a purely administrative arrangement to secure the peaceful and orderly administration of the center, only such investigation need be made as is requisite for an administrative determination by the Project Director."[10] Although a Fact Finding Committee, composed of project personnel, had long been in existence, it was required merely "to secure and examine any evidence which is available at the center, or which can without undue delay be secured from any other source, bearing upon the activities of any individual suspected of past or probable future interference with the peaceful and orderly processes of center administration."[11] To the Project Director was delegated the duty of reviewing "the evidence and recommendations submitted by the Committee," and of determining the final disposition of the cases. Theoretically, the detainee had recourse of appeal to the Director for an interview, but the Project Director "shall *at his convenience* hold [such] interviews,"[12] with wide discretionary powers in denying such interviews:

No interview need be held in cases in which the evidence supporting the [Fact Finding] Committee's recommendation is so clear as not to leave room for any reasonable doubt as to the correctness of the recommendation.[13]

after martial law was lifted, the Army in the main both arrested and released evacuees on information supplied by and as a "courtesy" to WRA.

[9] WRA, *Manual*, "Administrative Separation of Residents within Center," Section 110.15, April 26, 1944.

[10] *Ibid.*   [11] *Ibid.*   [12] *Ibid.* Italics ours.   [13] *Ibid.*

Restrictions upon the activities of the detainees, which had been operative by this time for more than five months, were formulated as follows:

All mail going into or coming from Area B . . . will be censored.

No visiting will be permitted between the residents or [sic] Area B . . . and the main area of the center except under extraordinary circumstances and with the express permission of the Project Director.

Visiting with the residents of Area B . . . will not in any event be permitted within the physical limits of Area B . . . but may take place only in rooms provided for the purpose outside the evacuee residential area and in the presence of witnesses if the Project Director so determines.

Families of individuals removed to Area B . . . will not be allowed to accompany such individuals into the separated area.[14]

Failure to have formal charges filed or formal hearings held was a continual cause of complaint among the detainees. Excerpts from the complaints of a number of detainees and former detainees follow. As one detainee stated, the reason for continued imprisonment "is a mystery to us."[15] Others said:

No reasons was ever given to me for my arrest.[16]

I was arrested by the Army on January 11, 1944, without any questioning and thrown in the place called "stockade." The reason I do not know and still is a question to my mind.[17]

Day after day we are being given the same line saying you might be released sometime soon. That is the only promise they say, which is very indefinite, and we ask for the reason of our detention, and they refuse to tell us. . . . We can't seem to budge that. We are forced at gun point, so there you are.[18]

I do not know the reason why I am being confined here. . . . Of course, I am a member of the Negotiating Committee, executive secretary, but what I did I acted in behalf of the people of the colony and because I was secretary I never said a word in a meeting anyway. . . . They [WRA] try to pin something about the November 4th incident. As far as that is concerned, I took no part in it.[19]

---

[14] *Ibid.*

[15] Letter from the files of the American Civil Liberties Union, Northern California Branch, August 20, 1944.

[16] Stenographic record of interview between Ernest Besig and detainees, July 11, 1944; from the files of the American Civil Liberties Union, Northern California Branch.

[17] Letter from the files of the American Civil Liberties Union, Northern California Branch, August 11, 1944.

[18] Stenographic record of interview between Ernest Besig and detainees, July 11, 1944; from the files of the American Civil Liberties Union, Northern California Branch.

[19] *Ibid.*

I got picked up on November 13th and released on April 7th. While I was in there they didn't tell me why I got picked up or why I have been kept in there for that length of time and when I got released there wasn't anything said, they simply, Mr. Best and Mr. Schmidt, have told me that they have confidence in me, that I am no longer any trouble maker and such and such and so have released me. . . . They simply said that I was one of the trouble makers, that's all. They haven't showed me any evidence or anything like that. Merely I was arrested on a mere accusation, and although they went through quite a bit of investigation about my activity and maybe they clarified their accusations themselves and brought my release, I guess.[20]

The only hearing I have had was just the other day with the Internal Securities. I don't know whether you call that a hearing or not . . . What they wanted to know—they just asked me a lot of questions like if I was a member of representatives [*Daihyo Sha Kai*] or if I participated in November 4th riot . . . I wanted to see Mr. Best. I asked him through a letter. He never answered it.[21]

The plight of the detainees bore heavily upon the community and did much to increase the rapidly developing sense of persecution. Agitation for release was carried on almost constantly by the detainees themselves, by their disturbed relatives, and by whatever group, radical or conservative, was in power or seeking power as representatives of the people or negotiators with the administration. The early radical group, the *Daihyo Sha Kai* and its supporters, had made strenuous efforts to give the issue an international aspect and, through appeals to the Spanish Consul, to obtain the intervention of the Japanese government. These efforts came to nothing because of the unwillingness and inability of the Spanish Consul to act on behalf of American citizens, who composed the bulk of the detainees. At the end of December, the detainees took matters into their own hands and instituted a six-day hunger strike directed both as a protest against the Army and the project administration and as an effort to speed up their release. Their act resulted in no administrative concessions and, coming as it did at a time when the residents, after weeks of unemployment, were ready to accede to a "back to normalcy" program, aroused little popular support.

The conservative Coördinating Committee, which came into power shortly after this hunger strike, had announced "justifiable

---

[20] *Ibid.*

[21] *Ibid.* Best, however, did grant interviews to some of the detainees. See Kuratomi's statement, p. 293.

release of detainees" as one of its major planks, and had negotiated
for this purpose with the Army and WRA throughout its tenure.
Its tactics of direct negotiation with the Army and WRA, rather
than appeal to the Spanish Consul or the Japanese government for
intervention, met with considerable success. It was able to bring
about the release of a contingent of twenty-six men as early as
January 19 and 20.[22] At almost every meeting with WRA officials
the committee nominated persons whose release it considered "justifiable" and pressed for action. Meantime, WRA assumed the
responsibility of determining the eligibility of detainees for release,
and releases other than those sanctioned by the committee were,
from time to time, authorized. When the Coördinating Committee
resigned at the end of April it reported that 257 stockade detainees
had been released. The committee, however, failed to receive credit
from the community for these releases; instead, criticisms were
heaped upon it for the slowness of releases, for its insistence on
the "justifiable" criterion, for its failure in obtaining releases for
the better-known detainees such as Abe, Kuratomi, Seki, etc., and
because residents suspected it of having a hand in recent arrests
and detainments.

After the resignation of the Coördinating Committee two groups
became conspicuous in fighting for release of the detainees—Tada
and his friends, and the radical Resegregationists.

Tada was released from the stockade in April and immediately
joined forces with Kodama, Yokota, and other *Daihyo Sha Kai*
adherents whose release had been obtained previously. They conferred with the Project Director and the Project Attorney at every
opportunity in an effort to persuade them to release Abe, Kuratomi,
Seki and others. Their efforts were not successful. According to
Tada:

They [WRA] do not tell me anything specific, all I get is a lot of
innuendos, "Well, you don't know what we know." That's what I hear
all the time.[23]

[22] Some men were released earlier. A WRA report, for instance, states, "In
some cases the wrong person was picked up and he was immediately returned
to the colony." WRA "History of Area B at Tule Lake—'The Stockade'" (manuscript), September 12, 1944.
[23] Stenographic record of interview between Ernest Besig and detainees, July
11, 1944; from the files of the American Civil Liberties Union, Northern California Branch.

The Resegregationists conducted a more concerted and extensive campaign in the camp. By the end of April they were the most powerful group on the project, although their activities were still for the most part shrouded in secrecy. New leaders had emerged, among whom were Yamashita, a parolee from Santa Fe, and Kira, who had arrived with the Manzanar contingent in February. Both of these men were experienced in the acts of agitation, and each was protected by "strong-arm" boys. The former had played a prominent role in Poston in support of the strike of November, 1942, and in the formation of a Kibei bloc to obstruct military registration in February, 1943. The latter had been leader of a gang in Terminal Island before evacuation and is said to have held this gang intact at Manzanar where it took a prominent part in the "riot" of December, 1942. They now stated that they were waiting until the center was "unified" to come out into the open with an ambitious plan for resegregation. Unification, they said, could be attained only after the stockade was liquidated. The motives underlying these tactics were apparently twofold: the hope of gaining the support of residents by championing a popular cause, and the desire to win the detained *Daihyo Sha Kai* leaders to their side and thus consolidate their position by forestalling the formation of an opposition group. The Resegregationist leaders had no more success in wringing concessions from the project administration than had the Tada group. By unceasing propaganda to the effect that peace would not come to the camp unless the detainees were released, they managed, however, to keep popular interest in the stockade issue alive.

Failing in his attempt to press the administration for release of the detainees, Tada decided to bring the matter before the American courts. The plan for legal action had been initiated by George Kuratomi and his close friends in March while Tada was still in the stockade. Kuratomi, Abe, Tada and others had agreed that the only hope of release for all of them would be through court action, and they made a pact that if any one of them were released he would seek legal aid. After he was released from the stockade in April, Tada approached Yamashita and Kira for advice and support in this plan, but he received little encouragement from them. Yamashita, who had hoped to incorporate the released detainees into the Resegregation Group, made a counterapproach to Tada pointing out that the organization had 9,000 members and promising "great power" if he would join it. Tada refused, stating later that he disapproved of the Resegregationists, doubted that they actually represented the wishes of the people, and disliked their policy of setting themselves apart from all other residents as the only "true Japanese" in camp.[23a] When Tada refused to join them, the Resegregationist leaders used the most powerful weapon at their command: they flooded the camp with rumors that he and his associates were *inu*. Coinciding as they did with the wave of general *inu* hatred in camp, these rumors brought Tada's overt activities to an effective end.

Shortly after Tada's unsuccessful attempt to obtain support for his plan of legal intervention, Kato and his intimates sent out a message to their relatives in the camp instructing them to hire a lawyer. The relatives, all of whom were Resegregationists, thereupon formed a loosely-knit organization called the *Saiban-iin* (Lawsuit Committee) and invited other prominent Resegregationists to join them. Because of its auspices Kira and Yamashita now threw their support behind the proposal, and it was agreed to ask the American Civil Liberties Union[24] to intercede on behalf of the detainees.

The *Saiban-iin* approached Ernest Besig, Director of the Northern California Branch of the A.C.L.U., who agreed to investigate the situation. He, however, met with considerable antagonism from WRA, at both the Washington and the project level, and did not obtain permission for a visit to Tule Lake until July 11. At this time meetings with relatives of the detainees were arranged, but Besig was not allowed to interview the stockade detainees themselves in private, being required to conduct all such interviews in the presence of members of the WRA Internal Security staff. Mr. Besig protested vigorously against this interference with the customary right of an attorney to interview his clients privately. The reason given by the project administration for its policy was the proximity of the time of Besig's arrival to the Noma murder.

[23a] Field Notes, March 6, 1945.

[24] The American Civil Liberties Union had recently been retained by Haruo Akahoshi, a brother-in-law of one of the members of the *Saiban-iin,* for defense in a case of alleged obstruction of Selective Service at Heart Mountain. Akahoshi had been transferred to Tule Lake, and it was upon his advice that help from the Union was sought also by the *Saiban-iin.*

It will be remembered that the detainees, who were now Besig's clients, were suspected by the administration of complicity in the murder. On July 12, before he could complete his interviews, Besig was forced to withdraw from the project.[25]

After returning to San Francisco Mr. Besig protested against WRA tactics in a letter to Secretary of the Interior Ickes, in which he outlined the problems arising from the continued detention of men against whom no charges had been filed. He also suggested to the detainees that one of them file an application for a writ of habeas corpus. At the same time the A.C.L.U. attorney brought the matter into the open through the public press:

Besig said . . . that he spent two days at the center interviewing his clients but that he was ordered out before he could finish the work.

"The project director, R. R. Best," Besig said, "simply decided he didn't want [my secretary and myself] around. . . . "

Besig explained that he was not concerned with the morals, guilt or innocence of any of the Japanese involved. He said, however, that they have been held in the stockade for some eight months without charges or hearings.

"These people are entitled to a hearing and a trial," he said. "If they are guilty, put them in prison or anywhere. But they have the basic right of every citizen for a fair trial."[26]

The *American Civil Liberties Union-News* elaborated on these complaints in an article headed "Tyranny Reigns at Tule Lake,"[27] in which it was stated that "two armed members of the Internal Security (Caucasian) police escorted the Union's representatives from the center"; that the right of counsel had been violated; and that "eighteen citizens"[28] had been imprisoned for over eight months "without the filing of charges or the granting of a hearing or trial of any kind."

"During these eight months," said Mr. Besig, "these citizens have not been allowed visits from their wives and children (some born since their

[25] The Project Attorney stated, in an interview, that Mr. Besig had not been forced out but had been asked to leave on the grounds that his presence interfered with the WRA investigation of the Noma murder. He claimed that Mr. Besig's visit had not been authorized by the central office of the American Civil Liberties Union. He said, further, that some evacuees had complained to Mr. Best that they were being threatened with beatings by their fellow residents unless they agreed to see Mr. Besig. Field Notes, July 14, 1944.

[26] *San Francisco Chronicle*, July 15, 1944.

[27] August, 1944.

[28] According to Kuratomi there were only sixteen citizens in the stockade at this time.

incarceration) and the War Relocation Authority only during the past month erected a beaver board wall around the Stockade to prevent the relatives of the men from occasionally waving to them from behind a wire fence about a hundred yards away."

WRA was then building a new stockade. Kuratomi said that Pearson, Internal Security officer in charge, told him (about July 15) the new stockade was to be a permanent one "to keep you there for the duration of the war." Best also had said repeatedly that he would not release the remaining detainees. According to Kuratomi:

I was able to see Mr. Best from time to time after May and almost every time he would repeat that the incident of November 4 and the demonstration of November 1 had resulted in such tremendous publicity. He would say "If I were to release any of you and anything should happen in the camp, the immediate cry from the public on the outside would be 'What was Kuratomi doing in the camp at large?' Or 'Why was Abe released?'" In other words, Mr. Best always seemed to be afraid that our release, instead of bringing peace and harmony to the camp, might become a source of further trouble and disturbances.[29]

By this time most of those still detained had been incarcerated for more than eight months, and, in spite of the efforts of several factions in camp and the interest of the American Civil Liberties Union, there seemed to be no hope of immediate release. Discouraged by Besig's reception on the project and by the evidences of WRA's intention to incarcerate them indefinitely, the detainees on July 19 took matters into their own hands and again embarked upon a hunger strike. Kato, who kept a diary, enumerated their grievances as follows:

After a most serious consideration we have finally decided that the only weapon and the only solution to let known our sincerity to all that we are not a trouble maker such as the WRA has branded us we plan to undergo another hunger strike. I shall refrain from writing minor reason for undertaking such steps. Some of the numerous grievances are:

1. Imprisoned for over eight months without the filing of charges or the granting of a hearing or trial of any kind.

2. No proof or evidence substantiating our guilt.

3. Living in a world of infamy for no reasons whatsoever.

4. During the entire time we have been in the stockade we have been denied all visiting privileges from our wives, children, fiancees or anyone else.

5. I was denied visits from my fiancee whom I was schedule to marry the day after my arrest on November 13.

[29] George Kuratomi, Statement, November 16, 1945.

6. Children born since our incarceration but to even see our wives were denied.

7. Third degree methods used on many of us.

8. Censorship of mails, including that coming from outside the center.

9. Since July 2, we were not permitted to receive cigarettes, toilet articles, and our daily needs.

10. Beaver board erected for no reasons whatsoever since July 2. Solitary confinement cannot be any worse.

11. Constant abusive words from the attending Internal Security staffs.

12. No medical or first aid facilities. Service to the base hospital denied.

13. Denied the constitutional right to counsel. Denial of due process of law to all of us.

14. In connection with the interview which we had with Mr. Ernest Besig of the American Civil Liberties Union, all right of privacy was denied to us.[30]

The hunger strike was undertaken by all sixteen citizens in the stockade. WRA shortly released two of them, claiming that the releases were granted "without regard for the hunger demonstration" after the cases in question had been thoroughly "reviewed."[31]

The attitude of project officials is described in a WRA-prepared manuscript as follows:

The hunger strike was not recognized as such by the administration for several days. In the first place, there was no formal declaration as there had been in January even though the leaders were the same as then. Secondly, there was an undetermined amount of food in the Area B Kitchen and missing supplies were unaccounted for. The administration had no way of knowing whether any of the men were eating as the Internal Security did not check minutely the food left at all times in the kitchen nor did they comb the premises of Area B, about 175 square yards, and they did not consider it important to do so and thereby build up a situation that harrassed the administration. Thirdly, it was hoped that the demonstration would be short-lived if no official recognition were taken of it.

On July 24, the 14 men were pursuing their fast and the Project Director and Reports Officer decided it was time to release the information to the public. This was done and thereafter the newspapers were informed of developments. The story was not given undue prominence in any paper.[32]

Unlike the Army, the WRA did not make daily medical checks of the men in the area. It was decided to consider the men in Area B on the same basis as the other evacuee residents of the Tule Lake Center. The WRA

[30] Bill Kato, "Diary since the Hunger Strike" (manuscript), July–August, 1944.
[31] WRA, "History of Area B at Tule Lake—'The Stockade'" (manuscript), September 12, 1944.
[32] The strike was, however, reported in most West Coast newspapers. The

considered Area B a part of the whole center, not a place of imprisonment
to which a man was committed for a definite length of time.[33]

The striking detainees hoped that their action would serve as
an effective protest to the administration against the injustices to
which they had been subjected and as a demonstration to their
fellow residents of their ability to undergo the ultimate in martyr-
dom. Kato's diary entries exemplify this dual motivation. On the
first day, he recorded that Internal Security officers "entered all
armed with clubs and pistols." On the third day, he attempted
to establish contact with the American Civil Liberties Union; and
various other detainees conferred with Internal Security officers.
On the fourth day, he felt "very lousy"; and on the fifth day he
and others "packed all our belongings, for most of us are really
getting weak . . . and too messy rooms gets on our nerves." One of
the detainees had to be carried to the washroom. On the sixth day,
interviews were again held with Internal Security officers and Kato
felt "that we cannot last too long." On the seventh day (July 25),
Sadao Endo fainted and was taken to the base hospital, while two
others went for treatment but returned. On the ninth day, Kato
and others requested that four ailing detainees be taken to the hospital "but my request denied." On the tenth day, the request was
granted, but others who had been taken to the hospital earlier for
treatment were returned "because they have refused to eat any
food." Endo, who had yielded to treatment and recovered, was also
returned. Seki was "permitted to see his wife." On the eleventh day
(July 29), all the strikers were ordered "to the hospital for a physical

San Francisco Examiner, for example, carried a two-column article on July 25,
1944:

Isolated as trouble makers, the Japanese, all men, have not eaten since last
Wednesday night, a spokesman for the group reported to camp officials.

And further, said the group's ultimatum, they will continue their self-imposed
fast until they are released from confinement in the isolated area.

Despite the declaration, however, Ray R. Best, project director, said food will
continue to be delivered to the strikers on the same basis as to other internees
in the camp.

"The day's supply of food is being left in the kitchen and will continue to be
delivered so that the men may resume eating if they wish," Best said. WRA, he
added, will take no further steps to force the fourteen to eat.

Best said that until yesterday he had been unable to obtain a definite statement from the group concerning their intentions. He expressed some doubt that
the strikers had gone completely without food since their kitchen contained
rice and other supplies at the time the strike assertedly started. This food, he
said, was gone after the men began refusing their daily rations.

[33] WRA, _op. cit._

checkup," stimulants were administered, and the strike was temporarily broken.

Details of the sort recorded by Kato reached the residents, and were magnified as they passed from one person to another. Expressions of sympathy for and identification with the strikers were frequent, although some residents deplored the strike as a foolish and useless gesture. J. Y. Kurihara said:

I think the hunger strike has made a very strong impression on the people. Those boys have been kept in there unjustly when they should have been released. The only solution which would bring the camp back to normal is release from the stockade.[34]

Yamashita stated:

I don't understand why Mr. Best is so stubborn in not releasing them.[35]

Tsuruda, discussing the strike at a later date, regarded the situation with mixed feelings:

I don't see why they went on a hunger strike. They weren't doing the WRA any harm. They were just harming themselves. It made us sad though. I kind of pitied them.[36]

While the strike was in progress, relatives and close friends of the detainees addressed frantic appeals to WRA officials in Washington and to the project administration; and they sought the advice of various evacuee leaders about steps that might be taken to bring the strike to an end. Responding to the appeals of these desperate relatives, the Resegregationist leaders prepared the following petition and immediately circulated it for signatures on July 28:

We were shocked to learn that fourteen residents confined in the stockade are on a Hunger Strike for their release and returned to this center. The Hunger Strike is on the 10th day on Friday, July 28, 1944.

Naturally we, as members of the Japanese race, are very worried and anxious about the lives of our racial brothers. Already several persons have collapsed from hunger. If any or several of our racial brothers should die on account of the Hunger Strike, we all would feel deeply grieved. Reverse the case; suppose Americans in an internment camp in Japan should die on a Hunger Strike, how would you feel? Would not the American people be deeply grieved? So will we if our racial brothers die of a Hunger Strike.

Therefore, we, the residents of the Tule Lake Center, request you, Mr. Raymond Best, to be merciful to our racial brothers and release the four-

[34] Field Notes, July 30, 1944.　　[36] Field Notes, August 19, 1944.
[35] Field Notes, July 28, 1944.

teen persons on a Hunger Strike from the stockade. Your mercy will never be forgotten.

By the evening of the next day (Saturday), the petition was said to have been signed by over 8,000 residents. It was circulated at a crucial moment: while the strikers were being transferred from the stockade to the hospital, and while rumors about the seriousness of their condition were passing from person to person. Resegregationist leaders, members of the *Saiban-iin,* and other friends of the strikers made announcements and speeches in various mess halls and exhorted the residents to sign. Concomitantly, sympathy for the detainees and antiadministration feeling again reached a high pitch. The petition was ready to be submitted to the administration on July 31 (Monday).

On July 28 when the petition was being presented for signatures, the Spanish Vice-Consul arrived from San Francisco on a routine inspection tour. Most residents, discouraged by the meager results of earlier appeals to the Consul, viewed his visit with indifference. A young Nisei remarked:

People believe that up to now the Spanish Consul hasn't been able to do anything. He hasn't been able to help the Nisei. They have lost interest in him.[37]

And Mr. Kira commented:

I don't think people have much confidence in him. He is a representative of such a small country—especially Spain.[38]

In spite of popular indifference, an evacuee committee was formed to meet with the Spanish representative. When the committee brought up the matter of the hunger strike, the Vice-Consul agreed to exert his utmost influence, although "he had hitherto maintained the point of view that the problems of Nisei were beyond his authority."[39] He pleaded with Mr. Best to free the detainees but to no avail. It is said that Mr. Best told the Vice-Consul that he could not release the men until the community returned to normal. While he was negotiating, the Vice-Consul received word that the hunger strike had ended. He left the center believing that the problem had been solved.

On July 30 (Sunday), the day after the Vice-Consul's departure,

---

[37] Field Notes, July 30, 1944.
[38] *Ibid.*
[39] *Newell Star,* Japanese Section, August 3, 1944.

Besig visited the project. He was refused permission to interview the stockade detainees, but was allowed to meet with some members of the *Saiban-iin*. He assured them that the contemplated habeas corpus proceedings would almost certainly result in freedom for the incarcerated men.

Besig's assurance immediately created a schism among the Resegregationists: the more extreme among them, such as Yamashita, Kira, Ishikawa, and Mrs. Tsuchikawa, tried to withhold the already completed petition, while the moderates, who had taken the more active role in the campaign for signatures, insisted that the petition be presented to the administration. The latter felt that for the benefit of the detainees the matter should be solved as expeditiously as possible by any means at their disposal. The former, however, did not want to give the administration an easy way out of the dilemma, and preferred to force it to an unwilling decision through legal action. They hoped that their prestige with the residents would be enhanced by the winning of a publicized victory over the administration. Kuratomi later commented:

> Yamashita and those people were afraid that the petition might successfully bring our releases. They didn't want that. They wanted the lawsuit so that they could say, "We got releases for those detainees." They were after laurels for themselves. They didn't care if we were kept in the stockade and suffered.[40]

Other informants attributed the extremists' shift in tactics to their apprehension of the possibility of capitalizing on popular sympathy for the detainees to raise a fund for defraying operating expenses of their Resegregationist organization. There is some evidence to support this contention, for a drive initiated at this time by Mrs. Tsuchikawa, Yamashita, and others is said to have yielded a fund of from $2,000 to $3,000, only $500 of which was allocated to the *Saiban-iin* for the attorney's fee.

The extremists succeeded in having the petition withheld for three days.[41] Meanwhile, on July 30, Yamashita managed to transmit a message to Besig surreptitiously, requesting him to initiate the lawsuit immediately and assuring him that a camp-wide drive to obtain funds was being undertaken.

---

[40] George Kuratomi, Statement, November 21, 1945.

[41] As a matter of fact, the petition was never submitted to the administration, for Ishikawa and an associate snatched it from its custodian and threw part of it into the fire.

Between August 4 and 8 all the detainees, having yielded to medical treatment, were discharged from the hospital and were again confined in the stockade. Upon being told by the Internal Security staff that they would not be released from the stockade, they immediately resumed the hunger strike. To inform their relatives of the situation they followed out a prearranged plan of nailing two red handkerchiefs to the outside walls of their barracks. The strike lasted from August 5 to August 13. Kato again kept a detailed diary, recording the progressive stages of physical weakness of himself and the other strikers. On the seventh day (August 11), he recorded that the strikers were informed "that there will be no hospital and medical service for us"; and that, on the ninth day, after promises from Internal Security officers that releases would be forthcoming in short order, an "amicable understanding" was reached and the strike ended. He wrote:

Rev. Abe and Mr. Seki conferred with Mr. Schmidt and we came to an amicable understanding whereby we agreed to eat commencing tonight. Dr. Sleath[42] came to check our physical condition. Six of us were consulted. One of the detainees was immediately transferred to the hospital. Dr. Sleath stated that we were on edge and that we probably will not last another day. The doctor recommended our transfer to the hospital but was denied by the Internal Securities. Mr. Schmidt stated that four or five will be released in about a day. The rest will eventually be released in about two weeks. Furthermore, he stated that all foods will be distributed from the hospital because we are all too weak to do anything. At 1:30 A.M. Mr. Schmidt and Dr. Sleath brought us warm milk and a baby's mush. Thus ended the nine-day hunger strike for me. I could not sleep all morning.[43]

Releases followed one another in quick order after the cessation of the strike. According to a WRA report, "Conditions in the center at the present time are such that isolation of individuals is no longer considered necessary."[44] One man was released on August 14, one on August 16, two on August 17, three on August 23, and the remaining seven on August 24. The WRA stated at this time that "the administration was considering the release of all the men in Area B at the time they started the hunger strike."[45]

---

[42] The chief medical officer, who succeeded Dr. Pedicord.
[43] Bill Kato, "Diary since the Hunger Strike" (manuscript), July–August, 1944.
[44] Newell Star, August 31, 1943.
[45] WRA, "History of Area B at Tule Lake—'The Stockade'" (manuscript), September 12, 1944.

According to the American Civil Liberties Union, however, WRA took this action to avoid defeat in the planned habeas corpus proceedings:

Faced with the prospect of habeas corpus proceedings, the War Relocation Authority . . . very quietly released 18 United States citizens of Japanese ancestry who had been imprisoned in the Stockade at the Tule Lake Segregation Center for more than eight months without charges or hearings, and without the privilege of receiving visits from their parents, wives, children and friends. The releases followed a conference on August 22 between Wayne M. Collins, American Civil Liberties Union Attorney, and WRA officials, including Dillon S. Myer, national director of the WRA, Philip Glick, solicitor, Robert Cozzens, area director, and Raymond Best, project director at Tule Lake. . . .

We venture to say that even the WRA is glad to be rid of the "Stockade problem" for that agency has acted as though it had a bear by the tail and did not know how to let go.[46]

It is impossible to determine the precise cause-effect relationships on the basis of these conflicting reports. There is, however, little evidence to support WRA's contention that improved conditions in the center led to liquidation of the stockade. That the action of the American Civil Liberties Union was an important factor in the conclusion of the matter seems clear; and the stockade detainees felt that this was the primary reason for their release. Kuratomi, for example, said:

As a result of the threat of a law suit from the ACLU, WRA turned us loose.[47]

News of the releases spread quickly throughout the camp and was received with universal approval. Kurihara said:

It makes the people feel much better. It releases a great deal of tension. Mr. Best should have released the men when the Army turned over the stockade to WRA.[48]

A young Nisei girl stated:

I think it's better that they were released. I don't see why they should be punished. They thought they were doing something good for the camp. I feel very relieved. It's a good thing they were released.[49]

[46] *American Civil Liberties Union-News*, September, 1944.
[47] Field Notes, March 6, 1945.
[48] Field Notes, August 21, 1944.
[49] Field Notes, August 30, 1944.

Administrative suspicion of the detainees did not, however, abate with their release. During the first week in September, the old matter of their alleged complicity in the Noma murder was raised once more. An investigator from the office of the District Attorney in Modoc County came to the project and undertook intensive questioning of Abe, Kuratomi, and Tada as well as such Resegregationist leaders as Mrs. Tsuchikawa, Kira, and Kubo. Several of them were taken to the County seat for further questioning. The belief that they would be indicted by the Grand Jury for complicity in the murder became widespread. They again appealed to Ernest Besig for legal counsel in a letter dated September 12, which in part read:

We were informed that sometime next week the Grand Jury of Modoc County will indict about half a dozen evacuees on charges of murder and conspiracy to murder. . . . We are not in receipt of summons or subpoena as yet but we should expect it any day.[50]

Kuratomi reacted to the threatened indictment as follows:

When I was questioned, I saw the statement accusing me of murder and conspiracy of murder and asking the County Grand Jury to indict me. One thing I am on the lookout for is a frameup. I'm playing safe and am going to have a lawyer come in and go over the situation.[51]

Legal intervention proved unnecessary, however, for no indictment was made and the matter was dropped.

In the latter part of September the released men issued a public statement called "Our Gratitude and Wishes," in which they said, in part:

During our long confinement we had two hunger strikes, never being fearful of fighting for just cause and always upholding our virtues as true Japanese.

Now that we are back in the colony, we solemnly pledge ourselves, however insignificant our efforts may be, to our fundamental objective of establishing a constructive and peaceful community here at Tule Lake. . . . We sincerely hope that every resident of this center, manifesting the traditional high ideal of our race will cooperate and work in unison for the peaceful functioning of this center.

Furthermore, in conclusion, we wish to express our most heartfelt gratitude to all the justice-loving residents who had given us such diligent and sacrificial support.

[50] Mrs. Tsuchikawa-Tomoichi Kubo, Letter, September 12, 1944. An almost identical letter was sent by Abe, Kuratomi, Tada, and others.
[51] Field Notes, September 18, 1944.

The men who were released at this time were Nisei and Kibei who had been incarcerated shortly after the November 4 incident. Their Issei counterparts had long since been removed to the Santa Fe detention camp for enemy aliens. The freed citizen detainees, recognizing the injustice of this discriminatory treatment of the alien members of their group, therefore added the following pledge to their statement:

In order that this incident [of November] which became international in significance and scope, come to a formal conclusion, we will give our most earnest efforts in uniting the families of the Issei sent to Santa Fe Detention Station in connection with this affair.

In this matter factions again competed against each other: on the one hand, Abe, Kuratomi, and Seki worked as a committee, and on the other hand Kato worked as a representative of the Resegregation Group. Both factions had meetings with Mr. Best to press for the return of the internees. They also made inquiries to Mr. Besig relative to obtaining the intervention of the American Civil Liberties Union. While these negotiations were proceeding, however, they discovered that the Issei internees did not wish to return to Tule Lake, having been promised reunion with their families in Crystal City, the Department of Justice internment camp for families. The issue was resolved when the family members of the Issei *Daihyo Sha Kai* representatives at Santa Fe left for Crystal City on the night of November 20, 1944.

Chapter XII

RESEGREGATION
Pressure Tactics of the "Disloyal"

THAT THE WRA PROGRAM of segregating evacuees into two groups—"those who wish to follow the American way of life" and "those whose interests are not in harmony with those of the United States"—was a failure, from the standpoint of the second of these groups, became apparent almost from the moment the first contingent of "disloyals" arrived at the Tule Lake Segregation Center from other projects. The cultural, behavioral, and attitudinal heterogeneity of the group administratively defined as having interests "not in harmony with the United States" has been discussed in preceding chapters. This heterogeneity arose from the fact that possession of "disharmonious interests" and eligibility for residence in the Tule Lake Segregation Center for the "disloyal" were determined on the basis (1) of a negative answer to a question regarding political allegiance, or (2) of refusal to answer this question, or (3) of an application for repatriation or expatriation to Japan, or (4) of an expressed desire to accompany or remain with a relative in any of the three preceding categories and thus preserve the family unit, or (5) in the case of the original Tulean population, of a mere refusal to move out of the center to a project designated for the "loyal." The loose definition of the group to be segregated as "disloyal" made it possible for many people, whose attitudes toward the future were quite undetermined, to wait out the war in the security of Tule Lake. Furthermore, the administrative practice of allowing, or even encouraging, changes of answers to the registration questionnaire prior to segregation led to a widespread belief that status as a "disloyal" could be transformed at will and at a more convenient time to status as a "loyal."

[303]

That the bulk of the evacuees at the Tule Lake Segregation Center were undetermined "disloyals" with little appreciation of the political implications of their status is a reasonable deduction from their behavior and expressions of attitudes. Among those segregated there was, however, a relatively small but very aggressive group, with a more positive appreciation of their status as "disloyals," who were determined to reject the America which had subjected them to the indignities of evacuation and confinement in concentration camps, to seek the earliest possible return to a victorious Japan, to give in the meantime all possible aid and comfort to the mother country, and to pursue to the limit the Japanese way of life which, the administration had implied, would be appropriate for "disloyal" segregants. This small group was overweighted with transferees, underweighted with old Tuleans. Many of the former had had to make a more definite commitment with respect to "disloyalty," and all of them had been forced to undergo the inconvenience and hardship of what was, in effect, another evacuation. The latter had, in large numbers, by mere refusal to answer the questionnaire or refusal to leave the project, avoided both the physical inconvenience of moving and the psychic distress of a definite commitment of future allegiance.

The new transferees, both the undetermined and the determined "disloyals," found themselves at an immediate disadvantage with respect to the old Tuleans, who had the best housing and the best jobs, were in positions of power and prestige and were favored by the administration. The resulting jealousies and dissatisfactions proved fertile ground for the growth of the belief, fostered by the more determined "disloyals," that the essential difficulty was that Tule Lake was not composed entirely of "like-minded" people or "true disloyals" who had cast themselves off from America and were devoted to the pursuit of the Japanese way of life. Soon, even the least determined "disloyals" among the transferees were blaming the lack of determined "disloyalty" among the old Tuleans for the frictions in camp. They felt that these undetermined "disloyals," whom some of them estimated in the thousands, should be forced to join others of like predispositions either in camps for the "loyal" or in the "outside world." A further clarification of status and a more rigid definition of "disloyalty" were called for, with a resegregation of "dissident elements." Accomplishment of this program would result in a community of "like-minded" people, strictly defined as "disloyal," who would be free to behave disloyally.

In describing their initial reactions to Tule Lake, statements such as the following were frequently made by transferees:

When we came to Tule Lake, we learned that the WRA had failed to carry out its program and to make this as a segregation center for disloyals. There were many loyal ones who remained here in large numbers and many uncertain ones in status, the No-Yes, the Yes-No, the nonregistrants. I thought that this dump certainly was no place for us.[1]

I was disappointed when I found a great number of Yes-Yes people and people who hadn't registered in camp. We had expected just one group and had expected to run this camp as we wanted to. We had had high hopes for that.[2]

As early as October 26, 1943, the desirability of working out a plan for the resegregation of the residents, involving the separation of the "sincere repatriates" and "others," was proposed by the Negotiating Committee of the *Daihyo Sha Kai,* the protest faction then in power. The question was again urgently raised by this faction at its meeting with Dillon Myer on November 1, when chairman Kuratomi attributed the unrest in camp to the fact that the population had not been differentiated rigidly into those "still loyal to this country" and those "who want to return to Japan sooner or later."

The matter was taken up repeatedly and unsuccessfully in meetings between *Daihyo Sha Kai* representatives and the Spanish Consul. On November 3, for example, the chairman of the Negotiating Committee told the Consul:

There are still some people here who are loyal and, naturally, are different from us. There are a number of volunteers who came with their relatives. A survey reveals that two to four thousand people are loyal Americans within this center. They asked that segregation be conducted as soon as possible. One thing they asked was, if possible, they would like to have some definite announcement made from Washington to this respect, and the date, anytime convenient—after the date, this center would be designated for only those persons who have intentions of going back to Japan.[3]

On November 4 a Gila transferee, a supporter of *Daihyo Sha Kai,* wrote the following editorial in the *Tulean Dispatch.*

---

[1] Statement by Mrs. Tsuchikawa, Field Notes, July 18, 1944.

[2] Statement by a young Nisei girl from Topaz, *Ibid.*

[3] Minutes of the meeting, November 3, 1943.

Is the reason why we were segregated into this center clear in the minds of all residents? If not, why not?

The WRA has definitely made this clear in our minds when they defined segregation as a movement to separate those who want to be JAPANESE from those who want to be AMERICAN.

We are here because we wish to be JAPANESE, because we desire to do things as Japanese. Our future does NOT lie in the American way of life; our future is in the Japanese way of life!

However, there are still many who by their actions and thoughts, insist upon reverting to the life they led prior to their decision! Are you one of those residents? If you are, it is about time that you have decided and act accordingly!

After the referendum and the narrow defeat of status quo in January, 1944, *Daihyo Sha Kai* remnants operated underground as proponents of plans (of unspecified details) for resifting the residents on the basis of loyalty and intention of early repatriation. Their efforts to win over the Manzanar contingent in March, 1944, emphasized that "nonclarification of status was the root of all center troubles" and implied strongly that further segregation would be the only solution of these troubles. Gaining strength and support from these and later transferees, they made an open bid for popular support of resegregation and preferential treatment of true "disloyals" in the Ishikawa petition in April, 1944. At the same time they emerged from the underground and adopted the name *Saikakuri Seigan* for their movement.[4]

The Ishikawa petition was specific in its demands that (1) the petitioners, being sincere repatriates, be given priority on the earliest exchange boat to Japan, and (2) in the meantime, they be permitted to segregate themselves within the Tule Lake center in a "designated section [of camp] among others of like inclination." In exhorting the residents to sign the petition, leaders of the movement urged separation from "a large number of heterogeneous elements, with whose thoughts our ideas could never harmonize."

The Ishikawa petition obtained some 6,500 signatures,[5] many of them as a result of pressure. The proponents in many cases silenced their critics by physical violence, or threat of violence, or by *inu* branding, or by the subtle use of clichés such as "We are all in the same boat. We are all Japanese, and should therefore act like true Japanese. Sign, if you are Japanese."

---

[4] See p. 235.

[5] Including, as noted previously, those of many young children for whom their parents signed.

On April 24 the completed petition was sent to the Spanish Embassy in Washington with a request for immediate consideration. And in May, when the Spanish Consul in San Francisco asked for an active list of applicants for repatriation and expatriation, the Resegregation Group sent him a more elaborate plea for resegregation, to which were attached the names on the Ishikawa petition, and a "supplementary list thereto." It was claimed that the two lists combined contained 7,500 names. Thereafter, Ishikawa and his cosigners, with such persons as Kira and Yamashita guiding them behind the scene, claimed the backing of these signers and assumed the authority of representing them as spokesmen.

As described in Chapter XI, the underground devoted its efforts for several months after the circulation of the Ishikawa petition toward pressing the administration and seeking the intervention of outside agencies for the release of the stockade detainees. At the same time, however, its leaders lost no opportunity of keeping the resegregation issue alive, and they put out a constant stream of propaganda to the effect that a peaceful and orderly way of life could not be attained until resegregation was carried out. They utilized the unrest and suspicion during the wave of violence against *inu* by branding their critics as "loyals" and informers. Because of the general belief that the "strong-arm boys" among the Resegregationists had been responsible for the *inu* beatings and murder, residents were reluctant to antagonize this group by reporting its activities. As a result the administration failed to obtain concrete evidence of the source of the terroristic tactics and the Resegregationists were enabled to proceed with their program without hindrance.

By the beginning of July the underground group had become a powerful and systematically integrated organization. Representatives had been appointed in every block and had been coördinated under ward representatives, who in turn formed a central committee. Ishikawa acted as the chairman of this committee, called *Jochi-iin* (Standing Committee), with Kira and Yamashita as advisors. The *Jochi-iin* met regularly and formulated policies, programs and propaganda which were passed along to the block representatives. Meetings of the *Jochi-iin* were soon dominated by Kira and Yamashita. Each of them had a well-organized group of "strong-arm boys," who frequently surrounded the barracks in

which *Jochi-iin* meetings were being held. It is reported that, whenever any dissent from Kira's or Yamashita's predetermined policies
was manifested in the audience, these boys would mill around, stick
their heads in the windows of the barracks, and make threatening
gestures until the dissent was withdrawn.

At about this time Kira and Yamashita also embarked upon a
series of "educational" lectures, which were held regularly in a
number of blocks. They expounded Japanese political ideology,
emphasized the Greater East Asia Co-Prosperity ideas, and re-
counted "news items" from Radio Tokyo. They convincingly presented Japan as victorious in the Pacific,[6] and exhorted the listeners
to be "true Japanese." Additional speakers were recruited and
similar lectures were given throughout the camp. This move was an
implementation of one of the arguments presented in the Ishikawa petition—that "the discipline and education of our children
adapted to the system of wartime Motherland are absolutely necessary." Such opportunities of "Japanization," resegregation proponents expected, would be a strong attraction for those "disloyals"
who hoped to pursue the Japanese way of life in Tule Lake, and
who had, soon after segregation, and with the consent of WRA,
established Japanese language schools to prepare their children
for a future in Japan. Most of these schools had adopted text books
used in Japan in recent years. In recreational activities emphasis
was more and more being placed on things Japanese, while typical
American activities were discouraged.

Meantime, the Resegregationists had failed to invoke any action
from the Spanish authorities on their appeals, and they decided to
reopen the issue of resegregation with WRA. On June 7 the nominal leaders addressed a letter to Dillon Myer, reiterating their
desire for separation from the "loyal" until they could achieve
their ultimate aim of repatriation. In this plea, the leaders advocated the removal of themselves and other like-minded "disloyals"
to another camp where they could wait for the exchange ship to
Japan. Without waiting for Myer's reply, they reported this move
to the residents through their organizational channels, and conveyed the impression that WRA would soon undertake resegregation. The effectiveness of their communication system was soon

---

[6] The Japanese reverses in the Pacific were presented as a part of the grand
strategy conceived by Japan, by which she was drawing the American forces
nearer to her home bases in order to achieve "decisive victory with one blow."

evidenced by the resultant wave of rumor of imminent resegregation that swept the camp. But the new plan of resegregation was contrary to the wishes of many of the signers of the Ishikawa petition, who had no desire to undergo the hardships of another move or the distress of resulting separation of family members and who wanted not themselves but the fence sitters and "loyals" removed.

There were many conflicting rumors about the probable destination of the "disloyal." Some claimed they would be sent to one of the existing WRA projects. Poston and Jerome were prominently mentioned. Others were sure they would be moved to Alaska. "Reliable" sources were quoted in detail, including newspaper and radio reports. Kurusu stated, "For more than two weeks everybody is saying we might be segregated again. First they said we would be sent to Poston, then they said Alaska."[7] Mrs. Kurusu added, "They told me that they had heard it over the radio and seen it in the *San Francisco Examiner* that the people are going to be sent to Jerome. It is the disloyal people who are going to be moved."[8] An elderly Issei woman said, "People heard it over the radio and the blocks are very upset. Children are crying. I have moved four times already and I don't want to move again. Jerome is bad, they say, too much rain."[9]

While these rumors were circulating,[10] the Resegregationists extended their program: (1) to advocate the renunciation of American citizenship; (2) to proselytize new members and enlarge the organization.

The question of renunciation had been brought up as early as December 13, 1943, in the meeting of the *Daihyo Sha Kai* remnants with the Spanish Consul, when a plea was made that "truly disloyal Nisei" be given the status of Japanese nationals and thus come within the jurisdiction of the protecting Spanish authorities. The plea was rejected by a representative of the State Department who accompanied the Consul, on the following grounds:

I would like to explain the status of the Nisei who have both Japanese and American citizenship. When you are in the United States you are an American citizen. When you are in Japan, you are a Japanese subject. When you are in Japan as Japanese subject, the American Government

---

[7] Field Notes, August 8, 1944.
[8] *Ibid.*
[9] Field Notes, August 10, 1944.
[10] The rumors did not die down until September, 1944.

does not protect you, and when you are in America as American subjects the Japanese Government does not protect you or in this case the Spanish Government will not protect you. You cannot by saying so throw off your American citizenship. You must do a specific act such as renouncing your citizenship. But you can do it in time of peace, but not in time of war. No American subject can throw off his citizenship.[11]

The question of renunciation remained dormant throughout the first half of 1944, although expressions such as "What's the use of having American citizenship?" were constantly heard. In July, however, the passage of the Denationalization Bill by Congress revitalized the issue. The *Newell Star* of July 13 reported that

a new law dealing with the relinquishment of their citizenship by American citizens has been passed by the Congress of the United States and signed by the President . . .

The new law provides that an American citizen may expatriate by "making in the United States a formal written renunciation of nationality in such form as may be prescribed by, and before such officer as may be designated by, the Attorney General, whenever the United States shall be in a state of war and the Attorney General shall approve such renunciation as not contrary to the interests of national defense."

It should be noted that a formal written renunciation of citizenship under the new law must be approved by the Attorney General before citizenship can be removed. The Department of Justice has indicated that the Attorney General will scrutinize each such renunciation with greatest care before an American citizen will be permitted to relinquish his citizenship under this law.[12]

Although the report added that detailed procedures had not yet been formulated, it was clear that the passage of the bill meant that American citizens could relinquish their citizenship, during wartime, while they were still on American soil. It also meant that "disloyal" Nisei and Kibei could achieve the status of "true Japanese" and come under the protection of the Japanese government.

The Resegregationists immediately made renunciation a focal point in their policies. On July 28, when the evacuee representatives met the Spanish Vice-Consul, Yamashita, Ishikawa, Tsuchikawa, and others among the representatives pressed the Vice-Consul

---

[11] Minutes of the meeting, December 13, 1943.

[12] It is to be noted that "the measure, which had the support of Attorney General Francis Biddle, was designed to provide legal means to denationalize between '300 to 1,000' persons of Japanese ancestry at the Tule Lake segregation center who had expressed a desire to renounce their United States citizenship and have asked for expatriation." (*Pacific Citizen*, July 8, 1944.)

for information as to whether those Japanese Americans in Tule Lake who renounced would be treated as Japanese nationals, what steps should be taken to restore Japanese citizenship for those who had been dual citizens and had subsequently canceled Japanese citizenship, and what procedure should be taken by those who had only American citizenship. The Vice-Consul merely stated that he had not received official interpretation of the bill and he therefore refused to answer the questions.

In their plans for expansion of their organization, Kira and Yamashita soon recognized the weakness of the plan of moving their followers to another center, and reverted to the earlier plan of removal of "loyals," whereby they and their followers could remain in Tule Lake, behave like "true Japanese," defy the administration and, if necessary, utilize force to expel from the camp those residents who did not share their views. Their proselytizing program was initiated with the organization of a young men's group, the *Sokoku Kenkyu Seinen-dan*, usually referred to merely as *Sokoku* (Young Men's Association for the Study of the Mother Country). The first meeting of the *Sokoku* was held on the night of August 12 in the high school auditorium,[13] with the permission of WRA. Approximately 500 youths, some older men and a few women attended this meeting and heard a lecture by Reverend Aramaki, the nominal founder,[14] behind whom Kira and Yamashita continued to manipulate the activities of the organization. The expressed aim of this organization was to prepare the members to be useful citizens of Japan after their expatriation. To this end they resolved to devote themselves to a study of Japanese language, Japanese history and Japanese political ideology. The formal aims of the group were announced in a manifesto on August 12 as follows:

Since the outbreak of war between Japan and America, citizens of Japanese ancestry have moved along two separate paths: (1) for the defense of their civil rights on legal principles, and (2) for the renunciation of their citizenship on moral principles. Each group has constantly expended its efforts for the fulfillment of its own aims.

[13] Subsequently, important ceremonies of the group were held on the eighth of each month, in commemoration of the anniversary of Pearl Harbor, which in Japan fell on that date.

[14] Some informants claimed that Kira and Yamashita appointed Aramaki as the leader so that his followers from Jerome could be brought into the organization.

After we were segregated to this center, we have, on moral principles, stood for renunciation, and have awakened the consciousness of racial heritage. Fortunately, the government, whose national policies are based on democracy, humanity and liberty, has now proclaimed by legislation that it officially approves our inclination. We are, indeed, delighted with this recognition. With the three principles listed below, we hereby organize the *Sokoku Kenkyu Seinen-dan* and resolve to devote ourselves for the achievement of our original aims.

1. To increase the appreciation of our racial heritage by a study of the incomparable culture of our mother country.

2. To abide by the project regulations and to refrain from any involvement in center politics. To be interested only in improving our moral life and in building our character.

3. To participate in physical exercises in order to keep ourselves in good health.

The important points in this manifesto are (1) emphasis on renunciation of citizenship by its members; (2) emphasis on the nonpolitical nature of the organization, and on the purely cultural context of its proposed activities. This second point was an attempt both to avert administrative objections which, it was believed, would be raised immediately if a political organization were formed, and also to allay the fears of potential members who would hesitate to join, since previous experience had shown that political activities were likely to lead to administrative repression.

To naïve residents who believed the organization's contention that it had no political aims, the proposed activities had a strong attraction. Many of the young Nisei who were contemplating expatriation had never been in Japan and had a very imperfect knowledge even of the rudiments of the language. It would obviously be of great practical value to them in their future if they learned something of the way of life which they would be expected to pursue. Their Issei parents were wholeheartedly behind such an endeavor, hoping thus to improve the young people's chances for economic and social acceptance in Japan. At the same time the pattern of life in Tule Lake was tending more and more to exalt the Japanese way of life and to disparage the American. To enter wholeheartedly into a study of Japanese culture was to act in conformity with this pattern and to erect a defense against being considered "loyal" to America by suspicious fellow residents.

The *Sokoku* scheduled frequent lectures for its members. On these occasions, emphasis was placed on *Yamato Damashii*, em-

peror worship and glorification of the war aims of Japan. Morning
outdoor exercises were initiated and participation was made compulsory for the members. These exercises gradually became more
and more exhibitionistically militaristic. Bugles and uniforms were
purchased and the young men, wearing grey sweat shirts and head
bands, stamped with the emblem of the rising sun, marched out
to the firebreaks, goose-stepping, and shouting *"Wash-sho! Wash-
sho!"* ("Hip! Hip!"), and drilled to the accompaniment of patriotic bugling. These exercises took place before six o'clock each
morning and, week by week, additional Japanese militaristic features were added to the routine.

The initial acceptance of the *Sokoku's* aims by residents was
widespread; if there was any disapproval, it was not openly expressed for fear of reprisal from the young members. Many residents
considered the expressed aims worthwhile. Some were articulate in
support of the organization. For example, Kurusu said, "The *Sokoku* is not a pressure group; they are not going into politics. They
are for the study of Japanese culture. That's why I joined them."[15]
And a Nisei woman remarked:

The *Sokoku* men have worked out some good things to educate young
men. Take these zoot-suiters, for instance, they're going to have a heck
of a time when they go to Japan. The *Sokoku* says, "We must train these
boys." And I think that's right. You must do something with these zoot-
suiters.[16]

There were, however, some who expressed their skepticism about
the sincerity of the organization. Kurihara, for example, said, "I
don't know the true motive behind it. I don't care to have any part
in it."[17]

And Wakida commented:

The *Sokoku* is big. It's well organized. It's good and strong. But if they
get too much power and can't control themselves, they might cause some
trouble. A lot of people are against it, but they are afraid to say anything.[18]

The administration was cognizant of the wave of resegregation
rumors and of the inception and subsequent overt activities of the
Sokoku. Although it was apparently unwilling to inhibit the formation of the organization or to interfere with its activities, which

[15] Field Notes, September 15, 1944.
[16] Field Notes, September 14, 1944.
[17] Field Notes, August 14, 1944.
[18] Field Notes, September 11, 1944.

were ostensibly in line with WRA-sanctioned "pursuance of the Japanese way of life," it made some effort to identify the leaders. The administration decided also to publicize Myer's communication dated July 14, which replied to the Resegregationists' letter of June 7 and denied any intention of resegregation.[19] Assistant Project Director Black, on August 30, called Ishikawa, Kubo and others, who signed the June 7 letter, into conference and announced emphatically that WRA would not embark upon such a program. It is reported that during this conference Black and the Resegregationists, who considered they had been "double crossed," engaged in heated arguments and parted with ill feeling.

Following this, the Resegregationists not only failed to make public the administrative denial, but they also, without knowledge of project officials, mimeographed and distributed Mr. Myer's letter and, in the Japanese translation, distorted it to their advantage and conveyed the false impression that their group was officially sanctioned and that plans for resegregation were under consideration by the administration. Myer's letter said in part:

> The policies under which the Tule Lake segregation center is operated have been carefully studied, both by Washington officials and by the Project Director at Tule Lake, and the policies presently in force are considered fair and equitable.
> Mr. Best, Project Director, will be glad to take up with representatives of the residents of Tule Lake, any specific problems relating to the administration of the Project. If necessary, Mr. Best will take such questions up with Washington, where you may be assured of considerate attention. I am sure Mr. Best will be glad to discuss with you the question of resegregation to which your communication refers.

The Japanese translation of the last paragraph read:

> However, I am sure that all problems in the Tule Lake segregation center that need attention and improvement will be studied and remedied *in consultation with the representatives of the Resegregation Group.*[20] Furthermore, whenever Director Best refers to the WRA headquarters in Washington any specific problem for consideration and approval, you may now be assured of considerate attention. Needless to say, I am sure Director Best will be glad to discuss frankly with you the question of resegregation about which your representatives have communicated.

---

[19] According to an Assistant Project Director, Meyer, Best, and others conferred in San Francisco on or about August 21 and agreed that WRA would not entertain any plan for resegregation. (Field Notes, August 24, 1944.)

[20] Italics ours.

After circulating this communication, the Resegregationists resumed pressure to force an administrative reconsideration of resegregation. On September 24 they brought forward a new petition accompanied by an explanatory pamphlet, written in both English and Japanese, and requested those who truly desired to return to Japan at the first opportunity to sign the petition. All who had signed the Ishikawa petition were urged to sign again; anyone who had not signed was impressed with the fact that this might be his last chance to join the group. In fact, the pamphlet stated that the group was preparing is final list of proposed repatriates and expatriates, and the list was to be presented to "both the American and the Japanese governments."

After reiterating the charge that WRA had failed to "clarify the distinctions between the loyals and the disloyals" and to make Tule Lake a segregation center for the latter, the pamphlet elaborated upon the aims of the Resegregationists. Pending repatriation to Japan they were prepared "to sacrifice everything . . . to the country we dearly love." Realizing "the uselessness of our American citizenship" they were ready to renounce it "as soon as possible." Their future being in Japan, they "do not desire to return ever . . . to the State of California or to others of our original places [of residence, but] instead we insist to remain within the center provided by the government." Determined as they were to "uphold highly our Japanese spirits and increasingly endeavor to cultivate ourselves both mentally and physically in order to fulfill the principle of being nothing but a real Japanese" they were prepared to expel from membership "those who act un-Japanese and who bring disgrace to other Japanese." And in stressing their determination to remain in camp until they were repatriated, the leaders played upon the constant fear of being forced to leave camp and resettle, which had recently been revitalized by rumors of imminent rescission of the orders excluding them from the West Coast and the possibility of closure of the relocation centers.

Several days before the distribution of the pamphlet, Mr. Yamashita, the Resegregationist leader, explained its purpose:

This petition will tell the administration exactly where we stand. We are certain that the administration and WRA cannot distinguish between the loyal and the disloyal people congregated in this camp. This is the reason for so much restlessness and unfortunate disturbances in camp.

We residents—the wiser people among us cannot wait for the administration to act. The time has come when the Japanese residents wish to formulate their beliefs.

You know that the people behind resegregation have been working underground for a long time. Anyone who would have come out openly for this earlier would have been put in the stockade. We have been working on this since April, awaiting the moment; but we had to keep it a secret. Now the time has come.

We are of the opinion that we cannot be loyal to two countries. As long as we are living here, why not make up our minds whether to be real Japanese or not? When this is fully impressed on the residents, this camp will become more peaceful than ever, and the loyal and the fence sitters will relocate according to WRA policy.

Those who refuse to sign this will have people asking them, "Are you loyal to Japan or not? If you are not loyal to Japan, why don't you go out?"

If they don't sign this they will be known to be not loyal to Japan and will be so told in public. Of course, many people who don't want to go back to Japan will sign, but then they will go in a corner and keep quiet.[21]

This is a revealing statement of the aims and outlook of the leader of the Resegregation Group, and is explicit in respect to the pressure which the petition was intended to put upon the residents.

The circulation of this petition was begun on Sunday, September 24, but the administration took no action on the matter for several days. On September 27 the Caucasian supervisor warned the block managers that the petition had no administrative sanction. Mr. Black, on September 30, followed with a memorandum emphasizing once more that "there will be no further segregation at Tule Lake or elsewhere because such a program is impractical and infeasible. . . . Contrary to a statement contained therein, resegregation is receiving no consideration, serious or otherwise, from WRA, either here or in Washington." He added a warning against signing the petition, pointing out that it was anonymous and unauthorized; that nothing could be gained by further petition since those who looked forward to a future in Japan and had applied for repatriation had "complied with all the requirements of either the American or the Japanese government" to achieve this end; and that "preferential treatment would not be obtained by further petition." He condemned scathingly the activities of the leaders which were, he said, detrimental to the residents and tended to "incite unrest, produce confusion, upset peace of mind, and con-

---

[21] Field Notes, September 21, 1944.

tribute to tension and nervousness." By this time, however, the Resegregationists had nearly completed the circulation of the petition. They paid no attention to the warning, but, on the contrary, increased their efforts to get more signatures.

When the petition was submitted to the Spanish Embassy and the State Department, it was said to have contained some 10,000 names, including those of minors and infants.[22] Itabashi, who did not sign it, explained:

My family of five have already applied through the Spanish Embassy to go back to Japan. So what more do we need? Resegregation means nothing when you analyze what the Resegregationists say. But the majority of people signed the petition under intimidation and ignorance.[23]

Wakida said:

When they circulated this petition, they said, "If you sign this paper, you won't be drafted into the Army and you'll be the first to get on the exchange boat. So everybody signed it.[24]

Many people were influenced to sign by a rumor, persistent at this time, that the Department of Justice would take over the operation of Tule Lake from WRA soon after the presidential election. This rumor is said to have originated with the Caucasian personnel but Resegregationists actively spread the story[25] among the evacuees and stated repeatedly that the pending transfer of the camp to the Department of Justice had been accomplished because of their activities, and would result ipso facto in resegregation. The Department of Justice, they pointed out, had custodial authority only over potentially dangerous aliens. If the Department took over Tule Lake it would certainly throw out "loyal" aliens and all citizens. The only people who would be allowed to remain would be aliens who had overtly demonstrated their loyalty to Japan and citizens who had renounced their American citizenship.

In soliciting signatures for the petition, the Resegregationists are also said to have used coercion and intimidation frequently.

---

[22] Less than a half of the persons whose names appeared on the petition were 17½ years of age or older.

[23] Field Notes, October 10, 1944.

[24] Field Notes, October 12, 1944.

[25] Dillon Myer denied the rumor publicly during a visit to the center on October 10. Resegregationists, however, continued to spread the story throughout the following month.

Some of the specific cases were reported by a Nisei transferee from Topaz:

I was pressured into signing up with the Resegregationist Group along with many others. We signed in order to prevent physical harm to ourselves and to the members of our family.[26]

By a Nisei anti-*Sokoku* girl, an old Tulean:

The *Sokoku* men had, in some wards, barred the children of parents who refused to sign the petition from participating in the morning exercises. The children were shamed in front of their friends.[27]

And by the Community Analyst:

Feeling ran so high in ward VII, that vocal anti-resegregationists or residents of "tough" blocks who had refused to sign were definitely on the spot. In block 73, the block manager . . . was forced by public opinion to move quietly out of his block and later resign; his secretary did likewise. In block 74, adjoining, in ward VII, we learned that one aged anti-resegregationist was hit over the back of the head and knocked unconscious (October 7).[28]

The general condition in camp was summarized by a high-ranking project official as follows:

There seems to be a very definite tension, worse than it has been since the Noma killing. Some groups are making threats against evacuee workers. My key workers resigned. It looks as if the young Kibei are doing the rough stuff now. They are hitting from several different angles.[29]

As was true in other periods of general tension in Tule Lake, the resurgence of violence was accompanied by widespread demoralization of the young people. Many cases of theft, vandalism, party crashing, and fist fights were reported. On the night of October 15, three elderly Issei returning from a meeting of a religious cult, were set upon by a gang of half a dozen young men. The men had refused to sign the resegregation petition and had advised other residents not to sign. At a meeting of the sect some time in September, they had made speeches calling upon the young men present to abstain from radical activities which might meet with administrative disapproval. One of them, Mr. Itabashi, had pointed out that nothing

---

[26] Field Notes, February 15, 1945.
[27] Field Notes, October 5, 1944.
[28] WRA, Community Analysis "Report on Center Trends (Oct. 8–16)" (manuscript), October 16, 1944.
[29] Field Notes, October 4, 1944.

would be gained by making trouble and that agitation only brought suffering upon the women and children in camp. He exhorted the Nisei to follow the higher ideals of Japan which, he stated, were not compatible with agitation or the making of unreasonable demands:

I said that this camp is no place for young men to make trouble. They should study. I said, "Young men, behave yourselves." What I said there was reported to the Resegregationist headquarters.[30]

The attack was described by Itabashi as follows:

The three of us were coming home from a religious meeting at block 52. I heard noisy footsteps. One of my friends was at my side, the other was 15 feet ahead. The first man who was attacked yelled. I turned around and saw that big stick. I can still see the club like a frozen picture, but I didn't know anything after that.[31]

Since the victims refused to name their assailants or give any description of them, the Caucasian Internal Security was able to accomplish nothing, and the evacuee police, following precedent, refused to handle the case.

On October 30 another case of violence, resulting from differences over the resegregation issue, was reported in Block 78, a strong proresegregation block in Ward VIII. Shinkichi Iwamoto, known to be Kira's right-hand man, knifed the son of a block resident who was said to be hostile to Kira and had criticized him. Presumably because of fear of the Resegregationists, the victim gave less and less incriminating evidence every time he testified in the hearings held by the Internal Security. The assailant was, however, turned over to Modoc County authorities, by whom he was sentenced to ninety days in jail. The Resegregationists claimed that their intervention on Iwamoto's behalf was responsible for the light sentence.

Meanwhile, Resegregationist leaders became increasingly arrogant. At the *Sokoku* ceremony held in Block 84 (Ward VIII) on October 21, Kira is said to have incited the young men to violence and to have promised that he would take care of them if they got into trouble. He quoted a Japanese proverb which, while characteristically flexible in interpretation, could be translated to mean: "To help the great cause, we have to kill those who stand in its

---

[30] Field Notes, November 9, 1944.   [31] *Ibid.*

way." The connotation to most of the residents seemed to be that the opponents of the Resegregationists would be liquidated.

The *Sokoku* had, together with the older Resegregationists, set up a staff in an office in Block 54. They plastered the walls with patriotic mottoes, Japanese flags and a sign to the effect that any person speaking English in the office would be fined at the rate of one cent a word. Its branches in various wards started publishing mimeographed weeklies or monthlies. With active support of the Resegregationist leaders the *Sokoku* continued, but now more overtly, with further elaboration of morning ceremonies, including drills, marching in goose step, and judo practice. Lectures with Yamashita, Kira, Aramaki, and other leaders as speakers, were given wide publicity, the most important taking place in the school auditorium on the eighth of each month. Group exercises of a more highly nationalistic character were initiated, including an early morning outdoor ceremony on the eighth of the month, at which prayers for Japanese victory were offered. The nature of such ceremonies is exemplified in the following announcement:

Hissho Kigan Shiki [Ceremony to Pray for Victory] is observed in Japan on every eighth day of the month. This is the day our motherland declared war against the allied nations. On this day the people of Japan offer a fervent prayer for total victory at any cost.

As Japanese subjects we shall observe *Hissho Kigan Shiki* this Sunday, October 8, 1944. Commencing at 6:30 A.M. at the outdoor stage. A request for all members to assemble at block 14 between barracks 1 and 13 by 6:00 A.M. is issued by the physical chairman. . . .

To purify the mind and body before attending the ceremony, the cabinet and block representatives shall take a cold shower Sunday morning at block 14 shower room at 5:00 A.M. Other members who are willing, are requested to meet at the same time and place.[32]

Yamashita discussed in detail the effects he and the other leaders hoped to obtain by encouraging these ceremonies and exercises. The young men, he said, were "preparing themselves physically and mentally" so that they could be utilized by the Japanese government "if they go on the exchange boat." He added that "by getting up early in the morning, by exercise and training after worshiping, and praying for victory and eternal life for our Japanese soldiers, these young people can be deeply impressed." He stated further that since the soldiers and civilians of Japan were

---

[32] *Sokoku Kenkyu Seinen-dan Ward I Weekly*, October 6, 1944.

making great sacrifices, it behooved the "true Japanese" in Tule Lake to give up their luxuries and show themselves willing to sacrifice also. "We must act parallel with what our brothers in Japan are doing."[33]

The ceremonies sponsored by the Resegregationists reached a climax in connection with *Meiji Setsu* on November 3. Although *Meiji Setsu* had been proclaimed a holiday by the administration and was celebrated by the general population, with each of the language schools as well as most blocks sponsoring festivals in the traditional manner, the *Sokoku* and the older Resegregationist members, pursuant to their policy of special dedication to Japan, held a separate ceremony. This ceremony was held on the outdoor stage of the main firebreak, with great solemnity and reverence. The young men marched in and ranged themselves in rows, standing without overcoats in the bitter November weather for more than an hour. Most of the older participants also lined up in rows. All the 2,000-odd participants bowed toward the rising sun, while a corps of buglers played Japanese national music.

In spite of the extensive proselytization and the apparent popular support of their activities, the Resegregationists at the end of October still constituted a minority in the center. Although they claimed 10,000 names on the resegregation petition of September, the active membership could not at the most have exceeded 2,000 evacuees, mostly transferees, and a few old Tuleans. Of these, about 750 evacuees belonged to the *Sokoku*, the young men's organization, which had gained some 200 new members during October. In the beginning of the month the *Sokoku* probably had only 550 members, as estimated by Wakida, who had

made a pretty thorough study of the strength of the *Sokoku*. They do not have more than sixty or seventy members in each ward, which would give them a membership of 550 at the outside. My ward, ward VII, has the largest membership, and they are also very strong in my block, block 68. Ward I has 52 members and ward III has only 50.[34]

The increase of membership during the month was largely credited to Kira, who decided at this time to affiliate his "Manzanar Gang" with the *Sokoku*. On October 21 a branch of the *Sokoku* was

---

[33] Field Notes, October 30, 1944.

[34] Field Notes, October 2, 1944. Reverend Aramaki, however, claimed that "the *Sokoku* has 1,000 members." (Field Notes, October 13, 1944.)

for the first time established in Ward VIII, which subsequently became the strongest proresegregation ward in the center.

Resegregationist leaders took further steps to increase their membership and to strengthen their group cohesion. They first replaced Reverend Aramaki with Nobuo Yamada as head of *Sokoku.* This move was an attempt by Kira and Yamashita to gain more complete control over the organization. They had, for some time, met difficulties in persuading Aramaki[35] to carry through some of their policies, while Yamada, a former member of the Negotiating Committee, an ex-stockade detainee, and chief instructor in judo for the *Sokoku,* was bound in closely with the leaders and was considered a more pliable instrument for their purposes.

The leaders then proceeded formally to organize the older Resegregationists who, up to this time, were still loosely organized as the *Saikakuri Seigan* into an association paralleling the *Sokoku.* In the *Jochi-iin* meeting on November 10 a plan to form a dues-paying organization called the *Sokuji Kikoku Hoshi-dan,* usually abbreviated to *Hoshi-dan* (Organization to Return Immediately to the Homeland to Serve), was formally adopted. Membership was limited to those who had signed the resegregation petition, who wished immediate return to Japan, who had pledged absolute loyalty to Japan, and who were willing "to sacrifice life and property in order to serve our mother country in time of unparalleled emergency." Officers were elected, and the interlocking relations of *Jochi-iin,* the highest ranking committee, with the *Sokoku* were described as follows: "The members of the *Jochi-iin* shall attend the meetings of the Central Executive Committee of the *Sokoku Kenkyu Seinen-dan* and shall guide the officers." Subscriptions were solicited for a mimeographed monthly magazine called the *Hokoku* (Service to Mother Country).

At about the same time, *Sokoku* changed its name to *Hokoku Seinen-dan,* usually abbreviated to *Hokoku* (Young Men's Organization to Serve Our Mother Country). This change of name reflected a change of the stated purpose of the organization from study of the culture (*Sokoku Kenkyu*) to service of the mother country. Resegregationists explained that the change of name sig-

---

[35] Aramaki submitted his resignation because of the circulation of widespread rumors imputing immorality. It is said that these rumors were started by Resegregationist leaders as a means of forcing Aramaki's resignation.

nified that the period of cultural preparation had been completed and that the young men were now ready to serve the mother country.

Thus, by September, the Resegregationists had emerged from the underground pressure group to a highly formalized, institutionalized organization, with a frankly nationalistic and exhibitionistically disloyal program. In the latter part of October they were enabled to push their program toward its ultimate goal—renunciation of American citizenship by the young men as a symbol of their complete rejection of America and identification with Japan.

The *Newell Star* of October 26 reported that the Department of Justice had, at last, set up procedures for accepting and processing applications for renunciation:

> The Citizenship Renunciation Law . . . is now operative. . . . Only individual applications will be considered. . . . The Department of Justice has indicated that no renunciation will be granted without careful examination of the facts and the reasons motivating the application. Request for renunciation from citizens who are motivated by a desire to avoid Selective Service or other legal obligations, will be subject to particular scrutiny. . . .
>
> The applicant forwards to the Attorney General his application for renunciation of citizenship, on the prescribed form, together with specified citizenship documents. Forms may be secured from the Attorney General as soon as they are printed. In the event the requested renunciation does not appear contrary to the interests of national defense, a hearing is conducted by a hearing officer whom the Attorney General designates. The applicant is notified of the time and place of hearing.
>
> After the hearing the applicant may file formal renunciation of citizenship on a prescribed form and request its approval. The hearing officer recommends approval or disapproval to the Attorney General. . . . A renunciation of citizenship does not become effective until the Attorney General approves it. Notice of approval or disapproval is given the applicant.[36]

As soon as the official procedures were announced, strong pressure was applied by the extremists within the organization to fur-

---

[36] Several proposals for deportation and denationalization of persons of Japanese ancestry were introduced in the 78th Congress. Of these only the denationalization bill, H.R. 4103, was enacted into law. This bill, however, did not have a provision for deportation, although, during the debate in the House of Representatives, Congressman J. L. Johnson from California stated, "If we get these people denaturalized, then deportation will follow after the war, as a matter of course. We will have conquered Japan so successfully that we can dictate the terms of the treaty which will undoubtedly include a provision that all these people shall be taken back to Japan." (Congressional Record, Volume 90, p. 2003, February 23, 1944.)

ther the symbolic repudiation of all things American by having
Hokoku members renounce. When a few official forms for renunciation were received from Washington in November, *Hokoku*
officers made dozens of carbon copies in order that the members
might renounce immediately en masse. Some minors also filed
applications. Both the applications on the typed forms[37] and those
by minors[38] were, however, soon declared invalid.

Delays in receiving prescribed forms slowed up the process of
renunciation, and during the whole of November the Department
of Justice received only 107 valid applications. By the middle of
December, it is estimated that the total number of applications
received approximated 600. Since *Hokoku* membership early in
December is estimated at about 1,500, it is clear that at most 40
per cent of the members were, at this time, willing to take the step
that would ultimately cut them off from America.[39] Thus, it is
evident that the new program, although accepted enthusiastically
by a large minority of *Hokoku* members, was as yet unsuccessful in
overcoming the inertia of the majority of the members.

Pressure for a wider acceptance of the program of renunciation
was now stepped up by an intensification of the nationalistic activities which became more ceremonial and more strictly regimented.
The number of buglers multiplied and bugling was indulged in
more loudly and more frequently. Morning exercises were elaborated. The short-clipped *bozu* haircut, in imitation of that required

[37] A WRA report states that approximately 117 applications were sent to the
Department of Justice on such typed forms. (WRA, Community Analysis Section, "Center Trend Report—November 17 to 25, 1944," manuscript, November
25, 1944.)

[38] Analysis of renunciants by age shows that "minors" were defined as those
under 17½ years of age.

[39] These estimates are based on data supplied by Assistant Attorney General
Herbert Wechsler (letter, August 4, 1945). Unfortunately the number of applications is tabulated only by calendar months, and the date refers to date of receipt
in Washington. During November, 107 applications were received, while the
December figure was 1,106. Including the invalidated forms, we estimate the
probable November total at 200. By graphic interpolation, we estimate some 500
applications during the first half of December. Deducting 100 from this figure
for substitution of valid forms in December for invalid forms received in November, we arrive at a figure of 400 for early December, or a total of 600 up to the
date of rescission of exclusion orders. (See pp. 358–361 for more complete analysis
of renunciation data.)

Documentary evidence leads us to believe that practically all these early applications for renunciation were from *Hokoku* members.

of Japanese soldiers, was made obligatory for the members as a symbol to set them off from dissenters. Members of *Hoshi-dan* tried to induce their children to leave the American schools and concentrate on Japanese studies. Young women relatives of members of the two organizations began to wear longer skirts, braid their hair in pigtails, and even to adopt the dress customary in Japan for working in the fields. Later these women were formally organized as a third Resegregationist group called *Hokoku Joshi Seinen-dan,* usually abbreviated to *Joshi-dan* (Young Women's Organization to Serve Our Mother Country), and, after a formal initiation ceremony on January 8, took up morning exercises similar to those of the *Hokoku.*

By December many nonmembers in certain blocks, especially those in wards VII and VIII and some blocks in Ward VI, where Resegregationists were numerous and strong, had begun to adopt these fashions in an attempt to act and look as much like "true Japanese" as possible, in order to give the impression that they had applied or would apply for renunciation, and thus avoid being called un-Japanese in their blocks. In these blocks this behavior was contagious, and it soon became difficult to differentiate from outward appearance the Resegregationists from their opponents. The underlying cause of this collective reaction was intimidation by the Resegregationists and fear of violence.

Propaganda took the form of spreading news of great Japanase naval victories, which were discussed avidly in almost every household. Among the items reported was the Japanese communique on October 16 from Radio Tokyo to the effect that the American fleet had fled from the scene of a naval engagement off the Philippines and that American losses included ten carriers, two battleships, three cruisers, and one destroyer sunk, and three carriers, one battleship, four cruisers, and eleven warships of unknown types damaged. Another popular short-wave news item reported that an American task force was annihilated off the coast of Formosa. Still another Radio Tokyo broadcast (November 28) claimed that the Japanese had launched a counterattack in Leyte, bombed Saipan and invaded Morotai Island. Despite quite contrary reports from American sources, many evacuees accepted these and other Japanese claims, interpreted them as "the last and final blow," which Japan had long been publicizing.

Rumors developed, also, bearing on the rewards of renouncing and the penalties of failure to renounce citizenship: (1) that those who did not renounce would be drafted into the Army; (2) that nonrenunciants would be ineligible for expatriation to Japan, and could not therefore accompany their repatriating parents; (3) that the Department of Justice would take over the administration of the Tule Lake center on January 15, 1945 (according to another version, January 1, 1945) and that after this transfer applications for renunciation would not be accepted and nonrenunciants would be forced to resettle.

Those who believed firmly in a future in victorious Japan were greatly influenced by these rumors of gains that would accrue to them by renunciation. And those who still held some unexpressed doubts about the outcome of the war or about the desirability of a future in Japan were comforted by a fourth prevalent rumor to the effect that after the war, renunciants would not be deported, but would be permitted to remain in the United States as aliens, if they so desired. This rumor was particularly attractive to many Issei parents who felt that their Nisei children had nothing to lose and perhaps much to gain by renouncing citizenship. The utilitarian view of denationalization was propounded by Yamashita and Kira, the Resegregationist leaders in the following terms. The former said:

Certainly, those who wish for immediate expatriation to Japan and at the same time don't wish to be inducted into the United States Army or don't wish to be forced to resettle should renounce their citizenship.[40]

And the latter:

The Denationalization Bill is a wartime law, and I think it's unconstitutional, because you can't discriminate against a certain portion of the people just because of their color and race. They evacuated us, and then they try to pin us down to a citizen's duties. Once a person is thrown into camp and pushed around, he looks at things emotionally. We cannot be held responsible for what we do in camp.

After the war the entire picture will be changed. The United States will not deport those who renounced their citizenship.[41]

In spite of the proselytizing activities of the leaders and the spread of rumors favorable to their program, the Resegregationists failed to win over the bulk of the population. As noted, appreciably

---

[40] Field Notes, September 7, 1944.   [41] Field Notes, September 21, 1944.

less than half of the young men members had yielded to their exhortations to renounce citizenship by the middle of December. Many of the other residents were irritated by the fanfare of bugles, the flag waving, the exhibitionistic performances of the young men and the constant stream of propaganda to which they were subjected.[42] Criticisms of Resegregationist activities began to be voiced, in spite of fear of terroristic tactics.

In November Mr. Kurusu, who had earlier been enthusiastic about the *Sokoku* activities, said:

I try to avoid the *Sokoku*. I haven't been going to the meetings. I'm afraid if that organization goes on as it is, it will get involved in more troubles.[43]

Similarly, Kurihara:

Resegregationists are not leading the residents in the right way. Just because I don't join their organization, they say I'm not loyal to Japan. How could they measure my loyalty that way? They have carried things too far. Knocking in the heads of people who are not for them is too much.[44]

And in the beginning of December, the daughter of a *Hoshi-dan* member, remarked:

They are not acting for the good of the people. They are trying to do everything in a spectacular way, such as cutting their hair. I believe there are lots of people in camp who wish more sincerely to return to Japan but aren't making such a noise about it.[45]

At about the same time, Murakami, the evacuee aide in the Legal Department of the project, said:

The *Hokoku* bunch is really the Kibei who returned to the United States in 1935–1937. They left Japan to escape the Japanese army draft. Japan doesn't want them. You can't deport them to Japan, because Japan won't take them.[46]

And Wakida, who taught in a Japanese language school:

After the *Sokoku* was organized, my students changed. They got very bad to teach. I don't care what the *Sokoku* do, but I don't like the fact that kids are not led right. The *Sokoku* boys are too hot headed. They say, "The Yes-Yes must get out of camp." But who can tell what the *Sokoku* boys think in their hearts? Who can tell whether they aren't dodging the draft.[47]

[42] See pp. 312–313.
[43] Field Notes, November 7, 1944.
[44] Field Notes, November 6, 1944.
[45] Field Notes, December 11, 1944.
[46] Field Notes, December 18, 1944.
[47] Field Notes, December 9, 1944.

By late 1944, only about 32 per cent of the population aged 17½ or older were listed as members of the combined Resegregationist organizations. The membership was, as indicated in Chart VIII, spread most unevenly throughout the project. Concentrations occurred in wards VIII and VII. In the former, nine out of ten blocks counted more than 50 per cent of the adult residents as members; in the latter, two out of nine. Extremes were reached in blocks 75

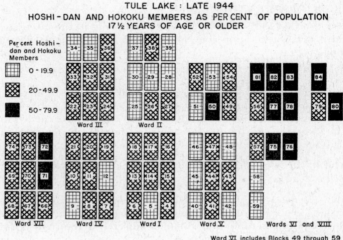

TULE LAKE : LATE 1944
HOSHI - DAN AND HOKOKU MEMBERS AS PER CENT OF POPULATION
17 ½ YEARS OF AGE OR OLDER

Ward VI includes Blocks 49 through 59
Ward VIII includes Bocks 75 through 84

Chart VIII

and 82, where more than three quarters of the residents were Resegregationists. The lowest proportions were reached in wards II and V: in the former, six out of nine, and in the latter, five out of nine blocks had fewer than 20 per cent membership. Three blocks (12, 25, and 28) had 5 per cent or less of their adult residents among the Resegregationists. In large part, these locational variations reflected the full-fledged emergence of the transferees as a protest faction and, correspondingly, the resistance of old Tuleans to pressure-group tactics, for 45 per cent of all transferees (40 per cent of the group entering in the first segregation movements, 56 per cent of those in the later movements) were Resegregationists, compared with scarcely more than 8 per cent of the old Tuleans. Cleavages that had begun shortly after segregation had not only persisted, but had widened, and resegregation had become the goal of the originally disadvantaged, still disgruntled transferees, who hoped thereby to force the removal of their advantaged competitors from the segregation center.

At the same time, a number of influential transferees and their followers developed informal, loosely-knit counterorganizations to combat Resegregationist pressure. Among these groups the more influential were the Abe-Kuratomi-Tada faction, Kurihara and his Manzanar friends, Wakida and his followers from Gila, and a group of moderate Resegregationists, including some old Tuleans who had entered the movement with Ishikawa but had subsequently broken away.

Of these groups the Abe-Kuratomi-Tada faction was the largest and the most effective force opposing the Resegregationists. Their opposition had begun as early as April, when the Resegregationists were operating underground. The animosity between Tada and the leaders of the Resegregation Group on the matter of obtaining the release of the members of the Negotiating Committee from the stockade, the Resegregation Group's unsuccessful attempt to make a convert of Tada, the campaign of gossip, which forced Tada's retirement from overt political activities, have already been described.

When Abe and Kuratomi were released from the stockade in late August, the Resegregationists did all in their power to draw them into the group, offering them positions of nominal leadership. Both Abe and Kuratomi, however, remained aloof and refused the positions offered them. Furthermore, they issued a statement of gratitude to "justice-loving residents" and gave no specific credit to the Resegregationists for their release from the stockade. The Resegregation Group was, in the end, able to induce only four of the fourteen released detainees to take an active part in their organization, among whom were Kato and Yamada, young "strong-arm" boys.

Early in September, relations between the factions were further strained when leaders of both (Kubo, Mrs. Tsuchikawa and others from the Resegregationists; Abe, Kuratomi, and Tada from the other faction) were threatened with indictment for complicity in the Noma murder.[48] Instead of bringing the two factions together,

---

[48] See p. 301.

this mutual trouble led to further disagreements. Deciding to initiate action which would bring them the services of a criminal lawyer, Kuratomi drafted a letter to Besig of the A.C.L.U., but after appending their signatures, the Resegregationists refused to act jointly in any situation involving Tada. The letter was therefore prepared in duplicate: Abe, Kuratomi, and Tada signing one copy, the Resegregationists the other. Nothing came of this incident and from this point on the two factions abandoned all pretense of coöperation or amicability.

Meanwhile, the Abe-Kuratomi faction had begun to organize its followers, but with great secrecy and caution. The Resegregationists, nevertheless, heard of the move, and saw to it that rumors of the consolidation of this "dangerous group," which, they claimed, was called *Dai Nippon Seinen-dan* (Great Japan Young Men's Organization),[49] reached the ears of the administration.

At the end of November, the Abe-Kuratomi group came into the open in opposition to the Resegregationists. The underlying cause was probably cumulative resentment over the gossip and the *inu* accusations to which they had been subjected by the Resegregationists. The immediate cause seems to have been a recently developed policy of the Resegregationists of expelling members who, in the opinion of the leaders, were obstructing their movement and were therefore un-Japanese. Among those expelled were the moderate charter members who had broken away from the more aggressive leaders of *Saikakuri,* and Hamaguchi and other friends of Abe and Kuratomi. Since a regulation of the Resegregation Group stipulated that the Japanese government, through the Spanish Consul, would be kept informed about changes in its membership list, the members expelled feared that they might not be eligible for repatriation.

The hostility resulting from expulsion came to a head on the evening of November 20, when the fifty-six relatives of Issei members of *Daihyo Sha Kai,* who had been interned, left Tule Lake for Crystal City. The Resegregation Group, the Abe-Kuratomi group, and the Ward VI language school all participated in an elaborate farewell ceremony. When the farewells were over, Tetsuo Kodama, a noted judo champion, some of whose close friends had

---

[49] Kuratomi denies both the appellation and the fact of formal organization, but admits that a strong informal group had been formed.

recently been expelled from *Hokoku,* accused Yamada, head of the organization, of having called him an *inu*. This was a challenge to fight, which Yamada ignored, but the news spread rapidly through the camp and interest in the state of open hostility which now existed between the rival groups ran high. Kodama's spectacular challenge was followed by similar incidents, in which groups of young men approached prominent Resegregationists and demanded to know the reason for the expulsion of some individual or other.

On December 15 the hostility resulted in violence. Tokuichi Matsubara, Ishikawa's successor as head of *Hoshi-dan* and a member of its inner clique, was attacked in Block 54 (headquarters of the Resegregationists) by Mr. Hamaguchi (a member of the Abe-Kuratomi faction) who had been expelled from *Hokoku*. Although the fight lasted only a few minutes, strong-arm boys of both factions and a crowd of several hundred spectators assembled. Called on for an explanation, Hamaguchi made a lengthy speech, denouncing the *Hokoku* for gangster tactics and for degradation of "the true spirit of Japan."

Presumably because they feared administrative suppression if they took the matter of vengeance into their own hands, Resegregationist leaders drew up a complaint against Hamaguchi and ten other men, who were forthwith arrested by the Caucasian police and taken to the jail at Klamath Falls.

The trial began on the project on December 19. In the short interval between attack and trial, the Resegregationists plastered latrines and laundry rooms with mimeographed statements to the general effect that their "peaceful organization" had been attacked by "gangsters." Yamashita is said to have reported to the administration that the attack was plotted by Abe, Kuratomi and Tada. The trial itself was marked by extreme hesitancy on the part of witnesses to make statements that might incriminate members of the *Hokoku*. Some of Hamaguchi's witnesses even failed to appear. So flagrant was the misrepresentation of facts that the Caucasian in charge warned, at the end of the trial, that those who had testified might be arrested for perjury. The verdict, announced ten days later, imposed a light sentence on Hamaguchi, two defendants were given suspended sentences, and the others were acquitted.

The fight and its aftermath did much to weaken the prestige and position of the Resegregationists. A number of members submitted resignations from the organization.

Meantime, the position of the Resegregationists had been threatened from another source. John Burling, representing the Department of Justice, had arrived on the project on December 6 to open hearings for renunciants. *Hokoku* members had taken the occasion to step up their militaristic ceremonies, apparently in an attempt to convince both Burling and their fellow-residents of their status as true renunciants. Burling, however, proceeded to investigate the group and to interview the leaders. He made it apparent, both to them and to other residents, that their activities were subversive and, if continued, would lead to internment in a Department of Justice camp for potentially dangerous enemy aliens.

Chapter XIII

RENUNCIATION

Mass Relinquishment of American Citizenship

As DESCRIBED IN THE preceding chapter, the Resegregationists had become an overtly organized pressure group during the fall of 1944. The parent group, *Hoshi-dan,* was operating in the main through the medium of the young men's organization, *Hokoku.* Members of these organizations had set for themselves, as the only "true Japanese" in America, the aim of immediate expatriation. The leaders had welcomed the recently passed Denationalization Bill and were attempting to have the Nisei and Kibei members renounce American citizenship en masse, and thus solidify their status as "disloyals."

Two administrative decisions announced simultaneously on December 17 transformed general reluctance to accept the pressure group program as a whole to popular support of the main Resegregationist issue—renunciation of American citizenship. The first of these decisions was the rescission by the Western Defense Command of the orders excluding Japanese Americans from the West Coast. The second was the decision by the War Relocation Authority to force resettlement by liquidating all relocation projects within a year.

Following the rescinding of the exclusion orders, the Western Defense Command made an extensive reclassification of Japanese Americans in camps and elsewhere.[1] As in other WRA camps, residents of Tule Lake were to be divided into two groups: (1) those

---

[1] Including not only evacuees still residing in relocation projects, but also those who had obtained leave clearance and resettled, as well as those who had been living continuously in areas not affected by evacuation orders.

[333]

free to resettle anywhere in the United States, and (2) those who would, after individual notification, continue to be restricted in their movements and places of residence.

The *Newell Star* announced, in an extra edition on December 19, that "the new system will permit the great majority of persons of Japanese ancestry to move freely anywhere in the U.S. that they wish to go." It added that "after January 20 all restrictions will be lifted except in the cases of individuals who will be specifically and individually notified."

No explanation of the basis of classification was made to the evacuees[2] other than that "those who have definitely indicated that they are not loyal to the U.S. or are considered potentially dangerous to the military security . . . will continue to be excluded."[3]

WRA's decision to force resettlement of persons classified by the Army as "free to move" was transmitted to the residents through a mimeographed statement by Dillon Myer, to the effect that

all relocation centers will be closed within a period of six months to one year after the revocation of the exclusion orders.

And Best announced, on the same day, that

the Tule Lake Center will be considered both a relocation center and a segregation center for some time to come. Those whom the Army authorities designate as free to leave here will be in the same status as residents of a relocation center.[4]

Thus Tule Lake residents were informed by the Army that most of them would presumably be free to move, by the Project Director that those free to move had the same status as residents of relocation

---

[2] On December 29, a document, which was never publicized in the camps, covering an "Understanding of Interior, Justice and War Departments on Japanese Relocation Program" was drawn up and, on January 2, 1945, was signed by representatives of the three departments. It specified that exclusion orders would be issued individually to about 10,000 persons, that about 5,000 others would be on a "detention" list, and not to be released from camps until their cases had been individually reviewed; that those still on the detention list, after review, would be segregated "at Tule Lake or elsewhere," together with "members of [their] . . . families who remain on a voluntary basis"; that all individual exclusion orders must be reviewed by Army hearing boards and were subject to revocation upon favorable recommendation; that all legal restrictions upon the departure of other than detainees be rescinded by WRA; that the Department of Justice would, in the course of time, take over responsibility for the detainees.

[3] *Newell Star,* December 19, 1944.   [4] *Ibid.*

projects, and by the National Director of WRA that all relocation projects would be closed within a year. These statements taken together imperiled the security of thousands of residents who, at the price of being branded "disloyal," believed they had attained a war-duration refuge. For all of them, forced resettlement, and for the young men of draft age induction into the armed forces, loomed if not as certainties at least as disturbingly high probabilities.

The immediate reaction of the Tule Lake residents was compounded of surprise, anxiety, doubt, and complacent rationalization. Most of them refused to accept the fact that they themselves might be obliged to leave the center. They expressed the conviction that they would be classified among those "who have definitely indicated that they are not loyal to the United States" and thus would "continue to be excluded." They assumed that exclusion would mean their continued detention by the Army or the Department of Justice at Tule Lake or some other segregation center.

Rationalizations regarding the security that Tule Lake segregants, compared with residents of other projects, would still enjoy are exemplified by the following statements:

By Murakami, a Nisei who worked in the Legal Department:

The announcement will mostly affect other relocation projects. The big trouble is going to be in those centers, where people will be afraid that now the WRA will force them to get out of the camps. It will disturb them very much.[5]

By Kurusu:

It's too late for WRA to change its policies regarding Tule Lake. I was segregated and I made up my mind to stay here for the duration.[6]

By a Nisei girl:

I and my family aren't really worrying, because we consider ourselves genuine segregants and are sure that we will be among those who will be left at Tule Lake.[7]

By a Nisei transferee from Manzanar:

We don't anticipate any special changes here. It will be just a change of people in Tule Lake. Some people will just go out, and other people will be sent in. I think that will make a strong turn toward betterment in this camp. Those who do not belong in this camp should go out. Then the

[5] Field Notes, December 19, 1944.   [7] Field Notes, December 24, 1944.
[6] *Ibid.*

people here will all be of one mind and it will be easier for the administration to oversee the camp.[8]

But that others could not accept these complacent rationalizations is suggested by such anxious questions as:

By Wakida:

Will the people who were excluded by the Army be allowed to remain in Tule Lake? Or will they be sent to some other center? People seem to be talking about this a great deal. I heard a rumor that only 4,000 people are expected to stay in Tule Lake.[9]

By a Nisei *Hokoku* member:

Does this mean that they're quickly going to call off the whole party; that the last few years [they] have just been kidding around; that repatriation and segregation, . . . which we were told to take seriously, is just a big joke?[10]

The Army moved quickly to notify residents of their status. The *Newell Star* of December 19 announced:

Representatives of the Western Defense Command have arrived at the center. . . . Starting tomorrow [they] will individually notify any individuals who are to be excluded. They will also notify those individuals whose cases have not yet been determined and will interview such individuals in order to determine their final status.

The Army team of some twenty officers immediately began to hold hearings at the rate of 400 to 500 a day, and, as the hearings progressed, anxiety of the residents about their security increased. "Loyalty" questions asked by some of the Army officers were identical with those on the registration questionnaire.[11] As at Military Registration, most aliens answered affirmatively, while most citizens reiterated the negative position they had taken on the earlier occasion. Reports quickly spread that irrespective of the statements made or the answers given, almost everybody called for a hearing was issued an individual exclusion order,[12] and that contrary to

---

[8] Field Notes, December 23, 1944.

[9] Field Notes, December 19, 1944.

[10] WRA, Community Analysis, "Center Trend Report (December 8–26)" (manuscript), December 26, 1944.

[11] See p. 58.

[12] There was a small number of cases where the individual exclusion orders were withheld. These were very unusual cases. For example, no order was issued to a person so long as he: declared himself loyal, expressed no intention of renouncing his citizenship, and had a brother or sister serving in the armed forces of the United States.

expectation individual exclusion orders did not involve continued detention, but meant that the persons concerned would be expected to resettle outside the zones of exclusion.

Informants reported:

A friend of my brother told the soldier that he was a repatriate and loyal to Japan, but he was still handed a permit to leave camp provided he does not go to certain excluded areas.[13]

One of the boys was saying he told the Army officer that he didn't know what country he wanted to live in after the war. He received a permit to leave the center anyway.[14]

I am worried by the results of the hearings of some of the young men I know. In spite of their pro-Japan statements, they were not told that they would be detained.[15]

Many of those who had not yet had their hearings reiterated that since they had originally been segregated as "disloyal" they would, when they had their hearings, certainly be given detention orders. But when the people who were making these self-reassuring statements were called in by the Army officers for hearings, most of them discovered that they, too, were "free" to resettle anywhere except in specified zones.[16] It was becoming apparent that Tule Lake residents were to have the same status as people in other relocation centers and correspondingly that they would be forced to leave camp and resettle. Furthermore, since only males[17] were given hearings, some residents inferred that induction via Selective Service was once more imminent.[18]

The means by which security could be safeguarded was suggested

---

[13] Statement by a Nisei girl, Field Notes, December 24, 1944.

[14] Statement by Mrs. Tsuchikawa, Field Notes, December 23, 1944.

[15] Statement by a Nisei girl, Field Notes, December 24, 1944.

[16] About the end of December, the project administration received a list of approximately 95,000 names of persons that were free to go out anywhere in the United States. There was no way of ascertaining the names of those to be detained in Tule Lake unless each name was checked with this voluminous list. Not until late January did the project receive a separate list of detainees, and the names on this list were not revealed to the residents.

[17] The Army issued no exclusion orders and held no hearings for females. It was apparently assumed that females would stay with or follow the males in the family.

[18] Selective Service procedures had been suspended for Tule Lake residents after the U.S. District Court in Eureka had dismissed an indictment against violators in July, 1944. (See pp. 239–240.)

by reports that the Army officers were asking citizens whether they wished to leave camp and resettle *or* to renounce their citizenship.[19] For example, an informant reported:

Four men whom I knew were called today by the Army. They asked them questions like "Do you want to go out or do you want to renounce citizenship?"[20]

Reports of this sort confirmed the belief that resettlement and renunciation were not compatible: a renunciant would not be forced to resettle; rather, he would be prevented from resettling and detained in camp.[21] The implication of choice between resettlement and renunciation was revealed by many other informants:

They can't force us out if we have signed for renunciation, can they?[22]

The majority of people who talked to me are convinced that renunciation of citizenship will keep them in Tule Lake.[23]

My brother said, at his hearing, that he wanted to renounce his citizenship, because he figured he could then stay in Tule Lake.[24]

Are they going to kick us out? What good will that do, when we don't want to get out? My mother said that segregation was a dirty trick, bringing us here with so much trouble and now it doesn't mean a thing. We hope that by renouncing citizenship, we will be allowed to stay here, but we are not sure. WRA should inform us about this.[25]

Since only Nisei and Kibei could renounce citizenship, Issei hoped and believed that security for the whole family could be

[19] Officers of the Western Defense Command, familiar with the hearing procedures, deny categorically that any question about resettlement was asked. The Project Attorney, however, reported that "Best talked to Army officers about the renunciation and resettlement questions. When Best inquired about the significance of asking if the evacuee had applied for renunciation of citizenship, they answered that it was instructions from the Presidio. And they said that they asked about resettlement just to be human." (Field Notes, April 17, 1945.)

[20] Statement by Kurusu, Field Notes, December 19, 1944.

[21] While the Army officers were uncommunicative on the subject WRA officials believed that "those who will be frozen in Tule Lake will be the ones who have renounced their citizenship, undesirable or dangerous aliens, and those who have been paroled from Department of Justice detention camps." (Field Notes, December 24, 1944.)

[22] Statement by Mrs. Wakida, Field Notes, December 27, 1944.

[23] Statement by a Caucasian social worker, Field Notes, December 24, 1944.

[24] Statement by a Nisei girl, Field Notes, December 24, 1944.

[25] Statement by a Nisei girl, Field Notes, December 29, 1944.

achieved by having their children renounce. They assumed that policies followed at the time of evacuation and segregation of keeping the family intact would operate again: Renunciation of even one citizen member in a family should provide a safeguard for all close relatives.

An Issei remarked:

People are going to swing in the direction which will keep them safe here. Then, when they're asked if they intend to renounce citizenship, a good many of the Nisei and Kibei will say yes . . . Put it this way. If you're a *Hakujin* (Caucasian), you take this matter of soiling your loyalty record seriously and would never say anything to [soil] it. But if you're a Jap and nobody believes your loyalty in this country anyway, you'll think about your future and your family. . . . We're going to have [our children] renounce citizenship just to stay here.[26]

The emerging belief that renunciation would solidify status as "disloyals" strengthened the hold of the Resegregationists on the residents, for pressure group leaders had been claiming for some time that membership in *Hokoku* was a sure means of obtaining preferential treatment on applications for renunciation. It was known that Burling of the Department of Justice had, during his visit in early December, recommended to the Attorney General immediate acceptance of applications for renunciation from *Hokoku* leaders. *Hokoku*'s position in this matter was further strengthened when, on December 27, seventy of the members of the two Resegregationist organizations (64 of whom were officers)[27] were removed to the detention camp at Santa Fe for internment as "undesirable enemy aliens." Most of those removed were *Hokoku* renunciants. This "punishment" of the leaders by the Department of Justice seemed to many of the residents to have many elements of undeserved reward: *Hokoku* leaders, among others, had applied to renounce their citizenship; their applications were being given priority in hearings and were receiving "favorable" action; they, and they alone, were being removed from the now insecure Tule Lake to the haven of an internment camp from which resettlement and military induction were alike impossible.

The removal of the internees was accomplished with an impres-

---

[26] WRA, Community Analysis, "Center Trend Report (December 8–26)" (manuscript), December 26, 1944.

[27] Among those removed were Yamashita, Kira, Matsubara, Tsuchikawa, Yamada, Aramaki, and Kato.

sive display of force on the part of the Department of Justice, forty-one armed guards removing the seventy men. On the part of the evacuees, it was accompanied by a spectacular farewell demonstration in which the Resegregationist organizations participated en masse, the young men marching up to the gate, standing in formation, singing patriotic songs, blowing bugles, and shouting loud *banzai*.

Immediately after the send-off, representatives of the Resegregationists met and selected a complete slate of new officers to replace the interned leaders.[28] These new officers issued a series of mimeographed statements, publicizing the internment and the elaborate farewell, and exhorting the members to carry out, "with the determination of being true Japanese, the aims and policies that had been laid out by our leaders."[29] They declared that "the internment of our leaders is the first step which will make possible for all of us . . . to become true Japanese nationals,"[30] and that the aim of resegregation for which they had been fighting so long was at last about to be achieved. Relatives of the internees reiterated these sentiments:

The parents of the people taken to Santa Fe are saying, "My child has now become a Japanese."[31]

People who went to sympathize with Mrs. Aramaki told me that she was happy about his internment, because it made him a real Japanese. They say every one of the wives is like that.[32]

My next door neighbor was a big shot in the *Hoshi-dan*. As soon as I heard he was picked up, I went to see his wife to say a few words of sympathy. Boy, she got mad and bawled me out for sympathizing. She said, "This is not sad. You should congratulate me." So, like a fool, I offered words of felicitation. It became a custom. Everytime anyone was picked up, we had to congratulate his relatives.[33]

After the internment, Resegregationists began to increase their pressure in two directions—upon the administration and upon the

[28] It was reported that, anticipating arrests, the interned leaders had named their successors (Field Notes, January 2, 1945).

[29] *Sokuji Kikoku Hoshi-dan* and *Hokoku Seinen-dan*, mimeographed statement, December 30, 1944.

[30] *Ibid.*

[31] Statement by Niiyama, Field Notes, January 8, 1945.

[32] Statement by Mrs. Wakida, Field Notes, January 4, 1945.

[33] Statement by June Yamaguchi, Field Notes, December 18, 1945.

general population. *Hokoku* members made repeated attempts to get administrative assurance that their applications for renunciation would be acted upon immediately and that they and members of *Hoshi-dan* would be forthwith interned. On December 28, the day after the leaders were removed, their representatives appealed to the project administration to intervene with the Department of Justice. To this request the Project Attorney replied,

> Mr. Best explained that he will consider your request that he tell Mr. Burling you and your entire group of the *Sokuji* and the *Hokoku Seinen-Dan* desire a preferential right to be taken to Santa Fe. . . . Mr. Best stated that although his recommendation may not make any difference to the Department of Justice, still he will make that recommendation to them. He will tell them that your whole group feels the same way they [the interned men] do, and that you desire to go to Santa Fe with them.[34]

And on January 2, they made a similar appeal:

> RESEGREGATIONIST REPRESENTATIVE: We definitely want to renounce our citizenship. Even though the Department of Justice does not recognize it, we consider ourselves Japanese and as far as our faith and fidelity is concerned, it is for the Japanese Government only. Therefore . . . we stress again, if you see Mr. Burling, will you please express to him how we feel about renouncing our citizenship? The members want preferential hearings so they can go to Santa Fe.
>
> PROJECT ATTORNEY: I will be very glad to do that. . . .
>
> RESEGREGATIONIST REPRESENTATIVE: We want to state again that our intentions are to be interned in one place as a group. You see there has been a lot of friction among the Japanese here. There is a certain Japanese group that seems to be loyal to both Japan and United States, others who are loyal to United States and unfaithful to Japan. Our only wish is to live with the Japanese whose intentions are the same with faith only toward the Japanese Government.[35]

Resegregationist pressure upon the general population involved intensification of nationalistic activities, coercive and terroristic tactics directed aganst dissenters, and extensive propaganda. Under their new leadership, Resegregationists discarded all restraint and became openly defiant. Morning exercises, goose-stepping, *"Wash-sho"* chants, bugling, were stepped up to fantastic proportions. Participants often numbered more than 1,500 daily and included women, children of elementary school age, and elderly Issei.

---

[34] Minutes of the meeting of the Project Attorney and representatives of the Resegregation Group, December 28, 1944.

[35] Minutes of the meeting of the Project Attorney and representatives of the Resegregation Group, January 2, 1945.

They are blasting their bugles louder than ever. And even old ladies are running around in slacks yelling *"Wash-sho!"*[36]

They used to march by my apartment. I would be wakened by the noise. They were all serious. They said they were training themselves to be useful to Japan when they go back. They were showing off that they alone were true Japanese, and we should act like they did if we wanted to be true Japanese, too. We were scared of them, we didn't dare complain about the noise.[37]

All of us wanted to get away from this pressure. So we shaved our heads to act as if we belonged to the *Hokoku*. At one time, there were only three long-haired men in my block. Even Issei shaved their heads, you know.[38]

When *Hokoku* members received notices from Washington approving their applications for denationalization they waved them ostentatiously in front of their friends and neighbors and exhorted them to send in their own applications without delay. They elaborated upon the advantages of renunciation and internment. Families of internees would soon be reunited. Resegregation would be accomplished, with the "true Japanese" enjoying the security of an internment camp, while the "loyals" and "fence sitters" would be forced by WRA to resettle.

The *Hoshi-dan* and *Hokoku* people are spreading the news that in less than fifty days the families of the interned men are to be united.[39]

They say they are glad to be picked up. They say we, who are left behind in camp, are going to be kicked around, while they will be safe and sound in internment camp.[40]

They keep on saying that anybody sent to Santa Fe is taking a step forward to becoming a real Japanese. If this propaganda takes effect, it will cause great trouble. A lot of people will start looking for trouble, trying to be sent to Santa Fe.[41]

I heard the rumor that all those who renounce their citizenship will be taken to Santa Fe.[42]

I heard a rumor that the Department of Justice is going to take over the camp on the 21st of January.[43]

[36] Statement by Mrs. Wakida, Field Notes, January 18, 1945.
[37] Statement by June Yamaguchi, Field Notes, December 18, 1945.
[38] Statement by a Kibei man, Field Notes, December 19, 1945.
[39] Statement by George Kuratomi, Field Notes, January 17, 1945.
[40] Statement by a Nisei woman, Field Notes, January 3, 1945.
[41] Statement by George Kuratomi, Field Notes, January 2, 1945.
[42] Statement by a Nisei girl, Field Notes, December 29, 1944.
[43] Statement by a prominent *Hoshi-dan* member, Field Notes, January 15, 1945. The *Pacific Citizen* also reported, on December 30, 1944, that "the Justice

There is a widespread rumor that all those persons who have not renounced their citizenship by January 20 will summarily be kicked out of camp.[44]

Meanwhile, WRA officials reiterated their intention of getting all "free" or "cleared" evacuees out of all centers. An official pamphlet containing information on WRA policies and procedures on the liquidation of centers, was distributed throughout the community on January 5. In it Mr. Myer reaffirmed his earlier statement that

the lifting of the blanket exclusion orders . . . signifies the beginning of the final phase of the relocation program. . . . Our prime objective in WRA, as always, is to restore the people residing in relocation centers to private life in normal communities. . . .

It is fortunate . . . that the WRA program enters its final phase at a time when there is a good demand for workers in war plants, in civilian goods production, in service occupations, and on the farms. Both from the standpoint of the national welfare and the evacuees' long-range economic security, it is highly important that the people now residing at the relocation centers make the transition back to private life at a time when employment opportunities are still plentiful. . . . In view of the funds that are available and the arrangements that are being made, the War Relocation Authority feels wholly confident that no evacuee will be deprived of adequate means of subsistence by reason of the closing of the centers. . . .[45]

Reactions of the residents to the "benefits" of WRA's program were almost universally unfavorable:

I have noticed that people are stiffening in their attitude. Last week some were saying, "If they make us get out, we'll go." Now they are determined not to leave.[46]

We wouldn't mind going back to San Francisco if we had everything as when we left. We'd jump right out. But we've lost everything.[47]

Department is expected to take over and operate the Tule Lake, California, segregation center."

[44] Statement by George Kuratomi, Field Notes, January 17, 1945.

[45] Travel grants and resettlement grants available to evacuees were defined as follows: "The *maximum of assistance* will be coach fare for each member of the family, plus $3.00 per person per day of travel for meals en route, plus five dollars per day for five days ($25.00) for each member of the family, the latter sum being designated to meet initial subsistence expenses at the place of destination. This maximum of assistance shall be given in all cases in which the family's resources in cash amount to $100 per family member or less." (WRA, Handbook, "Leave Assistance Grants," Section 60.13.2.A, March 4, 1944. Italics theirs.)

[46] Statement by Kurihara, Field Notes, January 5, 1945.

[47] Statement by a Nisei girl, Field Notes, January 2, 1945.

I heard that the German people who were interned during the first world war were paid $1,000 each when they were allowed to leave camp.

We have nothing now to depend on. We aren't sure of getting jobs. I feel the WRA plans for closing the camp will be a total failure, unless it increases financial assistance. I don't know one person who wants to go out.[48]

WRA wants us to get out with twenty-five dollars. But that's not going to get us anywhere. They've got a lot of nerve to offer us that.[49]

I don't know what's going to happen to us! It's very confusing. I think everybody feels that. They don't know what's what yet. In the first place, why do they want to kick us out? It was their fault we came here. They can't say, "We'll give you 25 dollars and coach fare. Get out by such and such day."

Since the people have been in camp three years, their funds are exhausted. It's all right for people who can afford it.[50]

The people are very much at a loss due to the fact that they can't make a decision. The WRA officials admit they're in the dark themselves. They don't know what to do or what it's all about.

I've got six children and my wife. Also my father and mother. To go outside you have to have a certain kind of home. If they want me to go out, the least they can do is to give me some kind of housing and say, "Now, you will take this?" Instead, they are saying, "America's going to help you. So you go out and do what you can." That's not dependable. We want some assurance, if we're to go out. By staying here, I'll have a roof over my children's heads and enough to eat, although I don't like the food.[51]

People with large families are worrying themselves to death. After all the wrongs they have done to the Japanese, nothing they do now will do any good.[52]

The decision to end all uncertainty by renunciation was more and more frequently being made:

When the Army came out to ask us to make this decision, I told the colonel, "If you set a deadline, I will renounce my citizenship due to the fact that I have no place to go."[53]

If this place becomes a relocation center, they'll draft us. In that case we must get busy and send in our renunciation of citizenship.[54]

---

[48] Statement by Hibashi, Field Notes, January 5, 1945.
[49] Statement by Murakami, Field Notes, January 9, 1945.
[50] Statement by a Nisei woman, Field Notes, January 3, 1945.
[51] Statement by Niiyama, Field Notes, January 8, 1945.
[52] Statement by Kurihara, Field Notes, January 15, 1945.
[53] Statement by Niiyama, Field Notes, January 8, 1945.
[54] Statement by Kurusu, Field Notes, January 12, 1945.

Quite a few of my girl friends are renouncing. I guess it's because they have applied for repatriation and want to accompany their families. Most of my friends at Japanese school all have the same sort of feeling. You know why the boys are renouncing? They are dodging the Army draft.[55]

Under the international agreement, they can't kick the aliens out of camp. That's the reason that so many people are renouncing their citizenship. If they were sincere about restoring our rights of citizenship, why didn't they call the women for Army hearings? They just want to get us in the Army. The trouble is that minority races always suffer one way or another.[56]

The ordinary resident of Tule Lake faced with "evacuation in reverse" had now become thoroughly disoriented. In confinement for more than two and a half years, he knew of the world outside only through newspapers[57] and radio reports. These reports led him to believe that the outside world was even more hostile and dangerous than it had been when he was evacuated. Just before rescission of the exclusion orders he was reading items such as the following:

President Roosevelt, Western Defense Command and the War Department yesterday were "strongly" urged by the State Senate's Committee on Japanese Resettlement "not to permit the return of Japanese to the Pacific Coast, and particularly California, for the duration of war. . . ."

The people of California, the committee declared, "are overwhelmingly opposed to the return of any Japanese during the war."

"We believe that because California is required to make an all-out war effort, that to allow the Japanese to return during the war is inadvisable because it would cause riots, turmoil, bloodshed and endanger the war effort."[58]

Return of Japanese Americans to the west coast is apt to result in "wholesale bloodshed and violence," Representative Engle, Democrat of California, said today.[59]

When rescission was announced, reports of statements by friendly government officials tended to reinforce his fears of violence:

Governor Warren yesterday called upon "all Americans" to comply "loyally, cheerfully and carefully" with the War Department order revoking

[55] Statement by a Nisei girl, Field Notes, January 24, 1945.
[56] Statement by Murakami, Field Notes, January 9, 1945.
[57] The *San Francisco Chronicle* and the *San Francisco Examiner* were most widely read in Tule Lake, along with the three vernacular newspapers, *Utah Nippo, Rocky Shimpo,* and *Colorado Times.* The *Pacific Citizen* (the JACL organ) also had many readers
[58] *San Francisco Chronicle,* December 13, 1944.
[59] *San Francisco Examiner,* December 13, 1944.

the mass Japanese evacuation, and notified chiefs of police, sheriffs and all public officials to join in developing uniform plans to prevent intemperate actions and civil disorder. . . .[60]

Secretary of the Interior Harold L. Ickes yesterday . . . warned . . . that any interference with [evacuees'] "right" to resettle on the west coast would be met with the full force of the Government.[61]

With the first of thousands of evacuated Japanese now trickling back into California, the State Advisory Committee on law enforcement today reiterated and reemphasized a previous plea to refrain from intemperate words or acts as the evacuees return.[62]

As the first contingent of evacuees returned to the Coast, after rescission, numerous "intemperate" acts were reported, e.g.,

Members of the anti-Nisei "Remember Pearl Harbor" League today were on record as determined to boycott all Japanese returned to the Puyallup and White river valleys [Washington] and anyone catering to them.[63]

At Auburn, approximately 300 residents of Placer county [California] signed a petition circulated under direction of Deputy Sheriff Jack Hannon, commander of Donner Post 1942, Veterans of Foreign Wars, according to United Press, agreeing not to do business or fraternize with returning Japanese.[64]

Steps were taken in Salinas [California] last week to organize the Monterey Bay Council on Japanese Relations, with officers and directors to be named from representative groups in Monterey, San Benito and Santa Cruz counties.
The purpose of the organization, according to E. M. Seifert, Jr., temporary chairman, will be for "sincere, unselfish and unprejudiced thinking" to "discourage the return" of persons of Japanese ancestry to the area.[65]

An unoccupied house at the Yamasaki nursery was destroyed by fire on the night of January 3, the third building owned or formerly occupied by persons of Japanese ancestry to burn in Placer county in the last six weeks.[66]

[In Caldwell, Idaho] three ruffians, accompanied by seventeen or eighteen persons, attacked three Nisei soldiers and their friends and relatives, who numbered about forty persons . . . at 1:30 A.M. [January 7, 1945],

[60] *San Francisco Chronicle,* December 18, 1944.
[61] *San Francisco Examiner,* December 22, 1944.
[62] *San Francisco Examiner,* January 5, 1945.
[63] *San Francisco Chronicle,* December 30, 1944.
[64] *San Francisco Chronicle,* January 18, 1945.
[65] *Pacific Citizen,* January 27, 1945.
[66] *Pacific Citizen,* January 13, 1945. See also *Rocky Shimpo,* January 17, 1945.

while they were waiting for a train.... They rushed into the waiting room, and socked a Nisei soldier ... who was standing at the entrance. The attackers shouted obscene words, and some of them said, "God damned Japs! I'm gonna kill all." They beat the Japanese at random and created a scene of utter confusion.[67]

[In Wells, Nevada], angered by the refusal of a loan of cash, a Caucasian, working for a railroad, shot and seriously injured three Japanese on January 20.[68]

Efforts to blow up the packing shed of a returned Japanese-American farmer with dynamite and to intimidate him and his family with gunshots were disclosed yesterday by Sheriff Charles Silva of Placer county. [Sumio] Doi, who returned to his place near Newcastle recently from Lamar, Colo., with his parents, called the sheriff's office early yesterday to report that several carloads of persons had parked on his property. Shots were being fired at the house, he said, in an effort to keep him and his family indoors.[69]

These and similar reports were distorted by rumor, and fears about the reception awaiting returnees increased:

Rumor is being circulated that five Japanese were killed in Fresno [California].[70]

People are saying that some Japanese were killed around Stockton [California]. Reading the papers and considering all other facts, the people have a feeling of not wanting to return to the Pacific Coast, even though the exclusion orders were lifted. California is not exactly dangerous, but still, it's not favorable to the Japanese.[71]

California is the last place I'd want to go back to, with all I've been reading. They say the Army will back us up. But that's only against mob violence, and not against what an individual might do. If some person beats us up, we can't do anything about it.[72]

What do they want us to do? Go back to California and get filled full of lead? I'm going to sit here and watch.[73]

Thus the residents were driven day by day nearer to the acceptance of the *Hokoku* program of renunciation as the only solution of their problems, and by January, renunciation had become a mass

---

[67] *Rocky Shimpo*, Japanese Section, January 24, 1945.

[68] *Colorado Times*, Japanese Section, January 27, 1945.

[69] *San Francisco Chronicle*, January 20, 1945. The Doi case was also sensationally reported in the vernacular press.

[70] Statement by Kurihara, Field Notes, January 15, 1945.

[71] Statement by Kurusu, Field Notes, January 12, 1945.

[72] Statement by a Nisei woman, Field Notes, January 3, 1945.

[73] Statement by a Nisei woman, Field Notes, January 14, 1945.

movement. In that month alone, 3,400 Nisei and Kibei in Tule Lake applied for denationalization. This number represented 40 per cent of the total citizen population over 17½ years of age, and combined with approximately 1,200 whose applications had been received earlier, meant that by this time one out of every two Nisei and Kibei in the center had attempted to withdraw from American citizenship. The reasons behind this act were rarely verbalized at the time. Months later, when the war was over and when the renunciants were threatened with deportation to a defeated Japan, retrospective explanations of the reasons for having given up citizenship poured in to the offices of all of the government agencies concerned. Although these explanations contain, of course, a certain amount of rationalization, they afford, as does no other source, an insight into the mental confusion and the social pressure that existed at this time.

Many of the letters,[74] and other documents prepared after the war had ended, show the extent to which brooding over the wrongs of evacuation and the "betrayal" of a minority group by a racially prejudiced majority, resulted in feelings of bitterness and hopelessness.

I attended East Florin Grammar School in the County of Sacramento, State of California. Even at this early age we were subject to discrimination for the school was for Japanese and Chinese only and apart from the Caucasians' school. We felt out of place and memories such as these remain deeply imbedded even at this time. We were not treated equally, we were inferior, and as children we felt lost and unwanted.

In 1935 I entered Elk Grove Union High in the County of Sacramento, State of California, and for the first time in our life we were able to mingle with the Caucasians, but this was to a limited extent, because we already had 3 strikes against us, as we were apart since grammar school . . .

War and evacuation forced us *American citizens* to leave *everything* we had worked and slaved for. Yes, we were bitter, can you blame us?[75]

My American friends . . . no doubt must have wondered why I renounced my citizenship. This decision was not that of today or yesterday. It dates back to the day when General DeWitt ordered evacuation. It was confirmed when he flatly refused to listen even to the voices of the former

---

[74] Letters cited in subsequent footnotes as from "the files of an attorney" were made available through the courtesy of a San Francisco law firm. Most of them were addressed to officials of the Department of Justice, and were written before the cases came into the hands of the attorney.

[75] Letter from the files of the American Civil Liberties Union, Northern California Branch, September 4, 1945. Italics his.

World War Veterans and it was doubly confirmed when I entered Manzanar. We who already had proven our loyalty by serving in the last World War should have been spared. The veterans asked for special consideration but their requests were denied. They too had to evacuate like the rest of the Japanese people, as if they were aliens.

I did not expect this of the Army. When the Western Defense Command assumed the responsibilities of the West Coast, I expected that at least the Nisei would be allowed to remain. But to General DeWitt, we were all alike. "A Jap's a Jap. Once a Jap, always a Jap." . . . I swore to become a Jap 100 percent, and never do another day's work to help this country fight this war. My decision to renounce my citizenship there and then was absolute.[76]

Please believe me I had renunciated because of the rash racial discrimination against us Japanese—toward us citizens of the United States also and had turned them into camps without giving them any chance to store their valuable possessions or properties while the Germans and Italians were free and as we at the Tule Lake Center were disloyal citizens of the United States, I did not want to be greedy enough to keep my United States citizenship and use it when necessary—when necessity claimed me. Since I was disloyal to the United States I wanted to be honest about it.[77]

Others, as might be expected, emphasized the fear of the outside world and the desire for the continued security of Tule Lake.

The rumors were that we would be forced out of here; whereas, the people outside would take arms and harm us. . . . As I am alone here, I was upset . . . The columns in the San Francisco newspaper spoke of violence displayed toward the returning evacuee.[78]

Everybody told me that I must renounce my citizenship of the United States, otherwise I will be forced to go outside of the camp to be murdered. Believe me, Sir, honest, I was scared and I applied for renouncement.[79]

With our large family nothing on hand, and no money to support ourselves, we have to do without foods, no house to live in. So I thought it was alright to renounce it for the duration.[80]

I have served in the U.S. Army for fifteen months and was given an Honorable Discharge . . . on account of my stomach ulcer. . . .
When I was discharged from the Army, I was quite sick and my wife . . .

[76] J. Y. Kurihara, manuscript, December, 1945.
[77] Letter from the files of the American Civil Liberties Union, Northern California Branch, September 5, 1945.
[78] Ibid., August 31, 1945.
[79] Letter from the files of an attorney, September 6, 1945.
[80] Letter from the files of the American Civil Liberties Union, Northern California Branch, September 13, 1945.

was pregnant, so both of us were unable to work; therefore, we could not do anything to earn our living. I had no money or a home to return to and take care of myself as my folks were evacuated to Tule Lake Center. As my parents were earning only $16.00 per month, it was impossible for me to plead for their help; therefore my wife and I decided to come to this center, thinking that this was the only place for us to make a living.

During our residence here a great many persons began encouraging us to renounce our citizenships, and ... rumors ... confused us altogether. One of these rumors was that if we did not renounce our citizenships, we would be forced out of this center. I believed that. Thinking that we would encounter hardships in earning our living because of my physical condition, in addition to our two little children, we applied for the renunciation of our citizenships in the confusion of our thoughts.[81]

Closely allied with the fear of forced resettlement was the oft-repeated fear of separation of family members. Many citizen children and citizen wives believed that their "disloyal" alien parents or husbands would be deported, and that only by becoming aliens through denationalization could they maintain family unity.

My Issei parents believed that all aliens here would be deported to Japan, while all the citizens would be forced to remain here. We were therefore confronted with the problem of preventing family separation.[82]

The reason for my renunciation was so that I'll be in the same classification as my alien husband. I feared, if in case there is a separation of aliens from the citizens, I will naturally be placed separate. I wouldn't mind if it was just myself, but I did not want to bring unhappiness to my little daughter.[83]

We were transferred [to Tule Lake] ... because my stepfather was considered a "disloyal" alien—not permitted to leave this camp under any circumstances.

After our arrival here, we were told that if an alien parent desired to return to Japan with his family, he must request for repatriation for himself and his family. So, on April 24, 1944, we sent our request to the Spanish Embassy.

Then, at the beginning of this year, we were told that if the parents are aliens and the children are citizens of this country, when the time came, the parents would be deported and the children detained in this country unless the citizens had requested for the renunciation of their citizenship. Or, if we chose to remain here, only the children could remain, but the parents would be deported due to their alien status. What choice

[81] *Ibid.*, August 22, 1945.

[82] Letter from the files of an attorney, August 31, 1945.

[83] Letter from the files of the American Civil Liberties Union, Northern California Branch, August 28, 1945.

did we have but to seek repatriation and renounce our citizenship because we do not have any desire whatsoever to have the family separated.[84]

I had no knowledge of the true consequence in renouncing; just as it is still indefinite. Before I went to hearing I understood that if I renounced I would be treated just like my parents, as an alien. By renouncing I had the impression that I would be just another alien hence would not be compelled to part from my parents who are also aliens.[85]

In other cases, there was evidence of reluctant yielding to family pressures:

I had the hardest time to make myself sign my signature on the special paper which meant that I was throwing away my citizenship. . . . Finally I signed it against my will due to the fact that whatever my husband do I have to be loyal to him.[86]

I never wished to renounce my citizenship but to stop my parents pleading and sobbing I went to an interview for renounciation.[87]

Communal pressure, often vague and ill-defined, was cited in a number of communications.

Everybody around me renounced. At least they said they did. They wouldn't speak to me. They treated me like an outcast. I felt alone and powerless in a huge dark place. I was afraid. Aloneness and powerlessness got worse and worse. What else could I do but renounce?[88]

We have been evacuated from Seattle, Washington . . . We did not transfer from one center to the other, but have remained here for the past three years and over. Before segregation took place the residents remained quiet and minded their own business but since the influx of segregants from the other centers the peoples' attitude and sentiment totally changed. The pressures, personal disturbances, and false rumors widely spread and aroused the innocents to obey and take commands or otherwise threatened. The atmosphere became uncomfortable and helpless.[89]

As in the case for mass request for renunciation, we were under strong pressure and the action, and with the upset minds followed through the hearing with the Department of Justice. I did not think the outcome would be so serious as to have our citizenship stripped from us. . . . You must believe me when I state that the camp pressures, rumors and built-up

[84] *Ibid.*, September 8, 1945.

[85] Letter from the files of an attorney, October 7, 1945.

[86] *Ibid.*, August 22, 1945.

[87] Letter from the files of the American Civil Liberties Union, Northern California Branch, August 21, 1945.

[88] Statement by a Kibei woman, Field Notes, December 19, 1945.

[89] Letter from the files of the American Civil Liberties Union, Northern California Branch, August 27, 1945.

advice led me into this confused situation. Under normal condition we would never think of doing what we have done.[90]

The following extract from a long letter illustrates the interplay of bitterness, fear of family separation, parental and communal pressures:

I am a Nisei girl, age 20, born and raised in Alameda, California, until the time of evacuation in Feb. 1942. My father passed away in May 1940. So there is my mother . . . 56 years old, and my brother [now] 18 years old. We were living a normal American life until we were uprooted from our beloved home. It was the home and security my father and mother worked so hard for when they came to America. This America was strange to them but they wanted to make their home here and raise us as good American citizens. Not knowing the language they had a hard time . . . My mother was especially taken back by [evacuation] since my father passed away, so you can imagine her bitterness. Being pushed from one WRA camp to another (Pleasanton, Turlock Assembly Center, Gila Center and Tule Center) only hardened her bitterness and I myself got pretty disgusted being shoved around but I reasoned that this would not happen under normal conditions. Life was not too hard up to Gila Center, but since segregation and coming here it has been a life of turmoil, anxiety and fear. My brother and I did not want to come here but we could not go against the wishes of our mother. She isn't young anymore so this life of moving about hasn't been easy for her so we obeyed her, thinking it was the only way to make up to all her unhappiness. We had life before us but mother's life is closer to end. . . . so we couldn't hurt her with any more worries. Since coming here I found out it was wrong in coming here. There are too many pro-Japanese organizations with too much influence. Naturally mother in the state of mind she was in would be greatly taken in by them. She had the family name in one of the organizations but we (my brother and I) absolutely refused to acknowledge it so she reluctantly withdrew our name. . . . When the renunciation citizenship came mother again wanted us to renounce. My brother luckily was under age but I could not fight against her this time. One [thing] that put a scare into me was that families would be separated. To me, I just had to sign on that paper, so I piled lies upon lies at the renunciation hearing. All horrid and untruthful lies they were. I didn't mean anything I said at that time, but fear and anxiety was too strong. I have regretted that I took such a drastic step—in fact I knew I would regret it before I went into it but I was afraid if I was torn away from the family I would never see them again in this uncertain world. I should have had more confidence in America but being torn away from my home and all made things so uncertain. I would never have renounced if . . . Administration made it clear that there would be no family separation. But the Administration could not assure us there would be no separation.[91]

[90] *Ibid.*, August 22, 1945.   [91] *Ibid.*, September 11, 1945.

The most prevalent explanation dealt with the pressure tactics of *Hokoku* and *Hoshi-dan* in forcing decisions to renounce upon members and unwilling nonmembers alike.

During the time of my hearing I was forced to [renounce] or else the "Pressure Group" continuously spoke evil of my family which I could not bear it.[92]

Some *Hokoku* boys threw rocks at our roof and windows after we had gone to sleep. It happened several times. I was really scared. We didn't have anyone to turn to for protection.[93]

Those *Hokoku* men somehow kept track of who had renounced and who had not. They knew that I had not. Everyday some of those men in my block would ask whether I had renounced or when I would renounce. In a short time block people refused to talk to me; it seemed that everyone was shunning me. When I finally decided to renounce, pressure was off me. I didn't get cold stares any more.[94]

Because of my completely American background and democratic principles, I began to get labeled . . . as a "loyal American," "informer," and whatnot . . . I was practically labeled as a sort of "voluntary segregant" who was on the American side. I lived in Block 50, which was unfortunately right next to Block 54, the headquarters of the fanatical *Hoshidan*. While I and the members of my family were able to withstand pressure to join the organization, I particularly was suspect to them. . . . During the mass renunciation program, they suspected anyone who did not request renunciation forms from Washington. And everyday watchers were stationed in the block office to check the incoming mail. They seemed to know . . . where everyone stood. I was practically told what to do and how to answer. There was no holding back at the hearing. At the height of the hysteria, they claimed they knew who would be accepted or not, and at the period they knew I was not a renouncee and they would activate even non-members who failed to do their biddings. I was so visibly upset during the hearing that it was hard to be myself as the hearing officer noted.[95]

There seemed to be a certain powerful group ruling the people of the center whom everyone feared. They were later called the *Hoshi Dan* and *Hokoku Seinen Dan*. . . . No one was free to act and think for himself. No one in our family was involved in these organizations until that fatal night of October, 1944. . . . As my friend, brother and I were on our way to night school, we came upon a man standing between the mess hall and

[92] *Ibid.*, August 30, 1945.

[93] Statement by a young Nisei man, Field Notes, December 19, 1945.

[94] Statement by a Kibei man, Field Notes, December 19, 1945.

[95] Letter from the files of the American Civil Liberties Union, Northern California Branch, August 21, 1945.

the barrack. His motions caused us to stop and investigate. Before I could call away my friend, he was slashed by a sharp knife on the left side of his face. Soon thereafter I learned that the man was influential in the *Hoshi Dan* and was a resident of the same block as our family. The brutality of the attack placed dreadful fear upon everyone in our block who were not connected with the *Hoshi Dan* for it was obvious what one may expect if one refused to recognize the organization as my friend, my brother and I had done. Hysteria of terrorism spread to other blocks in the colony and those who were nonmembers were helplessly driven to submit themselves to the influence of the *Hoshi Dan* members for fears of physical injuries. The knifer was soon apprehended but the rest of us were helplessly left in the colony with immediate fears of being the next prey of this merciless group in which this knifer was a member. Despite mother's pleas to stay out of this knifing case, I went to the trials as a witness of the incident because I felt it was my duty to prosecute the violator and to enforce peace in the center. I was placed in a dangerous position by acting as witness for I was eyed as an *inu* or informer of all the activities within this camp by the members of this group. Our whole family was wrapped in fears. Mother, who is forty-nine years old, was so nervous and upset about my safety so in the meantime she registered as a member of the *Hoshi Dan* to save me from possible beating or knifing. It wasn't long before everyone who had no intention at first, were coerced to become a member of the *Hoshi Dan* for fear of physical violence. We had no other choice for we had no way of moving out or away from terrorism in this fenced-in concentration camp. There were no other ways out because relocation was not permitted in Tule Lake at that time and also in such frenzy it was impossible to even mention the word "relocation." It was just maddening how much power that group was able to exert upon us against our wishes. Even at the trials, I was inhibited to express myself freely for fear of violence upon my immediate family as well as my innocent friends. After he was sentenced he later returned to our block which just added more horrifying mental strain upon us all.

The year ended quietly without another incident for we were superficially members of the organization. We complied by clipping our hair and abiding to the regulations of that organization. I was married in February, 1945, to a girl from the same block as ours whose family were members of the organization for the same reason as we were. Then on the 12th of February, my brother [Jack] was interned at Bismarck Internment Camp in North Dakota. At the time of his apprehension, he had just become a member but since he was listed on a membership list which was confiscated by WRA, he was taken. I remember he had his renunciation hearing just before mine. He was eighteen years old then having graduated in December, 1944, from Tri-State High on the project. Since he was only a kid, he was afraid to withdraw from the organization since the pressure placed upon him was too great. I regret very much that I sent my brother as a member of the [Hokoku] *Seinen Dan* but that was the only way out at that time, for he had sacrificed himself in order to protect our family.

He recently wrote that he will attempt to be released from Bismarck and join the family in Tule Lake.

As I recall now, I appeared at the renunciation hearing the first part of March when the camp was livelier than usual by the activities of the radical organizations to make us all renounce our citizenship. Their power was augmented by the fervor aroused by periodic removal of these agitators by the Department of Justice. Once a member of the organization, there was no way of withdrawing from that organization and of feeling safe to roam in the colony. It was so bad that those who did not renounce stated in public they had renounced in order to avoid the consequences of a person who did not renounce. During the time hearings were conducted in this center, these organizations were permitted to display their might and power so ostentatiously as though their selfish aim was the intention of everyone in this camp. It is just disgusting to believe that the Justice Department and the WRA remained on the sideline to watch us all renounce against our wishes when we couldn't act freely and express our true feelings toward this country. It may seem as though the hearings were conducted in privacy; however, when others within the block kept curious watch to see who did or who did not receive letters from the Justice Department, or who did or did not receive special hearing notices, there was the sad predicament of being eyed as a doublecrosser. I've never believed that such gangsterism could ever have been tolerated by any law-enforcing body.

Before I appeared at the hearing, I debated about appearing and pondered if there wasn't some way to avoid renunciation. There really was no way out with so much fear harassing me with additional worries over my brother [Jack's] apprehension, so I was compelled to appear at that hearing. At my hearing I was unable to express myself thoroughly except to say that I wanted to take mother to Japan so she will be able to join her daughter. I regret that I did not tell . . . my reasons for renouncing at that time. My hearing was about 2 minutes long. No doubt the Hearing Officer was aggravated by my hair clipped short which was no fault of mine. I avoided wearing regulation sweaters with the rising sun emblem.[96]

As the applications for renunciation continued to pour in, officials of the Department of Justice became alarmed at the momentum of the trend. The Department of Justice had sanctioned the Denationalization Bill for the following reasons: (1) the belief that continued detention in camps of American citizens not charged with crime would be declared unconstitutional; (2) the fear that, under these circumstances, the "militantly disloyal" (i.e., *Hokoku* members) would be forthwith released, contrary to "the real and demonstrable interests of national safety"; (3) the hope that the

---

[96] Letter from the files of an attorney, September 25, 1945. The assault and trial referred to in this letter have been described in Chapter XII.

Bill "would induce the members of the group to renounce their citizenship if given an opportunity to do so" and thus "permit the detention of that group which clearly had to be detained."[97] The Department had not expected other classes of the population to renounce.

When it became apparent that renunciation was by no means limited to the ardent *Hokoku* members but was also being used by the residents in general just as opportunistically as earlier declarations of "disloyalty" had been used, officials expressed fear that, within a short time, "about every family in Tule Lake would be involved in renunciation."[98] Burling, the Justice Department representative, attempted to stem the flood of applications by two devices: (1) to obtain a declaration from the National officials of WRA that Tule Lake would be a "refuge center" from which no one would be forced to resettle for the duration of the war, and (2) to stamp out the Resegregationist organizations.

WRA refused to yield in the matter of forced resettlement or to exempt Tule Lake from its plan of liquidating all relocation projects. The only concession Myer was willing to make was an assurance that "those who do not wish to leave the [Tule Lake] center *at this time* are not required to do so and may continue to live here or at some similar center until January 1, 1946."[99]

In an effort to stamp out Resegregationist pressure, Burling issued, on behalf of the Attorney General, an open letter to the chairmen of *Hoshi-dan* and *Hokoku*. Mimeographed copies of this letter, with a Japanese translation, were posted in all mess halls on January 24. In this letter he condemned the activities of *Hokoku* members, and of *Hoshi-dan* elders who "encourage the activities of the young men." Burling concluded with the warning that "since these activities are intolerable, they will not be tolerated but, on the contrary, will cease."

On the same day, January 24, Burling announced plans for a second internment, and two days later 171 more men were taken out of camp. At five-thirty in the morning, in a spectacular gesture of defiance, *Hokoku* bugles were blown loudly at dawn, and the

---

[97] Edward J. Ennis, Chief of Department of Justice Alien Enemy Control Unit, to Ernest Besig, Director of the American Civil Liberties Union, Northern California Branch, August 22, 1945.

[98] Statement by John Burling, Field Notes, January 17, 1945.

[99] *Newell Star*, January 29, 1945. Italics ours.

young members who were not being interned drilled and ordered themselves in ranks facing the fence. As each truck of internees left the gate a farewell shout of "Banzai!" arose.

On February 11, the Department of Justice ordered the arrest of another contingent of about 650 *Hokoku* and *Hoshi-dan* members. On this occasion the president of *Hokoku* was authorized to call an emergency meeting of the members. Answering bugle calls, the young men of the organization assembled immediately and each of those listed for removal accepted personal notice of internment.

On March 4 the Department of Justice arrested and interned a fourth contingent of 125 men.

On March 16 WRA decreed belatedly that all Resegregationist activities were unlawful and punishable by imprisonment:

> It had been the WRA policy at the Tule Lake Center to permit Japanese social and cultural activities except where they may lead to disturbances of the peace of the community. This policy will continue in effect. However, activities which are carried on under the guise of social or cultural objectives and which lead directly or indirectly through inducement, persuasion, coercion, intimidation and other action in the promotion of Japanese nationalistic and anti-American activities and the disruption of peace and security within the center, whether by individuals, groups or organizations, will not be tolerated.[100]

Bugling, wearing of Japanese emblems, and "assemblies, gatherings, parades, and group exercises, drilling or similar activities, designed to promote Japanese nationalistic" sentiment were prohibited.

All of these official actions came too late. Mass withdrawal from American citizenship had already taken place. Over a thousand applications were received in February. By this time, an overwhelming majority of those eligible to renounce citizenship[101] had attempted to do so, and only slightly over a hundred additions to the list were made in March. Most of these applications were approved,[102] and the final accounting for Tule Lake resulted in the denationalization of seven out of every ten citizens.

Whereas renunciation did not, as Burling had predicted, involve

---

[100] Tule Lake Segregation Center, Special Project Regulations, March 16, 1945.

[101] Nisei and Kibei 17½ years of age or older as of December 31, 1944.

[102] Renunciants were, however, often not notified of the approval of their applications for months.

"about every family in Tule Lake," it did involve a very large proportion. As Chart IX shows, there were some 4,390 families[103] containing at least one citizen member old enough to apply for renunciation. In 73 per cent of these families, at least one member renounced, and in only 27 per cent did no one renounce. The chart also shows strikingly that renunciation was, for the average family,

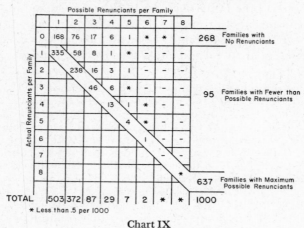

FREQUENCY DISTRIBUTION PER 1000 OF 4390 FAMILIES
HAVING CITIZEN MEMBERS ELIGIBLE TO RENOUNCE
BY POSSIBLE AND ACTUAL RENUNCIANTS

Possible Renunciants per Family

Actual Renunciants per Family	1	2	3	4	5	6	7	8		
0	168	76	17	6	1	*	*	–	268	Families with No Renunciants
1	335	58	8	1	*	–	–	–		
2		238	16	3	1	–	–	–		
3			46	6	*	–	–	–	95	Families with Fewer than Possible Renunciants
4				13	1	*	–	–		
5					4	*	–	–		
6						1	–	–		
7							–	–		
8								*	637	Families with Maximum Possible Renunciants
TOTAL	503	372	87	29	7	2	*	*	1000	

* Less than .5 per 1000

Chart IX

an "all or none" matter. In 80 per cent of the families where anyone renounced, every member who could renounce did so.[104]

That renunciation of any member was viewed as a protection for the whole family from forced resettlement, and that denationalization of all citizen members was often considered necessary to avoid separation of families containing both aliens and citizens, has been documented earlier in this chapter. These statistics show

[103] There were also 1,840 families containing no person who could renounce, i.e., no citizen member 17½ years of age or over. Of these families, 1,312 (71 per cent) consisted of only one person, usually a bachelor Issei. The other 528 consisted for the most part of elderly Issei couples. In an undetermined number of these cases, the family was "protected" by the renunciation of a citizen relative who did not live in the household.

[104] Leaving out of account the families where there was only one potential renunciant, and confining analysis to multiple-potential families, the proportion where all potentials renounced is still 70 per cent.

how extensively this protective device was used to achieve family security.

Within the individual family, however, there was greater need for the protection of the citizen husband or son than of the citizen wife or daughter because of the fear that nonrenunciant males would be inducted into the armed services. It is, therefore, not surprising to find that in families where all who could renounce did so, males comprised 65 per cent of the potential renunciants, and that in families where no one renounced, their proportion was only 49 per cent. Within the split families,[105] where there was evidently an attempt to keep a foothold in both America and Japan, males comprised 55 per cent of the potential renunciants. In these families, the daughter most frequently kept her foot in America, the son in Japan: 74 per cent of the males in such families renounced, compared with only 30 per cent of the females.

Family analysis indicated also the persistence of the old Tulean-transferee dichotomy, for 49 per cent of the families where no one renounced consisted of old Tuleans, as did 36 per cent of the "fence-sitting" split families, contrasted with only 19 per cent of the families where every one possible renounced.

Proceeding to more detailed analysis of renunciants, without regard to family composition, the most striking characteristic of the renunciant group is its youth. One out of five of the male renunciants and one out of four of the females were under 21 at the time of renunciation. Family security was thus achieved by the action of children who had been between 14 and 18 years old when they were removed from the outside world.

The punishment meted out by the Department of Justice also bore most heavily on the young, for 23 per cent of the male renunciants who were interned as "potentially dangerous enemy aliens" or "militantly disloyal" were under 21 years old when interned.

The second characteristic of the renunciant group was, as suggested by the family analysis, a concentration of males: 77 per cent of all males on the project renounced, as against 59 per cent of all females.

The third characteristic was the predominance of transferees among renunciants: for both sexes combined, 78 per cent of the transferees renounced, but only 49 per cent of the old Tuleans.

---

[105] Families where some but not all of those who could renounce did so.

The fourth characteristic was membership in one of the Resegregationist organizations: 91 per cent of the members of *Hokoku* and *Joshi-dan* renounced, compared with 59 per cent of nonmembers.

The fifth characteristic was locational concentration, which is illustrated in Chart X. The extremes are represented by Block 54[106] where 91 per cent renounced and Block 12 where the proportion was 34 per cent.[107]

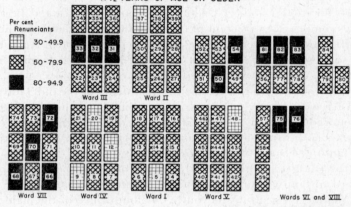

Chart X

The fact that these marked concentrations existed should not, however, draw attention from the equally remarkable fact that renunciation was a collective phenomenon, involving, in large proportions, all classes of the Tule Lake population. No quinquennial age group of male citizens from ages 20 to 24 to ages 35 to 39 contained less than 69 per cent renunciants; no comparable group of females less than 35 per cent. As noted, no block had less than 34 per cent renunciants, and in 68 out of the total 74 blocks at least

---

[106] Block 54 was headquarters of the Resegregationist organizations.

[107] The statistics cited are based on our own complete tabulations of data supplied by the Army. These data did not include information on the renunciants' education in Japan. Manuscript tables from WRA, based on a 10-per-cent sample, show, however, that over 80 per cent of the Kibei renounced, compared with 60 per cent of the "pure" Nisei.

50 per cent of the citizens were denationalized. Even among the old Tuleans, resistant as they were to pressure group tactics, the lowest proportion renouncing in any one block was 21 per cent in Block 48, and there were only two other blocks (12 and 29) in which the Tulean segment of the population had less than 30 per cent renunciants.

With mass renunciation of citizenship by Nisei and Kibei, the cycle which began with evacuation was complete. Their parents had lost their hard-won foothold in the economic structure of America. They, themselves, had been deprived of rights which indoctrination in American schools had led them to believe inviolable. Charged with no offense, but victims of a military misconception, they had suffered confinement behind barbed wire. They had been stigmatized as disloyal on grounds often far removed from any criterion of political allegiance. They had been at the mercy of administrative agencies working at cross-purposes. They had yielded to parental compulsion in order to hold the family intact. They had been intimidated by the ruthless tactics of pressure groups in camp. They had become terrified by reports of the continuing hostility of the American public, and they had finally renounced their irreparably depreciated American citizenship.

Many of them have since left the country, voluntarily, to take up life in defeated Japan. Others will remain in America, in the unprecedented and ambiguous status of citizens who became aliens ineligible for citizenship in the land of their birth.[108]

---

[108] Manuscript tables, obtained through the courtesy of WRA, show that about half of the renunciants had been released by February, 1946, to resettle in American communities. The total number of these "citizens with alien status" remaining in America will probably exceed 3,000.

APPENDIX

The Life History of a "Disloyal"

THE PRECEDING CHAPTERS have dealt with the collective aspects of the spoilage of evacuation. The process of attitude formation under the stress of racial discrimination, expulsion and detention has been analyzed cross-sectionally so far as the experience of individuals is concerned. The cumulative impact of circumstances in transforming attitudes of "loyalty" to those of "disloyalty" is also clearly evident in the life histories of individuals. This is illustrated by the following life history of a Nisei, who was highly articulate, intellectually honest, and embittered.

Joseph Yoshisuke Kurihara, a Hawaiian-born Nisei, was almost fifty years old at the time of evacuation. He had achieved a high measure of success in business and commercial activities in southern California. He had enlisted in the American Army during the first World War and served with an occupation unit in Germany. His political behavior and attitudes prior to evacuation are a matter of record, and all informants agree that he had no interest in and no connection with Japan. He had in fact never even visited the country. Although extremely sensitive to racial discrimination and slights to the minority group to which he belonged, he was known to be a firm advocate of democratic principles. He was a contributor to a vernacular newspaper with a pronounced "flag-waving" policy, and his contributions conformed to this policy. Following the outbreak of war between Japan and America, he made strenuous but unsuccessful efforts to participate actively in this country's war program. When evacuation came, Kurihara gave vehement expression to the embitterment he felt at his "betrayal" by America and, correspondingly, began to voice pro-Japan sentiments. He was a leader in the Manzanar riot. He was arrested and incarcerated, as described in Chapter II. He applied for expatriation to Japan in 1943. In Tule Lake, to which he was transferred in December, 1943, he was among the first to renounce American citizenship, and he successfully pressed immigration officials to be in the first contingent of voluntary deportees to Japan.

Kurihara agreed to prepare his life history for this study. Excerpts from this document, which are revealing of the emotional stress under which he made his decisions, will follow a brief, more formal account of his career.

Biographical Notes: Born in 1895 on Kauai Island, Hawaii. Single; no relatives in the United States. Short, stout and balding; square face, large jaw, resonant voice. Warm and friendly in manner, but self-assertive. Proud of his honesty and integrity and regarded by others as a man of his word. A devout Catholic.

Family moved to Honolulu when Kurihara was two years old. There he completed elementary school and graduated from a Catholic high school. Concurrently attended Japanese language schools for ten years. Hoped to become a doctor, and worked for a time in a road-construction crew to earn money to attend college.

Came to California in 1915; worked as fruit picker in Sacramento Valley prior to entrance in St. Ignatius College in San Francisco. Discouraged by evidence of racial discrimination on West Coast; migrated to middle west in early 1917.

Enlisted in U.S. Army while in Michigan in 1917. Served abroad. Honorably discharged in San Francisco in 1919. Visited Hawaii for brief period. Returned to California; entered a commercial college in Los Angeles and later Southwestern University from which he graduated in accounting in 1924.

Opened an accounting firm, serving Japanese community in Los Angeles, in 1924. In 1925, became partner in a wholesale produce firm and, at same time, operated retail fruit and vegetable store in Hollywood, which he sold at profit in 1927. Auditor and manager of Japanese-owned seafood packing company 1927–1928; salesman for a wholesale hardware company 1929–1931, earning on the average five hundred dollars a month. Opened retail fruit and vegetable store in Berkeley in an attempt to carry over to northern California a form of merchandising successful in Los Angeles area. Failed in this venture.

Studied navigation and television in Los Angeles. From 1934 to onset of war, employed as navigator of tuna-fishing boat. Arrived in San Diego from fishing expedition December 29, 1941. Remained there through January in effort to get clearance to navigate, which was denied. Went to San Pedro in attempt to enter merchant marine. Unsuccessful. Sought employment in two shipbuilding firms and was refused because of ancestry.

Witnessed expulsion of Japanese from Terminal Island on orders of Eleventh Naval District in February, 1942. Entered Manzanar with second volunteer contingent on March 23, 1942. Soon became active in antiadministration and anti-JACL movements. Arrested on December 7, 1942, during Manzanar riot. Sent to Moab and later to Leupp isolation camps. Transferred to Tule Lake in December, 1943, as segregant; inactive politically in Tule Lake, although had personal following. Renounced his citizenship; sailed for Japan in February, 1946.

Verbatim Excerpts from Kurihara's Manuscripts

His appraisal of his own personality:

I go from one extreme to the other. I sympathize, cry, and give my last penny to save a person in a worthy cause, but I can be mean and devilish when aroused.

Memories of Hawaii:

We, the boys of conglomerated races, were brought up under the careful guidance of American teachers, strictly following the principle of American Democracy. Let it be white, black, brown, or yellow, we were all treated alike. This glorious Paradise of the Pacific was the true melting pot of human races.

Early experiences of racial discrimination in California (around 1915):

My early experiences in Sacramento were of appalling nature. While walking on K Street from the Depot toward the Japanese district, suddenly a fairly well-dressed person came and kicked me in the stomach for no reason whatever. Luckily it glanced as I instinctively avoided it.

I watched his next move, maneuvering into position to fight it out the best I could. A crowd started to gather but no sooner than it did, another person coming out of a saloon in front of which we were about to tackle, stopped this public show. I went my way feeling terribly hurt.

In this same city of Sacramento, as my friend and I were walking in the residential district, a short distance away from the Japanese center, something came whizzing by, and then another and another. We noticed they were rocks being thrown at us by a number of youngsters. As we went toward them, the boys ran and hid. Feeling perplexed, I asked my friend, "Why do they attack us in such a manner?" He answered, "It's discrimina-

tion." No such thing ever happened where I came from. It was disgusting.
I felt homesick for my good old native land, Hawaii.

Enlistment in and experiences in American Army of occupation (1917–1919):

While in Michigan I was seized with an intense desire to join the Army.
I felt rather ashamed of myself in civilian attire. I had purchased $500
worth of Liberty Bonds to send to my five nieces and nephews in Hawaii,
but still not feeling satisfied, I finally went and enlisted. During the training period, I was befriended by many Caucasians. I made several visits to
their homes. I felt very happy. Knowing that they were going out of the
way to make me happy, I solemnly vowed to fight and die for the U.S. and
these good people, whose genuine kindness touched the very bottom of
my heart. In California my animosities against the Californians were growing with ever-increasing intensity, but in Michigan, my liking for the
American people was getting the best of me.

In the summer of 1918 I was sent to France with a medical corps. After
the armistice, I was assigned to Coblenz, Germany, with a medical corps
of the army of occupation. During my stay in Coblenz, I found out that
the German people were just as human as any other race. I learned to like
these people because they were kind and sincere. At every meal time, the
little German girls and boys would line the walk to the garbage can for
whatever scraps the boys were throwing away. I could not bear to see these
little ones suffer, so I always made it my duty to ask for as much as my
plate would hold and gave it to them. O Lord my God, so this is the price
of War. Why should these innocent children be made to suffer the hardships of war?

Experiences and attitudes immediately following Pearl Harbor:

After a fishing expedition off Mexico, we entered San Diego Bay immediately at daybreak on December 29. In the bay, the boat was stopped and
several officers in naval uniform came aboard. They scrutinized the papers,
and finding them satisfactory they left, but they took three of us (two
Portuguese and myself) along.

We were taken to the naval wharf and waited for orders but none came.
Around nine thirty, we again were asked to board the official launch and
this time were taken back to our own ship. No sooner when I boarded the
ship than a plain clothes man yelled, "Hey! you Jap, I want some information. You better tell me everything, or I'll kick you in the ————." My
blood boiled. I felt like clubbing his head off. It was just a hat rack and
nothing more.

Another gentleman came aboard, and seeing that I was an Oriental, he
said, "I want you to come with me to the Immigration Office."

At the office, I was told to take a seat in plain view of several officers.
Noon came, so they went for lunch while I sat there waiting. Three o'clock
came, I was feeling hungry and irritated. Finally I asked one of the officers

why they apprehended me and why they were keeping me waiting without lunch. He said the instruction was to bring all Japanese nationals in for questioning.

One of the officers obligingly took out some papers, called me to his side and started to ask the following questions:

"What do you think of the war?"

"Terrible."

"Who do you think will win this war?"

"Who knows? God only knows."

"Do you think Japan has the materials she needs to wage this war?"

"I never was there; so your guess is just as good as mine."

"Are you a navigator?"

"Yes, I navigated boats for the last eight years."

"Are you good at it?"

"Never missed my mark."

"Do you know all the bays along the coast?"

"Yes, nearly all the bays and coves along the entire coast from Seattle to Ecuador, South America."

"Have you been a good American citizen?"

"I was and I am."

"Will you fight for this country?"

"If I am needed, I am ready."

"Were you a soldier of any country?"

"Yes, I am Veteran of the Foreign Wars, U.S. Army."

I was released that evening.

Attempts to participate in the war effort:

I went to see the Port Master in San Diego to get a permit to sail the sea. Seeing that I was a Japanese, he said, "No permit for any Jap." We argued awhile. Losing his temper he said, "Get out or I'll throw you out." So I told him, "Say officer I wore that uniform when you were still unborn. I served in the U.S. Army and fought for Democracy. I may be a Jap in feature but I am an American. Understand!" I saw fire in his eyes, but he had no further words to say.

In San Pedro, when I applied at one shipbuilding company, I was told it would be better for me to try elsewhere because I will not enjoy working here. They said the fellow workmen were very antagonistic. They said they had two Japanese boys working as welders, but they did not think they would be here very long because of discrimination of the fellow workers.

The Terminal Island evacuation:

It was really cruel and harsh. To pack and evacuate in forty-eight hours was an impossibility. Seeing mothers completely bewildered with children crying from want and peddlers taking advantage and offering prices next to robbery made me feel like murdering those responsible without the slightest compunction in my heart.

The parents may be aliens but the children are all American citizens. Did the government of the United States intend to ignore their rights regardless of their citizenship? Those beautiful furnitures which the parents bought to please their sons and daughters, costing hundreds of dollars were robbed of them at the single command, "Evacuate!" Here my first doubt of American Democracy crept into the far corners of my heart with the sting that I could not forget. Having had absolute confidence in Democracy, I could not believe my very eyes what I had seen that day. America, the standard bearer of Democracy had committed the most heinous crime in its history.

The beginnings of his hatred of JACL leaders and other collaborators in the evacuation procedure:

Truly it was my intention to fight this evacuation. On the night of my return to Los Angeles from San Diego was the second meeting which the Citizens Federation of Southern California [sponsored by JACL] held to discuss evacuation. I attended it with a firm determination to join the committee representing the Nisei and carry the fight to the bitter end. I found the goose was already cooked. The Field Secretary of the JACL instead of reporting what actually transpired at a meeting they had had with General DeWitt just tried to intimidate the Nisei to comply with evacuation by stories of threats he claimed to have received from various parts of the State.

I felt sick at the result. They'd accomplished not a thing. All they did was to meet General DeWitt and be told what to do. These boys claiming to be the leaders of the Nisei were a bunch of spineless Americans. Here I decided to fight them and crush them in whatever camp I happened to find them. I vowed that they would never again be permitted to disgrace the name of the Nisei as long as I was about.

Initial experiences in and reactions to Manzanar:

The desert was bad enough. The mushroom barracks made it worse. The constant cyclonic storms loaded with sand and dust made it worst. After living in well furnished homes with every modern convenience and suddenly forced to live the life of a dog is something which one can not so readily forget. Down in our hearts we cried and cursed this government every time when we were showered with sand. We slept in the dust; we breathed the dust; and we ate the dust. Such abominable existence one could not forget, no matter how much we tried to be patient, understand the situation, and take it bravely. Why did not the government permit us to remain where we were? Was it because the government was unable to give us the protection? I have my doubt. The government could have easily declared Martial Law to protect us. It was not the question of protection. It was because we were Japs! Yes, Japs!

After corralling us like a bunch of sheep in a hellish country, did the government treat us like citizens? No! We were treated like aliens regardless of our rights. Did the government think we were so without pride to work for $16.00 a month when people outside were paid $40.00 to $50.00 a week in the defense plants? Responsible government officials further told us to be loyal and that to enjoy our rights as American citizens we must be ready to die for the country. We must show our loyalty. If such is the case, why are the veterans corralled like the rest of us in the camps? Have they not proven their loyalty already? This matter of proving one's loyalty to enjoy the rights of an American citizen was nothing but a hocus-pocus.

Decision to renounce citizenship:[1]

My American friends . . . no doubt must have wondered why I renounced my citizenship. This decision was not that of today or yesterday. It dates back the day when General DeWitt ordered evacuation. It was confirmed when he flatly refused to listen even to the voices of the former World War Veterans and it was doubly confirmed when I entered Manzanar. We who already had proven our loyalty by serving in the last World War should have been spared. The veterans asked for special consideration but their requests were denied. They too had to evacuate like the rest of the Japanese people, as if they were aliens.

I did not expect this of the Army. When the Western Defense Command assumed the responsibilities of the West Coast, I expected that at least the Nisei would be allowed to remain. But to General DeWitt, we were all alike. "A Jap's a Jap. Once a Jap, always a Jap." . . . I swore to become a Jap 100 percent, and never to do another day's work to help this country fight this war. My decision to renounce my citizenship there and then was absolute.

Just before he left for Japan, Kurihara wrote:

It is my sincere desire to get over there as soon as possible to help rebuild Japan politically and economically. The American Democracy with which I was infused in my childhood is still unshaken. My life is dedicated to Japan with Democracy my goal.

In connection with Kurihara's own account of the development of his attitudes, it is of interest to quote the opinions of administrators from our own field notes, recorded by Togo Tanaka in Manzanar during the fall of 1942:

WRA administrators familiar with Kurihara's case were, in general, sympathetic with him. In August, 1942, after Kurihara had made several public speeches which some listeners considered "subversive" and "anti-American" one project administrative officer said he had a talk with Kurihara. "I find Joe Kurihara very bitter about the entire situation, but

---

[1] This excerpt is also quoted in Chapter XIII but is repeated here for the sake of context.

he is bitter and sore in quite an American way," was his observation. The Assistant Project Director, in a conversation with a group at which Kurihara was not present, remarked: "If I were Joe Kurihara, I'd be mad too. He was a veteran of the World War, was discharged from the United States Army honorably, had done his part as a citizen. It's just as if I had saved one of you guys from getting stabbed or killed in a street brawl, and you rewarded me by kicking me into the gutter. Hell, sure I'd be bitter."

Biographical Notes

MOST OF THE political leaders who emerged in the Tule Lake Segregation Center were Kibei. This situation is partly to be explained by the high proportions of Kibei who were segregated. In normal Japanese American communities just before the war, and in relocation projects after evacuation, the ratio of Kibei to "pure" Nisei over 15 years of age was about 1 to 4. In the segregation center, however, the ratio was almost 1 to 1.

Kibei had leadership advantages over both Nisei and Issei. They were, on the average, older than the Nisei and, although they were much younger than the Issei, the recency of their education in Japan tended to make them more vigorous and effective exponents of the newer Japanese ideologies. Their superior bilingualism also operated in their favor. The medium of communication among the older residents was mainly Japanese (of which most Nisei had imperfect control), while a thorough working knowledge of English (which most Issei lacked) was essential in negotiating with the administration.

The following biographical notes on political leaders, grouped in terms of their main affiliation (*Daihyo Sha Kai,* Coördinating Committee and Coöp, Resegregationists) suggest the extent to which Kibei attained political leadership.

For reference purposes we include similar biographical notes on some of the less conspicuous residents who, along with the leaders, were among the informants for the study.

Daihyo Sha Kai Leaders

Abe, Shozo (pseudonym). A Kibei, and Buddhist priest. Born in 1912 in Hawaii. Married; two children. Of medium height and slender; physically unattractive. Manner forbidding in general and arrogant toward WRA officials and other Caucasians. Spoke little English, but reputed to be a good orator in Japanese.

Taken to Japan in 1913 and remained there until the age of nineteen. Thirteen years' schooling in Japan, including education at a Buddhist seminary and a college. Came to the United States, and attended Fresno State College for two years.

Served as a Buddhist priest in Seattle for two years, in Yakima for two years, in Fresno for a year and a half.

Evacuated to the Fresno Assembly Center in May, 1942, and later transferred to the Jerome Relocation Project. In both these camps, worked as a priest of the Buddhist church and gained a following, particularly among Kibei Buddhists. In Jerome, as noted in Chapter III, was a leader of group opposing military registration. Segregated to Tule Lake in the early transfer movement to that center. Did not renounce citizenship. Was released from Tule Lake late in 1945 for permanent resettlement in a city in the Pacific Northwest, where he resumed activities as a Buddhist priest.

Kuratomi, George Toshio. A Kibei, born in 1915 in San Diego, California. Married in Tule Lake; one child. Of medium height and slender. Quick intelligence; somewhat high-strung; dignified manner; an effective speaker, both in English and in Japanese. A devout Buddhist.

Taken to Japan at age of seven; returned to United States at age of fifteen in 1930. About seven years schooling in Japan. Graduated from high school in San Diego with honors.

Worked as helper and sales clerk in a fruit and vegetable store until November, 1937, when he made another short trip to Japan. Upon return to America, worked in San Diego successively as manager of a retail fruit and vegetable store, as salesman and truck driver in a wholesale produce store, as operator of his own produce store. Worked in spare time as Sunday school teacher and group leader in Buddhist church.

Evacuated in April, 1942, to the Santa Anita Assembly Center, and transferred in October to the Jerome Relocation Project. At Santa Anita, worked as translator and interpreter, at Jerome as foreman of a lumberjack crew. Continued Buddhist activities.

At Jerome, associated with Reverend Shozo Abe as a leader opposing military registration. Association with Abe continued in Tule Lake after segregation in September, 1943.

Did not renounce citizenship. Was released from Tule Lake in January, 1946, for resettlement in an Eastern city. Regarded evacuation as evidence of second-class American citizenship and, from time to time, considered possibility of career in the Orient.

Kato, Bill (pseudonym). A Kibei, born in 1918 in San Juan Batista, California. No relatives in America; claimed his family owned considerable property in Japan. In 1944, married daughter of prominent Resegregationist at Tule Lake. Of medium height, heavy set; affected *bozu* haircut. Boastful of leadership qualities, which were disputed by other informants. Conscientious and meticulous worker; unusually good command of both English and Japanese.

Elementary school education in Salinas. Taken to Japan at age of twelve; about eight years education there, including one year at a well-known Tokyo university. Returned to the United States in 1938 at the age of nineteen. Enrolled in 1938 in San Francisco Junior College, and in 1941 in San Francisco State College, majoring in economics.

Employed as a houseboy by a Caucasian woman while attending college in San Francisco, earning eighteen dollars a month.

Evacuated to the Santa Anita Assembly Center; claimed to have participated in Santa Anita "incident." Transferred to Topaz Relocation Project. Segregated to Tule Lake in September, 1943. Active in politics; aligned first with Taro Watanabe; later with pressure-group leaders.

Among the first to renounce his citizenship; an active propagandist for renunciation. Arrested in December, 1944, by the Department of Justice and interned. Left for Japan early in 1946.

Seki, Johnny (pseudonym). A Kibei, born in 1906 near Sacramento, California. Married; no children. Short and plump; gentle-mannered; genial and courteous; well liked by fellow evacuees. Good command of both English and Japanese. A Buddhist.

Taken to Japan in 1912; remained there until 1922; graduated from a middle school. Returning to the United States, entered high school in Courtland, California, and graduated in 1927. Later, enrolled in the Sacramento Junior College, majoring in electrical engineering; graduated in 1929.

Operated truck farms, first at Davis, later at Clarksburg, California.

Moved to San Bernardino County just before the war and was evacuated directly to Poston Relocation Project in May, 1942. Immediately became influential in politics; served on Temporary Community Council. Active role in the Poston strike; later appointed to evacuee board in advisory capacity to administration.

Segregated to Tule Lake in 1943; renounced citizenship in late 1944.

Tada, Mitsugu (pseudonym). A Kibei, born in 1902 in Sacramento, California. Married; one child. Slender and extremely tall for a Japanese; often addressed by nickname, "Slim." High-bridged nose; moustache; in appearance more like a person of Mexican extraction than a Japanese. Had pleasant manner and spoke excellent English. A Buddhist.

Taken to Japan in 1912; returned to the United States in 1920. Attended schools in Japan for seven years. In America attended evening school about six months.

Worked as a clerk in a Japanese general merchandise store in Sacramento. Moved in 1924 to Isleton and operated a large celery farm for two years. Later opened a wholesale fruit and vegetable store of his own in Sacramento.

Evacuated to the Walerga Assembly Center in May, 1942, and transferred to the Tule Lake Relocation Project in June. At Tule Lake served as head of the evacuee police force until arrested and incarcerated in the stockade in November, 1943. Associated with George Kuratomi and the Reverend Abe. Politically inactive after Resegregationists came into power; steadfastly refused to renounce his citizenship. Resettled in Sacramento with his family in 1945.

Coördinating Committee and Coöp Leaders

Sasaki, Milton (pseudonym). A Kibei, born in 1911 in Walla Walla, Washington. Married; two children. Short and slender; distinguished appearance; dressy and dandified. Good speaker in both English and Japanese; colorful and forceful style of English writing. Claimed also to be versed in Chinese, Spanish, Latin, and French.

Sent to Japan at age of five; about six years' schooling there. Graduated from high school in Seattle; attended University of Denver for two years; received A.B. degree from University of Chicago in 1931.

Various jobs in California cities in Sacramento and Los Angeles areas: bookkeeper, salesman, for retail hardware and grocery; buyer; grocery clerk; private tutor for Caucasian high school student; interviewer for Japanese-owned employment agency; manager of a Japanese grocery store.

Evacuated from Sacramento in May, 1942, to Walerga Assembly Center. Transferred in June to Tule Lake Relocation Project.

Politically inactive in presegregation period, except as member of hospital committee, which in the summer of 1943 submitted a complaint listing alleged misdeeds and malpractice of Caucasian Chief Medical Officer.

Employed as coal analyst in Tule Lake until shortly before first segregation movement. Was then appointed as the executive secretary of the Coöp. After dissolution of Coördinating Committee, again became inactive politically. Did not renounce citizenship, although his wife did. Resettled to Chicago in 1945.

Watanabe, Taro (pseudonym). An Issei, born in Japan in 1879. Entered United States in 1905. Heavy set; of medium height; impressive manner. Married; two grown daughters and one son of draft age. A Buddhist.

Twelve years' schooling in Japan, including three years in college, with major in law.

Employed in various menial jobs. Operated a laundry in Menlo Park, California, from 1925 until evacuation. Considered a leader of the Japanese community; at one time president of the Japanese Association.

Evacuated to Tanforan Assembly Center in May, 1942; transferred to Topaz Relocation Project in September. Reported to have occupied position of considerable prestige in Topaz. Segregated to Tule Lake in September, 1943. Elected to *Daihyo Sha Kai* from his block, but soon deserted the protest movement and joined Coördinating Committee group. After resignation of this body in the spring of 1943, became inactive politically. His son renounced his citizenship.

Noma, Takeo (pseudonym). An Issei, born in Japan in 1900; entered the United States at the age of eighteen. Married; three children. Taller than average and well built. Considered arrogant and blunt in manner; was said to have a number of enemies. A Buddhist.

Eleven years' education in Japan; graduated from a California high school.

From 1930 to evacuation acted as agent for a nationally known insurance company in Sacramento; claimed to have earned $300 a month.

Evacuated to the Walerga Assembly Center in May, 1942; transferred to the Tule Lake Relocation Project in June.

Not well known among evacuees in Tule Lake until shortly before the first segregation movement when he became general manager of the Coöp. Murdered during the wave of *inu* hatred in 1944.

Resegregationist and Pressure-Group Leaders

Yamashita, Koshiro (pseudonym). An Issei, born in Japan in 1904. Entered the United States at age of twenty. Married; no children. Of medium height and stout; large "handle-bar" moustache. Pompous and condescending manner; said to have tried unsuccessfully to achieve political career in Japan. Spoke and wrote Japanese well; fair command of English. A Christian.

Twelve years' schooling in Japan, including equivalent of junior college. Graduated from high school in Portland, Oregon; entered Stanford University in 1928; transferred to University of San Francisco, receiving A.B. degree. Returned to Stanford; received A.B. there in 1933. Claimed M.A. Stanford, but report denied by informants.

Teacher Japanese language school (Hawthorne); helper in wholesale fruit and vegetable store (Los Angeles); operator own fruit and vegetable store (San Gabriel).

Evacuated to Salinas Assembly Center, May, 1942; transferred to the Poston Relocation Project during the summer. Block manager and influential politically in Poston. Arrested by the FBI in February, 1943, for alleged obstruction of the registration program and complicity in beating the national president of JACL. Interned by the Department of Justice at Santa Fe, New Mexico. Released to Tule Lake Segregation Center in spring of 1943. Again arrested by the Department of Justice in December, 1943, and interned

Kira, Stanley Masanobu (pseudonym). A Kibei, born in Hawaii in 1897. Married; two children. Short and stout; effeminate appearance; small features; beard. Soft spoken and courteous to Caucasians; boastful and egotistical with fellow evacuees. Good command of both English and Japanese. Member of the American Legion and A. F. of L.

Attended elementary school and high school in Hawaii. Brief visit to Japan at the age of fifteen. Served in Medical Corps of the United States Army 1918 to 1919. Employed from 1920 to 1924 as assistant cashier in a bank in Hawaii; and until 1935 as postmaster at a monthly salary of eighty dollars.

In Japan 1935–1938; studied political science in a well-known Tokyo university.

Came to California in 1938; secretary of union local of Japanese fishermen in Terminal Island.

Filed suit against General DeWitt, contesting legality of evacuation.

Evacuated to Santa Anita Assembly Center in May, 1942. Reported by several informants to have been a leading participant in Santa Anita incident. Transferred to Manzanar Relocation Center in August, 1942. Claimed to have organized a gang of young strong-arm boys there. Involved in the Manzanar riot of December, 1942. Segregated to Tule Lake in February, 1944. Renounced his citizenship in the fall of 1944; interned by the Department of Justice.

Ishikawa, Torakichi (pseudonym). An Issei, born in Japan in 1893. Came to United States in 1912. Married; six young children. Tall and well built. Argumentative and self-assertive. Spoke English fairly well.

Thirteen years' schooling in Japan. Received B.S. degree in agriculture from College of Agriculture, University of California, Davis, in 1918.

Grower of tomatoes and apricots in Merced from 1920 to 1934. Employed concurrently as manager of a growers' association for three years. Taught Japanese language school in Mt. Eden, California, from 1934 to evacuation.

Evacuated to Tanforan Assembly Center in May, 1942. Worked as a police warden. Transferred to the Topaz Relocation Project in September, 1942. Segregated to Tule Lake in September, 1943. Not well known among evacuees until Ishikawa petition (Chapter VIII). Interned by Department of Justice in December, 1944.

Yamada, Nobuo (pseudonym). A Kibei, born in Imperial County, California, in 1915. Single; three brothers, one of whom serving in the United States Army. Of medium height and slender. Arrogant and self-assertive. Boastful of his physical prowess and skill in judo. Claimed a large personal following. English defective. A Buddhist.

Taken to Japan in 1920 and remained there until the age of thirteen; eight years' schooling in Japan, 1920–1928. Graduated high school in Orange County, California, in 1936.

Helped on father's farm in Orange County until evacuation.

Evacuated directly to Poston Relocation Project in May, 1942. Worked as judo instructor and organized informal group of young Kibei. Role in Poston strike is described in Chapter II. Segregated to Tule Lake in October, 1943. Renounced his citizenship; interned by Department of Justice in December, 1944.

Tsuchikawa, Mrs. Hanako (pseudonym). A Kibei, born in Hawaii in 1914. Married to an Issei; three children. Sister of Sadao Endo, who was imprisoned in the stockade for complicity in the November disturbance at Tule Lake. Another brother in the U.S. Army. Very short and slender; physically attractive; often called "Madame Chiang Kai-shek" by fellow evacuees. Proud and stubborn; argumentative. Spoke English with accent. A Buddhist.

In Japan 1924–1931 and 1939–1941; attended schools there. Three years of schooling in Fresno, California.

Evacuated to Fresno Assembly Center in May, 1942; transferred to Jerome Relocation Project in October; segregated to Tule Lake in September, 1943. Renounced her citizenship.

Other Informants

Wakida, George (pseudonym). A Kibei, born in 1914 in Stockton, California. Married; no children. Short and well built. A Buddhist.

In Japan 1916–1931; eleven years' schooling there. Graduated elementary school and high school in Stockton; also attended San Francisco State College 1938–1939.

Operated tomato farm in northern California from 1940 until evacuation.

Evacuated to Turlock Assembly Center in May, 1942; employed as recreational director; also taught English to Issei. Transferred to Gila Relocation Project in August, 1942. Became block manager. Influential among the Kibei faction and organized a powerful Kibei club. Arrested and sent to the Leupp Isolation Center in

February, 1943, for antiregistration activities. Segregated to Tule Lake in December, 1943. Politically inconspicuous in Tule Lake, although influential among many Gila transferees. Renounced his citizenship.

Niiyama, Sam (pseudonym). A Nisei, born in Seattle in 1908. Married; five children. Lived with aged parents. Short and somewhat stout. Practical and cynical. A Buddhist.

Finished second year high school in Winslow, Washington. Also attended Japanese language school for five years.

Worked in Portland as salesman for a wholesale produce company. Later operated berry farms in Oregon and Washington.

Evacuated directly to Tule Lake Relocation Project in June, 1942. Became a block manager; influential among evacuee administrative workers. Remained in Tule Lake after segregation. Became head of Civic Organizations in 1944. Did not renounce his citizenship.

Tsuruda, Bob (pseudonym). A Nisei, born in Sacramento, California, in 1914. Married; one child. Medium height and slender; attractive in appearance. Conceited, but good sense of humor; talkative. Spoke Japanese fairly well, but could not read or write it. No religious affiliation.

Graduated from junior college in Sacramento.

Worked in drug store and soda fountain in Stockton and Sacramento.

Evacuated to Turlock Assembly Center in May, 1942; transferred to Gila Relocation Project in August, 1942; segregated to Tule Lake in October, 1943. Was permitted to resettle to a town in the Middle West in September, 1944.

Kurusu, Isamu (pseudonym). A Kibei, born in Sacramento, California, in 1913. Married; no children. Tall and slender. Gentle in manner and courteous. Spoke English with accent. A Buddhist.

In Japan 1920–1932; attended schools for twelve years. Graduated Pasadena (California) Junior College; one year in California Institute of Technology studying engineering.

Employed as draftsman.

Evacuated from San Marino, California, to Tulare Assembly Center in May, 1942; transferred to Gila Relocation Project in September, 1942; segregated to Tule Lake in October, 1943. Renounced his citizenship.

Higashi, Thomas (pseudonym). A Nisei, born in Monterey, California, in 1918. Married; one child. Short, medium build.

Attended schools in San Pedro, California. Five months in Compton Junior College. Twelve years' attendance Japanese language school.

Employed as radio operator on fishing boat, and as clerk in fruit and vegetable store in Los Angeles Harbor district.

Evacuated to Tulare Assembly Center in April, 1942; transferred to Gila Relocation Project in September, 1942; segregated to Tule Lake in October, 1943. Both he and his wife renounced citizenship.

Itabashi, Kazuhiko (pseudonym). An Issei, born in Japan in 1887. Married; three children. Short and slender. Neat in appearance; spry and alert. Straightforward; kind manner. Spoke English fairly well.

Segregated to Tule Lake from Manzanar in February, 1943. All three of his children renounced citizenship.

A Note on Terminology

ASSEMBLY CENTERS, relocation projects, and the segregation center are referred to in documents indiscriminately as *camp, project, center,* and *community.* The evacuee section in Tule Lake is occasionally called the *colony* or the *village.*

The primary physical unit in the evacuee section of each project was the *block,* composed of *barracks,* divided into *apartments.* Each block had communal facilities, including *mess hall, latrine* and *washroom, laundry room,* and *recreation hall.* Blocks were grouped into *sections, quads,* or *wards,* separated by wide *firebreaks.*

Project administration was in charge of Caucasian employees, sometimes referred to as *appointed personnel.* The chief officer was the *Project Director.* Under him were various assistants in charge of such functions as *Community Management* (including welfare, education, internal security); *Operations* (including agriculture, industry); and *Administrative Management* (including finance, personnel, mess operations, supply).

Evacuee residents of the projects are referred to in the text and documents as *evacuees* or *residents.* After segregation, residents of Tule Lake are also called *segregants.* Segregants remaining in Tule Lake are called *old Tuleans;* those transferring to Tule Lake from other projects, *transferees*. *Internee* is used in the text to apply only to persons interned in enemy alien camps administered by the Department of Justice. Occasionally, however, documentary quotations use the word indiscriminately as synonymous with either "resident" or "a person confined in the stockade." The latter are properly called *detainees*. After rescission of the exclusion orders, however, *detainees* refers, in official documents, to persons prohibited by the Army from leaving camps; and *excludees* to persons prohibited from residing in specified areas but free to resettle elsewhere.

Liaison between administration and residents was accomplished by evacuee *block managers,* each of whom occupied a *block manager's office.*

Each project had an evacuee-operated but administration-controlled newspaper, for example, the Minidoka project published *Minidoka Irrigator;* the Topaz project, *Topaz Times;* Tule Lake, prior to the period of martial law, published the *Tulean Dispatch,* and after the period of martial law the *Newell Star.*

INDEX

Names

(Names in italics are pseudonyms)

Abe, S., 71, 113, 113n, 116, 125n, 132, 137, 138, 145, 158, 160, 164, 165, 166, 196n, 197, 231, 244, 246, 289, 290, 293, 299, 301, 301n, 302, 329, 330, 331

Aramaki, 71, 311, 311n, 320, 322, 322n, 339n

Austin, V., 148, 149, 153, 153n, 155n, 157, 162, 164, 165, 173, 175, 188n, 220n, 254

Besig, E., 285n, 287n, 289n, 291, 292, 292n, 294, 298, 301, 302, 330, 356n

Best, R., 38n, 100, 101, 121, 122, 123, 124, 125, 125n, 126, 127, 128, 129, 130, 133, 134, 135, 137, 140, 140n, 141, 144, 145, 157, 163, 178, 192, 196, 197, 200, 201, 212, 216, 217, 223, 230, 237, 242, 248, 249, 252, 253, 254, 256, 257, 258, 259, 278, 281, 288, 288n, 292, 292n, 293, 295n, 296, 297, 300, 302, 314, 314n, 334, 338n, 341

Billigmeier, R., 89n, 90n, 96n

Black, H., 192, 205, 211, 218, 230, 231, 233, 234, 241, 256, 258, 314, 316

Burling, J. L., 332, 339, 341, 356, 356n, 357

Coverley, H. M., 38n, 73

Cozzens, R. B., 134, 155, 155n, 157, 162, 300

DeWitt, J. L., 7, 8n, 9, 9n, 10, 10n, 11, 12, 19, 20n, 348, 349, 367, 368

Doi, H., 113, 113n, 116, 119

Eisenhower, M. S., 24, 25, 33n, 34, 38

Endo, S., 137, 138, 223, 295

Higashi, I., 177, 207, 209, 237, 239, 245

Huycke, L., 188, 189, 190, 211

Ishikawa, T., 230, 231, 234, 298, 298n, 306, 307, 309, 310, 314, 331

Itabashi, K., 247, 278, 279, 281, 282, 317, 318, 319

Kami, 160, 161, 179, 179n, 180, 196, 205, 212, 259, 261, 269, 270, 276, 276n

Kato, B., 113, 113n, 116, 120n, 121n, 122n, 140, 140n, 158, 161, 161n, 173, 174, 175, 291, 293, 294n, 295, 296, 299, 302, 329, 339n

Kira, S., 259, 290, 291, 297, 298, 301, 307, 308, 311, 311n, 319, 320, 321, 322, 326, 339n

Kitagawa, 178, 180, 195, 259, 261, 262

Kodama, T., 71, 146, 158, 198, 203, 289, 330, 331

Koike, 164, 198

Kubo, T., 234, 301, 301n, 314, 329

Kuratomi, G., 71, 71n, 119, 122n, 124, 125, 125n, 126, 127, 128, 133, 134, 135, 136, 137, 138, 141, 142, 146, 146n, 149, 154, 155, 158, 160, 164, 165, 173, 174, 175n, 178n, 188n, 196n, 197, 223, 246, 288n, 289, 290, 292n, 293, 293n, 298, 298n, 301, 301n, 302, 305, 329, 330, 330n, 331, 342n, 343n